THE MOST-GLORIOUS HOLY QUR'AN

Qur'an-i Quds-si El-ABHA

*"Blessed be He who sent down the Furqân on His servant
that he might be (or: become) a Warner for the worlds!"*

*"tabâraka lladhî nazzala l-furqâna 'alâ 'abdihi
li-yakûna li-l-'âlamîna nadhîran"*

THE MOST-GLORIOUS HOLY QUR'AN:

Qur'an-i Quds-si El-ABHA!

FOREWORD

Muhammad the Prophet was an orphan. Like all orphans prophets need to be taken care of too. After the calamity, Muhammad was taken into the care of the childhood home of his uncle. Later Khadijih the owner of the Camel Trading Company in which he was employed, took Muhammad not only into her business, but into her home as her man. He was ever a faithful servant of his Lord (*rabb*).

When he received Revelation--He was shattered and shaking. Khadijih did not forsake him, but took him into the bosom of her cloak and wrapped him with her own veils. Thus Allah gave him succor and comfort in the days of the great dividing!

Later as those gathered around him, he was taken care of by his own community. This is similar to the care given to Jeane Dixon and Black Elk, and the other ones smitten of the visionary of God: what the Bible states is the Gift of Prophecy.[*] Unlike these others, Muhammad is numbered amongst the Nine: The great Holy Prophets of Independent Manifestationhood. But unlike the Universal Manifestations of God that give a message for all humanity globally, Islam was given, like the Gita and the Torah and the Avesta and the Tripitaka within the context of only a specific local group of folks of a certain specific community of hearts and souls. Nevertheless, 'Abdu'l-Baha states all Revelation has the potential to be translated into the Universal Manifestation.

---

[*]For more on Jeane Dixon see *Jeane Dixon Was Right!* by Dr. Leland Jensen; and also *Black Elk Speaks* by John G. Neihardt. For those interested in the prophecies of Nostradamus see Victor Woods's, *Nostradamus Prophecy: New York City Nuked!*

This resurrection of the true and Holy Qur'an in the correct order fulfills 'Abdu'l-Baha's injunction to prepare the world for the universality of the Revelation of the Holy Prophet of Islam. For this reason it is the full and complete and whole (holy: *quds*) Revelation of The Most Glorious Holy Qur'an: **Qur'an-i Quds-si El-ABHA**!

TESTIMONY OF THE RECEPTION
OF THE MOST-HOLY AND ALL-GLORIOUS QU'RAN

I testify, I received this Holy Qur'an in one single **Night of Power** (it was 50,000 years "better than a thousand months" by Muhammad's reckoning). I transcribed the HQ in one single **Night of Power** the eclipse of the Blue Blood Super Moon (1/30-31/2018 AD). For 30 Days, each according to one Juz, I perfected and arranged and purified the parchments of the work into the Most Perfect Form and True arrangement in the style and brocades of the eternal Songs of Allah. During those days of Ramada'in-ontic Heat and effulgent star-spangled nights of cool breezes and tumultuous winds, I remained enraptured in the company of God, and his prophets, and felt the Messengers of Allah and the angels of heaven ascending and descending the ladders of the sublime lattice workings of God.

I testify--and my testimony is faithful and true--that this is the true and correct copy of the Holy Qur'an, revealed by the Prophet Muhammad, assembled in correct order by his son-in-law and successor Imam Ali; presented to and re-jected by Sunni Caliphs Abu Bakr, Omar, and Uthman Ibn Affan; and again presented to and accepted by my own ancestor, the Exilarch (Exiled monarchs of King David: Ar. *Ras al-Jalut*; Heb. *Resh Galutha*) Bostanai al-Raza by the person of Imam Ali himself in the presence of his own son and successor Husayn: **The Prince of Martyrs.**

To the best of my knowledge at least two original parchment copies (possibly a third) of this sacred book exist as transcribed by the hand of Imam Ali. Upon the uncovering of any of these holy artifacts a work of comparison can then be made about the scientific efficacy of the Revelations of the Holy Qur'an and how the mystery of the reversal of the sign of the sovereign operates and is made known.

My testimony is TRUE *(al-Amin)*.

Neal Chase,
Council Tree of the Farthest Remote
Fort Collins, CO.
January 30 thru March 21, 2018
The Month Girded by the appearance of the Double-Twin Super-Moons.
As upheld in the prophecy of God whence
the Moons were *split* in Twain.

POST SCRIPT:
Of Ins and Jinns. A Dialogic!

I.
Dear Muhammad!

Allah'u'Abha! We are heading out to the Memorial and will be out of office for about a week.

Apparently *jinn* (Ar.) is cognate with the Latin *gen*. Here the Latin translated the Hebrew *goyyim* as **GEN**tiles--which came to mean the non-Jews (but meant the people outside the Covenant (*tawhid*) of God): and jinn in this sense meant the non-Arab people or foreigners: *Ajnabi*. All cultures have in-group and out-group terms. The world of Muhammad was an isolated pocket and most everything outside of it was jinn: *Ajnabi* and *Faranji*.

Thus Nimrod (and his descendants) was a jinn (*iblis*) as he was Ajnabi and Faranji: not of the lineage of SHEM and ABRAHAM. The 56 ethnic groups of North China know those apart from them as of the *Qai-Lo* (*gweilo*); in Japan they actually use the word *jinn* as those natives on-Island are *Nihon-JIN* (*naan-jin*) and those off-Island are Gai-JIN (*gaijin*). The "*Gai*" in *Gai-Jin* is the same "*Qai*" in *Qai-Lo* and in Hebrew is *Goy* (*Qai/Gai*) of the *Goyyim*.

"**Gweilo** or **gwailou** (Chinese: 鬼佬; Cantonese Yale: *gwáilóu*, pronounced [kʷěi lǒu] is a common Cantonese slang term for Westerners. In its unmodified form, it applies only to European ethnicities and has a history of racially deprecatory use. Cantonese speakers frequently use *gwailou* to refer to Westerners in general use, in a non-derogatory context, although whether this type of usage is offensive is disputed by both Cantonese and Westerners alike" [1, 2].

"*Gwái* (鬼) means 'ghost,' and *lóu* (佬) means 'man.' The term *gwáilóu* therefore literally means 'ghostly man,' [3] and is sometimes translated into English as 'foreign devil' [4]. The term [allegedly] arose due to European's pale white complexion, which was seen as being ghost-like. The term *ghost* has also been used to describe other ethnic groups, for example, a 17th-century writer from Canton Qu Dajun (Qu-**Djinn**) wrote that Africans 'look like ghosts,' and *gwáinòu* (Chinese: 鬼奴; literally: 'ghost slave') was once used to describe African slaves" [5].

The reference to "ghost" means the "white" people. In Africa they also saw the pale-face as white-ghosts (see *muzungu, wazungu, zungu,* and *zunguka* for more). "In Swahili, the word muzungu (plural, wazungu) has its root in the word for ghost or spirit, and cognates of the word--mzungu in Chichewa and murungu in Shona and other Bantu languages--have the meaning of a powerful spirit, even a god. Foreigners had once seemed godlike when they first appeared in some places" [6].

This (other sense) gave rise to the Islamic understanding of many contexts of jinn as "spiritual beings" and also as "a separate intelligent species of invisible beings predating mankind." Likewise certain gods and goddesses and other supernatural entities bore the titles of jinn: "Archeological evidence found in Northwestern Arabia seems to indicate the worship of jinn, or at least their tributary status, hundreds of years before Islam: an Aramaic inscription from Beth

Fasi'el near Palmyra pays tribute to the '*ginnaye,*' the 'good and rewarding gods,' [7] and it has been argued that the term is related to the Arabic *jinn"* [8].

Thus the Qur'an also mentions that Muhammad was sent as a prophet to both "humanity and the jinn,",", and that prophets and messengers were sent to both communities [9].

"*Jinn* is an Arabic collective noun deriving from the Semitic root JNN (Arabic: جُنّ / جَنّ, *jann*), whose primary meaning is 'to hide.' Some authors interpret the word to mean, literally, 'beings that are concealed from the senses' [10]. Cognates include the Arabic *majnūn* ('possessed,' or generally 'insane'), *jannah* ('garden'), and *janīn* ('embryo') [11]. *Jinn* is properly treated as a plural, with the singular being *jinni*. Some claim a Persian origin of the word, for in the form of the Avestic '*Jaini*,', a wicked (female) spirit. *Jaini* were among various creatures in the possibly even pre-Zoroastrian mythology of peoples of Iran [12]. The anglicized form *genie* is a borrowing of the French génie, from the Latin *genius*, a guardian spirit of people and places in Roman religion. It first appeared [13] in 18th-century translations of the _Thousand and One Nights_ from the French [14], where it had been used owing to its rough similarity in sound and sense."

"And I did not create the jinn and mankind except to worship Me"
(Q. *adh-Dhariyat: THE SCATTERERS.* Sahih).

Thus the first meaning (the grounded meaning) in Holy Qur'an as to Jinn and Men--means it (The Message) was for the ALL the people of the world both the in-groups (indigenous peoples of the Manifestations) that the Manifestations appeared within and the people of the outgaard: the outer expanses. Thus the "mystery of the Kingdom" according to Paul is that the "gentiles/goyyim/gai-jinn/gwai-lo" are fellow heirs of the Kingdom" (See Eph. 3:6, etc. for more).

This reading is correct and true! It sets the scientific foundation for what this really is all about!

It is from this foundation that the "hidden" jinn make reference to the hidden effects of the jinn (foreigners) in our world (and other hidden processes) and that which is hidden of the past that still influence our culture and society today as that which is hidden (dialogically) of our collective and personal futures. These unseen psychological and spiritual forces--the relational forces operating between the peoples--and also Those like Ghosts from the Past or Spirits of the Present. They have no supernatural effect as of actual departed souls who cannot come back and make meddle in our affairs. But as the grateful dead: there is still unfinished work that needs to be accomplished (by us) upon this plane of existence: unfinished business. In any rate--from this scientific foundation the JINN (and the constellation of etymological and morphological word groupings (and cross-culturally) as such have come to be understand in many various forms and varieties. But this letter gives the true foundations and sense of the word. May God unite all the worlds! So we can have association with all, for all, by the all, in the all and through the all: **"that God may become all and all to everyone!"**

your servant,
Neal.

ps Jinn also relates to *genius* in Latin and to *daemon* in Greek. It is our belief that all people have an inner hidden true genius (*jn*) maybe more than one. Thus the Prophet stated (when asked of his own personal jinn): that the moment the Revelation appeared: his jinn (without hesitation in the least preformed Sujud al-Takbir and) surrendered.

REFERENCES

1. Yu, Irene. (7 November 2006). "MP shouldn't generalize." *Richmond News.* Archived from the original on 12 March 2007.

2. Brown, Jules; Lee, Helen & Gardner, Dinah. (2002). The Rough Guide to Hong Kong and Macau , p. 399.

3. Cummings, Patrick J.; Wolf, Hans-Georg. (2011). A Dictionary of Hong Kong English: Words from the Fragrant Harbor, . p. 69.

4. De Mente, Boyé Lafayette. (2000). The Chinese Have a Word for It: The Complete Guide to Chinese Thought and Culture, p. 145..

5. Zhidong Hao (2011). Macau History and Society, p. 86.

6. Theroux, Paul. (2012). The Tao of Travel: Enlightenments from Lives on the Road. Boston, MA: Mariner Books.

7. Hoyland, R. G. (2001). Arabia and the Arabs: From the Bronze Age to the Coming of Islam, p. 145; see also Brown, Jonathan A.C. (2011). Muhammad: A Very Short Introduction.

8. Teixidor, Javier. (1979). *The Pantheon of Palmyra*, p. 6.

9. Q. adh-Dhariyat: THE SCATTERERS; Muḥammad ibn Ayyūb al-Ṭabarī, Tuḥfat al-gharā'ib, I, p. 68; Abū al-Futūḥ Rāzī, Tafsīr-e rawḥ al-jenān va rūḥ al-janān, pp. 193, 341.

10. Lane, Edward William. (1863). *An Arabic-English Lexicon*, p. 462.

11. Wehr, Hans. (1994). Dictionary of Modern Written Arabic (4 ed.), p. 164.

12. See Tisdall, William St. Clair. (1905). *The Original Sources of the Qur'an.* London, UK: Society for Promoting Christian Knowledge.; and Tisdall, W. St. Clair. (1895). *The Religion of the Crescent or Islam: Its Strength, Its Weakness, Its Origin, Its Influence.*

13. "genie, n." (2014). Oxford English Dictionary (3rd ed).

14. Anonymous. (1706). *Arabian Nights' Entertainments, Vol. I,* p. 14. ("Grub Street Version.").

II.
Dear Neal,

Allah'u'Abha!

This is an astounding email! Thank you for sharing this incredible information. I have shared it with a close friend of mine who came to visit me this evening and he also found in interesting.

The problem is that Muslims can only see one sense of the Jinn which you have quoted as "a separate intelligent species of invisible beings predating mankind" [comment in reply: yes! that is THOSE WHO return--now!!]. Although I am greatly impressed by [this] perspective on the Jinn and the scientific explanation you have offered rooted in the anthropological and etymological study and roots of the word and concept, I am non-the-less inclined to believe in the above popular concept also due to an experience I have had personally in which some shadowy figures came to me one morning and caused me a great deal of pain by squeezing my back and my neck. Later, I came across some research by a Western scholar, Rosemary Ellen Guiley, described as "one of the leading experts on the paranormal today," who also came across many accounts from numerous people regarding a similar or identical experience of seeing certain shadowy figures. She concluded that the best term that could describe this phenomenon was the Eastern concept of the Djin. She spells it with a D. This is because the Islamic description of many characteristics of the Jinn such as the ability of Jinns to come in different colours and shapes corresponded to the accounts she heard from the various people who had been affected. She also refers to them as the shadow man. you may be familiar with this already. I would like you to check out the following Youtube video and web links below which go into this a bit and refer to what I am telling you:

(A) https://www.youtube.com/watch?v=cyaHgawWgNM
(B) https://www.psychologytoday.com/blog/shadow-boxing/201307/shadow-people
(C) http://djinnuniverse.com/faqs-about-the-djinn

I would be interested to know your perspective on the above both from a Psychological as well as religious viewpoint, as you are an expert on both. Mind you, Rosemary only claims that the shadow people are one aspect or manifestation of the Djinn and not that it is its exclusive meaning and representation.

It is also interesting that you have brought this up at this time, as I have recently completed a small research and observation on the passage of the Qur'an which I have written about in my book. I will attach the whole chapter that contains this information with this email, so you can see it and give me your thoughts on it. I have found it very interesting.

So far, your findings are the most astounding perspective on the Jinn that I have seen and it indeed seems to be a very well-grounded perspective and explanation of the origins of this concept. I thank God for this knowledge and you for sharing it.

Your Brother,
Muhammad.

ps basically, I want to know whether the Jinn the Muslims believe in is true or untrue. Is it real or unreal. I feel silly asking this because in a way I have experienced something which seems to me support it. But then again, a very clear perspective is important for me, as living in this community, I come across this idea quite often and have been questioned about it recently. I just told them that I believed in it because I have had personal experience of it, but that there were many interpretations of the Jinn besides this one.

Salam upon you O Beloved Guardian! I pray that God always blesses you!

****

1. Ibn Dirris brings the following report in his Book of Virtues, Bish b. Musa-Hawtha b. khalifah-Awf-Muhammad b. Sirin-Ikramah-Ikramah says:

After people gave allegiance to Abu Bakr, Ali sat in his house. Somebody said to Abu Bakr, "Ali dislikes giving allegiance to you." Abu Bakr sent somebody asking Ali, "do you dislike giving allegiance to me?" He replied, "No! I swear by God." Then, he asked, "What stops you from giving alliegence to me?" Ali then said, "I saw that the BOOK OF GOD was being added to, so I swore not to wear my cloak except for my prayers until I have compiled the Qur'an." So, Abu Bakr said to him, "What a good thing you have chosen to do."

2. Ali said, "I surely brought them the Book comprising the Revelation and the Interpretation." "Not a verse of the Qur'an was revealed to the Messenger of God without his reciting and dictating it to me, and without my writing it in my own hand. He taught me its (the Qur'an's) interpretation and exposition, its *nasikh* and *manasukeh*, and its *muhkam* and *mutashabih*. He prayed to God Almighty to teach me to comprehend and memorize it. Hence, I neither forgot a verse from the **Book of God Almighty** nor any knowledge that he dictated to me and which I wrote. Imam Ja'far Al-Sadiq says: "No one among the people, except a liar, can claim having compiled the whole Qur'an as it was revealed AND NO ONE EXCEPT 'ALI AND THE IMAMS SUCCEEDING HIM HAVE COMPILED AND PRESERVED IT AS IT WAS REVEALED?"

3. Ali compiled the Qur'an as it was revealed after the death of the Prophet and brought it before Abu Bakr and Umar and a group of people. When he presented it before them, they said, "We have **no need for you** or for **your Qur'an**. We have a sufficient amount of Qur'an." Ali then said, "Behold! I swear by God! You will **not see it after today** until our **Qaim** rises!"

4. Imam Ja'far Sadiq and Muhammad Baqir said: Ali compiled the Qur'an as Allah had revealed it and brought it to them and said, "This is the Book of your Lord just as He revealed it to your Prophet. It neither adds nor takes away a word from it." They responded, "We **do not need it**, as we have the like of what you have." Ali left while reciting the following verse, "They cast the book of God behind their backs and bought a small gain for it. What an awful a gain it was" (Ali Imran 187).

5. Abu Zar Ghifari says: When the messenger of God passed away, Ali compiled the Qur'an and brought it to the Muhajirin and Ansaar (Immigrants and helpers from among the companions). He presented it to them **following the Prophet's advice and instruction to him**. When Abu Bakr opened it, on the first page that opened, there appeared grave faults and infamies about the people. So, Umar sprang up and said, "Ali! Take it back. We do not need it!" So, Ali took it and left. Then, they called Zaid Ibn Thabit who knew how to recite the Qur'an. Umar said to him, "Ali has brought the Qur'an but it exposes a lot of iniquities of the Muhajirin and the Ansaar. So, zaid agreed to their request.

6. Imam Baqir says: "When the Qaim rises, he will set up camps for those who will teach the Qur'an **as it had been revealed by Allah**. It will be most difficult for those who have memorised the Qur'an today because it will be compiled in a different way."

7. HERE IS THAT WAY!...

The Qur'an...Comprehendeth All Religions

THIS is indeed a NOBLE QUR'AN in a BOOK kept HIDDEN which none toucheth save the PURIFIED, a REVELATION from the Lord of the Worlds.

Say: Perused ye not the Qur'an? Read it, that haply ye may find the Truth, for this Book is verily the Straight Path. This is the Way of God unto all who are in the heavens and all who are on the earth. (Baha'u'llah, Gleanings XVIII)

The most distinguished of God's chosen Ones, hath likened the Dispensation of **the Qur'an** unto heaven, by reason of its loftiness, its paramount influence, its majesty, and the fact that it **comprehendeth all religions.** (Baha'u'llah, Iqan, p. 40)

The Purpose of the one true God, exalted be His glory, in revealing Himself unto men is to lay bare those gems that lie hidden within the mine of their true and inmost selves. That the divers communions of the earth, and the manifold systems of religious belief, should never be allowed to foster the feelings of animosity among men, is, in this Day, of the essence of the Faith of God and His Religion. **These principles and laws, these firmly-established and mighty systems, have proceeded from one Source, and are the rays of one Light.** That they differ one from another is to be attributed to the varying requirements of the ages in which they were promulgated. (Baha'u'llah, Gleanings CXXXII)

O contending peoples and kindreds of the earth! Set your faces towards unity, and let the radiance of its light shine upon you. Gather ye together, and for the sake of God resolve to root out whatever is the source of contention amongst you. Then will the effulgence of the world's great Luminary envelop the whole earth, and its inhabitants become the citizens of one city, and the occupants of one and the same throne. This wronged One hath, ever since the early days of His life, cherished none other desire but this, and will continue to entertain no wish except this wish. **There can be no doubt whatever that the peoples of the world, of whatever race or religion, derive their inspiration from one heavenly Source, and are the subjects of one God. The difference between the ordinances under which they abide should be attributed to the varying requirements and exigencies of the age in which they were revealed. All of them, except a few which are the outcome of human perversity, were ordained of God, and are a reflection of His Will and Purpose.** Arise and, armed with the power of faith, shatter to pieces the gods of your vain imaginings, the sowers of dissension amongst you. Cleave unto that which draweth you together and uniteth you. This, verily, is the most exalted Word which the Mother Book hath sent down and revealed unto you. To this beareth witness the Tongue of Grandeur from His habitation of glory. (Baha'u'llah, Gleanings CXI)

ALIF!

------preface------

"There is no compulsion in religion.
The right direction is henceforth distinct from error.
And he who rejecteth false deities and believeth in Allah
hath grasped a firm handhold which will never break.
Allah is Hearer, Knower."
(*Q. Manzil al-Houris, al Baqarah*)

This preface is of the utmost importance! It includes for the first time in history--bound in one single volume--all the essential Holy Documents of the sacred Religion of Islam--in true order and the Most Great Perfection!

Yet before we magnify upon these subtile, sultry and intriguing themes, we must first announce the faithful reproduction of THE OATH OF MUHAMMAD. This document is still extant in the Capital City of the Ottoman Empire of Turkey's archives, and is here published for the first time in the correct position as preface to THIS HOLY QUR'AN. This arrangement being **the Most Glorious of all Qur'ans** because indeed IT IS--in and of itself--THE MOST-GLORIOUS HOLY QUR'AN!

THE OATH
OF THE
PROPHET MOHAMMED
TO THE
FOLLOWERS OF THE NAZARENE
(*The Astiname of Muhammad* Translated by Anton Haddad)

As an evidence of the injustice and intolerance which has characterized the attitude of Christians toward the Great Prophet Mohammed, and to prove how unfortunate is their error in attributing hatred and cruelty to Him in His dealings with the Nazarene, I wish, for the sake of truth and Christian enlightenment, to quote Mohammed's words, His valid oath and Covenant, concerning them.

This oath, entrusted by *MUHAMMAD* to His Caliphs, is an expression of His Authoritative Command to them as to their attitude toward the followers of Christ throughout the whole world. The oath referred to was issued by the Prophet Mohammed to the Christian Monks of Saint Catherine at Mount Sinai. A copy of it was translated into Turkish, while the original is still preserved in the treasury of the Sultan in Constantinople. This same Turkish copy was translated into Arabic by Naufal Effendi Naufal, a Christian of Tripoli, Syria; which translation is recorded in a book written by him and known as Sunnajat-ut-Tarab. The oath is as follows:

MUHAMMAD'S OATH
TO THE CHRISTIANS (NAZARENES)

THIS is a letter that was issued by *MUHAMMAD* Ibn Abdullah, the Messenger, the Prophet, the Faithful, Who is sent to all the people as a trust on the part of God, to all His creatures, that they may have no plea against God hereafter--Verily God is The Mighty, The Wise. This letter is directed to the embracers of Islam, as a Covenant given to the followers of Nazarene in the East and West, the far and the near, the Arabs and foreigners, the known and the unknown.

THIS letter contains the oath given unto them, and he who disobeys that which is therein will be considered a disobeyor and a transgressor to that whereunto he is commanded. He will be regarded as one who has corrupted the oath of God, disbelieved His Testament, rejected His Authority, despised His Religion, and made himself deserving of His Curse, whether he is a Sultan or any other believer of Islam.

Whenever monks, devotees and pilgrims gather together, whether in a mountain or valley, or den, or frequented place, or plain, or church, or in houses of worship, Verily We are back of them and shall protect them, and their properties and their morals, by Myself, by My friends and by My assistants, for they are of My subjects and under My protection.

The Astiname of Muhammad

I shall exempt them from that which may disturb them; of the burdens which are paid by others as an oath of allegiance. They must not give anything of their income but that which pleases them--they must not be offended, or disturbed, or coerced or compelled. Their judges should not be changed or prevented from accomplishing their offices, nor the monks disturbed from exercising their religious order, or the people of seclusion stopped from dwelling in their cells.

No one is allowed to plunder their pilgrims, or destroy or spoil any of their churches, or houses of worship, or take any of the things contained within any of these houses and bring it to the houses of Islam. And he who takes away anything therefrom, will be one who has corrupted the oath of God, and, in truth, disobeyed His Messenger.

Poll-taxes should not be put upon their judges, monks, and those whose occupation is the worship of God; nor is any other thing to be taken from them, whether it be a fine, a tax or any unjust right. Verily I shall keep their compact, wherever they may be, in the sea or on the land, in the East or West, in the North or South, for they are under My protection and the testament of My safety, against all things which they abhor.

No taxes or tithes should be received from those who devote themselves to the worship of God in the mountains, or from those who cultivate the Holy Lands. No one has the right to interfere with their affairs, or bring any action against them--Verily this is for aught else and not for them; rather, in the seasons of crops, they should be given a Kadah for each Ardab of wheat (about five bushels and a half) as provision for them, and no one has the right to say to them this is too much or ask them to pay any tax.

As to those who possess properties, the wealthy and merchants, the pol-tax to be taken from them must not exceed twelve Dirhams a hear per year (i.e. about 45 cents).

They shall not be imposed upon by anyone to undertake a journey, or to be forced to go to war or to carry arms; for the Islams have to fight for them. Do not dispute or argue with them, but deal according to the verse recorded in the Koran, to wit; 'Do not dispute or argue with the people of the Book but in that which is best.' Thus they will live favored and protected from everything which may offend them by the Callers to religion (Islam), wherever they may be and in any place they may dwell.

Should any Christian woman be married to a Musluman, such marriage must not take place except after her consent, and she must not be prevented from going to her church for prayer. Their churches must be honored and they must not be prevented from building churches or repairing convents.

They must not be forced to carry arms or stones; but the Islams must protect them and defend them against others. It is positively incumbent upon every one of the Islam nation not to contradict or disobey this oath until the Day of Resurrection and the end of the world.

THIS is the oath which *MUHAMMAD* Ibn Abdullah gave to the Christian nation, the fulfillment and promulgation of which has been agreed upon by all the witnesses who have hitherto attached their names. It was signed by the great Assistants of *MUHAMMAD*, as follows:

Ali Ibn Abi Talib
Abu Bekhr Ibn Kahafat
Omar Ibn El-Khattab
Ottman Ibn Affan
Aboul Darda
Abou Harirat
Abdullah Ibn Masood
Abbas Ibn Abdoul Mottaleb
El-Fadhl Ibn Abbas
Ezzobier Ibn El-Awam
Talhat Ibn Abdullah
Said Ibn Maath
Said Ibn Abada
Thabit Ibn Nafees
Zied Ibn Thabit
Abou Hanifa Ibn Attaba
Hashim Ibn Obied
Maazam Ibn Kariesh
El-Harith Ibn Thabit
Abdoul Azim Ibn Haasan
Abdullah Ibn Omar Ibn El-Aas
Aamir Ibn Yasir

"This oath was written by the hand of Ali Ibn Abi Talib in the worship place of the Prophet on the third day of Muharram in the second year of El-Hajrih."

INSHIRAH!

INSHIRAH![*]

---THE DILATING-EXPANSION OF THY HEART---
Manzil al-Awwal
'Idál

Bism'illah Ar-Rahman Ar-Rahim!

Alif. Dal. Dal. Dal. Dal. Dal. Dal. Vav.

"O Rasul! Have We not opened Thine heart for Thee
and caused Thy bosom to dilate,
and eased Thee of the burden
Which galled down Thy back;
And have We not, for Thee, exalted Thy name in fame?
Then verily along with trouble and hardship cometh ease,
Verily! with trouble and hardship cometh ease;
So when Thou art relieved, still toil
And strive to please the Pleasure of Thy Lord,
the Lord of All the Worlds!" (Q. al-Inshirah)

Bism'illah Ar-Rahman Ar-Rahim!

READ ALOUD: RECITE! *(aq-Qaara): In the name of Thy Lord Who createth,*
Createth man from a clot (al-'Alaq).
RECITE: *And Thy Lord is the Most Bounteous,*
Who teacheth by the **PEN**,
Teacheth man that which he knew not.

Bism'illah Ar-Rahman Ar-Rahim!

When Allah's succour (an-Nasr) and the triumph cometh
And Thou seest mankind Entering the religion of Allah in Troops,
Then hymn the praises of Thy Lord, and seek forgiveness of Him.
Lo! He is ever ready to show mercy.

---

[*]***THE OPENING!***

I. JUZ'UN SIPARA PRIMO:

1. Bism'illah Ar-Rahman Ar-Rahim! al-Hadid: THE ROD OF IRON.

All that is in the heavens and the earth **GLORIFIETH ALLAH;**[*] and He is the Mighty, the All-Wise.

His is the Sovereignty of the heavens and the earth; He quickeneth and He giveth death; and He is Able to do all things.

He is the First and the Last, and the Outward and the Inward; and He is Knower of all things.

He it is Who created the heavens and the earth in six Days; then He mounted the Throne. He knoweth all that entereth the earth and all that emergeth therefrom and all that cometh down from the sky and all that ascendeth therein; and He is with you wheresoever ye may be. And Allah is Seer of what ye do.

His is the Sovereignty of the heavens and the earth, and unto Allah (all) things are brought back and do return.

He causeth the night to pass into the day, and He causeth the day to pass into the night, and He is knower of all that is in the breasts.

Believe in Allah and His messenger, and spend of that whereof He hath made you trustees; and such of you as believe and spend (aright), theirs will be a great reward.

What aileth you that ye believe not in Allah, when the messenger calleth you to believe in your Lord, and He hath already made a Covenant with you, if ye are believers?

He it is Who sendeth down Clear Revelations [Will and Testament of] unto His slave ['Abdu'l-Baha], that He may bring you forth from darkness unto light; and Lo! For you, Allah is Full of Pity, Merciful.

And what aileth you that ye spend not in the way of Allah when unto Allah belongeth the inheritance of the heavens and the earth? Those who spent and fought before the Victory (*al-Fath*) are not upon a level (with the rest of you). Such are greater in rank than those who spent and fought afterwards. Unto each hath Allah promised good. And Allah is Informed of what ye do.

Who is he that will **lend unto Allah a goodly loan**, that He may double it for him and his may be a rich reward?

---

[*]**Al-Musabbihat** refer to the collective name of the seven surahs that begin with Allah's *glorification* 'Subhana,' 'Sabbaha,' and 'Yusabbihu:' *al-Hadid* ; *al-Hashr* ; *as-Saff* ; *al-Jumua*; *at-Taghabun*; *al-Isra*; and *al-Ala*.

On the day when Thou wilt see the believers, men and women, their light shining forth before them and on their right hands, (and wilt hear it said unto them): Glad news for you this day: Gardens underneath which rivers flow, wherein ye are immortal. That is the supreme triumph.

On the day when the hypocritical men and the hypocritical women will say unto those who believe: "Look on us that we may borrow from your light!" It will be said: "Go back and seek for light!" *Then* there will **separate them a wall** wherein *is* a **GATE, the inner side whereof containeth mercy, while the outer side thereof is toward the doom.**

They will cry unto them (saying): "Were we not with you?" They will say: "Yea, verily; but ye tempted one another, and hesitated, and doubted, and vain desires beguiled you till the ordinance of Allah came to pass; and the deceiver deceived you concerning Allah; So this day no ransom can be taken from you nor from those who disbelieved. Your home is the Fire; that is your patron, and a hapless journey's end."

Is not the time ripe for the hearts of those who believe to submit to Allah's reminder and to the truth which is revealed, that they become not as those who received the scripture of old but the term was prolonged for them and so their hearts were hardened, and many of them are evil-livers.

Know that Allah quickeneth the earth after its death. We have made clear Our Revelations for you, that haply ye may understand.

Lo! Those who give alms, both men and women, and **lend unto Allah a goodly loan**, it will be doubled for them, and theirs will be a rich reward.

And those who believe in Allah and His messengers, they are the loyal, and the martyrs are with their Lord; they have their reward and their light; while as for those who disbelieve and deny Our Revelations, they are owners of hell-fire.

Know that the life of the world is only play, and idle talk, and pageantry, and boasting among you, and rivalry in respect of wealth and children; as the likeness of vegetation after rain, whereof the growth is pleasing to the husbandman, but afterward it drieth up and Thou seest it turning yellow, then it becometh straw. And in the Hereafter there is grievous punishment, and (also) forgiveness from Allah and His good pleasure, whereas the life of the world is but matter of illusion.

Race one with another for forgiveness from your Lord and a Garden whereof the breadth is as the breadth of the heavens and the earth, which is in store for those who believe in Allah and His messengers. Such is the bounty of Allah, which He bestoweth upon whom He will, and Allah is of Infinite Bounty.

Naught of disaster befalleth in the earth or in yourselves but it is in a Book before we bring it into being--Lo! That is easy for Allah--That ye grieve not for the sake of that which hath escaped you, nor yet exult because of that which hath been given. Allah loveth not all prideful boasters, who hoard and who enjoin upon the people avarice. And whosoever turneth away, still Allah is the Absolute, the Owner of Praise.

We verily sent Our messengers with THIS RIGHTEOUS BOOK, and revealed with them the Scripture and the Balance, that mankind may observe right measure; and He revealed **IRON** (*al-Hadid*), wherein is mighty power and (many) uses for mankind, and that Allah may know him who helpeth Him and His messengers, though unseen. Lo! Allah is Strong, Almighty.

And We verily sent Noah and Abraham and placed the prophethood and the scripture among their seed, and among them there is he who goeth right, but many of them are evil-livers.

Then We caused Our messengers to follow in their footsteps; and We caused *JESUS*, son of Miriam, to follow, and gave him the Gospel, and placed compassion and mercy in the hearts of those who followed him. But monasticism they invented--We ordained it not for them--only seeking Allah's pleasure, and they observed it not with right observance. So We give those of them who believe their reward, but many of them are evil-livers.

O ye who believe! Be mindful of your duty to Allah and put faith in His messenger. He will give you twofold of His mercy and will appoint for you a light wherein ye shall walk, and will forgive you. Allah is Forgiving, Merciful;

That the People of the Scripture may know that they control naught of the bounty of Allah, but that the bounty is in Allah's hand to give to whom He will. And Allah is of Infinite Bounty.

2. Bism'illah Ar-Rahman Ar-Rahim! aq-Qaara: THE FIRST REVELATION READ ALOUD! RECITE!

READ ALOUD: RECITE! (aq-Qaara): In the name of Thy Lord Who createth,
Createth man from a clot (al-'Alaq).
RECITE: And Thy Lord is the Most Bounteous,
Who teacheth by the **PEN**,
Teacheth man that which he knew not.

3. Bism'illah Ar-Rahman Ar-Rahim! an-Nasr: THE DIVINE SUPPORT--ENTRY BY TROOPS.

When Allah's succour (an-Nasr) and the triumph cometh
And Thou seest mankind Entering the religion of Allah in Troops,
Then hymn the praises of Thy Lord, and seek forgiveness of Him.
Lo! He is ever ready to show mercy.

4. Bism'illah Ar-Rahman Ar-Rahim! al-Mudathir: THE CLOAKED ONE.

O Thou enveloped in the cloak of Thy mantle,[*]
Arise and warn!
Thy Lord magnify,

---

[*]The mantle is kept in Afghanistan, the area from which Bin Laden sent the 19 in 4 "birds" (planes).

Thy raiment purify,
Pollution shun!

And show not favor, seeking worldly gain!

For the sake of Thy Lord, be patient!

For when the trumpet shall sound,
Surely that day will be a day of anguish,
Not of ease, for disbelievers.

Leave Me (to deal) with him whom I created lonely[*],
And then bestowed upon him ample means,[†]
And sons abiding in his presence[‡]
And made (life) smooth for him.

Yet he[§] desireth that I should give more.

Nay! For Lo! He hath been stubborn to Our Revelations.[**]

On him I shall impose a fearful doom.

For Lo! He did consider; then he planned[††]--
Self-destroyed is he[‡‡], how he planned!
Again self-destroyed is he, how he planned! -

Then looked he,
Then frowned he and showed displeasure.

Then turned he away in pride
And said: "This is naught else than magic from of old;
This is naught else than speech of mortal man."

Him shall I fling unto the burning. Ah, what will convey unto Thee what that burning is!--It leaveth naught; it spareth naught. It shrivelleth the man.

Above it are nineteen[§§] We have appointed only angels to be wardens of the Fire, and their number (19) have We made to be a stumbling-block for those who disbelieve; that those to whom the Scripture hath been given may have certainty, and that believers may increase in faith;

---

[*] Bush & Bin Laden
[†] Saudi & Bush Fortunes
[‡] *Mujahidin* fighters brothers and sons at arms & UNCLE SAM, that is ALUS (ALlied US/NATO/UN forces)
[§] UNCLE SAM: the US, Bush, and current POTUS
[**] Our Press Releases Announcing the Revelation of Baha'u'llah that accurately predict all these things.
[††] Planned the 9-11.
[‡‡] UNCLE SAM who knew about it before it happened.
[§§] The 19 that flew the 4 birds (planes) at the 9-11.

and that those to whom the Scripture hath been given and believers may not doubt; and that those in whose hearts there is disease, and disbelievers, may say: "What meaneth Allah by this similitude (parable)?" Thus Allah sendeth astray whom He will, and whom He will He guideth. None knoweth the hosts of Thy Lord save Him. This is naught else than a Reminder unto mortals.[*]

Nay, by the Moon
And the Night when it withdraweth
And the Dawn when it shineth forth,

Lo! This is one of the greatest (portents)[†]
As a warning unto men.

Unto him of you who will advance or hang back.
Every soul is a pledge for its own deeds;

Save those who will stand on the right hand.
In gardens they will ask one another

Concerning the guilty:
"What hath brought you to this burning?"

They will answer: "We were not of those who prayed
Nor did we feed the wretched.
We used to wade (in vain dispute) with (all) waders,
And we used to deny the Day of Judgment,
Till the Inevitable came unto us."

The mediation of no mediators will avail them then.

Why now turn they away from the Admonishment,
As they were frightened asses
Fleeing from a lion?

Nay, but everyone of them desireth that he should be given open pages (from Allah).

Nay, verily. They fear not the Hereafter.

Nay, verily. Lo! This is an Admonishment. So whosoever will may heed.

And they will not heed unless Allah willeth (it). He is the fount of fear. He is the fount of Mercy.

---

[*] Thus is the 9-11 Event prophesied in the Qur'an openely in the outset.
[†] The prediction of the 9-11 by God as promised and foreseen in this Holy Qur'an (HQ).

5. Bism'illah Ar-Rahman Ar-Rahim! al-Fatihah: THE STRAIGHT PATH.

In the name of Allah, the Beneficent, the Merciful.
Praise be to Allah, the Lord of All the Worlds,
The Beneficent, the Merciful.
Master of the Day of Judgment,
Thee (alone) we worship; Thee (alone) we ask for help.
Show us **The Straight Path**,
The path of those whom Thou hast favored; Not the (path) of those who earn Thine anger nor of those who go astray.

6. Bism'illah Ar-Rahman Ar-Rahim! al-Inshirah: THE EXPANSION: THE OPENING DILATION OF THY HEART.

O *RASUL*! Have We not opened Thine heart for Thee
and caused Thy bosom to dilate,
and eased Thee of the burden
Which galled down Thy back;
And have We not, for Thee, exalted Thy name in fame?
Then verily along with trouble and hardship cometh ease,
Verily! with trouble and hardship cometh ease;
So when Thou art relieved, still toil
And strive to please the pleasure of Thy Lord,
the Lord of All the Worlds!

7. Bism'illah Ar-Rahman Ar-Rahim! al-Kafrun: THE UNBELIEVERS.

Say: O disbelievers!
I worship not that which ye worship;
Nor worship ye that which I worship.
And I shall not worship that which ye worship.
Nor will ye worship that which I worship.
Unto you your religion, and unto me my religion.

8. Bism'illah Ar-Rahman Ar-Rahim! at-Takwir: BURIED ALIVE.

When the sun is overthrown,
And when the stars fall,
And when the hills are moved,
And when the camels big with young are abandoned,
And when the wild beasts are herded together,
And when the seas rise,
And when souls are reunited,
And when (by their religion--not mine!)

the girl-child that was **buried alive**[*]
is asked
For what sin she was slain,
And when the pages are laid open,
And when the sky is torn away,
And when hell is lighted,
And when the Garden is brought nigh,
(Then) every soul will know what it hath made ready.

Oh, but I call to witness the planets,
The stars which rise and set,
And the close of night,
And the breath of morning
That this is in truth the word of an honored messenger,
Mighty, established in the presence of the Lord of the Throne,
(One) to be obeyed, and trustworthy;
And your comrade is not mad.
Surely he beheld Him on the clear horizon.
And he is not avid of the Unseen.
Nor is this the utterance of a devil worthy to be stoned.
Whither then go ye?
This is naught else than The Reminder unto creation,
Unto whomsoever of you willeth to walk straight.
And ye will not, unless (it be) that Allah willeth, the Lord of Creation.

9. Bism'illah Ar-Rahman Ar-Rahim! al-Humazah: THE BACKBITING SLANDERER.

Woe unto every slandering traducer,
Who hath gathered wealth (of this world) and arranged it.
He thinketh that his wealth will render him immortal.
Nay, but verily he will be flung to the Consuming One.
Ah, what will convey unto Thee what the Consuming One is!
(It is) the fire of Allah, kindled,
Which leapeth up over the hearts (of men).
Lo! It is closed in on them
In outstretched columns.

10. Bism'illah Ar-Rahman Ar-Rahim! al-Kauthar: ABUNDANCE.

Lo! We have given Thee Abundance;
So pray unto Thy Lord, and sacrifice.
Lo! It is Thy insulter (and not Thou) who is without posterity.

---

[*] Or shot in the head: Malala Yousafzai.

11. Bism'illah Ar-Rahman Ar-Rahim! al-Lahab: THE FLAME.

The power of Abu Lahab will perish, and he will perish.
His wealth and gains will not exempt him.
He will be plunged in flaming Fire,
And his wife, the wood-carrier,
Will have upon her neck a halter of palm-fibre.

12. Bism'illah Ar-Rahman Ar-Rahim! al-Ma'un: OUR DAILY BREAD

What thinkest Thou of him who treateth our religion as a lie?
That is he who repelleth the orphan,
And urgeth not the feeding of the needy.
Ah, woe unto worshippers
Who are heedless of their prayer;
Who would be seen (at worship)
Yet refuse to help the needy!

13. Bism'illah Ar-Rahman Ar-Rahim! at-Takthur: WORLDLY GAIN.

Rivalry in worldly increase distracteth you
Until ye come to the graves.
Nay, but ye will come to know!
Nay, but ye will come to know!
Nay, would that ye knew (now) with a sure knowledge!
For ye will behold hell-fire.
Aye, ye will behold it with sure vision.
Then, on that day, ye will be asked concerning pleasure.

14. Bism'illah Ar-Rahman Ar-Rahim! ad-Duha: THE BRIGHTNESS.

By the morning *hours*
And by the night when it is stillest,
Thy Lord hath not forsaken Thee nor doth He hate Thee,
And verily the latter portion will be better for Thee than the former,
And verily Thy Lord will give unto Thee so that Thou wilt be content.
Did He not find Thee an orphan and protect?
Did He not find Thee wandering and direct?
Did He not find Thee destitute and enrich?
Therefore the orphan oppress not,
Therefore the beggar drive not away,
Therefore of the bounty of Thy Lord be Thy discourse.

II. JUZ'UN SIPARA SECUNDO:

15. Bism'illah Ar-Rahman Ar-Rahim! as-Saffat: THE RANGERS

By those who set the Ranks in battle order
And those who drive away (the wicked) with reproof
And those who read (the Word) for The Reminder,
Lo! Thy Lord is surely One;
Lord of the heavens and of the earth and all that is between them, and **Lord of the Sun's Risings**.

Lo! We have adorned the lowest heaven with an ornament, the planets;
With security from every froward devil.
They cannot listen to **the Highest Chiefs** for they are pelted from every side,
Outcast, and theirs is a perpetual torment;
Save him who snatcheth a fragment, and there pursueth him a piercing flame.

Then ask them: "Are they stronger as a creation, or those (others) whom we have created?" Lo! We created them of plastic clay.
Nay, but Thou dost marvel when they mock
And heed not when they are reminded,
And seek to scoff when they behold a portent.

And they say: "Lo! This is mere magic; when we are dead and have become dust and bones, shall we then, forsooth, be raised again? And our forefathers?"

Say: "Ye, in truth; and ye will be brought low."

There is but ONE SHOUT, and Lo! They behold, and say: "Ah, Woe for us! This is the Day of Judgment." This is **the Day of Separation**, which ye used to deny.

And it is said unto the angels (ye are the angels): "Assemble those who did wrong, together with their wives and what they used to worship instead of Allah, and lead them to the path to hell; and stop them, for they must be questioned."

What aileth you that ye help not one another?

Nay, but this day they make FULL SUBMISSION.

And some of them draw near unto others, mutually questioning. They say: "Lo! Ye used to come unto Us, imposing, swearing that ye spoke the truth."

They answer: "Nay, but ye yourselves were not believers. We had no power over you, but ye were wayward folk. Now the Word of our Lord hath been fulfilled concerning Us. Lo! We are about to taste the DOOM. Thus we misled you. Lo! We were ourselves astray."

Then Lo! This day they both are sharers in the doom.

Lo! Thus deal We with the guilty. For when it was said unto them, There is no God save Allah, they were scornful and said: "Shall we forsake our gods for A MAD POET?"

Nay, but he brought the Truth, and he confirmed those sent before him.

Lo! Now verily ye taste the painful doom--
Ye are requited naught save what ye did--
Save single-minded slaves of Allah;
For them there is a known provision,
Fruits. And they will be honored
In the Gardens of Na'im (Heb. *Nahum*),
On couches facing one another;

A cup from a gushing spring is brought round for them,
White, delicious to the drinkers,
Wherein there is no headache nor are they made mad thereby.

And with them are those of modest gaze, with lovely eyes,
PURE as they were hidden eggs (of the ostrich).

And some of them draw near unto others, mutually questioning.

A speaker of them saith: "Lo! I had a comrade who used to say: 'Art Thou in truth of those who put faith in his words? Can we, when we are dead and have become mere dust and bones--can we then verily be brought to BOOK?'"

He saith: "Will ye look?"

Then looketh he and seeth him in the depth of hell. He saith: "By Allah, Thou verily didst all but cause my ruin, and had it not been for the favor of my Lord, I too had been of those haled forth (to doom). Are we then not to die saving our former death, and are we not to be punished?"

Lo! This is the supreme triumph.

For the like of this, then, let the workers work.

Is this better as a welcome, or the Tree of Zaqqum? Lo! We have appointed it a torment for wrong-doers. Lo! It is a Tree that springeth in the heart of hell. Its crop is **as it were the heads of devils**.[*] And Lo! They verily must eat thereof, and fill their bellies therewith. And afterward, Lo! Thereupon they have a drink of boiling water. And afterward, Lo! Their return is surely unto hell.

---

[*] The heads stamped on coins and money: "The love of money is the root of all evil" (1 Tim. 6:10 KJV).

They indeed found their fathers astray, but they make haste to follow in their footsteps. And verily most of the Old Ones went astray before them, and verily We sent among them warners. Then see the nature of the consequence for those warned, save single-minded slaves of Allah.

And Noah verily prayed unto Us, and gracious was the Hearer of his prayer and We saved him and his household from the great distress, and made **his seed** the survivors, and left for him among the later folk the salutation: "Blessings Be unto Noah among the peoples!" Lo! Thus do We reward the good. Lo! He is one of Our believing slaves. Then We did drown the others.

And Lo! Of his persuasion verily was Abraham when he came unto his Lord with a whole heart; When he said unto his father and his folk: "What is it that ye worship? Is it a falsehood--gods beside Allah--that ye desire? What then is your opinion of the Lord of the Worlds?"

And he glanced a glance at the stars then said: "Lo! I feel sick!" And they turned their backs and went away from him. Then turned he to their gods and said: "Will ye not eat? What aileth you that ye speak not?" Then he attacked them, striking with his right hand.

And his people came toward him, hastening. He said: "Worship ye that which ye yourselves do carve when Allah hath created you and what ye make?"

They said: "Build for him a building and fling him in the red-hotfire." And they designed a snare for him, but We made them the undermost.

And he said: "Lo! I am going unto my Lord Who will guide me. My Lord! Vouchsafe me of the righteous." So We gave him tidings of **a Gentle Son**.

And when he was old enough to walk with him, Abraham said: "**O My Dear Son**, I have seen in a dream that I must sacrifice Thee. So look, what thinkest Thou?" He said: "O my Father! Do that which Thou art commanded. Allah willing, Thou shalt find me of the steadfast."

Then, when they had **both Surrendered** to Allah, and he had flung him down upon his face, we called unto him: "O Abraham! **Thou hast already fulfilled The Vision**!" Lo! Thus do We reward the good.

Lo! That verily was a CLEAR TEST.

Then We ransomed him with a tremendous victim. And We left for him among the later folk the salutation: "Blessings Be unto Abraham!" Thus do We reward the good. Lo! He is one of Our believing slaves. And we gave him tidings of the birth of Isaac, a prophet of the righteous. And We blessed him and Isaac. And of their seed are some who do good, and some who plainly wrong themselves.

And We verily gave grace unto *MOSES* and Aaron, and saved them and their people from the great distress, and helped them so that they became the Victors. And We gave them the CLEAR Scripture and showed them the right path. And We left for them among the later folk the salutation: "Blessings Be unto *MOSES* and Aaron!" Lo! Thus do We reward the good. Lo! They are two of Our believing slaves.

And Lo! Elijah was of those sent to warn, when he said unto his folk: "Will ye not ward off? Will ye cry unto Baal and forsake **the Best of Creators**, Allah, your Lord and Lord of your forefathers?" But they denied him, so they surely will be haled forth to the doom save single-minded slaves of Allah. And we left for him among the later folk the salutation: "Blessings Be unto Eliajh!" Lo! Thus do We reward the good. Lo! He is one of our believing slaves.

And Lo! Lot verily was of those sent to warn. When We saved him and his household, every one, save an old woman among those who stayed behind; Then We destroyed the others. And Lo! Ye verily pass by the ruin of them in the morning and at night-time; have ye then no sense?

And Lo! Jonah verily was of those sent to warn when he fled unto **The Laden Ship**, and then drew lots and was of those rejected; and the fish swallowed him while he was blameworthy; and had he not been one of those who glorify Allah he would have tarried in its belly till the day when they are raised; Then We cast him on a desert shore **while he was sick**; and We caused a Tree of gourd to grow above him; and We sent him to a hundred Thousand folk or more and they believed, therefore We gave them comfort for a while.

Now ask them (O *AL-AMIN*): "Hath Thy Lord daughters whereas they have sons? Or created We the angels females while they were present?"

Lo! It is of their falsehood that they say: "Allah hath begotten." Allah! Verily they tell a lie. And again of their falsehood: "He hath preferred daughters to sons." What aileth you? How judge ye? Will ye not then reflect? Or have ye a clear warrant? Then produce your writ, if ye are truthful.

And they imagine kinship between him and the jinn, whereas the jinn know well that they will be brought before Him. Glorified be Allah from **ALL THAT** which they attribute unto Him, save single-minded slaves of Allah. Lo! Verily, ye and that which ye worship, ye cannot excite anyone against Him.

Save him who is to burn in hell, there is not one of us but hath his known position.

Lo! We, even we are they who set the ranks,
Lo! We, even we are they who hymn His praise!

And indeed they used to say: "If we had but a reminder from the men of old We would be single-minded slaves of Allah."

Yet they disbelieve therein; but they will come to know.

And verily Our word went forth of old unto Our bondmen sent to warn that they verily would be helped, and that Our Host, they verily would be the Victors.

So withdraw from them (O *AL-AMIN*) awhile, and watch, for they will soon see.

Would they hasten on Our doom?

But when it cometh home to them, then it will be a hapless morn for those who have been warned.

Withdraw from them awhile and watch, for they will soon see.

Glorified be Thy Lord, the Lord of Majesty, from ALL THAT which they attribute unto Him and Blessings Be unto those sent to warn.

And praise be to Allah, Lord of All the Worlds!

16. Bism'illah Ar-Rahman Ar-Rahim! al-Qalam: THE PEN.

Nun.

By the pen and that which they write therewith, Thou art not, for Thy Lord's favor unto Thee, a madman.

And Lo! Thine verily will be a reward unfailing.
And Lo! Thou art of a tremendous nature.

And Thou wilt see and they will see
Which of you is <u>The Demented</u>.

Lo! Thy Lord is Best Aware of him who strayeth from His way, and He is Best Aware of those who walk aright.

Therefore obey not Thou the rejecters who would have had Thee compromise, that they may compromise.

Neither obey Thou each feeble oath-monger, detracter, spreader abroad of slanders, hinderer of the good, transgressor, malefactor greedy therewithal, intrusive. It is because he is possessed of wealth and children that, when Our Revelations are recited unto him, he saith: "Mere fables of the Old Ones." We shall brand him on the nose.

Lo! We have tried them as We tried the owners of the garden when they vowed that they would pluck its fruit next morning, and made no exception for the Will of Allah; Then a visitation from Thy Lord came upon it while they slept and in the morning it was as if plucked. And they cried out one unto another in the morning, saying: "Run unto your field if ye would pluck the fruit." So they went off, saying one unto another in low tones: "No needy man shall enter it to-day against you." They went betimes, strong in this purpose. But when they saw it, they said: "Lo! We are in error! Nay, but we are desolate!"

The best among them said: "Said I not unto you: 'Why glorify ye not Allah?'"

They said: "Glorified be our Lord! Lo! We have been wrong-doers."

Then some of them drew near unto others, self-reproaching. They said: "Alas for us! In truth we were outrageous. It may be that our Lord will give us better than this in place thereof. Lo! We beseech our Lord."

Such was the punishment. And verily the punishment of the Hereafter is greater if they did but know.

Lo! For those who keep from evil are **Gardens of Na'im** (Heb. *Nahum*) with their Lord. Shall We then treat those who have surrendered as We treat the guilty? What aileth you? How foolishly ye judge! Or have ye a scripture wherein ye learn that ye shall indeed have all that ye choose?

Or have ye a Covenant on OATH FROM US[*] **that reacheth to the Day of Judgment**, that yours shall be all that ye ordain? Ask them (O *AL-AMIN*) which of them will vouch for that!

Or have they other gods? Then let them bring their other gods if they are truthful on the day when it befalleth in earnest, and they are ordered to prostrate themselves but are not able, with eyes downcast, abasement stupefying them. And they had been summoned to prostrate themselves while they were yet unhurt. **Leave Me to deal with those who give the lie to this pronouncement.** We shall lead them on by steps from whence they know not.

Yet I bear with them, for Lo! My scheme is firm.

Or dost Thou ask a fee from them so that they are heavily taxed? Or is the Unseen theirs that they can write thereof?

But wait Thou for Thy Lord's decree, and be **not like him of the fish,**[†] who cried out in despair. Had it not been that favor from his Lord had reached him he surely had been cast into the wilderness while he was reprobate. But his Lord chose him and placed him among the righteous.

And Lo! Those who disbelieve would fain disconcert Thee with their eyes when they hear THE REMINDER, and they say: "Lo! He is indeed mad;" When he is naught else than THE REMINDER to creation.

Nay, but verily man is rebellious that he thinketh himself independent! Lo! Unto Thy Lord is the return.

Hast Thou seen him who dissuadeth a slave when he prayeth? Hast Thou seen if he relieth on the guidance of Allah or enjoineth piety? Hast Thou seen if he denieth Allah's guidance and is froward? Is he then unaware that Allah seeth?

---

[*] **The Astiname of *MUHAMMAD*.**
[†] The "Sign of Jonah" as *JESUS* cried out on the cross!

Nay! But if he cease not We will seize him by the forelock--the lying, sinful forelock--Then let him call upon his henchmen! We will call **The Guards of Hell** (19).

Nay! Obey not Thou him. But prostrate Thyself, and draw near unto Allah.

III. JUZ'UN SIPARA TERZO/TERTIO:

17. Bism'illah Ar-Rahman Ar-Rahim! al-Imran: THE FAMILY OF 'IMRAN!

Alif. Lam. Mim. (ELOHIM: *Alim*). I AM (*ana*) THE LORD GOD KING OF THE UNIVERSE (*Allah*), THE ALL-KNOWING (*al-Alim*) THE ALL-GLORIOUS (*al-Majid*)!

Allah! There is no God save Him, the Alive, the Eternal!

He hath Revealed unto Thee the Scripture with truth, confirming that which was revealed before it, even as He revealed the Torah and the Gospel aforetime, for a guidance to mankind; and hath revealed THE GOLDEN CRITERIA. Lo! Those who disbelieve the Revelations of Allah, theirs will be a heavy doom. Allah is Mighty, able to Requite the wrong.

Lo! Nothing in the earth or in the heavens is hidden from Allah. He it is Who fashioneth you in the wombs as pleaseth Him. There is no God save Him, the Almighty, the Wise.

He it is Who hath revealed unto Thee the Scripture wherein are CLEAR REVELATIONS--they are **the Substance of the BOOK**--and others which are allegorical. But those in whose hearts is doubt pursue, forsooth, that which is allegorical seeking to cause dissension by seeking to explain it. None knoweth its explanation save Allah. And those who are of sound instruction say: "We believe therein! The whole is from our Lord!" but only men of understanding really heed.

Our Lord! Cause not Our hearts to stray after Thou hast guided Us, and bestow upon Us Mercy from Thy Presence. Lo! Thou, only Thou, art the Bestower.

Our Lord! Lo! It is Thou Who gatherest mankind together to a Day of which there is no doubt. Lo! Allah faileth not to keep the tryst. On that Day neither the riches nor the progeny of those who disbelieve will aught avail them with Allah. They will be fuel for Fire.

Like Pharaoh's folk and those who were before them, they disbelieved Our Revelations and so Allah seized them for their sins. And Allah is severe in punishment.

Say unto those who disbelieve: "Ye shall be overcome and gathered unto Hell, an evil resting-place."

Here is a token for you in two hosts which met: one army fighting in the way of Allah, and another disbelieving, whom they saw as twice their number, clearly, with their very eyes. Thus Allah strengtheneth with His succor whom He will. Lo! Herein verily is a lesson for those who have eyes.

BEAUTIFIED for humankind is love of the joys that come from women and offspring; and stored-up heaps of gold and silver, and horses branded with their mark, and cattle and land. That is comfort of the life of the world. Allah! With Him is a more excellent abode.

Say: "Shall I inform you of something better than that? For those who keep from evil, with their Lord, are Gardens underneath which rivers flow wherein they will abide, and pure companions, and contentment from Allah." Allah is Seer of His bondmen, those who say: "Our Lord! Lo! We believe. So forgive us our sins and guard us from the punishment of Fire;" the steadfast, and the truthful, and the obedient, those who spend (and hoard not), those who pray for pardon in **The Watches of the Night.**

Allah Himself is Witness that there is no God save Him. And the angels and **The Men[*] of Learning** (*Alim*) too are witness. Maintaining His creation in justice, there is no God save Him the Almighty, the Wise.

Lo! Religion with Allah is the SURRENDER (to His Will and Guidance). Those who received the Scripture differed **only after knowledge came unto them**, through transgression among themselves. Whoso disbelieveth the Revelations of Allah (will find that) Lo! Allah is swift at reckoning.

And if they argue with Thee, (O *AL-AMIN*), say: "I have ***surrendered my purpose*** to Allah and so have those who follow me." And say unto those who have received the Scripture and those who read not: "Have ye too surrendered?" If they surrender, then truly they are rightly guided, and if they turn away, then it is Thy duty only to convey the message unto them. Allah is Seer of His bondmen.

Lo! Those who disbelieve the Revelations of Allah, and slay the prophets wrongfully, and slay those of humankind who enjoin equity: promise them a painful doom. Those are they whose works have failed in the world and the Hereafter; and they have no helpers. Hast Thou not seen how those who have received a portion of the Scripture invoke the Scripture of Allah in their disputes that it may judge between them; then a faction of them turn away, being opposed to it?

That is because they say: "The Fire will not touch us save for a certain number of days." That which they used to invent hath deceived them regarding their religion.

How will it be with them when We have brought them all together to a Day of which there is no doubt, when every soul will be paid in full what it hath earned, and they will not be wronged. Say: "O Allah! Owner of Sovereignty! Thou givest sovereignty unto whom Thou wilt, and Thou withdrawest sovereignty from whom Thou wilt. Thou exaltest whom Thou wilt, and Thou abasest whom Thou wilt. In Thy hand is the good. Lo! Thou art Able to do all things. Thou causest the night to pass into the day, and Thou causest the day to pass into the night. And Thou bringest forth the living from the dead, and Thou bringest forth the dead from the living. And Thou givest sustenance to whom Thou choosest, without stint."

---

[*]*Rijal*: the men and women who are The Leaders of Learning: *The Alim.*

Let not the believers take disbelievers for their friends **in preference to** believers. Whoso doeth that hath no connection with Allah unless it be that ye but guard yourselves against them, taking as it were security. Allah biddeth you beware only of Himself. Unto Allah is the journeying.

Say, (O *AL-AMIN*): "Whether ye hide that which is in your breasts or reveal it, Allah knoweth it. He knoweth that which is in the heavens and that which is in the earth, and Allah is Able to do all things."

On the Day when every soul will find itself confronted with all that it hath done of good and all that it hath done of evil every soul will long that there might be a mighty space of distance between it and that evil. Allah biddeth you beware of Him. And Allah is Full of Pity for His bondmen.

Say: "If ye love Allah, follow me; Allah will love you and forgive you your sins. Allah is Forgiving, Merciful."

Say: "Obey Allah and the messenger. But if they turn away, Lo! Allah loveth not the disbelievers.

Lo! Allah preferred *ADAM* and Noah and the Family of Abraham and the Family of 'Imran above all His creatures.

They are descendants one of another. Allah is Hearer, Knower.

When the wife of 'Imran said: My Lord! I have vowed unto Thee that which is in my belly as a consecrated offering). Accept it from me. Lo! Thou, only Thou, art the Hearer, the Knower!"

And when she was delivered she said: "My Lord! Lo! I am delivered of a female"--Allah knew best of what she was delivered--the male is not as the female; and Lo! "I have named her Miriam," and Lo! "I crave Thy protection for her and for her offspring from Satan the outcast."

And her Lord accepted her with full acceptance and vouchsafed to her a goodly growth; and made Zachariah her Guardian. Whenever Zachariah went into the sanctuary where she was, he found that she had food. He said: "O Miriam! Whence cometh unto Thee this food?" She answered: "It is from Allah. Allah giveth without stint to whom He will."

Then Zachariah prayed unto his Lord and said: "My Lord! Bestow upon me of Thy bounty goodly offspring. Lo! Thou art the Hearer of Prayer."

And the angels called to him as he stood praying in the sanctuary: "Allah giveth Thee glad tidings of (a son whose name is) John, who cometh to confirm a word from Allah lordly, CHASTE, a prophet of the righteous."

He said: "My Lord! How can I have a son when age hath overtaken me already and my wife is barren?" The angel answered: "So it will be. Allah doeth what He will."

He said: "My Lord! Appoint a token for me." The angel said: "The token unto Thee shall be that Thou shalt not speak unto mankind three days except by signs. Remember Thy Lord much, and praise Him in the early *hours* of twilight night and morning's Alpenglow."

And when the angels said: "O Miriam! Lo! Allah hath chosen Thee and made Thee PURE, and hath preferred Thee above all the women of creation."

O Miriam! Be obedient to Thy Lord, prostrate Thyself and bow with those who bow in worship. This is of the tidings of things hidden. We reveal it unto Thee. **Thou wast not present with them when they threw their pens to know which of them should be the Guardian of Miriam, nor wast Thou present with them when they quarrelled thereupon.**

When the angels said: "O Miriam! Lo! Allah giveth Thee glad tidings of a word from him, whose name is the Messiah, *JESUS*, son of Miriam, illustrious in the world and the Hereafter, and one of those brought near unto Allah. He will speak unto mankind in his cradle and in his manhood, and he is of the righteous."

She said: "My Lord! How can I have a child when no mortal hath touched me?"

He said: "So it will be."

Allah createth what He will. If He decreeth a thing, He saith unto it only: "Be! and it is."

"And He will teach him the Scripture and Wisdom (*Hikmat/Chokhmah*), and the Torah and the Gospel, and will make him a messenger unto the Children of Israel, saying: 'Lo! I come unto you with a sign from your Lord. Lo! I fashion for you out of clay the likeness of a bird, and I breathe into it and it is a bird,[*] by Allah's leave. I heal him who was born blind, and the leper, and I raise the dead, by Allah's leave. And I announce unto you what ye eat and what ye store up in your houses. Lo! Herein verily is a portent for you, if ye are to be believers. And I come confirming that which was before me of the Torah, **and to make lawful some of that which was forbidden unto you**. I come unto you with a sign from your Lord, so keep your duty to Allah and obey me. Lo! Allah is my Lord and your Lord, so worship Him. That is a straight path.'"

But when *JESUS* became conscious of their disbelief, he cried: "Who will be my helpers in the cause of Allah?" The disciples said: "We will be Allah's helpers. We believe in Allah, and bear Thou witness that we have Surrendered unto Him. Our Lord! We believe in that which Thou hast revealed and we follow him whom Thou hast sent. Enrol us among those who witness to the truth."

And they (the disbelievers) schemed, and Allah schemed (against them): and **Allah is the best of schemers.**[†]

When Allah said: "O *JESUS*! Lo! I am gathering Thee and causing Thee to ascend unto Me, and am cleansing Thee **of those who disbelieve** and am setting those who follow Thee above those

---

[*] An airplane that flies.
[†] Man plans and God plans. And God is the best of planners!

who disbelieve until the Day of Resurrection. Then unto Me ye will all return, and I shall judge between you as to that wherein ye used to differ. As for those who disbelieve I shall chastise them with a heavy chastisement in the world and the Hereafter; and they will have no helpers. And as for those who believe and do good works, He will pay them their wages in full." Allah loveth not wrong-doers.

This which We recite unto Thee is a Revelation and a wise REMINDER!

Lo! The likeness of *JESUS* with Allah is as the likeness of *ADAM*. He created him of dust, then He said unto him: "Be! and he is."

This is the truth from Thy Lord (O *AL-AMIN*), so be not Thou of those who waver. And whoso disputeth with Thee concerning him, after the knowledge which hath come unto Thee, say unto him: "Come! We will summon our sons and your sons, and our women and your women, and ourselves and yourselves, then we will pray humbly to our Lord and **solemnly invoke the curse of Allah** upon those who lie."

Lo! This verily is the True Narrative. There is no God save Allah, and Lo! Allah, He verily is, is the Mighty, the Wise.

And if they turn away, then Lo! Allah is Aware of who are the corrupters.

Say: "O People of the Scripture! Come to an agreement between us and you: that we shall worship none but Allah, and that we shall ascribe no partner unto Him, and that none of us shall take others for lords beside Allah." And if they turn away, then say: "Bear witness that we are they who have Surrendered (unto Him)."

O People of the Scripture! Why will ye argue about Abraham, when the Torah and the Gospel were not revealed till after him? Have ye then no sense?

Lo! Ye are those who argue about that whereof ye have some knowledge: Why then argue ye concerning that whereof ye have no knowledge? Allah knoweth. Ye know not.

Abraham was not a Jew, nor yet a Christian; but he was an upright man who had Surrendered (to Allah), and he was not of the idolaters.

Lo! Those of humankind who have the best claim to Abraham are those who followed him, and *THIS PROPHET* and those who believe with him; and Allah is **the Protecting Guardian** of the believers.

A party of the People of the Scripture long to make you go astray; and they make none to go astray except themselves, but they perceive not.

O People of the Scripture! Why disbelieve ye in the Revelations of Allah, when ye yourselves bear witness to their Reality?

O People of the Scripture! Why confound ye truth with falsehood and knowingly conceal the truth?

And a party of the People of the Scripture say: "Believe in that which hath been revealed unto those who believe at the opening of the day, and disbelieve at the end thereof, in order that they may return; and believe not save in one who followeth your religion"--Say (O *AL-AMIN*): "Lo! The guidance is Allah's Guidance"--that anyone is given the like of that which was given unto you or that they may argue with you in the presence of their Lord. Say: "Lo! The bounty is in Allah's hand. He bestoweth it on whom He will. Allah is All-Embracing, All-Knowing. He selecteth for His mercy whom He will. Allah is of Infinite Bounty."

Among the People of the Scripture there is he who, if Thou trust him with a weight of treasure, will return it to Thee. And among them there is he who, if Thou trust him with a piece of gold, will not return it to Thee unless Thou keep standing over him. That is because they say: "We have no duty to the Gentiles." They speak a lie concerning Allah knowingly.

Nay, but the chosen of Allah is the one who fulfilleth their pledge and wardeth off evil; for Lo! Allah loveth those who ward off evil.

Lo! Those who purchase a small gain **at the cost of Allah's Covenant** and **their Oaths**, they have no portion in the Hereafter. Allah will neither speak to them nor look upon them on the Day of Resurrection, nor will He make them grow. Theirs will be a painful doom.

And Lo! There is a party of them who distort the Scripture with their tongues, that ye may think that what they say is from the Scripture, when it is not from the Scripture. And they say: "It is from Allah," when it is not from Allah; and they speak a lie concerning Allah knowingly.

It is not possible for any human being unto whom Allah had given the Scripture and Wisdom and the prophethood that he should afterwards have said unto mankind: "Be slaves of me instead of Allah;" but what he said was: "Be ye faithful servants of the Lord by virtue of your constant teaching of the Scripture and of your **constant study** thereof." And he commanded you not that ye should take the angels and the prophets for lords. Would he command you to disbelieve after ye had Surrendered to Him?

When Allah made His **Covenant** with the prophets, He said: "Behold that which I have given you of the Scripture and knowledge. And afterward there will come unto you a messenger, confirming that which ye possess. Ye shall believe in him and ye shall help him." He said: "Do ye agree, and will ye take up My burden which I lay upon you in this matter?" They answered: "We agree." He said: "Then bear ye witness. I will be a witness with you." Then whosoever after this shall turn away: they will be miscreants.

Seek they other than the religion of Allah, when unto Him submitteth whosoever is in the heavens and the earth, willingly or unwillingly, and unto Him they will be returned.

Say: "We believe in Allah and that which is revealed unto us and that which was revealed unto Abraham and Ishmael and Isaac and Jacob and the tribes, and that which was vouchsafed unto

MOSES and *JESUS* and the prophets from their Lord. **We make no distinction between any of them**, and unto Him we have surrendered." And whoso seeketh as religion other than the Surrender (to Allah) it will not be accepted from him, and he will be a loser in the Hereafter.

How shall Allah guide a people who disbelieved after their belief and after they bore witness that the messenger is true and after THIS RIGHTEOUS BOOK had come unto them. And Allah guideth not wrongdoing folk. As for such, their guerdon is that on them rests the CURSE of Allah and of angels and of men combined.[*] They will abide therein. Their doom will not be lightened, neither will they be reprieved; save those who afterward repent and do right. Lo! Allah is Forgiving, Merciful.

Lo! Those who disbelieve after their profession of belief, and afterward grow violent in disbelief: their repentance will not be accepted. And such are those who are astray.

Lo! Those who disbelieve, and die in disbelief, the whole earth full of gold would not be accepted from such an one if it were offered as a ransom for his soul. Theirs will be a painful doom and they will have no helpers. Ye will not attain unto piety until ye spend of that which ye love. And whatsoever ye spend, Allah is Aware thereof.

ALL FOOD was lawful unto the Children of Israel, save that which Israel forbade himself, in days before the Torah was revealed. Say: "Produce the Torah and read it unto us if ye are truthful."

And whoever shall invent a falsehood after that concerning Allah, such will be wrong-doers.

Say: "Allah speaketh truth. So follow the religion of Abraham, the upright. He was not of the idolaters."

Lo! The first Sanctuary appointed for humankind was that at Mecca, a blessed place, a guidance to the peoples; wherein are **Plain Memorials**[†] of Allah's guidance; the place where Abraham stood up to pray; and whosoever entereth it is safe. And pilgrimage to the House is a duty unto Allah for humankind, for him who can find a way thither. As for him who disbelieveth, let him know that Lo! Allah is Independent of all creatures.

Say: "O People of the Scripture! Why disbelieve ye in the Revelations of Allah, when Allah Himself is Witness of what ye do?"

Say: "O People of the Scripture! Why drive ye back believers from the way of Allah, seeking to make it crooked, when ye are witnesses to Allah's guidance? Allah is not unaware of what ye do."

O ye who believe! If ye obey a party of those who have received the Scripture they will make you disbelievers after your belief. How can ye disbelieve, when it is ye unto whom Allah's

---

[*]See Deuteronomy chapters 28 and 30.
[†]The acceptance of al-Islam by the Exilarchs (Ar. *Ras al-Jalut*; Heb. *Resh Galutha*; Persian: *Ispahbud*: Abu Muluk) is recorded in the stone thereof.

Revelations are recited, and His messenger is in your midst? He who holdeth fast to Allah, he indeed is guided unto a right path.

O ye who believe! Observe your duty to Allah with right observance, and die not save as those who have surrendered unto Him and hold fast, all of you together, to **The Cable of Allah** (*Urvatu'l-Vuthqa*: The Firm Cord) and do not separate. And remember Allah's favors unto you: How ye were enemies and He made friendship between your hearts so that ye became as brothers by His grace; and how ye were upon the brink of an abyss of fire, and He did save you from it. Thus Allah maketh clear His Revelations unto you, that haply ye may be guided, and there may spring from you a nation who invite to goodness, and enjoin right conduct and forbid indecency. Such are they who are successful. And be ye not as those who separated and disputed *after* THIS RIGHTEOUS BOOK had come unto them. For such there is an awful doom,

On the Day when some faces will be whitened and some faces will be blackened; and as for those whose faces have been blackened, it will be said unto them: "Disbelieved ye after your profession of belief? Then taste the punishment for that ye disbelieved." And as for those whose faces have been whitened, in the mercy of Allah they dwell for ever. These are Revelations of Allah. We recite them unto Thee in truth. Allah willeth no injustice to His creatures. Unto Allah belongeth whatsoever is in the heavens and whatsoever is in the earth; and unto Allah all things are returned.

Ye are **the best Community** that hath been raised up for mankind. Ye enjoin right conduct and forbid indecency; and ye believe in Allah. And if the People of the Scripture had believed it had been better for them. Some of them are believers; but most of them are evil-livers. They will not harm you save a trifling hurt, and if they fight against you they will turn and flee. And afterward they will not be helped. Ignominy shall be their portion wheresoever they are found save where they grasp a rope from Allah and a rope from men. They have incurred anger from their Lord, and wretchedness is laid upon them. That is because they used to disbelieve the Revelations of Allah, and slew the prophets wrongfully. That is because they were rebellious and used to transgress. **They are not all alike**.

Of the People of the Scripture there is a staunch community who recite the Revelations of Allah in the night season, falling prostrate before Him. They believe in Allah and the Last Day, and enjoin right conduct and forbid indecency, and vie one with another in good works. These are of the righteous. And whatever good they do, they will not be denied the meed thereof. Allah is Aware of those who ward off evil.

Lo! The riches and the progeny of those who disbelieve will not avail them aught against Allah; and such are rightful owners of the Fire. They will abide therein. The likeness of that which they spend in this life of the world is as the likeness of a biting, icy wind which smiteth the harvest of a people who have wronged themselves, and devastateth it. Allah wronged them not, but they do wrong themselves.

O ye who believe! Take not for intimates others than your own folk, who would spare no pains to ruin you; they love to hamper you. Hatred is revealed by the utterance of their mouths, but that which their breasts hide is greater. We have made plain for you the Revelations if ye will understand.

Lo! Ye are those who love them though they love you not, and ye believe in all the Scripture. When they fall in with you they say: "We believe;" but when they go apart they bite their finger-tips at you, for rage. Say: "Perish in your rage!"* Lo! Allah is Aware of what is hidden in your breasts. If a lucky chance befall you, it is evil unto them, and if disaster strike you they rejoice thereat. But if ye persevere and keep from evil their guile will never harm you. Lo! Allah is Surrounding what they do.

And when Thou settedst forth at daybreak from Thy housefolk to assign to the believers their positions for the battle, Allah was Hearer, Knower.

When two parties of you almost fell away, and Allah was their Protecting Friend. In Allah let believers put their trust. Allah had already given you the Victory at Badr, when ye were contemptible. So observe your duty to Allah in order that ye may be thankful.

When Thou didst say unto the believers: "Is it not sufficient for you that your Lord should support you with three thousand angels sent down to your help? Nay, but if ye persevere, and keep from evil, and the enemy attack you suddenly, your Lord will help you with five thousand angels sweeping on." Allah ordained this only as a message of good cheer for you, and that thereby your hearts might be at rest--Victory (*al-Fath*) cometh only from Allah, the Mighty, the Wise--That He may cut off a part of those who disbelieve, or overwhelm them so that they retire, frustrated.

It is no concern at all of Thee (O *AL-AMIN*) whether He relent toward them or punish them; for they are evil-doers. Unto Allah belongeth whatsoever is in the heavens and whatsoever is in the earth. He forgiveth whom He will, and punisheth whom He will. Allah is Forgiving, Merciful.

O ye who believe! Devour not usury, doubling and quadrupling the sum lent. Observe your duty to Allah, that ye may be successful. And ward off (from yourselves) the Fire prepared for disbelievers. And obey Allah and the messenger, that ye may find mercy. And vie one with another for forgiveness from your Lord, and for a paradise as wide as are the heavens and the earth, prepared for those who ward off evil; Those who spend (of that which Allah hath given them) in ease and in adversity, those who control their wrath and are forgiving toward mankind; Allah loveth the good; And those who, when they do an evil thing or wrong themselves, remember Allah and implore forgiveness for their sins--Who forgiveth sins save Allah only?-- and will not knowingly repeat the wrong they did. The reward of such will be forgiveness from their Lord, and Gardens underneath which rivers flow, wherein they will abide for ever--a bountiful reward for workers!

Systems have passed away before you. Do but travel in the land and see the nature of the consequence for those who did deny the messengers. This is a **Declaration for Humankind**, a guidance and an admonition unto those who ward off evil. Faint not nor grieve, for ye will overcome them if ye are (indeed) believers. If ye have received a blow, the (disbelieving) people

_____

*"Say: Die in your wrath O evil ones."

have received a blow the like thereof. These are only the vicissitudes which We cause to follow one another for mankind, to the end that Allah may know those who believe and may choose witnesses from among you; and Allah loveth not wrong-doers.

And that Allah may prove those who believe, and may blight the disbelievers. Or deemed ye that ye would enter paradise while yet Allah knoweth not those of you who really strive, nor knoweth those of you who are steadfast? And verily ye used to wish for death before ye met it (in the field). Now ye have seen it with your eyes!

MUHAMMAD is but a messenger, messengers the like of whom have passed away before him. Will it be that, when he dieth or is slain, ye will turn back on your heels? He who turneth back on his heels doth no hurt to Allah, and Allah will reward the thankful.

No soul can ever die except by Allah's leave and at a term appointed. Whoso desireth the reward of the world, We bestow on him thereof; and whoso desireth the reward of the Hereafter, We bestow on him thereof. We shall reward the thankful.

And with how many a prophet have there been a number of devoted men who fought (beside him). They quailed not for aught that befell them in the way of Allah, nor did they weaken, nor were they brought low. Allah loveth the steadfast.

Their cry was only that they said: "Our Lord! Forgive us for our sins and wasted efforts, make our foothold sure, and give us victory over the disbelieving folk." So Allah gave them the reward of the world and the good reward of the Hereafter. Allah loveth those whose deeds are good.*

O ye who believe! If ye obey those who disbelieve, they will make you turn back on your heels, and ye turn back as losers. But Allah is your Protector, and He is the Best of Helpers.

We shall cast terror into the hearts of those who disbelieve because they ascribe unto Allah partners, for which no warrant hath been revealed. Their habitation is the Fire, and hapless the abode of the wrong-doers.

Allah verily made good His promise unto you when ye routed them by His leave, until the moment when your courage failed you, and **ye DISAGREED *about* THE ORDER** (of the Qur'anic Revelation of the Divine Order (*Sirat-Ayat*) of the Holy (*Suwar*) and Sacred *Surahs*!) and *ye* **disobeyed, _after_** He had shown you that for which ye long (this parchment in the correct order and Most Perfect Form: indeed this is the Best and Most Superior of all Qur'ans. "Say: To Museum, Antiquarian, Collector, and Archive go the Furqan: into homes and gardens and dilating hearts and growing bountiful souls receive THIS HOLY QUR'AN†"). Some of you

---

* The good things of thyis world and of the next.
† The meaning of this verse is that the true believers should PURGE, BIND and BANISH (get rid of) the STRANGER of the Furqan (Firkin) from their homes and hearts. Purify themselves, their hearts and homes, and hearths and make ready to receive this Most-Glorious Holy Qur'an (*Qur'an-i Quds El-ABHA*) into their homes, their hearts, their souls, their minds and their very own selves. They are also required to have a physical parchment copy (not digital) of this perfected text of THE TRUE NARRATIVE of *AL-AMIN*! Qur'an means to Recite this visually stabilized parchment copy by chanting aloud! Blessed are they who know! For scholars needing access to the Firkin,

25

desired the world, and some of you desired the Hereafter. Therefore He made you flee from them, that He might try you. Yet now He hath forgiven you. Allah is a Lord of Kindness to believers.

When ye climbed (the hill) and paid no heed to anyone, while the messenger, in your rear, was calling you (to fight). Therefore He rewarded you grief for his grief, that He might teach you not to sorrow either for that which ye missed or for that which befell you. Allah is Informed of what ye do.

Then, after grief, He sent down security for you. As slumber did it overcome a party of you, while (the other) party, who were anxious on their own account, Thought wrongly of Allah, the Thought of ignorance. They said: "Have we any part in the Cause?" Say: "The Cause belongeth wholly to Allah." They hide within themselves (a thought) which they reveal not unto Thee, saying: "Had we had any part in the Cause we should not have been slain here." Say: "Even though ye had been in your houses, those appointed to be slain would have gone forth to the places where they were to lie. All this hath been in order that Allah might try what is in your breasts and prove what is in your hearts. Allah is Aware of what is hidden in the breasts of men."

Lo! Those of you who turned back on the day when the two hosts met, Satan alone it was who caused them to backslide, because of some of that which they have earned. Now Allah hath forgiven them. Lo! Allah is Forgiving, Clement.

O ye who believe! Be not as those who disbelieved and said of their brethren who went abroad in the land or were fighting in the field: "If they had been with us they would not have died or been killed": that Allah may make it anguish in their hearts. Allah giveth life and causeth death; and Allah is Seer of what ye do.

And what though ye be slain in Allah's way or die therein? Surely pardon from Allah and mercy are better than all that they amass.

What though ye be slain or die, when unto Allah ye are gathered?

It was by the mercy of Allah that Thou wast lenient with them (O *AL-AMIN*), for if Thou hadst been stern and fierce of heart they would have dispersed from round about Thee. So pardon them and ask forgiveness for them and consult with them upon the conduct of affairs. And when Thou art resolved, then put Thy trust in Allah. Lo! Allah loveth those who put their trust in Him. If Allah is your helper none can overcome you, and if He withdraw His help from you, who is there who can help you after Him? In Allah let believers put their trust.

It is not for any prophet to embezzle. Whoso embezzleth will bring what he embezzled with him on the Day of Resurrection. Then every soul will be paid in full what it hath earned; and they will not be wronged. Is one who followeth the pleasure of Allah as one who hath earned condemnation from Allah, whose habitation is the Fire, a hapless journey's end?

---

this single copy in their possession must be held secure in their possession according *The Hygienic Laws of at-Tahrim va at-Taharah.*

There are degrees (of grace and reprobation) with Allah, and Allah is Seer of what they do. Allah verily hath shown grace to the believers by sending unto them a messenger of their own who reciteth unto them His Revelations, and causeth them to grow, and teacheth them the Scripture and Wisdom (*hikmat/chokhmah*); although before he came to them they were in flagrant error.

And was it so, when a disaster smote you, though ye had smitten them with a disaster twice as great, that ye said: "How is this?" Say unto them: "It is from yourselves." Lo! Allah is Able to do all things.

That which befell you, on the day when the two armies met, was by permission of Allah; that He might know the true believers;

And that He might know the hypocrites, unto whom it was said: "Come, fight in the way of Allah, or defend yourselves." They answered: "If we knew aught of fighting we would follow you." On that day they were nearer disbelief than faith. They utter with their mouths a thing which is not in their hearts. Allah is Best Aware of what they hide.

Those who, while they sat at home, said of their brethren: "If they had been guided by us they would not have been slain." Say: "Then avert death from yourselves if ye are truthful." Think not of those, who are slain in the way of Allah, as dead. Nay, they are living. With their Lord they have provision.

Jubilant (are they) because of that which Allah hath bestowed upon them of His bounty, rejoicing for the sake of those who have not joined them but are left behind: That there shall no fear come upon them neither shall they grieve. They rejoice because of favor from Allah and kindness, and that Allah wasteth not the wage of the believers.

As for those who heard the call of Allah and His messenger after the harm befell them; for such of them as do right and ward off, there is great reward. Those unto whom men said: "Lo! The people have gathered against you, therefore fear them." The threat of danger but increased the faith of them and they cried: "Allah is Sufficient for us! Most Excellent is He in Whom we trust!"

So they returned with grace and favors from Allah, and no harm touched them. They followed the good pleasure of Allah, and Allah is of Infinite Bounty. It is only the devil who would make souls fear his partisans. Fear them not; fear Me! If ye are true believers!

Let not their conduct grieve Thee, who run easily to disbelief, for Lo! They injure Allah not at all. It is Allah's Will to assign them no portion in the Hereafter, and theirs will be an awful doom. Those who purchase disbelief at the price of faith harm Allah not at all, but theirs will be a painful doom.

And let not those who disbelieve imagine that the rein We give them bodeth good unto their souls. We only give them rein that they may grow in sinfulness. And theirs will be a shameful doom.

It is not the purpose of Allah to leave you in your present state till He shall separate the wicked from the good. And it is not the purpose of Allah to let you know the Unseen. But Allah chooseth of His messengers whom He will, to receive knowledge thereof. So believe in Allah and His messengers. If ye believe and ward off evil, yours will be a vast reward. And let not those who **hoard up** that which Allah hath bestowed upon them of His bounty think that it is better for them. Nay, it is worse for them. That which they hoard will be their collar on the Day of Resurrection. Allah's is the heritage of the heavens and the earth, and Allah is Informed of what ye do.

Verily Allah heard the saying of those who said, when asked for contributions to the war: "Allah, forsooth, is poor, and we are rich!" We shall record their saying with their slaying of the prophets wrongfully and We shall say: "Taste ye the punishment of burning!" This is on account of that which your own hands have sent before you to the judgment. Allah is no oppressor of His bondmen.

The same are those who say: "Lo! Allah hath charged us that we believe not in any messenger until he bring us an offering which fire from heaven shall devour." Say unto them: "Messengers came unto you before me with miracles, and with that very miracle which ye describe. Why then did ye slay them? Answer that if ye are truthful!" And if they deny Thee, even so did they deny messengers who were before Thee, who came with miracles and with the Psalms[*] and with the Scripture giving light. Every soul will taste of death. And ye will be paid on the Day of Resurrection only that which ye have fairly earned. Whoso is removed from the Fire and is made to enter paradise, he indeed is triumphant. **The life of this world is but comfort of illusion**.

Assuredly ye will be tried in your property and in your persons, and ye will hear much wrong from those who were given the Scripture before you, and from the idolaters. But if ye persevere and ward off evil, then that is of the steadfast heart of things. And remember when Allah laid a charge on those who had received the Scripture He said: "Ye are to expound it to humankind and not to hide it." But they flung it behind their backs and bought thereby a little gain. Verily evil is that which they have gained thereby.

Think not that those who exult in what they have given, and love to be praised for what they have not done--Think not, they are in safety from the doom. A painful doom is theirs. Unto Allah belongeth the Sovereignty of the heavens and the earth. Allah is Able to do all things.

Lo! In the creation of the heavens and the earth and in the difference of night and day are tokens of His Sovereignty for people of understanding, such as remember Allah, standing, sitting, and reclining, and consider the creation of the heavens and the earth, and say: "Our Lord! Thou createdst not this in vain. Glory be to Thee! Preserve us from the doom of Fire. Our Lord! Whom Thou causest to enter the Fire: him indeed Thou hast confounded. For evil-doers there will be no helpers. Our Lord! Lo! We have heard a crier calling unto Faith: 'Believe ye in your Lord!' So we believed. Our Lord! Therefore forgive us our sins, and remit from us our evil deeds, and make us die the death of the righteous. Our Lord! And give us that which Thou hast promised to us by Thy messengers. Confound us not upon the Day of Resurrection. Lo! Thou breakest not the tryst."

---

[*]Pslams 89

And their Lord hath heard them and He saith: "Lo! I suffer not the work of any worker, male or female, to be lost. Ye proceed one from another. So those who fled and were driven forth from their homes and suffered damage for My cause, and fought and were slain, verily I shall remit their evil deeds from them and verily I shall bring them into Gardens underneath which rivers flow"--A reward from Allah. And with Allah is the fairest of rewards.

Let not the vicissitude of the success of those who disbelieve, in Leland (*the land*), deceive Thee. It is but a brief comfort. And afterward their habitation will be hell, an ill abode. But those who keep their duty to their Lord, for them are Gardens underneath which rivers flow, wherein they will be safe for ever. A gift of welcome from their Lord. That which Allah hath in store is better for the righteous.

And Lo! Of the People of the Scripture there are some who believe in Allah and that which is revealed unto you and that which was revealed unto them, humbling themselves before Allah. They purchase not a trifling gain at the price of the Revelations of Allah. Verily their reward is with their Lord. Lo! Allah is swift to take account.

O ye who believe! Endure, outdo all others in endurance, be ready, and observe your duty to Allah, in order that ye may succeed.

18. Bism'illah Ar-Rahman Ar-Rahim! at-Tahrim: THE PROHIBITION.

O *PROPHET*! Why bannest Thou that which Allah hath made lawful for Thee, seeking to please Thy wives? And Allah is Forgiving, Merciful.

Allah hath made lawful for you absolution from your oaths (of such a kind), and Allah is your Protector. He is the Knower, the Wise.

When the *PROPHET* confided a fact unto one of his wives and when she afterward divulged it and Allah apprised him thereof, he made known to her part thereof and passed over part. And when he told it to her she said: "Who hath told Thee?" He said: "The Knower, the Aware hath told me."

If ye TWAIN turn unto Allah repentant, (ye have cause to do so) for your hearts desired (the ban); and if ye aid one another against him (*AL-AMIN*) then Lo! Allah, even He, is his Protecting Friend, and Gabriel and the righteous among the believers; and furthermore the angels are his helpers.

It may happen that his Lord, if he divorce you, will give him in your stead wives better than you, Submissive (to Allah), believing, pious, penitent, devout, inclined to fasting, widows and maids.

O ye who believe! Ward off from yourselves and your families a Fire whereof the fuel is men and stones, over which are set angels strong, severe, who resist not Allah in that which He commandeth them, but do that which they are commanded.

Then it will be said: "O ye who disbelieve! Make no excuses for yourselves this day. Ye are only being paid for what ye used to do."

O ye who believe! Turn unto Allah in sincere repentance! It may be that your Lord will remit from you your evil deeds and bring you into Gardens underneath which rivers flow, on the day when Allah will not abase the Prophet and those who believe with him. Their light will run before them and on their right hands; they will say: "Our Lord! Perfect our light for us, and forgive us! Lo! Thou art Able to do all things."

O *PROPHET*! Strive against the disbelievers and the hypocrites, and be stern with them. Hell will be their home, a hapless journey's end.

Allah citeth an example for those who disbelieve: the wife of Noah and the wife of Lot, who were under two of Our righteous slaves yet betrayed them so that they (the husbands) availed them naught against Allah and it was said unto them: "Enter the Fire along with those who enter."

And Allah citeth an example for those who believe: the wife of Pharaoh (Asiyih) when she said: "My Lord! Build for me a home with Thee in the Garden, and deliver me from Pharaoh and his work, and deliver me from evil-doing folk;" And Miriam, daughter of 'Imran, whose body was CHASTE, therefore We breathed therein something of Our Spirit. And she put faith in the words of her Lord and His scriptures, and was of the obedient.

19. Bism'illah Ar-Rahman Ar-Rahim! al-Qari'ah: THE TERRIBLE CALAMITY!

The Calamity!
What is the Calamity?
Ah, what will convey unto Thee what the Calamity is!

A day wherein mankind will be as thickly-scattered moths
And the mountains will become as carded wool.

Then, as for him whose scales are heavy (with good works),
He will live a pleasant life.

But as for him whose scales are light,
A bereft and Hungry One will be his mother,

Ah, what will convey unto Thee what she is!--
Raging Fire!

IV. JUZ'UN ISPARA QUARTO:

20. Bism'illah Ar-Rahman Ar-Rahim! al-Layli: THE NIGHT.

By the night enshrouding
And the day resplendent
And Him Who hath created male and female,
Lo! Your effort is dispersed (toward divers ends).

As for him who giveth and is dutiful (toward Allah)
And believeth in goodness;
Surely We will ease his way unto the state of ease.

But as for him who hoardeth and deemeth himself independent,
And disbelieveth in goodness;
Surely We will ease his way unto adversity.
His riches will not save him when he perisheth.

Lo! Ours it is (to give) the guidance
And Lo! Unto Us belong the latter portion and the former.

Therefore have I warned you of the raging-flaming Fire
Which only the most wretched must endure,
He who denieth and turneth away.

Far removed from it will be the righteous
Who giveth his wealth that he may grow (in goodness).

And none hath with him any favour for reward,
Except as seeking (to fulfill) the purpose of his Lord Most High.

He verily will be Content.

21. Bism'illah Ar-Rahman Ar-Rahim! ash-Shams: THE SUN.

By the sun and his brightness,
And the moon when she followeth him,
And the day when it revealeth him,
And the night when it enshroudeth him,
And the heaven and Him Who built it,
And the earth and Him Who spread it,
And a soul and Him Who perfected it
And inspired it (with conscience of) what is wrong for it and what is right for it.
He is indeed successful who causeth it (the soul) to grow,
And he is indeed a failure who stunteth it.

Thamud denied the truth in their rebellious pride,
When the basest of them broke forth
And the messenger of Allah, said: "It is the she-camel of Allah, so let her drink!"
But they denied him, and they hamstrung her, so Allah doomed them for their sin and razed their dwellings.

He dreadeth not the SEQUEL of events.

22. Bism'illah Ar-Rahman Ar-Rahim! al-Qamar: THE MOON.

The HOUR drew nigh and the moon was rent in TWAIN.

And if they behold a portent they turn away and say: "Prolonged illusion."

They denied the Reality and followed their own lusts. Yet everything will come to a decision and surely there hath come unto them news whereof the purport should deter, Effective Wisdom; but warnings avail not.

So withdraw from them (O *AL-AMIN*) on the day when **The Summoner** summoneth unto a painful thing.

With downcast eyes, they come forth from the graves as they were locusts spread abroad, hastening toward **The Summoner**; the disbelievers say: "This is a hard day."

The folk of Noah denied before them, yea, they denied Our slave ['Abdu'l-Baha] and said: "A madman;" and he was repulsed.

So he cried unto his Lord, saying: "I am vanquished, so give help."

Then opened We the GATES OF HEAVEN with pouring water
And caused the earth to gush forth springs, so that the waters met for a predestined purpose.

And We carried him upon a thing [a train on tracks] of planks and nails, [and on a ship]
That ran (upon the waters) in Our sight, as a reward for him who was rejected.

And verily We left it as a token;[*] but is there any that remembereth?

Then see how dreadful was My punishment after My warnings!

And in truth We have made THIS QUR'AN easy to remember; but is there any that remembereth?

A'ad rejected warnings. Then how dreadful was My punishment after My warnings.

---

[*] The Ark is on Mt. Ararat.

Lo! We let loose on them a raging wind on a day of constant calamity, sweeping men away as though they were uprooted trunks of palm-trees. Then see how dreadful was My punishment after My warnings!

And in truth We have made THIS QUR'AN easy to remember; but is there any that remembereth?

Thamud rejected warnings for they said: "Is it a mortal man, **alone among us**, that we are to follow? Then indeed we should fall into error and madness. Hath THE REMEMBRANCE been given unto him alone among us? Nay, but he is a rash liar."

To the warner it was said: "To-morrow they will know who is the rash liar. Lo! We are sending the she-camel as a test for them; so watch them and have patience; and inform them that the water is to be shared between (her and) them. Every drinking will be witnessed."

But they call their comrade and he took and hamstrung her. Then see how dreadful was My punishment after My warnings!

Lo! We sent upon them ONE SHOUT, and they became as the dry twigs rejected by the builder of a cattle-fold.

And in truth We have made THIS QUR'AN easy to remember; but is there any that remembereth?

The folk of Lot rejected warnings. Lo! We sent a storm of stones upon them all save the family of Lot, whom We rescued in the last watch of the night, as grace from Us. Thus We reward him who giveth thanks. And he indeed had warned them of Our blow, but they did doubt the warnings. They even asked of him his guests for an ill purpose. Then We blinded their eyes and said: "Taste now My punishment after My warnings!" And in truth the punishment decreed befell them early in the morning.

Now taste My punishment after My warnings!

And in truth We have made THIS QUR'AN easy to remember; but is there any that remembereth?

And warnings came in truth unto the house of Pharaoh who denied Our revelations, every one. Therefore We grasped them with the grasp of the Mighty, the Powerful. Are your disbelievers better than those, or have ye some immunity in the scriptures? Or say they: "We are a host victorious?" The hosts will all be routed and will turn and flee. Nay, but the HOUR is their appointed tryst, and the HOUR will be more wretched and more bitter (than their earthly failure).

Lo! The guilty are in error and madness.

On the day when they are dragged into the Fire upon their faces it is said unto them: "Feel the touch of hell!" Lo! We have created every thing by measure.

And Our commandment is but ONE,[*] as the twinkling of an eye.
And verily We have destroyed your fellows; but is there any that remembereth?

And every thing they did is in the scriptures, and every small and great thing is recorded.

Lo! The righteous will dwell among gardens and rivers, firmly established in the favor of **a Mighty King.**

23. Bism'illah Ar-Rahman Ar-Rahim! an-Najm: THE STAR.

By the Star when it setteth, your comrade erreth not, nor is deceived; nor doth he speak of his own desire. It is naught save an inspiration that is inspired, which one of mighty powers hath taught him, One vigorous; and he grew clear to view when he was on the uppermost horizon.

Then he drew nigh and came down till he was distant two bows' length or even nearer, and He revealed unto His slave ['Abdu'l-Baha] that which He revealed [sacred Will and Testament of 'Abdu'l-Baha]. The heart lied not in seeing what it saw.

Will ye then dispute with him concerning what he seeth?[†]

And verily he saw him yet another time by **The Lote-Tree of the Utmost Boundary** (*Sadratu'l Muntaha*) nigh unto which is the Garden of Abode.

When that which shroudeth did enshroud the Lote-Tree, the eye turned not aside nor yet was overbold. Verily he saw one of the greater Revelations of his Lord.

Have ye thought upon Al-Lat and Al-'Uzza and Manat, the third, the other? Are yours the males and His the females? That indeed were an unfair division! They are but names which ye have named, ye and your fathers, for which Allah hath revealed no warrant. They follow but a guess and that which they themselves desire. And now the guidance from their Lord hath come unto them.

Or shall man have what he coveteth? But unto Allah belongeth the after-life, and the former.

And how many angels are in the heavens whose intercession availeth naught save after Allah giveth leave to whom He chooseth and accepteth.

Lo! It is those who disbelieve in the Hereafter who name the angels with the names of females. And they have no knowledge thereof. They follow but a guess, and Lo! A guess can never take the place of the truth.

---

[*]Save Iblis (and those like him) who refuse to surrender.
[†]Leland.

Then withdraw (O *AL-AMIN*) from him who fleeth from Our REMEMBRANCE and desireth but the life of the world. Such is their sum of knowledge. Lo! Thy Lord is Best Aware of him who strayeth, and He is Best Aware of him whom goeth right.

And unto Allah belongeth whatsoever is in the heavens and whatsoever is in the earth, that He may reward those who do evil with that which they have done, and reward those who do good with goodness.

Those who avoid enormities of sin and abominations, save the unwilled offences--(for them) Lo! Thy Lord is of vast mercy. He is Best Aware of you from the time when He created you from the earth, and when ye were hidden in the bellies of your mothers. Therefore ascribe not purity unto yourselves. He is Best Aware of him who wardeth off evil.

Didst Thou (O *AL-AMIN*) observe him who turned away, and gave a little, then was grudging? Hath he knowledge of the Unseen so that he seeth? Or hath he not had news of what is in the books of *MOSES* and Abraham (*Sefer Yetzirah*) who paid his debt: that no laden one shall bear another's load, and that man hath only that for which he maketh effort, and that his effort will be seen.

And afterward he will be repaid for it with fullest payment; and that Thy Lord, He is the GOAL; and that He it is who maketh laugh, and maketh weep, and that He it is Who giveth death and giveth life; and that He createth the TWO SPOUSES, the male and the female, from a drop of goo when it is poured forth; and that He hath ordained the second bringing forth; and that He it is Who enricheth and contenteth; and that He it is Who is **The Lord of Sirius**; and that He destroyed the former people of A'ad, and Thamud He spared not; and the folk of Noah aforetime, Lo! They were more unjust and more rebellious; and Al-Mu'tafikah He destroyed so that there covered them that which did cover.

Concerning which then, of the bounties of Thy Lord, canst Thou dispute?

This is a warner of the warners of old.

The threatened HOUR is nigh: None beside Allah can disclose it.

Marvel ye then at this statement, and laugh and not weep, while ye amuse yourselves?

Rather prostrate yourselves before Allah and serve Him.

24. Bism'illah Ar-Rahman Ar-Rahim! al-Inshiqaq: THE RENDING.

When the heaven is split asunder
And attentive to her Lord in fear,
And when the earth is spread out
And hath cast out all that was in her, and is empty
And attentive to her Lord in fear!
Thou, verily, O man, art working toward Thy Lord

a work which Thou wilt meet in His presence.

Then whoso is given his account in his right hand
He truly will receive an easy reckoning
And will return unto his folk in joy.

But whoso is given his account behind his back,
He surely will invoke destruction
And be thrown to scorching fire.

He verily lived joyous with his folk,
He verily deemed that he would never return.
Nay, but Lo! His Lord is ever looking on him!

Oh, I swear by the afterglow of sunset,
And by the night and all that it enshroudeth,
And by the moon when she is at the full,
That ye shall journey on from plane to plane.

What aileth them, then, that they believe not
And, when THIS QUR'AN is recited unto them, worship not?

Nay, but those who disbelieve will deny;
And Allah knoweth best what they are hiding.
So give them tidings of a painful doom,
Save those who believe and do good works, for theirs is a reward unfailing.

25. Bism'illah Ar-Rahman Ar-Rahim! al-Waqi'ah: THAT WHICH IS COMING.

When the event befalleth--
There is no denying that it will befall--
Abasing some, exalting others;

When the earth is shaken with a shock
And the hills are ground to powder
So that they become a scattered dust,
And ye will be three kinds:

First those on the right hand; what of those on the right hand?
And then those on the left hand; what of those on the left hand?
And the foremost in the race, the foremost in the race:

Those are they who will be brought nigh in Gardens of Delight (*Na'im*); a multitude of those of
old and a few of those of later time. On lined couches, reclining therein face to face. There wait
on them **immortal youths** with bowls and ewers and a cup from a PURE SPRING Wherefrom

36

they get no aching of the head nor any madness, and fruit that they prefer and flesh of fowls that they desire.

And there are fair ones with wide, lovely eyes, like unto hidden pearls, reward for what they used to do. There hear they no vain speaking nor recrimination naught but the saying: "Blessings!"And again: "Blessings!"

And those on the right hand; what of those on the right hand?

Among thornless Lote-Trees and clustered plantains, and spreading shade, and water gushing, and fruit in plenty neither out of reach nor yet forbidden, and raised couches; Lo! We have created them a NEW CREATION; and made them virgins, lovers, friends, for those on the right hand; A multitude of those of old and a multitude of those of later time.

And those on the left hand: What of those on the left hand?

In scorching wind and scalding water and shadow of black smoke, neither cool nor refreshing. Lo! Heretofore they were effete with luxury and used to persist in the awful sin. And they used to say: "When we are dead and have become dust and bones, shall we then, forsooth, be raised again, and also our forefathers?"

Say (unto them, O *AL-AMIN*): "Lo! Those of old and those of later time will all be brought together to the tryst of an appointed day. Then Lo! Ye, the erring, the deniers, ye verily will eat of a Tree called Zaqqum and will fill your bellies therewith; And thereon ye will drink of boiling water, drinking even as the camel drinketh." This will be their welcome on the Day of Judgment. We created you. Will ye then admit the truth?

Have ye seen that which ye emit? Do ye create it or are We the Creator?

We mete out death among you, and We are not to be outrun, that We may **transfigure you** and make you what ye know not. And verily ye know the first creation. Why, then, do ye not reflect? Have ye seen that which ye cultivate? Is it ye who foster it, or are We the Fosterer? If We willed, We verily could make it chaff, then would ye cease not to exclaim: "Lo! We are laden with debt! Nay, but we are deprived!"

Have ye observed the water which ye drink? Is it ye who shed it from the raincloud, or are We the Shedder? If We willed We verily could make it bitter. Why then, give ye not thanks?

Have ye observed the fire which ye strike out; was it ye who made the Tree thereof to grow, or were We the grower? We, even We, appointed it **A Memorial** and a comfort for the dwellers in the wilderness. Therefore (O *AL-AMIN*), praise the name of Thy Lord, the Tremendous.

Nay, I swear by the places of the stars--And Lo! That verily is a tremendous oath, if ye but knew--That *THIS* is indeed a NOBLE QUR'AN in a BOOK kept HIDDEN which none toucheth save the PURIFIED, a REVELATION from the Lord of the Worlds.

Is it *this* Statement that ye scorn, and make denial thereof your livelihood?

Why, then, when the soul cometh up to the throat (of the dying) and ye are at that moment looking--and We are nearer unto him than ye are, but ye see not--why then, if ye are not in bondage (unto Us), do ye not force it back, if ye are truthful?

Thus if he is of those brought nigh, then breath of life, and plenty, and the Gardens of Pleasureable Delight (Na'im). And if he is of those on the right hand, then the greeting "Blessings Be unto Thee" from those on the right hand.

But if he is of the rejecters, the erring, then the welcome will be boiling water and roasting at hell-fire. Lo! This is certain truth.

Therefore (O *AL-AMIN*) praise the name of Thy Lord, the Tremendous.

26. Bism'illah Ar-Rahman Ar-Rahim! al-Infitar: THE CLEAVING ASSUNDER.

When the heaven is cleft asunder,
When the planets are dispersed,
When the seas are poured forth,
And the sepulchres are overturned,
A soul will know what it hath sent before (it) and what left behind.

O man! What hath made Thee careless concerning Thy Lord, the Bountiful,
Who created Thee, then fashioned, then proportioned Thee?
Into whatsoever form He will, He casteth Thee.
Nay, but ye deny the Judgment.

Lo! There are above you Guardians,
Generous and recording,
Who know all that ye do.

Lo! the righteous verily will be in delight.
And Lo! the wicked verily will be in hell;
They will burn therein on the Day of Judgment,
And will not be absent thence.

Ah, what will convey unto Thee what the Day of Judgment is!
Again, what will convey unto Thee what the Day of Judgment is!

A day on which no soul hath power at all for any other soul. The COMMAND on that day is Allah's.

27. Bism'illah Ar-Rahman Ar-Rahim! al-Haqqah: THE ULTIMATELY REAL.

The Reality!
What is the Reality ?
Ah, what will convey unto Thee what the Reality is!

Thamud and A'ad disbelieved in the judgment to come.

As for Thamud, they were destroyed by the lightning. And as for A'ad, they were destroyed by a fierce roaring wind, which He imposed on them for **seven long nights** and **eight long days** so that Thou mightest have seen men lying overthrown, as they were hollow trunks of palm-trees. Canst Thou (O *AL-AMIN*) see any remnant of them?

And Pharaoh and those before him, and the communities that were destroyed, brought error, and they disobeyed the messenger of their Lord, therefore did He grip them with a tightening grip.

Lo! When the waters rose, We carried you upon the ship that We might make it a memorial for you, and that remembering ears (that heard the story) might remember.

And when the trumpet shall sound ONE BLAST and the earth with the mountains shall be lifted up and crushed with one crash, then, on that day will the Event befall.

And the heaven will split asunder, for that day it will be frail. And the angels will be on the sides thereof, and **eight will uphold the Throne of Thy Lord** that day, above them.

On that day ye will be exposed; not a secret of you will be hidden.

Then, as for him who is given his record in his right hand, he will say: "Take, read my book!" Surely I knew that I should have to meet my reckoning.

Then he will be in blissful state in a high garden whereof the clusters are in easy reach. And it will be said unto those therein: "Eat and drink at ease for that which ye sent on before you in past days."

But as for him who is given his record in his left hand, he will say: "Oh, would that I had not been given my book and knew not what my reckoning! Oh, would that it had been death!" My wealth hath not availed me, my power hath gone from me. It will be said: "Take him and fetter him and then expose him to hell-fire and then insert him in a chain whereof the length is seventy cubits."

Lo! He used not to believe in Allah the Tremendous, and urged not on the feeding of the wretched. Therefore hath he no lover here this day, nor any food save filth which none but sinners eat.

But nay! I swear by all that ye see and all that ye see not that it is indeed the speech of an illustrious messenger. It is not poet's speech--little is it that ye believe! Nor diviner's speech--little is it that ye remember! It is A REVELATION from the Lord of the Worlds.

And if he had invented false sayings concerning Us, we assuredly had taken him by the right hand and then severed his life-artery, and not one of you could have held Us off from him.

And Lo! It is a warrant unto those who ward off evil.
And Lo! We know that some among you will deny it.
And Lo! It is indeed an anguish for the disbelievers.
And Lo! It is absolute truth.

So glorify the Name of Thy Tremendous Lord.

28. Bism'illah Ar-Rahman Ar-Rahim! al-Ghashiya: THE OVERWHELMING CALAMITY.

Hath there come unto Thee tidings of the Overwhelming?
On that day faces will be downcast, toiling, weary, scorched by burning fire, drinking from a boiling spring, no food for them save bitter thorn-fruit which doth not nourish nor release from hunger.

In that day other faces will be calm, glad for their effort past, in a high Garden where they hear no idle speech, wherein is a gushing spring, wherein are couches raised and goblets set at hand and cushions ranged and silken carpets spread.

Will they not regard the camels, how they are created?
And the heaven, how it is raised?
And the hills, how they are set up?
And the earth, how it is spread?

Remind them, for Thou art but a REMEMBRANCER,
Thou art not at all a warder over them.
But whoso is averse and disbelieveth,
Allah will punish him with direst punishment.

Lo! Unto Us is their return
And Ours their reckoning.

29. Bism'illah Ar-Rahman Ar-Rahim! al-Zilzal: THE SHAKING.

When Earth is shaken with her Great Earthquake
And Earth yieldeth up her burdens,
And man saith: "What aileth her?"
That day she will relate her chronicles,
Because Thy Lord inspireth her.

That day humankind will issue forth in scattered groups to be shown their deeds.
And whoso doeth good an atom's weight will see it then,
And whoso doeth ill an atom's weight will see it then.

30. Bism'illah Ar-Rahman Ar-Rahim! al-Mulk: THE KINGDOM.

Blessed is He in Whose hand is the Sovereignty, and, He is Able to do all things. Who hath created life and death that He may try you which of you is best in conduct; and He is the Mighty, the Forgiving,

Who hath created **seven heavens in harmony**. Thou (O *AL-AMIN*) canst see no fault in the Beneficent One's creation; then look again: Canst Thou see any rifts?

Then look again and yet again, Thy sight will return unto Thee weakened and made dim. And verily We have beautified the world's heaven with lamps, and We have made them missiles for the devils, and for them We have prepared the doom of flame.

And for those who disbelieve in their Lord there is the doom of hell, a hapless journey's end! When they are flung therein they hear its roaring as it boileth up, as it would burst with rage. Whenever a (fresh) host is flung therein the wardens thereof ask them: "Came there unto you no warner?"

They say: "Yea, verily, a warner came unto us; but we denied and said: 'Allah hath naught revealed; ye are in naught but a great error.'"

And they say: "Had we been wont to listen or have sense, we had not been among the dwellers in the flames." So they acknowledge their sins; but far removed from mercy are the dwellers in the flames.

Lo! Those who fear their Lord in secret, theirs will be forgiveness and a great reward.
And keep your opinion secret or proclaim it, Lo! He is Knower of all that is in the breasts.

Should He not know what He created? And He is the Subtile, the Aware. He it is Who hath made the earth subservient unto you, so Walk in the paths thereof and eat of His providence. And unto Him will be the resurrection (of the dead). Have ye taken security from Him Who is in the heaven that He will not cause the earth to swallow you when Lo! It is convulsed?

Or have ye taken security from Him Who is in the heaven that He will not let loose on you a hurricane? But ye shall know the manner of My warning. And verily those before them denied, then see the manner of My wrath with them! Have they not seen the birds above them spreading out their wings and closing them? Naught upholdeth them save the Beneficent. Lo! He is Seer of all things.

Or who is he that will be an army unto you to help you instead of the Beneficent? The disbelievers are in naught but illusion.

Or who is he that will provide for you if He should withhold His providence? Nay, but they are set in pride and frowardness.

Is he who goeth groping on his face more rightly guided, or he who walketh upright on a straight road?

Say (unto them, O *AL-AMIN*): "He it is who gave you being, and hath assigned unto you ears and eyes and hearts. Small thanks give ye!"

Say: "He it is Who multiplieth you in the earth, and unto Whom ye will be gathered." And they say: "When will this promise be fulfilled, if ye are truthful?"

Say: "The knowledge is with Allah only, and I am but a plain warner; but when they see it nigh, the faces of those who disbelieve will be awry, and it will be said (unto them): "This is that for which ye used to call."

Say (O *AL-AMIN*): "Have ye Thought: Whether Allah causeth me and those with me to perish or hath mercy on us, still, who will protect the disbelievers from a painful doom?"

Say: "He is the Beneficent. In Him we believe and in Him we put our trust. And ye will soon know who it is that is in error manifest."

Say: "Have ye thought: If all your water were to disappear into the earth, who then could bring you gushing water?"

31. Bism'illah Ar-Rahman Ar-Rahim! at-Tariq: THE NIGHT-COMER.

By the heaven and the Morning Star
--Ah, what will tell Thee what the Morning Star is!
--The piercing Star!
No human soul but hath a Guardian over it.
So let man consider from what he is created.

He is created from a gushing fluid
That issued from between the loins and ribs.

Lo! He verily is Able to return him unto life
On the day when hidden thoughts shall be searched out.

Then will he have no might nor any helper.

By the heaven which giveth the returning rain,
And the earth which splitteth (with the growth of trees and plants)
Lo! THIS QUR'AN is a conclusive word,
It is no pleasantry.

Lo! They plot a plot (against Thee, O *AL-AMIN*)
And I plot a plot (against them).

So give a respite to the disbelievers. Deal Thou gently with them for a while.

32. Bism'illah Ar-Rahman Ar-Rahim! ad-Dahr: THE MAN.

Hath there come upon man any period of time in which he was a thing unremembered? Lo! We create man from a drop of thickened fluid to test him; so We make him hearing, knowing.

Lo! We have shown him the way, whether he be grateful or disbelieving.

Lo! We have prepared for disbelievers manacles and carcans and a raging fire.

Lo! The righteous shall drink of a cup whereof the mixture is of Kafur, a spring wherefrom the slaves of Allah drink, making it gush forth abundantly, because they perform the vow and fear a day whereof the evil is wide-spreading, and feed with food the needy wretch, the orphan and the prisoner, for love of Him, saying: "We feed you, for the sake of Allah only. We wish for no reward nor thanks from you;* Lo! We fear from our Lord a day of frowning and of fate." Therefore Allah hath warded off from them the evil of that day, and hath made them find brightness and joy; and hath awarded them for all that they endured, a Garden and silk attire; reclining therein upon couches, they will find there neither (heat of) a sun nor bitter cold. The shade thereof is close upon them and the clustered fruits thereof bow down. Goblets of silver are brought round for them, and beakers as of glass bright as glass but made of silver, which they themselves have measured to the measure of their deeds.

There are they watered with a cup whereof the mixture is of Zanjabil, the water of a spring therein, named Salsabil!

There wait on them immortal youths, whom, when Thou seest, Thou wouldst take for scattered pearls. When Thou seest, Thou wilt see there bliss and high estate. Their raiment will be fine green silk and gold embroidery. Bracelets of silver will they wear. Their Lord will slake their thirst with a pure drink. And it will be said unto them: "Lo! This is a reward for you. Your endeavour upon earth hath found acceptance."

Lo! We, even We, have revealed unto Thee THIS QUR'AN, A REVELATION: so Submit patiently to Thy Lord's command, and obey not of them any guilty one or disbeliever.

Remember the NAME of Thy Lord at morn and evening. And worship Him of the night. And glorify Him through the livelong night.

Lo! These love fleeting life, and put behind them the remembrance of a grievous day. We, even We, created them, and strengthened their frame. And when We will, We can replace them, bringing others like them in their stead.

---

* We seek no reward nor recompense.

Lo! This is an Admonishment, that whosoever will may choose a way unto his Lord. Yet ye will not, unless Allah willeth. Lo! Allah is Knower, Wise.

He maketh whom He will to enter His mercy, and for evil-doers hath prepared a painful doom.

33. Bism'illah Ar-Rahman Ar-Rahim! ad-Dukhan: THE EVIDENT SMOKE.

Ha. Mim.

By the Scripture that maketh plain Lo! We revealed it on a BLESSED NIGHT--Lo! We are ever warning--Whereon every wise command is made clear as a command from Our presence--Lo! We are ever sending--A mercy from Thy Lord.

Lo! He, even He is the Hearer, the Knower, Lord of the heavens and the earth and all that is between them, if ye would be sure. There is no God save Him. He quickeneth and giveth death; your Lord and Lord of your forefathers.

Nay, but they play in doubt.

But watch Thou (O *PROPHET*) for the day when the sky will produce visible smoke that will envelop the people. This will be a painful torment. Then they will say: "Our Lord relieve us of the torment. Lo! We are believers."

How can there be THE REMEMBRANCE for them, when a messenger making plain the Reality had already come unto them, and they had turned away from him and said: "One taught (by others), a madman?"

Lo! We withdraw the torment a little. Lo! Ye return to disbelief.

On the day when We shall seize them with the greater seizure, (then) in truth We shall punish. And verily We tried before them Pharaoh's folk, when there came unto them a Noble Messenger, Saying: "Give up to me the slaves of Allah. Lo! I am a faithful messenger unto you." And saying: "Be not proud against Allah. Lo! I bring you a clear warrant. And Lo! I have sought refuge in my Lord and your Lord lest ye stone me to death. And if ye put no faith in me, then let me go."

And he cried unto his Lord, saying: "These are guilty folk!"

Then (his Lord commanded): "Take away My slaves by night. Lo! Ye will be followed, and leave the sea behind at rest, for Lo! They are a drowned host." How many were the gardens and the watersprings that they left behind, and the cornlands and the goodly sites and pleasant things wherein they took delight!

Even so (it was), and We made it an inheritance for other folk; and the heaven and the earth wept not for them, nor were they reprieved.

And We delivered the Children of Israel from the shameful doom; from Pharaoh. Lo! He was a tyrant of the wanton ones. And We chose them, purposely, above all creatures. And We gave them portents wherein was a clear trial.

Lo! These, forsooth, are saying: "There is naught but our first death, and we shall not be raised again. Bring back our fathers, if ye speak the truth!" Are they better, or the folk of Tubb'a and those before them? We destroyed them, for surely they were guilty.

And We created not the heavens and the earth, and all that is between them, in play. We created them not save with truth; but most of them know not. Assuredly the **Day of Decision** is the term for all of them, a day when friend can in naught avail friend, nor can they be helped, save him on whom Allah hath mercy. Lo! He is the Mighty, the Merciful.

Lo! The Tree of Zaqqum, the food of the sinner! Like molten brass, it seetheth in their bellies As the seething of boiling water. And it will be said: "Take him and drag him to the midst of hell, then pour upon his head the torment of boiling water." Saying: "Taste! Lo! Thou wast forsooth the mighty, the noble! Lo! This is that whereof ye used to doubt."

Lo! Those who kept their duty will be in a place secured. Amid gardens and watersprings, attired in silk and silk embroidery, facing one another. Even so it will be. And We shall wed them unto fair ones with wide, lovely eyes. They call therein for every fruit in safety. They taste not death therein, save the first death. And He hath saved them from the doom of hell, a bounty from Thy Lord. That is the supreme triumph.

And We have made this Scripture easy in Thy language only that they may heed.

Wait then (*O AL-AMIN*) Lo! They too are waiting.

34. Bism'illah Ar-Rahman Ar-Rahim! at-Tin: THE FIG.

By the fig and the olive,
By Mount Sinai,
And by this land made safe;
Surely We created man of the best stature
Then we reduced him to the lowest of the low,
Save those who believe and do good works, and theirs is a reward unfailing.
So who henceforth will give the lie to Thee about the judgment?
Is not Allah the most conclusive of all judges?

35. Bism'illah Ar-Rahman Ar-Rahim! al-'Asr: TIME.

By the declining day,
Lo! Man is a state of loss,
Save those who believe and do good works, and exhort one another to truth
and exhort one another to **Endurance.**

36. Bism'illah Ar-Rahman Ar-Rahim! at-Tur: THE MOUNTAIN.

By the Mount,
And a Scripture inscribed
On fine parchment unrolled,
And the House frequented,
And the roof exalted,
And the sea kept filled,
Lo! The doom of Thy Lord will surely come to pass;
There is none that can ward it off.

On the day when the heaven will heave with (awful) heaving,
And the mountains move away with (awful) movement,
Then woe that day unto the deniers
Who play in talk of grave matters;
The day when they are thrust with a (disdainful) thrust, into the fire of hell
(And it is said unto them): "This is the Fire which ye were wont to deny.
Is this magic, or do ye not see?"

Endure the heat thereof, and whether ye are patient of it or impatient of it is all one for you. Ye are only being paid for what ye used to do.

Lo! Those who kept their duty dwell in Gardens and Delight (*Na'im*), happy because of what their Lord hath given them, and because their Lord hath warded off from them the torment of hell-fire. (And it is said unto them): "Eat and drink in health for what ye used to do, reclining on ranged couches." And we wed them unto fair ones with wide, lovely eyes. And they who believe and whose seed follow them in faith, We cause their seed to join them there, and We deprive them of nought of their life's work. Every man is a pledge for that which he hath earned.

And We provide them with fruit and meat such as they desire. There they pass from hand to hand a cup wherein is neither vanity nor cause of sin. And there go round, waiting on them menservants of their own, as they were hidden pearls. And some of them draw near unto others, questioning, saying: "Lo! Of old, when we were with our families, we were ever anxious;" but Allah hath been gracious unto us and hath preserved us from the torment of the breath of Fire. Lo! We used to pray unto Him of old. Lo! He is the Benign, the Merciful."

Therefore warn (men, O Thou *APOSTLE & PROPHET*). By the grace of Allah Thou art neither soothsayer nor madman.

Or say they: "He is a poet, one for whom we may expect the accident of time?" Say (unto them): "Except your fill! Lo! I am with you among the expectant!"

Do their minds command them to do this, or are they an outrageous folk? Or say they: "He hath invented it?" Nay, but they will not believe!

Then let them produce speech the like thereof, if they are truthful.

Or were they created out of naught? Or are they the creators? Or did they create the heavens and the earth? Nay, but they are sure of nothing!

Or do they own the treasures of Thy Lord? Or have they been given charge thereof? Or have they any **Stairway to Heaven** by means of which they overhear (decrees). Then let their listener produce some warrant manifest!

Or hath He daughters whereas ye have sons? Or askest Thou a fee from them so that they are plunged in debt? Or possess they the Unseen so that they can write it down? Or seek they to ensnare the messenger? But those who disbelieve, they are the ensnared!

Or have they any god beside Allah? Glorified be Allah from all that they ascribe as partner unto Him!

And if they were to see a fragment of the heaven falling, they would say: "A heap of clouds." Then let them be till they meet their day, in which they will be **thunder-stricken**, a DAY in which their guile will naught avail them, nor will they be helped. And verily, for those who do wrong, there is a punishment beyond that. But most of them know not.

So wait patiently (O *APOSTLE*) for Thy Lord's decree, for surely **Thou art in Our sight**; and *Hymn* the Praise of Thy Lord when Thou uprisest, and in the night-season also *Hymn* His Praise, and at the setting of the stars!!

CHINVAT-SIRAT: Bism'illah Ar-Rahman Ar-Rahim!

When Allah's succour (an-Nasr) and the triumph cometh
And Thou seest mankind Entering the religion of Allah in Troops,
Then hymn the praises of Thy Lord, and seek forgiveness of Him.
Lo! He is ever ready to show mercy.

-Sabe'a

MIRAJ!

MIRAJ!

---ADORATIONS OF THE SACRED NIGHT JOURNEY---
(al-'Isrā' wal-Mi'rāj)
Manzil-i-Salat va Wudu
Fiḍál

Bism'illah Ar-Rahman Ar-Rahim!

RECITE! (aq-Qaara): In the name of thy Lord Who createth,
Createth man from a clot (al-'Alaq).
RECITE: And thy Lord is the Most Bounteous,
*Who teacheth by the **PEN**,*
Teacheth man that which he knew not.

V. JUZ'UN SIPARA QUINTO:

37. Bism'illah Ar-Rahman Ar-Rahim! bani Isra'il: O THOSE WHO STRIVE WITH GOD!

GLORIFIED BE HE[*] Who carried His servant by night from the sacred Temple of Mecca to the Far Distant Temple [of Ezekiel[†]] the neighborhood whereof [Rocky Mountains of the USA] We have blessed, that We might show him of Our tokens! Lo! He, only He, is the Hearer, the Seer.

We gave unto *MOSES* the Scripture, and We appointed it a guidance for the children of Israel, saying: "Choose no Guardian [Psalm 89] beside Me."

The seed of those whom We carried (in the ship) along with Noah. Lo! He was a grateful slave.

And We decreed for the Children of Israel in the Scripture: "Ye verily will work corruption in the earth twice [attacks against the first and second Temples; the first and second IBC/UHJ; first and second attacks on the Trade Towers], and ye will become great tyrants."

So when the time for the first of the two came, We roused against you slaves of Ours of great might who ravaged your country, and it was a threat performed [Shalamanasser III and Titus of Rome; the Covenant-breaking "Hands" former-members of first and second IBCs; underground explosion/four planes]

---

[*]**Al-Musabbihat** refer to the collective name of the seven surahs that begin with Allah's *__glorification__* 'Subhana,' 'Sabbaha,' and 'Yusabbihu:' *al-Hadid*; *al-Hashr*; *as-Saff*; *al-Jumua*; *at-Taghabun*; *al-Isra*; and *al-Ala*.
[†]Here on his journey Muhammad met with the Mormon Prophet George Williams in Utah in 1863 and then proceeded on his way in his own continuing Night Journey to the Deer Lodge Sanctuary and then the vicinity of THE CITY (Missoula, MT) and beyond. See my *EZEKIEL'S TEMPLE IN MONTANA*, for more.

Then we gave you once again your turn against them, and We aided you with wealth and children and made you more in soldiery. Saying: "If ye do good, ye do good for your own souls, and if ye do evil, it is for them. So, when the time for the second (of the judgments) came (We roused against you others of Our slaves) to ravage you, and to enter the Temple even as they entered it the first time, and to lay waste all that they conquered with an utter wasting.

It may be that your Lord will have mercy on you, but if ye repeat (the crime) We shall repeat (the punishment), and We have appointed hell a dungeon for the disbelievers.

Lo! THIS QUR'AN guideth unto that which is straightest, and giveth tidings unto the believers who do good works that theirs will be a great reward. And that those who believe not in the Hereafter, for them We have prepared a painful doom. Man prayeth for evil as he prayeth for good; for man was ever hasty.

And We appoint the night and the day two portents. Then We make dark the portent of the night, and We make the portent of the day sight-giving, that ye may seek bounty from your Lord, and that ye may know the computation of the years, and the reckoning; and everything have We expounded with a clear expounding.

And every man's augury have We fastened to his own neck, and We shall bring forth for him on the Day of Resurrection a BOOK which he will find wide open. And it will be said unto him: "Read Thy BOOK!" Thy *soul* sufficeth as reckoner against Thee this day.

Whosoever goeth right, it is only for the good of his own soul that he goeth right, and whosoever erreth, erreth only to its hurt. No laden soul can bear another's load, We never punish until we have sent a messenger. And when We would destroy a township We send commandment to its folk who live at ease, and afterward they commit abomination therein, and so the WORD hath effect for it, and we annihilate it with complete annihilation.

How many generations have We destroyed since Noah! And Allah sufficeth as Knower and Beholder of the sins of His slaves. Whoso desireth that which hasteneth away, We hasten for him therein what We will for whom We please. And afterward We have appointed for him hell; he will endure the heat thereof, condemned, rejected. And whoso desireth the Hereafter and striveth for it with the effort necessary, being a believer; for such, their effort findeth favor (with their Lord). Each do We supply, both these and those, from the bounty of Thy Lord. And the bounty of Thy Lord can never be walled up.

See how We prefer one of them above another, and verily the Hereafter will be greater in degrees and greater in preferment. Set not up with Allah any other god lest Thou sit down reproved, forsaken. Thy Lord hath decreed, that ye worship none save Him, and that ye show kindness to parents. If one of them or both of them attain old age with Thee, say not "FIE!" unto them nor repulse them, but speak unto them a gracious word. And lower unto them the wing of Submission through mercy, and say: "My Lord! Have mercy on them both as they did care for me when I was little!" Your Lord is Best Aware of what is in your minds. If ye are righteous, then Lo! He was ever Forgiving unto those who turn unto Him.

Give the kinsman his due, and the needy, and the wayfarer, and squander not Thy wealth in wantonness. Lo! The Squanderers were ever brothers of the devils, and the devil was ever an ingrate to his Lord. But if Thou turn away from them, seeking mercy from Thy Lord, for which Thou hopest, then speak unto them a reasonable word. And let not Thy hand be chained to Thy neck nor open it with a complete opening, lest thou sit down rebuked, denuded. Lo! thy Lord enlargeth the provision for whom He will, and straiteneth it for whom He will. Lo, He was ever Knower, Seer of His slaves.

Slay not your children, fearing a fall to poverty, We shall provide for them and for you. Lo! The slaying of them is great sin. And come not near unto adultery. Lo! It is an abomination and an evil way. And slay not the life which Allah hath forbidden save with right. Whoso is slain wrongfully, We have given power unto his heir, but let him not commit excess in slaying. Lo! He will be helped. Come not near the wealth of the orphan save with that which is better till he come to strength; and **Keep the COVENANT**. **Lo! Of** the **COVENANT** it will be **asked.**

Fill the measure when ye measure, and weigh with a right balance; that is meet, and better in the end. Follow not that whereof Thou hast no knowledge. Lo! The hearing and the sight and the heart--of each of these it will be asked.

And walk not in the earth exultant. Lo! Thou canst not rend the earth, nor canst Thou stretch to the height of the hills. The evil of all that is hateful in the sight of Thy Lord. This is of that Wisdom wherewith Thy Lord hath inspired Thee. And set not up with Allah any other god, lest Thou be cast into hell, reproved, abandoned.

Hath your Lord then distinguished you by giving you Sons, and hath chosen for Himself females from among the angels? Lo! Verily ye speak an awful word! We verily have displayed Our warnings in THIS QUR'AN that they may take heed, but it increaseth them in naught save aversion.

Say: "If there were other gods along with Him, as they say, then had they sought a way against the **Lord of the Throne**. Glorified is He, and High **Exalted above what they say**!

The **seven heavens** and the earth and all that is therein praise Him, and there is not a thing but hymneth His praise; but ye understand not their praise. Lo! He is ever Clement, Forgiving.

And when Thou recitest THIS QUR'AN we place between Thee and those who believe not in the Hereafter a hidden barrier; and We place upon their hearts veils lest they should understand it, and in their ears a deafness; and when Thou makest mention of Thy Lord alone in THIS QUR'AN, they turn their backs in aversion.

We are Best Aware of what they wish to hear when they give ear to Thee and when they take secret counsel, when the evil-doers say: "Ye follow but a man bewitched."

See what similitudes they coin for Thee, and thus are all astray, and cannot find a road! And they say: "When we are bones and fragments, shall we forsooth, be raised up as a new creation?"

Say: "Be ye stones or iron or some created thing that is yet greater in your thoughts!" Then they will say: "Who shall bring us back." Say: "He Who created you at the first." Then will they shake their heads at Thee, and say: "When will it be?" Say: "It will perhaps be soon; a day when He will call you and ye will answer with His praise, and ye will think that ye have tarried but a little while." Tell My bondmen to speak that which is kindlier. Lo! The devil soweth discord among them. Lo! The devil is for man an open foe.

Your Lord is Best Aware of you. If He will, He will have mercy on you, or if He will, He will punish you. We have not sent Thee as a warden over them.

And Thy Lord is Best Aware of all who are in the heavens and the earth. And we preferred some of the prophets above others, and <u>unto David</u> We gave <u>the Psalms</u>.[*]

Say: "Cry unto those whom ye assume to be gods beside Him, yet they have no power to rid you of misfortune nor to change." Those unto whom they cry seek the way of approach to their Lord, which of them shall be the nearest; they hope for His mercy and they fear His doom. **<u>Lo! The DOOM of Thy Lord is to be shunned.</u>**

There is not a township but We shall destroy it ere the Day of Resurrection, or punish it with dire punishment. That is set forth in the BOOK.

Naught hindereth Us from sending portents save that the folk of old denied them. And We gave Thamud the *she-camel*[†]--a clear portent save to warn.

And when we told Thee: "Lo! Thy Lord encompasseth mankind, and We appointed not **The Vision** which we showed you but as a TEST for humankind! And likewise **The Accursed Tree** in THIS QUR'AN. We warn them, but it increaseth them in naught save gross impiety.

And when We said unto the angels: "Fall down prostrate before *ADAM*" and they fell prostrate all save Iblis, he said: "Shall I fall prostrate before that which Thou hast created of clay?" He said: "Seest Thou this whom Thou hast honoured above me, if Thou give me grace until the Day of Resurrection I verily will seize his seed, save but a few."

He said: "Go, and whosoever of them followeth Thee--Lo! Hell will be your payment, ample payment. And excite any of them whom Thou canst with Thy voice, and urge Thy horse and foot

---

[*]Psalm 89:1-4; 26-29; 35-37 KJV: "I will sing of the mercies of the LORD for ever: with my mouth will I make known Thy faithfulness to all generations. For I have said, Mercy shall be built up for ever: Thy faithfulness shalt Thou establish in the very heavens. **I have made a Covenant with my chosen, I have sworn <u>unto David my servant</u>, Thy seed will I establish for ever, and build up <u>Thy throne</u> to all generations. Selah**... He shall cry unto me, Thou art my Father, my God, and the Rock of my Salvation. Also I will make him my firstborn, higher than the kings of the earth. My mercy will I keep for him for evermore, and **my covenant shall stand fast with him**. His seed also will I make to endure for ever, and his throne as the days of heaven... Once have I sworn by my holiness that **I will not lie unto David**. His seed shall endure for ever, and his **throne** as the sun before me. **It shall be established for ever** as the moon, and as a faithful witness in heaven. Selah."

[†] The Avestan "Hustra" literally means "camel" and refers to the Pure Revelation of *ZOROASTER* (*zarathustra*) that immediately preceded the Revelation (vehicle: *Vahana*) of *THE BUDDHA* and immediately followed the Revelation of *KRISHNA*.

against them, and be a partner in their wealth and children, and promise them." Satan promiseth them only to deceive. Lo! My faithful bondmen--over them Thou hast no power, and Thy Lord sufficeth as their Guardian.

O Humanity! Your Lord is He Who driveth for you the ship upon the sea that ye may seek of His bounty. Lo! He was ever Merciful toward you. And when harm toucheth you upon the sea, all unto whom ye cry for succor fail save Him alon), but when He bringeth you safe to land, ye turn away, for man was ever thankless. Feel ye then secure that He will not cause a slope of the land to engulf you, or send a sand-storm upon you, and then ye will find that ye have no protector? Or feel ye secure that He will not return you to that plight a second time, and send against you a hurricane of wind and drown you for your thanklessness, and then ye will not find therein that ye have any avenger against Us?

Verily we have honored the Children of *ADAM*. We carry them on the land and the sea, and have made provision of good things for them, and have preferred them above many of those whom We created with a marked preferment. On the day when We shall summon all men with their RECORD, whoso is given his BOOK in his right hand--such will read their BOOK and they will not be wronged a shred. Whoso is blind here will be blind in the Hereafter, and yet further from the road.

And they indeed strove hard to beguile Thee (O *AL-AMIN*) away from that wherewith We have inspired Thee, that Thou shouldst invent other than it against Us; and then would they have accepted Thee as a friend. And if We had not **made Thee wholly firm** Thou mightest almost have inclined unto them a little. Then had we made Thee taste a double punishment of living and a double punishment of dying, then hadst Thou found no helper against Us. And they indeed **wished to scare Thee from the land** that they might drive Thee forth from thence, and then they would have stayed there but a little after Thee. Such was Our method in the case of those whom We sent before Thee, and Thou wilt not find for OUR METHOD aught of power to change.

Establish worship at the going down (*Maghrib*) of the Sun--before the nightfall and during the twilights of the first seen lights of the Starry, Starry Night--establish worship in the Dark of Night (*Ishaa*), and *Hear* (the recital of) THIS HOLY QUR'AN after dawn (*Zhur*). Lo! *Hear!* (the recital of) THIS HOLY QUR'AN after dawn (*Asr*) is ever witnessed. And some part of the night awake (*Fajr*) for *it*--before the sunrise and before the twilights of the daybreak: a largess for Thee. It may be that thy Lord will raise Thee to a praised estate.[*]

And say: "My Lord! **Cause me to come in with a firm incoming and to go out with a firm outgoing.** And give me from Thy Presence a sustaining Power." And say: "Truth hath come and falsehood hath vanished away." Lo! Falsehood is ever bound to vanish.

---

[*]These are the five orders of prayers given by Allah to Muhammad in consequence of this Night Journey. These correspond to the Five Movements (Chinese: 五行; pinyin: *Wŭ Xíng*): The five overcoming fluid interactions and overlapping modalities of melting, penetrating, separating, absorbing, and quenching. These five are in Order of the Day: (a) *Maghrib* (the Twilight Glow after the Sundisk is hidden till Dark); (b) *Ishaa* (from Dusk till Dawn); (c) *Fajr* (the Twilight Glow *before* the Sundisk peaks its first Direct-Ray till Daybreak); (d) *Zuhr* (NoonDay); (e) *Asr* (Afternoon). Like the Jews and the Baha'is, the Muslim day begins and ends at Sunset. The same is true for many other cultures, peoples, and ways.

And We reveal of THIS QUR'AN that which is a healing and a mercy for believers though it increase the evil-doers in naught save ruin. And when We make life pleasant unto man, he turneth away and is averse; and when ill toucheth him he is in despair. Say: "Each one doth according to his rule of conduct, and Thy Lord is Best Aware of him whose way is right."

They are asking Thee concerning the Spirit. Say: "The Spirit is by command of my Lord, and of knowledge ye have been vouchsafed but little." And if We willed We could withdraw that which We have Revealed unto Thee, then wouldst Thou find no Guardian for Thee against Us in respect thereof. It is naught save mercy from Thy Lord. Lo! His kindness unto Thee was ever great.

Say: "Verily, though humankind and the jinn should assemble to produce the like of THIS QUR'AN, they could not produce the like thereof though they were helpers one of another." And verily We have displayed for humankind in THIS QUR'AN all kind of similitudes, but most of humankind refuse aught save disbelief. And they say: "We will not put faith in Thee till Thou cause a spring to gush forth from the earth for us; or Thou have a garden of date-palms and grapes, and cause rivers to gush forth therein abundantly; or Thou **cause the heaven to fall upon us piecemeal**, as Thou hast pretended, or bring Allah and the angels as a warrant; or Thou have a house of gold; or Thou **ascend up into heaven**, and even then we will put no faith in **Thine Ascension** till Thou bring down for us a BOOK that we can read." Say: "My Lord be Glorified! Am I aught save a mortal messenger?" And naught prevented mankind from believing when the guidance came unto them save that they said: "Hath Allah sent a mortal as His messenger?"

Say: "If there were in the earth angels walking secure, We had sent down for them from heaven an angel as messenger." Say: "Allah sufficeth for a witness between me and you. Lo! He is Knower, Seer of His slaves." And he whom Allah guideth, he is led aright; while, as for him whom He sendeth astray, for them Thou wilt find no protecting friends beside Him, and We shall assemble them on the Day of Resurrection on their faces, blind, dumb and deaf; their habitation will be hell; whenever it abateth, We increase the flame for them. That is their reward because they disbelieved Our Revelations and said: "When we are bones and fragments shall we, forsooth, be raised up as a new creation?"

Have they not seen that Allah Who created the heavens and the earth is Able to create the like of them, and hath appointed for them an end whereof there is no doubt? But the wrong-doers refuse aught save disbelief. Say: "If ye possessed the treasures of the mercy of my Lord, ye would surely hold them back for fear of spending, for man was ever grudging."

And verily We gave unto *MOSES* nine tokens, and THIS RIGHTEOUS BOOK. Do but ask the Children of Israel how he came unto them, then Pharaoh said unto him: "Lo! I deem Thee one bewitched, O *MOSES*."

He said: "In truth Thou knowest that none sent down these portents save the Lord of the heavens and the earth as proofs, and Lo! For my part, I deem Thee lost, O Pharaoh." And he wished to scare them from the land, but We drowned him and those with him, all together.

And We said unto the Children of Israel after him: "Dwell in the land;" but when the promise of the Hereafter cometh to pass We shall bring you as a crowd gathered out of various nations. With truth have We sent it down, and with truth hath it descended. And We have sent Thee as naught else save a bearer of good tidings and a warner.

And *THIS* is *THE* QUR'AN that WE have divided (*7 Manzil|30 Juz|60 Hizb|240 Maqra*): THAT Thou mayst recite it unto HUMANKIND at intervals, and We have revealed it by Progressive Revelation.

Say: "Believe therein or believe not, Lo! Those who were given knowledge before it, when it is read unto them, fall down prostrate on their faces, adoring, saying: "Glory to our Lord! **Verily the promise of our Lord must be fulfilled!**" They fall down on their faces, weeping, and it increaseth humility in them.

Say: "Cry unto Allah, **or cry unto the Beneficent** (*Ar-Rahman*), unto whichsoever ye cry (it is the same). His are **The Most Beautiful Names**. And Thou, be not loud-voiced in Thy worship nor yet silent therein, but **follow A WAY between**.

And say: "Praise be to Allah, Who hath not taken unto Himself a Son, and Who hath no partner in the Sovereignty, nor hath He any protecting friend through dependence." And magnify Him with all Magnificence!

38. Bism'illah Ar-Rahman Ar-Rahim! al-Quraysh: THE ASSOCIATION.

For the taming of Quraysh: the people of the Association of the Covenant (*Hisb'Ahd-ullah*),
For their taming We cause the caravans to set forth in winter and summer.
So let them worship the **Lord of this House**,
Who hath fed them against hunger and hath made them safe from fear.

39. Bism'illah Ar-Rahman Ar-Rahim! al-Aliyah: THE ASCENT.

Nay, I swear by THIS CITY *(al-Balad)*
And Thou art an indweller of THIS CITY (*Baladeh an-Nur*)--
And the begetter and that which he begat,
We verily have created man in an atmosphere:
Thinketh he that none hath power over him?
And he saith: "I have destroyed vast wealth:"
Thinketh he that none beholdeth him?
Did We not assign unto him two eyes
And a tongue and two lips,
And guide him to the parting of the mountain ways?
But he hath not attempted the Ascent (*al-Aliyah*)--
Ah, what will convey unto Thee what the Ascent is!--
It is to free a slave,
And to feed in the day of hunger.
An orphan near of kin,

Or some poor wretch in misery,
And to be of those who believe
and exhort one another to perseverance
and exhort one another to pity.
Their place will be on the right hand.
But those who disbelieve Our Revelations,
their place will be on the left hand.
Fire will be an awning over them.

VI. JUZ'UN SIPARA SEXTO:

ba. Bism'illah Ar-Rahman Ar-Rahim! Hadith al-'Isrā' wal-Mi'rāj: THE NIGHT JOURNEY!

In the Name of Allah Most Merciful Most Beneficient!

Blessings and Peace upon the Messenger of Allah and his Family and Companions.

As the Prophet, upon him blessings and peace, was in al-Hijr at the House (the semi-circular space under the waterspout which is open on both sides on the Northwest side of the Ka'ba), lying down at rest between two men (his uncle Hamza and his cousin Ja'far ibn Abi Talib), Gabriel and Michael came to him. With them was a third angel (Israfil). They carried him until they brought him to the spring of Zamzam, where they asked him to lie on his back and Gabriel took him over from the other two. The Prophet said: "The roof of my house was opened and Gabriel descended."

He split the Prophet's chest from his throat to the bottom of his belly. Then Gabriel said to Michael: "Bring me a *tast* (a vessel, usually made of copper) of water from Zamzam so that I will purify his heart and expand his breast." He took out his heart and washed it three times, removing from it what was wrong. Michael went back and forth to him with the vessel of water from Zamzam three times.

Then he brought him a golden vessel filled with Wisdom and Belief which he emptied into his chest. He filled his chest with *hilm* (intelligence, patience, good character), knowledge, certainty, and submission, then he closed it up. He sealed it between his shoulders with the seal of Prophethood.

Then he brought **the Buraq** (lightning-mount), handsome-faced and bridled, a tall, white beast, bigger than the donkey but smaller than the mule. He could place his hooves at the farthest boundary of his gaze. He had long ears. Whenever he faced a mountain his hind legs would extend, and whenever he went downhill his front legs would extend. **He had two wings** on his thighs which lent strength to his legs.

He bucked when the Prophet came to mount him. Gabriel put his hand on his mane and said: "Are you not ashamed, O Buraq? By Allah, no-one has ridden you in all creation more dear to Allah than he is." Hearing this he was so ashamed that he sweated until he became soaked, and he stood still so that the Prophet mounted him.

The other Prophets used to mount the Buraq before. Sa'id ibn al-Musayyib said: "It is the beast of Abraham which he used to mount whenever he travelled to **The Sacred House**."

Gabriel departed with him. He placed himself on his right while Michael was on his left. The one holding his stirrup was Gabriel and the one holding the reins of the Buraq was Michael.

They travelled until they reached a land filled with datepalms. Gabriel said to the Prophet: "Alight and pray here." He did so and remounted, then Gabriel said: "Do you know where you prayed?" He said no. Gabriel said: "You prayed in a *tayba* (land of pastures) and the Migration will take place there."

The Buraq continued his lightning flight, placing his hooves wherever his gaze could reach. Gabriel then said again: "Alight and pray here." He did so and remounted, then Gabriel said: "Do you know where you prayed?" He said no. Gabriel said: "You prayed in the City of Madyan at the Tree of *MOSES*."

The Buraq continued his lightning flight, then Gabriel said again: "Alight and pray here." He did so and remounted, then Gabriel said: "Do you know where you prayed?" He said no. Gabriel said: "You prayed at the MOUNTAIN OF SINA' (Mount Sinai) where Allah addressed *MOSES*."

Then he reached a land where the palaces of Syria became visible to him. Gabriel said to him: "Alight and pray." He did so and remounted, then the Buraq continued his lightning flight and Gabriel said: "Do you know where you prayed?" He said no. Gabriel said: "You prayed in Bayt Lahm (Bethlehem), where *JESUS* son of Miriam was born."

As the Prophet was travelling mounted on the Buraq he saw a devil from the jinn who was trying to get near him holding a firebrand. Everywhere the Prophet turned he would see him. Gabriel said to him: "Shall I teach you words which, if you say them, his firebrand will go out and he will fall dead?" The Prophet said yes. Gabriel said:

"Say: I seek refuge in the Face of Allah the Munificent and in Allah's perfect words which neither the righteous nor the disobedient overstep from the evil of what descends from the heaven and the evil of what ascends to it and the evil of what is created in the earth and the trials of the night and the day and the visitors of the night and the day except the visitor that comes with goodness, O Beneficent One!"

At this the devil fell dead on his face and his firebrand went out.

They travelled until they reached a people who sowed in a day and reaped in a day. Every time they reaped, their harvest would be replenished as before. The Prophet said: "O Gabriel, what is this?" He replied: "These are *al-mujahidun*--those who strive--in the path of Allah the Exalted. Every good deed of theirs is multiplied for them seven hundred times, and whatever they spend returns multiplied."

The Prophet then noticed a fragrant wind and said: "O Gabriel, what is this sweet scent?" He replied: "This is the scent of the lady who combed the hair of Pharaoh's daughter and that of her children. As she combed the hair of Pharaoh's daughter the comb fell and she said: "In the name of Allah, may Pharaoh perish!" whereupon Pharaoh's daughter said: "Do you have a Lord other than my father?" She said yes. Pharaoh's said: "Shall I tell my father?" She said yes. She told him and he summoned her and said: "Do you have a Lord other than me?" She replied: "Yes, my Lord and your Lord is Allah."

This woman had two sons and a husband. Pharaoh summoned them and he began to entice the woman and her husband to renegade on their religion, but they refused. He said: "Then I shall kill you." She said: "Be so good as to bury us all together in a single grave if you kill us." He replied: "Granted, and it is your right to ask us." He then ordered that a huge cow made of copper be filled with boiling liquid (oil and water) and that she and her children be thrown into it. The children were taken and thrown in one after the other. The second and youngest was still an infant at the breast. When they took him he said: "Mother! Fall and do not tarry for verily you are on the right." Then she was thrown in with her children.

Then the Prophet saw people whose heads were being shattered, then every time they would return to their original state and be shattered again without delay. He said: "O Gabriel, who are these people?" He replied: "These are the people whose heads were too heavy (on their pillows) to get up and fulfill the prescribed prayers."

Then he saw a people who wore loincloths on the fronts and on their backs. They were roaming the way camels and sheep roam about. They were eating thistles and **Zaqqum** (*Basmala 15: as-Saffat*) and white-hot coals and stones of Gehenna. He said: "Who are these, O Gabriel?" He replied: "These are the ones who did not meet the obligation of paying *zakat* from what they possessed, whereas Allah never kept anything from them."

Then he saw a people who had in front of them excellent meats disposed in pots and also putrid, foul meat, and they would eat from the foul meat and not touch the good meat. He said: "What is this, O Gabriel?" He replied: "These are the men from your Community who had an excellent, lawful wife at home and who would go and see a foul woman and spend the night with her; and the women who would leave her excellent, lawful husband to go and see a foul man and spend the night with him."

Then he came to a plank in the middle of the road which not even a piece of cloth nor less than that could cross except it would be pierced. He said: "What is this, O Gabriel?" He replied: "This is what happens to those of your Community who sit in the middle of the road and cut it" and he recited: "Lurk not on every road to threaten wayfarers and to turn away from Allah's path him who believes in Him, and to seek to make it crooked." (*Basmala 105: al-A'raf*).

The Prophet saw a man swimming in a river of blood and he was being struck in his mouth with rocks which he then swallowed. The Prophet asked: "What is this, O Gabriel?" He replied: "This is what happens to those who eat usury."

Then he saw a man who had gathered a stack of wood which he could not carry, yet he was adding more wood to it. He said: "What is this, O Gabriel?" He replied: "This is a man from your Community who gets people's trusts when he cannot fulfill them, yet he insists on carrying them.

He then saw people whose tongues and lips were being sliced with metal knives. Every time they were sliced they would return to their original state to be sliced again without respite. He said: "Who are these, O Gabriel?" He replied: "These are the public speakers of division in your Community: they say what they don't do."

Then he passed by people who had copper nails with which they scratched their own faces and chests. He asked: "Who are these, O Gabriel?" He replied: "These are the ones who ate the flesh of people (backbiters) and tarnished their reputations."

Then he saw a small hole with a huge bull coming out of it. The bull began to try entering the hole again and was unable. The Prophet said: "What is this, O Gabriel?" He replied: "This is the one in your Community who tells an enormity, then he feels remorse to have spoken it but is unable to take it back."

He then came to a valley in which he breathed a sweet, cool breeze fragrant with musk and he heard a voice. He said: "What is this, O Gabriel?" He replied: "This is the voice of Paradise saying: 'O my Lord, bring me what You have promised me for too abundant are my rooms, my gold-laced garments, my silk, my brocades, my carpets, my pearls, my coral, my silver, my gold, my goblets, my bowls, my pitchers, my couches, my honey, my water, my milk, my wine!' And He says: 'You will have every single Muslim and Muslima, every Mu'min and Mu'mina, and everyone who has believed in Me and My Messengers and did excellent deeds without associating a partner to Me nor taking helpers without Me. Anyone who fears Me will be safe, and whoever asks Me I shall give him, and whoever lends Me something I shall repay him, and whoever relies on Me I shall suffice him. I am Allah besides Whom there is no god. I never fail in My promise. Successful indeed are the believers! Blessed is Allah, therefore, the best of Creators!' And Paradise answered: 'I accept.'"

Then he came to a valley in which he heard a detestable sound and smelled a stench-carrying wind. He said: "What is this, O Gabriel?" He replied: "This is the sound of Gehenna saying: 'O Lord, give me what You promised me, for abundant are my chains, my yokes, my punishments, my fires, my thistles, my pus, my tortures! My depth is abysmal, my heat is extreme, therefore give me what You promised me!' And He replied: 'You will have every idolater and idolatress, every male and female disbeliever and foul one, and every tyrant who does not believe in the Day of Reckoning.'"

The Prophet saw the Dajjal in his actual likeness. He saw him with his own eyes not in a dream. It was said to him: "O Messenger of Allah, how was he when you saw him?" He replied: "Mammoth-sized (*faylamaniyyan*), extremely pale and white (*aqmaru hijan*), one of his eyes is protuberant as if it were a twinkling star. His hair is like the branches of a tree. He resembles 'Abd al-'Uzza ibn Qatan who died in Jahiliyya."

The Prophet saw a pearl-like white column which the angels were carrying. He said: "What is this you are carrying?" They replied: "**The Column of Islam**. We have been ordered to place it **in SYRIA**-- the quintessence of Allah's lands."

The Prophet said: "I saw on the **Night that I was Enraptured (Miraj)** a white column resembling a pearl, which the angels were carrying. I said to them: What are you carrying? They replied: **The Column of the Book**. We have been ordered to place it in Syria. Later, in my sleep, I saw that **The Column of the Book** was snatched away from under my headrest. I began to fear lest Allah the Almighty had abandoned the people of the earth. My eyes followed where it went. It was a brilliant light in front of me. **Then I saw it was placed in Syria**."

As the Prophet was travelling he heard someone calling him from his right: "O *MUHAMMAD*, look at me, I want to ask you something!" But the Prophet did not respond. Then he said: "Who was this, O Gabriel?" He replied: "This is the herald of the Jews. If you had answered him your Community would have followed Judaism."

The Prophet continued travelling and he heard someone calling him from his left: "O *MUHAMMAD*, look at me, I want to ask you something!" But the Prophet did not respond. Then he said: "Who was this, O Gabriel?" He replied: "This is the herald of the Christians. If you had answered him your Community would have followed Christianity."

The Prophet continued travelling and then passed by a woman with bare arms, decked with every female ornament Allah had created. She said: "O *MUHAMMAD*, look at me, I need to ask you something." But he did not look at her. Then he said: "Who was this, O Gabriel?" He replied: "This was the world, *(al-dunya)*. If you had answered her, your Community would have preferred the world to the hereafter."

As the Prophet travelled on, he passed by an old man who was a distance away from his path saying: "Come hither, O *MUHAMMAD*!" But Gabriel said: "Nay, go on, O *MUHAMMAD*!" The Prophet went on and then said: "Who was this, O Gabriel?" He replied: "This was Allah's enemy, Iblis. He wanted you to incline towards him."

He went on and passed by an old woman on the roadside who said: "O *MUHAMMAD*, look at me, I need to ask you something." But he did not look at her. Then he said: "Who was this, O Gabriel?" He replied: "The world has as much left to live as the remaining lifetime of this old woman."

As he went on he was met by some of Allah's creatures who said: "Peace be upon you, O First One! Peace upon you, O Last One! Peace be upon you, O Gatherer!" Gabriel said to him: "Return their greeting," and he did. Then he saw them another time and they said the same thing. Then he saw them a third time and again they greeted him. He said: "Who are they, O Gabriel?" He replied: "Abraham, *MOSES* and *JESUS*."

The Prophet then passed by *MOSES* as he was praying in his grave at a place of red sandhills. He was tall, with long hair and brown complexion, similar to one of the *shanu'a*--the Yemeni men of pure lineage and manly virtue. He was saying with a loud voice: "You have honored him and preferred him!" Then the Prophet greeted him and he returned his greeting. *MOSES* said: "Who is this with you, O Gabriel?" He replied: "This is Ahmad." He said: "Welcome to the Arabian Prophet who acted perfectly with his Community!" and he made an invocation for blessing on his behalf. Then he said: "Ask ease for you Community."

They continued travelling and the Prophet said: "O Gabriel, who was this?" He replied: "This is *MOSES* the son of 'Imran." The Prophet asked: "Who was he reprimanding?" He said: "He is reprimanding his Lord." The Prophet said: "He reprimands his Lord and raises his voice against his Lord?!" Gabriel said: "Allah the Exalted knows *MOSES*'s bluntness."

He passed by a large tree whose fruit seemed like a thornless berry (of the kind that gives shade to men and cattle). Under it an old man was resting with his dependents. There were lamps and a great light could be seen. The Prophet said: "Who is this, O Gabriel?" He replied: "Your father Abraham." The Prophet greeted him and Abraham returned his greeting and said: "Who is this with you, O Gabriel?" He replied: "This is your son Ahmad." He said: "Welcome to the unlettered Arabian Prophet who has conveyed the message of his Lord and acted with perfect sincerity with his Community! O my son, **you are going to meet your Lord tonight**, and your Community is the last and the weakest of all Communities--therefore, if you are able to have your need fulfilled concerning your Community, or most of it, be sure to do it!" Then he invoked for goodness on his behalf.

They continued travelling until they reached the valley that is in THE CITY--that is: **The Hallowed House** in New Jerusalem--when Lo and Behold! The Gehenna was shown to them like a carpet unfolded. They said: "O Messenger of Allah, how was it?" He replied: "Like cinders."

He continued travelling until he reached THE CITY of **The Hallowed House** and he entered it by its Southern gate. Gabriel came to the Rock and placed his fingers in it, piercing it. The Prophet then dismounted the Buraq and tied it at **The Gate of the House**, using the ring by which the Prophets tied it before him using the spot that Gabriel had hollowed out.

The Prophet entered the mosque from a gate through which the sun and the moon could be seen when they set. He prayed two cycles of prayer and did not tarry long before a large throng of people had gathered.

Gabriel raised the call to prayer. The angels descended from the heaven. Allah gathered all the Messengers and Prophets. Then the Prophet prayed as the leader of the angels and Messengers. When he left Gabriel asked him: "O *MUHAMMAD*, do you know who prayed behind you?" He said no. Gabriel said: "Every single Prophet whom Allah has ever sent."

The Prophet recognized all the Prophets, some standing in prayer, some bowing, some prostrating. Then a caller called out to the prayer and the final call to prayer was made. They rose and stood in lines, waiting for the one who would lead them. Gabriel took the hand of the Prophet and brought him forward. He led them in two cycles of prayer.

Then the Prophet met the spirits of the Prophets. They glorified their Lord, after which Abraham said: "Praise to Allah Who has made taken me as His intimate friend, Who has given me an immense Kingdom, Who has made me a prayerful Community and one by whom prayer is led, Who has rescued me from the fire and made it cool and safe for me!"

Then *MOSES* glorified his Lord and said: "Praise be to Allah Who has spoken to me directly, Who has brought to pass the destruction of Pharoah and the salvation of the Children of Israel at my hands, and Who has made from among my Community a people who guide others through truth and establish justice upon it!"

Then David glorified his Lord and said: "Praise be to Allah Who has brought me an immense Kingdom, Who has softened iron for my hands, and subjected to me the mountains and the birds which laud Him, and has given me wisdom and unmistakable judgment in my speech!"

Then Solomon glorified his Lord and said: "Praise be to Allah Who has subjected the winds to my command as well as the devils, so that they did as I wished and constructed for me elevated sanctuaries, images, large bowls the size of ponds, and vessels fixed in their spot (due to their size), Who has taught me **the language of birds** and has brought me a part of every good thing, Who has subjected to me the armies of the devils and the birds and has preferred me over many of His believing servants, Who has brought me an immense Kingdom which no one after me may possess, and Who has made my kingdom a goodly one wherein there is no reckoning nor punishment!"

Then *JESUS* son of Miriam glorified his Lord and said: "Praise be to Allah Who has made me His word, Who has fashioned me after *ADAM*'s likeness whom He created out of earth then said to him: 'Be,' and he was, Who has taught me the Book and the Wisdom and the Torah and the Evangel, Who has caused me to heal the blind and the leper and to raise the dead by Allah's permission, Who has raised me and cleansed me and granted me and my mother protection against the cursed devil, so that the devil had no path by which to harm us!"

Every Prophet then glorified his Lord in the best of language, and the Prophet said: "All of you have glorified their Lord and I am going to glorify my Lord also:

"Praise belongs to Allah Who has sent me--a Mercy to the worlds sent **to all without exception**, a bearer of glad tidings and a warner--Who has caused to descend upon me THIS ALL-GLORIOUS HOLY QUR'AN in which there is a perfect exposition of all things, Who has made my Community the best Community ever brought out for the benefit of mankind, Who has made my Community a mean and a middle, Who has made my Community in truth the first and the last of all Communities, Who has expanded my breast and has relieved me of my burden, Who has exalted my name, And has made me the Opener and the Sealer!"

Upon hearing this Abraham said: "In this has *MUHAMMAD* bested you!"

Then they brought up the matter of the HOUR and referred it to Abraham, but he said: "I have no knowledge of it." They turned to *MOSES* but he said: "I have no knowledge of it." They turned to *JESUS* and he said: "As for the time when it shall befall, no one knows it except Allah.[*]

"As for what my Lord has assured me, then: the Dajjal (Antichrist) will come forth and I will face him with two rods. At my sight he shall melt like lead: Allah shall cause his destruction as soon as he sees me. It will be so that the very stones will say: 'O those who have Submission, behind me hides a disbeliever, therefore come and slay him[†] (with the breath of his lips)! And Allah shall cause them all to die. People will then return to their countries and nations. At that time Gog and Magog shall come out. They will come from every direction. They will trample all nations underfoot. Whatever they come upon they will destroy. They will drink up every body of water.

"At last **the people will <u>come to me</u> complaining about them**. At that time I will invoke Allah against them so that He will destroy them and cause their death until the whole earth will reek of their stench. Allah will send down rain which shall carry their bodies away and hurl them into the sea.

"I have been assured by my Lord that once all this takes place then the HOUR will be as the pregnant mother at the last stages of her pregnancy. Her family does not know when she shall suddenly give birth by night or by day."

The Prophet then felt the greatest thirst that he had ever felt, whereupon Gabriel brought him a vessel of wine, a vessel of water, a vessel of honey, and a vessel of milk. He chose the latter. Gabriel said: "You have chosen *fitra*--**natural disposition**--and if you had drunken the wine, your Community would have strayed from the right way and none but a few of them would have followed you." And "If you had drunk the water your Community would have perished by drowning." And

The Prophet said, "Every child is born with **a natural disposition** (*al-fitra*); then his parents convert him to Judaism, or Christianity, or Zoroastrianism or something else. It is the same with the animal which delivers a perfect baby animal. Do you find it missing anything?" "O Messenger of Allah, what if the child dies before that?" He replied: "Allah knows best what they would have done."

And when he was given the vessel of honey he then saw the wide-eyed maidens of Paradise to the left of the Rock. He greeted them and they returned his greeting. Then he asked them something and they replied with an answer that cools the eyes.

Then the Prophet was brought the ladder by which the spirits of the children of *ADAM* ascend. Creation never saw a more beautiful object. It had alternate stairs of silver and gold and came

---

[*]"But of that day and HOUR no one knows, not even the angels of heaven, **nor the Son**, but the Father **only** (Gk. *monos*)" (Matt. 24:36 RSV).
[†]"He will strike the earth with <u>the rod of his mouth</u> (his tongue); with *the **breath of his lips*** (his words) he will *slay* the wicked" (Is. 11:4 NIV); "And then the Lawless One will be **revealed**, and the Lord Jesus will slay him with **the breath of his mouth** (his words) and destroy him by his appearing and his coming" (2 Thess. 2:8 RSV).

down from the Highest and Amplest Garden of Paradise (*Jannat al-firdaws*). It was incrusted with pearls and surrounded with angels on its right and left.

The Prophet began his ascent with Gabriel until they reached **one of the Gates of the Nearest Heaven** called *Bab al-Hafazha*. There an angel stood guard, named Ishmael, who was the custodian of the nearest heaven. He inhabits the wind. He never ascends to the heaven nor descends to earth except on the day that the Prophet died, blessings and peace upon him. In front of him stood seventy thousand angels, each angel commanding an army of seventy thousand more. Gabriel asked for the Gate to be opened. Someone said: "Who is this?" He answered: "Gabriel."

"Who is with you?"
"*MUHAMMAD.*"
"Has he been sent for?"
"Yes."

"Welcome to him, from his family! May Allah grant him long life, a brother of ours and a deputy of Allah, and what excellent brother and deputy! What an excellent visit is this!"

The Gate was opened. When they came in they saw *ADAM*, peace be upon him, the father of humanity, as he was on the day Allah created him in his Most Perfect Form. The spirits of the Prophets and of his believing offspring were being shown to him, whereupon he would say: "A goodly spirit and a goodly soul, put her in the Highest (*'illiyyin*)!" Then the spirits of his unbelieving offspring would be shown to him and he would say: "A foul spirit and a foul soul, put her in the lowest layer of Hell (*sijjin*)!"

The Prophet saw to *ADAM*'s right great dark masses and a Gate exuding a fragrant smell, and to his left great dark masses and a Gate exuding a foul, malodorant smell. Whenever *ADAM* looked to his right he would smile and be happy, and whenever he looked to his left he would be sad and weep. The Prophet greeted him and *ADAM* returned his greeting and said: "Welcome to the righteous son and the righteous Prophet!"

The Prophet said: "What is this, O Gabriel?" He replied: "This is your father *ADAM* and the dark throngs are the souls of his children. Those on the right are the people of Paradise and those on the left are the people of the Fire. Whenever he looks to his right he smiles and is glad, and whenever he looks to his left he is sad and weeps. The door to his right is the Gate of Paradise. Whenever he sees those of his offspring enter it he smiles happily. The door to his left is the Gate of Gehenna. Whenever he sees those of his offspring enter it he weeps sadly.

Then the Prophet continued for a little while. He saw a tablespread on which there were pieces of good meat which no one approached, and another tablespread on which were pieces of rotten meat which stank, surrounded by people who were eating it. The Prophet asked: "O Gabriel, who are these?" He replied: "These are those of your Community who abandon what is lawful and go to what is unlawful."

Then the Prophet went on for a little while. He saw groups of people who had bellies as large as houses, and there were snakes in them which could be seen through their skins. Every time one of those people stood up he would fall again and he would say: "O Allah, don't make the HOUR of Judgment rise yet!" Then they meet the people of Pharoah on the road and the latter trample them underfoot. The Prophet said: "I heard them clamoring to Allah." He asked: "O Gabriel, who are these?" He replied: "They are those of your Community who eat up usury. They cannot stand up except in the manner of those whom the Satan touches with possession."

Then the Prophet went on for a little while. He saw groups of people whose lips resembled the lips of camels. Their mouths were being pried open and they would be stoned. A rock from Gehenna was placed in their mouths and then it would come out again from their posteriors. The Prophet said: "I heard them clamoring to Allah." He asked: "O Gabriel, who are these?" He replied: "They are those of your Community who eat up the property of orphans and commit injustice. They are eating nothing but a fire for their bellies, and they shall be roasted in it."

Then the Prophet went on for a little while. He saw women suspended by their breasts and others hanging upside down, and the Prophet said: "I heard them clamoring to Allah." He asked: "Who are these, O Gabriel?" He replied: "These are the women who commit fornication and then kill their children."

Then the Prophet went on for a little while. He saw groups of people whose sides were being cut off for meat and they were being devoured. They were being told: "Eat, just as you used to eat the flesh of your brother." The Prophet said: "O Gabriel, who are these?" He replied: "They are the slanderers of your Community who would bring shame to others."

Then the Prophet continued for a little while, and he found the consumers of usury and of the property of orphans, and the fornicators and adulterers, and others, in various loathsome states as those that have been described, and worse.

Then they ascended to the second heaven. Gabriel asked for the Gate to be opened. Someone said "Who is this?" He answered: "Gabriel."

"Who is with you?"
"*MUHAMMAD.*"
"Has he been sent for?"
"Yes."

"Welcome to him, from his family! May Allah grant him long life, a brother of ours and a deputy of Allah, and what excellent brother and deputy! What an excellent visit is this!"

The Gate was opened. When they came in they saw the sons of the two sisters: *JESUS* son of Miriam and John son of Zechariah. They resembled each other in clothing and hair. Each had with him a large company of their people. *JESUS* was curly-haired, of small build, leaning towards fair complexion, with hair let down as if he were coming out of the bath. He resembles 'Urwa ibn Mas'ud al-Thaqafi.

The Prophet greeted them and they returned his greeting. Then they said: "Welcome to the righteous brother and the righteous Prophet!" Then they invoked for goodness on his behalf.

After this the Prophet and Gabriel **ascended to the third heaven**. Gabriel asked for the Gate to be opened. Someone said: "Who is this?"He answered: "Gabriel."

"Who is with you?"
"*MUHAMMAD.*"
"Has he been sent for?"
"Yes."

"Welcome to him, from his family! May Allah grant him long life, a brother of ours and a deputy of Allah, and what excellent brother and deputy! What an excellent visit is this!"

The Gate was opened. When they came in they saw Joseph, and with him stood a large company of his people. The Prophet greeted him and he returned his greeting and said: "Welcome to the righteous brother and the righteous Prophet!" Then he invoked for goodness on his behalf. Joseph had been granted the gift of beauty. He was the most handsome creation that Allah had ever created and he surpassed people in beauty the way the full moon surpasses all other stars.

The Prophet asked: "Who is this, O Gabriel?" He replied: "Your brother Joseph."

Then they ascended to the fourth heaven. Gabriel asked for the Gate to be opened. Someone said: "Who is this?" He answered: "Gabriel."

"Who is with you?"
"*MUHAMMAD.*"
"Has he been sent for?"
"Yes."

"Welcome to him, from his family! May Allah grant him long life, a brother of ours and a deputy of Allah, and what excellent brother and deputy! What an excellent visit is this!"

The Gate was opened. When they came in they saw Enoch (Idris: *'Akhnukh*). Allah exalted him to a lofty place. The Prophet greeted him and he returned his greeting and said: "Welcome to the righteous brother and the righteous Prophet!" Then he invoked for goodness on his behalf.

Then they ascended to the fifth heaven. Gabriel asked for the Gate to be opened. Someone said: "Who is this?" He answered: "Gabriel."

"Who is with you?"
"*MUHAMMAD.*"
"Has he been sent for?"
"Yes."

"Welcome to him, from his family! May Allah grant him long life, a brother of ours and a deputy of Allah, and what excellent brother and deputy! What an excellent visit is this!"

The Gate was opened. When they came in they saw Aaron. Half of his beard was white and the other half was black. It almost reached his navel due to its length. Surrounding him were a company of the children of Israel listening to him as he was telling them a story. The Prophet greeted him and he returned his greeting and said: "Welcome to the righteous brother and the righteous Prophet!" Then he invoked for goodness on his behalf.

The Prophet asked: "Who is this, O Gabriel?" He replied: "This is the man who is beloved among his people, Aaron son of 'Imran."

Then they ascended to the sixth heaven. Gabriel asked for the Gate to be opened. Someone said: "Who is this?" He answered: "Gabriel."

"Who is with you?"
"*MUHAMMAD.*"
"Has he been sent for?"
"Yes."

"Welcome to him, from his family! May Allah grant him long life, a brother of ours and a deputy of Allah, and what excellent brother and deputy! What an excellent visit is this!"

The Gate was opened. The Prophet passed by Prophets who had with them less than ten followers in all, while others had a large company, and others had not even one follower.

Then he saw a huge dark mass (*sawad 'azhim*) that was covering the firmament. He said: "What is this throng?" He was told: "This is *MOSES* and his people. Now raise your head and look." He raised his head and saw another huge dark mass that was covering the firmament from every direction he looked. He was told: "These are your Community, and besides these there are seventy thousand of them that will enter Paradise without giving account."

As they went in the Prophet saw *MOSES* son of 'Imran, a tall man with brown complexion, similar to one of the *shanu'a*-- the Yemeni men of pure lineage and manly virtue--with abundant hair. If he had two shirts on him, still his hair would exceed them. The Prophet greeted him and he returned his greeting and said: "Welcome to the righteous brother and the righteous Prophet!" Then he invoked for goodness on his behalf and said: "The people claim that among the sons of *ADAM* I am more honored by Allah than this one, but it is he who is more honored by Allah than me!"

When the Prophet reached him *MOSES* wept. He was asked: "What is it that makes you weep?" He replied: "I weep because a child that was sent after me will enter more people in Paradise from his Community than will enter from mine. The children of Israel claim that among the children of *ADAM* I am the one most honored by Allah, but here is one man among the children of *ADAM* who has come after me in the world while I am in the next world (and is more honored). If he were only by himself I would not mind, but he has his Community with him!"

67

Then they ascended to the seventh heaven. Gabriel asked for the Gate to be opened. Someone said: "Who is this?" He answered: "Gabriel."

"Who is with you?"
"*MUHAMMAD*."
"Has he been sent for?"
"Yes."

"Welcome to him, from his family! May Allah grant him long life, a brother of ours and a deputy of Allah, and what excellent brother and deputy! What an excellent visit is this!"

The Gate was opened. The Prophet saw Abraham the Friend sitting at the Gate of Paradise on a **throne of gold** the back of which was leaning against **The Inhabited House** (*al-Bayt al-Ma'mur*). With him were a company of his people. The Prophet greeted him and he returned his greeting and said: "Welcome to the righteous son and the righteous Prophet!"

Then Abraham said: "Order your Community to increase their seedlings of Paradise for its soil is excellent and its land is plentiful." The Prophet said: "What are the seedlings of Paradise?"

He said: "Convey my greetings to your Community and tell them that Paradise has excellent soil and sweet water, and that its seedlings are: *Subhan Allah*: Glory to Allah; *wa al-Hamdu lillah*: and Praise to Allah; *wa La ilaha illallah*: and There is no god but Allah; and *wallahu akbar*: and Allah is Greatest." He said: "There is no change nor might except with Allah the High, the Almighty."

With Abraham were sitting a company of people with pristine faces similar to the whiteness of a blank page, and next to them were people with something in their faces. The latter stood and entered a river in which they bathed. Then they came out having purified some of their hue. Then they entered another river and bathed and came out having purified some more. Then they entered a third river and bathed and purified themselves and their hue became like that of their companions. They came back and sat next to them.

The Prophet said: "OGabriel, who are those with white faces and those who had something in their hues, and what are these rivers in which they entered and bathed?" He replied: "The ones with white faces are a people who never tarnished their belief with injustice or disobedience; those with something in their hues are a people who would mix good deeds with bad ones, then they repented and Allah relented towards them. As for these rivers, then the first is Allah's mercy (*Rahmat'u'llah*), the second his favor (*Ni'mat'u'llah*), and the third **'and their Lord gave them a pure beverage to drink'** *(wa saqahum rabbuhum sharaban tahuran)* (*Basmala 32: ad-Dahr*)."

Then the Prophet was told: "This is your place and the place of your Community." He saw that his Community were divided into two halves: one half were wearing clothes that seemed as white as a blank page, the other were wearing clothes that seemed the color of ashes or dust. He

---

Ma'mur means inhabited with the remembrance of Allah and the great number of angels.

entered **The Inhabited House** and those who were wearing the white clothes entered with him. Those that wore ash-colored clothes were no longer able to see him, and yet they were in the best of states. The Prophet prayed in **The Inhabited House** together with those of the believers that were with him.

Every day seventy thousand angels enter **The Inhabited House**, who shall never return to it until the Day of Resurrection. This **House** is exactly superposed to the Ka'ba. If one stone fell from it it would fall on top of the Ka'ba. The angels who have entered it never see it again.

The Prophet said: "**The Night I was Enraptured** I passed by the Heavenly Host, and Lo and Behold! Gabriel was like the worn-out saddle-cloth on the camel's back from fear of his Lord-- like a saddle-blanket that clings to the ground--Be one of the saddle blankets of your house, that is: keep to it in times of dissension."

VII. JUZ'UN SIPARA SETTIMO:

ha. Bism'illah Ar-Rahman Ar-Rahim! Sharh-i-Shajarih Namih-i-Mubarakih: THE LOTE TREE OF THE FARTHEST LIMIT!!

Then the Prophet was raised up to the Lote-Tree of the Farthest Limit. There ends whatever ascends from the earth before it is seized, and whatever descends from above before it is seized.

It is a tree from the base of which issue rivers whose water is never brackish (it does not change in taste, or color, or smell, and the sweat of those who drink it in Paradise has the fragrance of musk); and rivers of milk whose taste does not change after it is drunk; and rivers of wine which brings only pleasure to those who drink it; and rivers of purified honey. Someone on his mount could travel under its shade for seventy years and still not come out of it. The lotus fruit that grows on it resembles the jars of Hijar. Its leaves are shaped like the ears of the she-elephant, and each leaf could wrap up this Community entirely. One of its leaves could wrap up all creatures. The prophet said: "Date pastry is from paradise," that is: it resembles the fruit of Paradise.

On top of each leaf there was an angel who covered it with colors which cannot be described. Whenever he covered it by Allah's order it would change. It would turn into sapphire and chrysolite the beauty of which it is impossible for anyone to praise according to what its merit. On it were moths of gold.

From the base of the tree issued four rivers: two hidden rivers and two visible ones. The Prophet asked: "What are these, O Gabriel?" He replied: "As for the hidden ones, they are two rivers of Paradise. The visible ones are the Nile and the Euphrates."

At the base of the tree ran a source called Salsabil. From it issued two rivers: one is the Kawthar. The Prophet said: "I saw it flowing impetuously, roaring, at the speed of arrows. Near it were pavilions of pearl (*lu'lu'*), sapphire (*yaqut*), and chrysolite (*zabarjad*) on top of which nested green birds more delicate than any you have ever seen. On its banks were vessels of gold and silver. It ran over pebbles made of sapphire and emerald (*zumurrud*). Its water was whiter than milk."

The Prophet took one of the vessels and scooped some water and drank. It was sweeter than honey and more fragrant than musk. Gabriel said to him: "This is the river which Allah has given you as a special gift, and the other river is the River of Mercy." The Prophet bathed in it and his past and future sins were forgiven.

At the Lote-Tree of the Farthest Limit the Prophet saw Gabriel in his angelic form. He had six hundred wings. Every single wing could cover the entire firmament. From his wings embellishments were strewn in all directions, such as rare pearls and sapphires of a kind Allah alone knows. Then the Prophet was taken to the Kawthar and entered Paradise. Lo and behold! It contains what no eye has seen, nor ear heard, nor human mind ever imagined. On its Gate he saw written: "Charity is repaid tenfold, and the loan eighteenfold."

The Prophet said: "O Gabriel, how can the loan be more meritorious than charity?" He replied: "Because one asking for charity may still have some need left, while the borrower does not borrow except his need is fulfilled."

The Prophet continued to travel until he reached rivers of milk whose taste does not change, and rivers of wine which bring only pleasure to those who drink it, and rivers of honey purified, and overhanging those rivers were domes of hollowed pearl whose circumference is like the Aquarius star.

Above the rivers were pommels resembling the hides of the humped camels. Its birds were like the Bactrian camel. Upon hearing this Abu Bakr said: "O Messenger of Allah, they are certainly delicate!" The Prophet replied: "And daintier to eat yet, and certainly I hope that you shall eat from them."

The Prophet then saw the Kawthar and on its banks were domes of hollowed pearl. The soil of its banks was overfragrant musk. Then the Fire was shown to him. In it he saw Allah's wrath and His punishment and sanction. Were rocks and iron to be thrown into it the Fire would consume them completely. In it were a people who were eating carrion. The Prophet said: "Who are these, O Gabriel?" He replied: "Those who ate the flesh of people."

Then the Prophet saw **al-Malik**, the **Custodian of the Fire**. He was a grim figure whose face expressed anger. The Prophet greeted him first.[*] Then the Gates of the Fire were closed as he stood outside, and he was raised up beyond the Lote-Tree of the Farthest Limit, and a cloud concealed him from everything else, and Gabriel stayed back.

The Prophet was taken up to a point where he heard the **Screeching of the Pens** (Revelation Writing of the Divine Decree). He saw **a man who had disappeared into the light of the Throne**. He said: "Who is this? Is this an angel?" It was said to him, no. He said: "Is it a Prophet?" Again the answer was no. He said: "Who is it then?" The answer was: "This is a man whose tongue was moist with Allah's remembrance in the world, and his heart was attached to the school of the Holy Places of Worship and Teachings, and he never incurred the curse of his father and mother."

---

[*]The Prophet said: "I greeted him and he returned my greeting and welcomed me, but he did not smile at me."

Then the Prophet saw his Lord, the Glorious, the Exalted, and he fell prostrate, and at that time his Lord spoke to him and said: "O *MUHAMMAD!*" He replied: "At your service, O Lord!" Allah said: "Ask!" The Prophet said: "You have taken to Yourself Abraham as a friend, and You have given him an immense Kingdom. You have spoken to *MOSES* directly, and have given David an immense Kingdom and softened iron and subjected the mountains to him. You have given Solomon an immense Kingdom, and subjected the jinn and humans and devils to him, as well as the winds, and You have given him a Kingdom the like no one may have after him. You have taught *JESUS* the Torah and the Evangel, and made him heal those born blind and the lepers, and raise up the dead with Your permission, and You have protected him and his mother from the cursed devil so that the devil had no path by which to harm them!"

Allah said: "And I have taken you to Myself as My beloved."[*] He said: "And I have sent you for all people without exception, a bearer of glad tidings and a warner; and I have expanded your breast for you and relieved you of your burden and exalted your name; and I am not mentioned except you are mentioned with Me; and I have made your Community the best Community ever brought out for the benefit of mankind; and I have made your Community a mean and a middle; and I have made your Community in truth the first and the last of all Communities; and I have made public address (*al-khutba*) impermissible for your Community unless they first witness that you are My servant and Messenger; and I have placed certain people in your Community with Evangels for Hearts--Repositories of Allah's Book; and I have made you the first Prophet created and the last one sent and the first one heard in My court; and I have given you **Seven of the Oft-Repeated** which I gave to no other Prophet before you; and I have given you the last verses of Surat al-Baqara which constitute a treasure from under My Throne which I gave to no other Prophet before you!

"And I have given you the Kawthar; and I have given you eight arrows (i.e. shares in good fortune): Islam, Emigration (*hijra*), Jihad, Charity (*sadaqa*), Fasting Ramadan, Ordering Good, and Forbidding Evil; and the day I created the heavens and the earth **I made obligatory upon you and upon your Community FIFTY PRAYERS: therefore establish them, you and your Community.**"

The Prophet said: "My Lord has preferred me over everyone else (*faddalani rabbi*): He has sent me as a mercy to the worlds and to all people without exception, a bearer of glad tidings and a warner; He has thrown terror into the hearts of my enemies at a distance of a month's travel; He has made spoils of war lawful for me while they were not lawful for anyone before me; the entire earth has been made a ritually pure place of prostration for me; I was given the words that open, those that close, and those that are comprehensive in meaning. I was given the apex of eloquence; My Community was shown to me and there is none of the followers and the followed but he is known to me; I saw that they would come to a people that wear hair-covered sandals; I saw that they would come to a people of large faces and small eyes as if they had been pierced with a needle; nothing of what they would face in the future has been kept hidden from me; and I have been ordered to perform fifty prayers daily."

---

[*] As it is written in the Torah: *Habib 'u 'llah* --Allah's Beloved.

Then the cloud that cloaked him was dispelled and Gabriel took him by the hand and hurried away with him until he reached Abraham, who did not say anything. Then the Prophet reached *MOSES* who asked: "What did you do, O *MUHAMMAD*? What obligations did your Lord impose on you and your Community?" He replied: "He imposed **fifty prayers** every day and night on me and my Community." *MOSES* said: "Return to your Lord and ask Him to lighten your burden and that of your Community for in truth your Community will not be able to carry it. Verily I myself have experienced people's natures before you. I tested the Children of Israel and took the greatest pains to hold them to something easier than this, but they were too weak to carry it and they abandoned it. Your Community are even weaker in their bodies and constitutions, in their hearts, in their sight, and in their hearing."

The Prophet turned to Gabriel to consult him. The latter indicated to him that yes, if you wish, then return. The Prophet hurried back until he reached the Tree and the cloud cloaked him and he fell prostrate. Then he said: "Lord, make lighter the burden of my Community for verily they are the weakest of all Communities." He replied: "I have removed five prayers from their obligation."

Then the cloud was dispelled and the Prophet returned to *MOSES* and told him: "He has removed five prayers from my obligation." He replied: "Go back to your Lord and ask him to make it less, for in truth your Community will not be able to carry that." The Prophet did not cease to go back and forth between *MOSES* and his Lord, while Allah each time reduced it by five prayers, until Allah said: "O *MUHAMMAD*!" The Prophet said: "At Your service, O Lord!" He said: "**Let them be five prayers every day and night, and let every prayer count as ten. That makes fifty prayers.** This word of Mine shall not be changed nor shall My Book be abrogated. Let whoever is about to perform a good deed, even if he does not ultimately do it, receive the reward of doing it, while if he does it, he shall receive it tenfold. Let whoever is about to commit a bad deed, and he does not ultimately do it, let not anything be written against him, while if he does it, let one misdeed be written against him."

Then the cloud was dispelled and the Prophet returned to *MOSES* and told him: "He has removed five prayers from my obligation." He replied: "Go back to your Lord and ask him to make it less, for in truth your Community will not be able to carry that." The Prophet said: "I have gone back again to my Lord until I feel shy from Him. Rather, I accept and submit." At this a herald called out: "I have decreed My obligation and have reduced the burden of My servants." *MOSES* then said to the Prophet: "Go down in the name of Allah."

The Prophet did not pass a throng of angels except they said to him: "You must practice cupping (*'alayka bi al-hijama*)--and "Order cupping to your Community."[*]

---

[*]Cupping: The process of drawing blood from the body by scarification (scratches or superficial incisions in the skin) and the application of a cupping glass (in which a partial vacuum is created, as by heat) without scarification, as for relieving internal congestion (*Webster's*).

As the Prophet was descending he asked Gabriel: "Why did I not see any of the people of heaven except they welcomed me and smiled at me **except one**: I greeted him and he greeted me back and welcomed me, but he did not smile at me?" He replied: "That was **al-Malik** the **Custodian of the Fire**. He never smiled once since the day he was created. If he had ever smiled for anyone, it would have been you."

When the Prophet reached the Nearest Heaven he looked below it and he saw a dense cloud of smoke filled with din. He asked: "What is this, O Gabriel?" He replied: "These are the devils that swarm over the eyes of human beings so that they will not think about the dominions of the heavens and the earth, or else they would have seen wonders."

Then he mounted the Buraq again and departed. He passed by a caravan of the Quraysh and saw a camel upon which were tied two containers, a black one and a white one. When he came face to face with the caravan there was a stampede in which the caravan turned around and that camel was thrown down to the ground and its freight broke.

Then the Prophet passed by another caravan who had lost one of their camels which were rounded up. The Prophet greeted them and one of them said: "This is the voice of *MUHAMMAD*!" after which the Prophet returned to his Companions in Mecca shortly before morning.

When morning came he remained alone and, knowing that people would belie him, sat despondently.

The enemy of Allah Abu Jahl was passing by and he approached and sat down next to him, saying in the way of mockery: "Has anything happened?" The Prophet replied: "Yes." Abu Jahl said: "And what is that?" The Prophet replied: "I was enraptured last night." Abu Jahl said: "To where?" The Prophet replied: "To **The Hallowed House**." Abu Jahl said: "Then you woke up here among us?" He replied: "Yes."

Abu Jahl decided not to belie the Prophet for fear the Prophet would deny having said this to him if he went and told the people of Mecca, so he said: "What do you think if I called your people here? Will you tell them what you just told me?" The Prophet said yes. Abu Jahl cried out: "O assembly of the Children of Ka'b ibn Lu'ay, come hither!" People left their gatherings and came until they all sat next around the two of them. Abu Jahl said: "Tell your people what you just told me." Allah's Messenger said: "I was enraptured last night." They said: "To where?" The Prophet replied: "To **The Hallowed House**." They said: "Then you woke up here among us?" He replied: "Yes." There was no one left except he clapped his hands, or held his head in amazement, or clamored and considered it an enormity.

Al-Mut'im ibn 'Adi (he died a disbeliever) said: "All of your affair before today was bearable, until what you said today. I bear witness that you are a liar (*ana ashhadu annaka kadhibun*). We strike the flanks of the she-camels for one month to reach **The Hallowed House**, then for another month to come back, and you claim that you went there in one night! By al-Lat, by al-'Uzza! I do not believe you."

Abu Bakr said: "O Mut'im, what an evil thing you said to the son of your brother when you faced him thus and declared him a liar! As for me I bear witness that he spoke the truth (*ana ashhadu annahu sadiqun*)."

The people said: "O *MUHAMMAD*, describe **The Hallowed House** for us. How is it built, what does it look like, how near is it to the mountain." [*] There were some among them who had travelled there. He began to describe it for them: "Its structure is like this, its appearance like this, its proximity to the mountain is such-and-such," and he did not stop describing it to them until he began to have doubt about the description. He was seized with an anxiety he had not felt before, whereupon he was immediately brought to **The HOUSE** itself and saw it in front of him.

He was placed outside the gate of 'Aqil or 'Iqal. The people said: "How many gates does the mosque have?" He had not counted them before. He looked at the gates and began to count them one by one and to inform them. All the while Abu Bakr was saying: "You have spoken the truth. You have spoken the truth. I bear witness that you are the Messenger of Allah (*sadaqta sadaqta ashhadu annaka rasulullah*)!"

The people said: "As for the description, then, by Allah, he is correct." They turned to Abu Bakr and said: "But do you believe what he said, that he went last night to **The Hallowed House** and came back before morning?" He replied: "Yes, and I do believe him regarding what is farther than that. I believe the news of heaven he brings, whether in the space of a morning or in that of an evening journey." Because of this Abu Bakr was named al-Siddiq: the Most Truthful, the One Who Never Lies.

Then they said: "O *MUHAMMAD*, tell us about our caravans." He replied: "I saw the caravan of the tribe as I was coming back. They had lost one of their camels and were searching for it everywhere. I reached their mounts and there was no one with them. I found a water bottle and I drank from it.

"Then I reached the other caravan at that appointed place. I saw a red camel carrying one black container and one white one. When I came face to face with the caravan there was a stampede and that camel fell and its freight broke. Then I reached the caravan in al-Tan'im. It was headed by a grayish camel on which was a black hair-cloth and two blackish containers and here are the three caravans about to reach you from the mountain pass." They said: "When will they arrive?" He replied: "On the fourth day of the week." On that day the Quraysh came out, expecting the caravans. The day passed and they did not arrive. The Prophet made an invocation and *the day was extended one more hour during which the sun stood still,* (Double Day of Joshua) and the caravans came.

They went to meet the riders and asked them: "Did you lose a camel?" They said yes. They asked the second caravan: "Did one red camel of yours shatter her freight?" They said yes. They asked the first caravan: "Did anyone lose a water bottle?" One man said: "I did, by Allah, I had prepared it but none of us drank it nor was it spilled on the ground!" At this they accused the Prophet of sorcery and they said: "al-Walid spoke the truth." And Allah revealed the verse: "We

---

[*] See The Last Nine Chapters of the Book of Ezekiel (chapters 40 through 48) for the full description--and my book *EZEKIEL'S TEMPLE IN MONTANA* for more.

appointed not **The Vision** which we showed you but as a TEST for humankind"(*Basmala 37: bani Isra'il*)!

When the fair was due, a number of the Quraysh came to al-Walid ibn al-Mughira, who was a man of some standing, and he addressed them in those words: "The time of the fair has come round again and representatives of the Arabs will come to you and they will have heard about this fellow of yours, so agree upon one opinion without dispute so that none will give the lie to the other." They replied: "You give us your opinion about him." He said: "No, you speak and I will listen." They said: "He is a *kahin* (seer or giver of oracles)." He said: "By Allah, he is not that, for he has not the unintelligent murmuring and rhymed speech of the *kahin*." "Then he is possessed," they said. "No, he is not that," he said, "we have seen possessed ones, and here is no choking, spasmodic movements and whispering." "Then he is a poet," they said. "No, he is no poet, for we know poetry in all its forms and meters." "Then he is a sorcerer." "No, we have seen sorcerers and their sorcery, and here is no blowing and no knots." "Then what are we to say, O Abu 'Abd al-Shams?" they asked. He replied: "By Allah, his speech is sweet, his root is a palm-tree whose branches are fruitful, and everything you have said would be known to be false. The nearest thing to the truth is your saying that he is a sorcerer, who has brought a message by which he separates a man from his father, or from his brother, or from his wife, or from his family."

At this point they left him, and began to sit on the paths which men take when they come to the fair. They warned everyone who passed them about the Prophet's doings. Allah revealed concerning al-Walid:

"Leave Me to deal with him whom I created lonely, and then bestowed upon him ample means, and sons abiding in his presence and made life smooth for him. Yet he desires that I should give more. Nay, for Lo! He has been stubborn to Our Revelations. On him I shall impose a fearful doom. For Lo! He did consider; then he planned--Self-destroyed is he, how he planned! Again, self-destroyed is he, how he planned!--Then looked he, then frowned he and showed displeasure. Then turned he away in pride and said: 'This is naught else than magic from of old; This is naught else than speech of mortal man. Him shall I fling unto the burning" (*Basmala 11: al-Lahab*)!

The Account is finished with praise to Allah and by His grace.

VIII. JUZ'UN SIPARA OTTAVO:

40. Bism'illah Ar-Rahman Ar-Rahim! bani Isra'il: al-Fatir: THE CREATOR.

Praise be to Allah, the Creator of the heavens and the earth, Who appointeth the angels messengers having wings two, three and four. He multiplieth in creation what He will. Lo! Allah is Able to do all things.

That which Allah openeth unto humankind of mercy none can withhold it; and that which He withholdeth none can release thereafter. He is the Mighty, the Wise.

O People of the Human Race! Remember Allah's grace toward you! Is there any creator other than Allah who provideth for you from the sky and the earth? There is no God save Him. Whither then are ye turned?

And if they deny Thee, (O *AL-AMIN*), messengers of Allah were denied before Thee. Unto Allah all things are brought back.

O Humankind! Lo! The promise of Allah is true. So let not the life of the world beguile you, and let not the avowed beguiler beguile you with regard to Allah.

Lo! The devil is an enemy for you, so treat him as an enemy. He only summoneth his faction to be owners of the flaming Fire. Those who disbelieve, theirs will be an awful doom; and those who believe and do good works, theirs will be forgiveness and a great reward. Is he, the evil of whose deeds is made fairseeming unto him so that he deemeth it good, (other than Satan's dupe)? Allah verily sendeth whom He will astray, and guideth whom He will; so let not Thy soul expire in sighings for them. Lo! Allah is Aware of what they do!

And Allah it is Who sendeth the winds and they raise a cloud; then We lead it unto a dead land and revive therewith the earth after its death. Such is the Resurrection.

Whoso desireth power (should know that) **all power belongeth to Allah**. Unto Him good words ascend, and the pious deed doth He exalt; but those who plot iniquities, theirs will be an awful doom; and the plotting of such folk will come to naught.

Allah created you from dust, then from a little fluid, then He made you pairs (the male and female). No female beareth or bringeth forth save with His knowledge. And no-one groweth old who groweth old, nor is aught lessened of his life, but it is recorded in a Book, Lo! That is easy for Allah.

And the two seas are not alike: this, fresh, sweet, good to drink, this other bitter, salt. And from them both ye eat fresh meat and derive the ornament that ye wear. And Thou seest the ship cleaving them with its prow that ye may seek of His bounty, and that haply ye may give thanks. He maketh the night to pass into the day and He maketh the day to pass into the night. He hath subdued the sun and moon to service. Each runneth unto an appointed term. Such is Allah, your Lord; His is the Sovereignty; and those unto whom ye pray instead of Him own not so much as the white spot on a date-stone. If ye pray unto them they hear not your prayer, and if they heard they could not grant it you. On the Day of Resurrection they will disown association with you. None can inform you like Him Who is Aware.

O Humankind! Ye are the poor in your relation to Allah. And Allah! He is the Absolute, the Owner of Praise. If He will, He can be rid of you and bring (instead of you) some new creation. That is not a hard thing for Allah.

And no burdened soul can bear another's burden, and if one heavy laden crieth for (help with) his load, naught of it will be lifted even though he (unto whom he crieth) be of kin. Thou warnest only those who fear their Lord in secret, and have established worship. **He who groweth, groweth only for himself**, (he cannot by his merit redeem others). Unto Allah is the journeying.

The blind man is not equal with the seer; Nor is darkness tantamount to light; Nor is the shadow equal with the sun's full heat; Nor are the living equal with the dead. Lo! Allah maketh whom He will to hear. Thou canst not reach those who are in the graves. Thou art but a warner.

Lo! We have sent Thee with the Truth, a bearer of glad tidings and a warner (*nadhîr*); and there is not a nation but a warner (נזיר) hath passed among them.

And if they deny Thee, those before them also denied. Their messengers came unto them with THIS RIGHTEOUS BOOK, and with the Psalms and the Scripture giving light. Then seized I those who disbelieved, and how intense was My abhorrence!

Hast Thou not seen that Allah causeth water to fall from the sky, and We produce therewith fruit of divers hues; and among the hills are streaks white and red, of divers hues, and others raven-black; And of men and beasts and cattle, in like manner, divers hues? The **erudite** among His bondmen fear Allah alone. Lo! Allah is Mighty, Forgiving.

Lo! Those who read the Scripture of Allah, and establish worship, and spend of that which We have bestowed on them secretly and openly, they look forward to imperishable gain, that He will pay them their wages and increase them of His grace. Lo! He is Forgiving, Responsive.

As for that which We inspire in thee of the Scripture, it is the Truth confirming that which was before it. Lo! Allah is indeed Observer, Seer of His slaves. Then We gave the Scripture as inheritance unto those whom We elected of Our bondmen. But of them are some who wrong themselves and of them are some who are lukewarm, and of them are some who outstrip others through good deeds, by Allah's leave.

That is the great favor! Gardens of Eden! They enter them wearing armlets of gold and pearl and their raiment therein is silk. And they say: "Praise be to Allah Who hath put grief away from us. Lo! Our Lord is Forgiving, Bountiful, Who, of His grace, hath installed us in the mansion of eternity, where toil toucheth us not nor can weariness affect us."

But as for those who disbelieve, for them is fire of hell; it taketh not complete effect upon them so that they can die, nor is its torment lightened for them. Thus We punish every ingrate.
And they cry for help there, saying: "Our Lord! Release us; we will do right, not the wrong that we used to do." Did not We grant you a life long enough for him who reflected to reflect therein? And the warner came unto you. Now taste (the flavor of your deeds), for evil-doers have no helper. Lo! Allah is the Knower of the Unseen of the heavens and the earth. Lo! He is Aware of the secret of people's breasts.

He it is Who hath made you regents in the earth; so he who disbelieveth, his disbelief be on his own head. Their disbelief increaseth for the disbelievers, in their Lord's sight, naught save abhorrence. Their disbelief increaseth for the disbelievers naught save loss.

Say: "Have ye seen your partner-gods to whom ye pray beside Allah? Show me what they created of the earth! Or have they any portion in the heavens? Or have We given them a scripture so they act on clear facts therefrom? Nay, the evil-doers promise one another only to deceive. Lo! Allah graspeth the heavens and the earth that they deviate not, and if they were to deviate there is not one that could grasp them after Him. Lo! He is ever Clement, Forgiving."

And they swore by Allah, their most binding oath, that if a warner came unto them they would be more tractable than any of the nations; yet, when a warner came unto them it aroused in them naught save repugnance, shown in their behaving arrogantly in the land and plotting evil; and the evil plot encloseth but the men who make it. Then, can they expect aught save the treatment of the folk of old? Thou wilt not find for Allah's way of treatment any substitute, nor wilt Thou find for Allah's way of treatment aught of power to change. Have they not travelled in the land and seen the nature of the consequence for those who were before them, and they were mightier than these in power? Allah is not such that aught in the heavens or in the earth escapeth Him. Lo! He is the Wise, the Mighty.

If Allah took mankind to task by that which they deserve, He would not leave a living creature on the surface of the earth; but He reprieveth them unto an appointed term, and when their term cometh--then verily they will know that Allah is ever Seer of His slaves.

41. Bism'illah Ar-Rahman Ar-Rahim! al-Ma'arij: THE LADDERS AND ASCENDING STAIRWAYS!

A questioner questioned concerning the DOOM about to fall upon the disbelievers, **which none can repel**, from Allah, **Lord of the Ascending Stairways** whereby the angels and the Spirit ascend unto Him in a Day whereof the span is fifty thousand years!

But be patient (O *AL-AMIN*) with a patience fair to see. Lo! They behold it afar off! While we behold it nigh:

The day when the sky will become as molten copper,
And the hills become as flakes of wool,
And no familiar friend will ask a question of his friend
Though they will be given sight of them.

The guilty soul will long to be able to ransom himself from the punishment of that day at the price of his children and his spouse and his brother and his kin that harbored him and all that are in the earth, if then it might deliver him.

But nay! For Lo! it is the fire of hell EAGER TO ROAST! It calleth him who turned and fled (from The Reality), and hoarded (wealth: goods, property, land, money, labor and made slaves) and withheld it.

Lo! Man was created anxious,
Fretful when evil befalleth him
And, when good befalleth him, grudging;

Save worshippers. Who are constant at their worship and in whose wealth there is a right acknowledged for the beggar and the destitute; and those who believe in the Day of Judgment, and those who are fearful of their Lord's DOOM:

Lo! The DOOM of their Lord is that before which none can feel secure--And those who preserve their chastity save with their wives and those whom their right hands possess, for thus they are not blameworthy; But whoso seeketh more than that, those are they who are transgressors!

And those who keep their pledges and **their Covenant**,
And those who stand by their Testimony
And those who are attentive at their worship:
These will dwell in Gardens, honored.

What aileth those who disbelieve, that they keep staring toward Thee (O *AL-AMIN*), open-eyed, on the right and on the left, in groups?

Doth every man among them hope to enter the Garden of Delight?

Nay, verily. Lo! We created them from what they know.

But nay! I swear by the Lord of the rising-places and the setting-places of the planets that We verily are Able to replace them by (others) better than them. And we are not to be outrun.

So let them chat and play until they meet their Day which they are promised:

The DAY when they come forth from the graves in haste, as racing to a goal,
with eyes AGHAST, abasement stupefying them:

Such is **THE DAY** which they are promised!

42. Bism'illah Ar-Rahman Ar-Rahim! Ha Mim Sajdah: REVELATIONS WELL EXPOUNDED.

Ha. Mim.

A Revelation from the Beneficent, the Merciful, A Scripture whereof the verses are expounded, a Lecture in Arabic for people who have knowledge: Good tidings and a warning. But most of them turn away so that they hear not.

And they say: "Our hearts are protected from that unto which Thou callest us, and in our ears there is a deafness, and between us and Thee **there is a Veil**. Act, then. Lo! We also shall be acting.

Say unto them: "I am only a mortal like you. It is **inspired in me** that your God is One God, therefore take the straight path unto Him and seek forgiveness of Him. And Woe unto the idolaters (materialists), who give not the poor-due (zakat), and who are disbelievers in the Hereafter. Lo! As for those who believe and do good works, for them is a reward enduring.

Say: "Disbelieve ye verily in Him Who created the earth in two Days, and ascribe ye unto Him rivals? He is the Lord of the Worlds.

He placed therein firm hills rising above it, and blessed it and measured therein its sustenance in four Days, alike for all who ask; Then turned He to the heaven when it was smoke, and said unto it and unto the earth: "Come both of you, willingly or loth." They said: "We come, obedient."

Then He **ordained them seven heavens** in two Days and inspired in each heaven its **mandate**; and We decked the nether heaven with lamps, and rendered it inviolable. That is the measuring of the Mighty, the Knower.

But if they turn away, then say: "I warn you of a thunderbolt like the thunderbolt which fell upon A'ad and Thamud; when their messengers came unto them from before them and behind them, saying: "Worship none but Allah!" They said: "If our Lord had willed, He surely would have sent down angels unto us, so Lo! We are disbelievers in that wherewith ye have been sent."

As for A'ad, they were arrogant in the land without right, and they said: "Who is mightier than us in power?" Could they not see that Allah Who created them, He was mightier than them in power? And they denied Our Revelations.

Therefore We let loose on them **a raging wind in evil days**,*that We might make them taste the torment of disgrace in the life of the world. And verily the doom of the Hereafter will be more shameful, and they will not be helped.

And as for Thamud, We gave them guidance, but they preferred blindness to the guidance, so the bolt of the **doom of humiliation** overtook them because of what they used to earn.

And We delivered those who believed and used to keep their duty to Allah.

And THE DAY when the enemies of Allah are gathered unto the Fire, they are driven on till, when they reach it, their ears and their eyes and their skins testify against them as to what they used to do. And they say unto their skins: "Why testify ye against us?" They say: "Allah hath given us speech Who giveth speech to all things, and Who created you at the first, and unto Whom ye are returned."

Ye did not hide yourselves lest your ears and your eyes and your skins should testify against you, but ye deemed that Allah knew not much of what ye did. That, your thought which ye did think about your Lord, hath ruined you; and ye find yourselves among the lost. And though they are resigned, yet the Fire is still their home; and if they ask for favor, yet they are not of those unto whom favor can be shown.

And We assigned them comrades (in the world), who made their present and their past fairseeming unto them. And the Word concerning nations of the jinn and humankind who passed away before them hath effect for them. Lo! They were ever losers.

---

*Agnia Fire-Weapon.

Those who disbelieve say: Heed not THIS QUR'AN, and **drown the hearing of it**; haply ye may Conquer. But verily We shall cause those who disbelieve to taste an awful doom, and verily We shall requite them the worst of what they used to do.

That is the reward of Allah's enemies: THE FIRE. Therein is their immortal home, payment forasmuch as they denied Our Revelations.

And those who disbelieve will say: "Our Lord! Show us those who beguiled us of the jinn and humankind. We will place them underneath our feet that they may be among **the nethermost-Gloom**.*

Lo! Those who say: "Our Lord is Allah," and afterward are upright, the angels descend upon them, saying: "Fear not nor grieve, but hear good tidings of the paradise which ye are promised. We are your protecting friends in the life of the world and in the Hereafter. **There ye will have all that your souls desire**, and there ye will have all for which ye pray. A GIFT of welcome from One Forgiving, Merciful.

And who is better in speech than him who prayeth unto his Lord and doeth right, and saith: "Lo! I am of those who SURRENDER!"

The good deed and the evil deed are not alike. Repel the evil deed with one which is better, then lo! He, between whom and Thee there was enmity will become as though he was a bosom friend. But none is granted it save those who are steadfast, and none is granted it save the owner of **Great Happiness**.

And if a whisper from the devil reach Thee (O *AL-AMIN*) then seek refuge in Allah. Lo! He is the Hearer, the Knower.

And of His portents are the night and the day and the sun and the moon. Adore not the sun not the moon; but adore Allah Who created them, if it is in truth Him Whom ye worship. But if they are too proud--still those who are with Thy Lord glorify Him night and day, and tire not.

And of His portents is this: That Thou seest the earth lowly, but when We send down water thereon it thrilleth and groweth. Lo! **He Who quickeneth it is verily the Quickener of the Dead**. Lo! He is Able to do all things.

Lo! Those who distort Our Revelations are not hid from Us. Is he who is hurled into the Fire better, or he who cometh secure on the Day of Resurrection? Do what ye will. Lo! He is Seer of what ye do.

Lo! Those who disbelieve in THE REMINDER when he cometh unto them are guilty, for Lo! It is an unassailable Scripture.

---

*For if God did not spare the angels when they sinned, but cast them into hell and committed them to pits of **Nether Gloom** to be kept until the judgment...then the Lord knows how to rescue the godly from trial, and to keep the unrighteous under punishment until the day of judgment, and especially those who indulge in the lust of defiling passion and despise authority" (2 Peter 2:4, 9-10 RSV).

Falsehood cannot come at it from before it or from behind it. It is the Revelation from the Wise, the Owner of Praise.

Naught is said unto Thee (O *AL-AMIN*) save what was said unto the messengers before Thee. Lo! Thy Lord is owner of forgiveness, and owner also of dire punishment.

And if We had appointed it a Lecture in a foreign tongue they would assuredly have said: "If only its verses were expounded (so that we might understand)?" What! A foreign tongue and an Arab?--Say unto them (O *AL-AMIN*): "For those who believe it is a guidance and a healing; and as for those who disbelieve, there is a deafness in their ears, and it is blindness for them. Such are called to from afar."

And We verily gave *MOSES* the Scripture, but there hath been dispute concerning it; and but for a WORD* that had already gone forth from Thy Lord, it would ere now have been judged between them; but Lo! They are in hopeless doubt concerning it.

Whoso doeth right it is for his soul, and whoso doeth wrong it is against it. And Thy Lord is not at all a tyrant to His slaves. Unto Him is referred all knowledge of the HOUR. And no fruits burst forth from their sheaths, and no female carrieth or bringeth forth but with His knowledge. And on the day when He calleth unto them: "Where are now My partners?" they will say: "We confess unto Thee, not one of us is a witness for them." And those to whom they used to cry of old have failed them, and they perceive they have no place of refuge.

Man tireth not of praying for good, and if ill toucheth him, then he is disheartened, desperate. And verily, if We cause him to taste mercy after some hurt that hath touched him, he will say: "This is my own; and I deem not that the HOUR will ever rise, and if I am brought back to my Lord, I surely shall be better off with Him"--But We verily shall tell those who disbelieve all that they did, and We verily shall make them taste hard punishment.

When We show favor unto man, he withdraweth and turneth aside, but when ill toucheth him then he aboundeth in prayer.

Bethink you: "If it is from Allah and ye reject it--Who is further astray than one who is at open feud with GOD?"

We shall show them Our portents on the horizons and within themselves until it will be manifest unto them that it is the Truth. Doth not thy Lord suffice, since He is Witness over all things? How! Are they still in doubt about the meeting with their Lord? Lo! Is not He surrounding all things?

---

*Jude 1:9-11 RSV: "But when the archangel Michael, contending with the devil, **disputed about the BODY of MOSES**, he did not presume to pronounce a reviling judgment upon him, but said, 'The Lord rebuke you' (see Zech. 3:1 for more). But these men **revile whatever they do not understand**, and by those things that they know by instinct as irrational animals do, they are destroyed. Woe to them! For they walk in the way of Cain, and abandon themselves for the sake of gain to Balaam's error, and perish in Korah's rebellion."

43. Bism'illah Ar-Rahman Ar-Rahim! al-Qadr: THE MAJESTY.

Lo! We revealed it on the Night of Predestination and Power!
Ah, what will convey unto Thee what **The Night of Power** is!
The Night of Power is better than a thousand months.
The angels and the Spirit descend therein, by the permission of their Lord, with all decrees.
The night is: **Peace** until the rising of the **Dawn**.

44. Bism'illah Ar-Rahman Ar-Rahim! an-Naba': THE TIDING NEWS.

Whereof do they question one another?
It is of the awful tidings,
Concerning which they are in disagreement.

Nay, but they will come to know!
Nay, again, but they will come to know!

Have We not made the earth an expanse,
And the high hills bulwarks?

And We have created you in pairs,
And have appointed your sleep for repose,
And have appointed the night as a cloak,
And have appointed the day for livelihood.

And We have built above you **Seven** **Strong**,
And have appointed a **Dazzling LAMP**,[*]
And have sent down from the rainy clouds abundant water,
Thereby to produce grain and plant,
And gardens of thick foliage.

Lo! the Day of Decision is a fixed time,
A day when the trumpet is blown and ye come in multitudes,
And the Heaven is Opened (at night and in the day-season too) and becometh as GATES,
And the hills are set in motion and become as a mirage.

Lo! Hell lurketh in ambush,
A home for the rebellious.
They will abide therein for ages.
Therein taste they neither coolness nor any drink
Save boiling water and a paralysing cold:
Reward proportioned (to their evil deeds).

For Lo! They looked not for a reckoning;

---

[*]"And THE CITY has no need of sun or moon to shine upon it, for **The Glory of God** (Baha'u'llah) is its Light (*an-Nur*), and its **LAMP** is the LAMB" (Revelation 21:23 RSV).

They called Our Revelations false with strong denial.
Everything have We recorded in a Book.
So taste of that which ye have earned. No increase do We give you save of torment.

Lo! For the duteous is achievement--
Gardens enclosed and vineyards,
And maidens for companions,
And a full cup.

There hear they never vain discourse, nor lying--Requital from Thy Lord--a gift in payment--
Lord of the heavens and the earth, and all that is between them, the Beneficent; with Whom none
can converse.

On the day when the angels and the Spirit stand arrayed, they speak not, saving him whom the
Beneficent alloweth and who speaketh right.That is the True Day. So whoso will should seek
recourse unto his Lord.

Lo! We warn you of a DOOM at hand, a day whereon a man will look on that which his own
hands have sent before, and the disbeliever will cry: "Would that I were **dust!**"

45. Bism'illah Ar-Rahman Ar-Rahim! Qaf-i Kuh: THE GRAND MESA SIMURGH RUKH.

QAF: The Thunderbird-Phoenix! BY THIS GLORIOUS QUR'AN!

NAY, but they marvel that a warner of their own hath come unto them; and the disbelievers say:
"This is a strange thing: When we are dead and have become **dust** shall we be brought back
again? That would be a far return!"

We know that which the earth taketh of them, and with Us is a recording BOOK. Nay, but they
have denied the truth when it came unto them, therefore they are now in troubled case. Have they
not then observed the sky above them, how We have constructed it and beautified it, and how
there are no rifts therein? And the earth have We spread out, and have flung firm hills therein,
and have caused of every lovely kind to grow thereon, A VISION and a reminder for every
penitent slave.

And We send down from the sky blessed water whereby We give growth unto gardens and the
grain of crops, and lofty date-palms with ranged clusters, provision made for men; and therewith
We quicken a dead land. Even so will be the resurrection of the dead.

The folk of Noah denied before them, and so did the dwellers at Ar-Rass and Thamud, and A'ad,
and Pharaoh, and the brethren of Lot, and the **Dwellers in the Wood**, and the folk of Tubb'a:
every one denied their messengers, therefore My threat took effect.

Were We then worn out by the first creation? Yet they are in doubt about THIS NEW
CREATION.

We verily created man and We know what his soul whispereth to him, and **We are nearer to him than his jugular vein**. When **The Two Receivers** receive him, seated on the right hand and on the left, he uttereth no word but there is with him an observer ready. And the agony of death cometh in truth. And it is said unto him: "This is that which Thou wast wont to shun."

And the trumpet is blown. This is the threatened Day.

And every soul cometh, along with it a driver and a witness.

And unto the evil-doer it is said: "Thou wast in heedlessness of this. Now We have removed from Thee Thy covering, and piercing is Thy sight this day." And his comrade saith: "This is that which I have ready as testimony."

He saith: "Do ye TWAIN hurl to hell each rebel ingrate, hinderer of good, transgressor, doubter, who setteth up another god along with Allah. Do ye TWAIN hurl him to the dreadful doom."

His comrade saith: "Our Lord! I did not cause him to rebel, but he was himself far gone in error."

He saith: "Contend not in My presence, when I had already proffered unto you the warning. The sentence that cometh from Me cannot be changed, and I am in no wise a tyrant unto the slaves."

On the day when We say unto hell: "Art Thou filled?" and it saith: "Can there be more to come?" And the Garden is brought nigh for those who kept from evil, no longer distant. And it is said: "This is that which ye were promised." It is for every penitent and heedful one, who feareth the Beneficent in secret and cometh with a contrite heart. Enter it in peace. This is the **Day of Immortality**. There they have all that they desire, and there is more with Us.

And how many a generation We destroyed before them, who were mightier than these in prowess so that they overran the lands! Had they any place of refuge when the judgment came? Lo! Therein verily is a reminder for him who hath a heart, or giveth ear with full intelligence. And verily We created the heavens and the earth, and all that is between them, in six Days, and naught of weariness touched Us.

Therefore bear with what they say, and *hymn the praise* of thy Lord before the rising (*Fajr*) and before the setting (*Maghrib*) of the sun; And in the night-time (*Ishaa*) *hymn His praise*, and after the (prescribed) prostrations. And *prayerfully-listen* on the day (*Zhur*) when the crier crieth from a near place, The day (*Asr*) when ye all will *prayerfully-hear* the Awesome Cry in truth. That is **The Day of Coming Forth** from **The Coffer**.[*]

---

[*]These are the five orders of prayers given by Allah to Muhammad in consquence of this Night Journey. These correspond to the Five Movements (Chinese: 五行; pinyin: *Wǔ Xíng*): The five overcoming fluid interactions and overlapping modalities of melting, penetrating, separating, absorbing, and quenching. These five are in Order of the Day: (a) *Maghrib* (the Twilight Glow after the Sundisk is hidden till Dark); (b) *Ishaa* (from Dusk till Dawn); (c) *Fajr* (the Twilight Glow *before* the Sundisk peaks its first Direct-Ray till Daybreak); (d) *Zuhr* (NoonDay); (e) *Asr* (Afternoon). Like the Jews and the Baha'is, the Muslim day begins and ends at Sunset. The same is true for many other cultures, peoples, and ways.

Lo! We it is Who quicken and give death, and unto Us is the journeying.

On the Day when the earth splitteth asunder from them, hastening forth they come. That is a gathering easy for Us to make.

We are Best Aware of what they say, and Thou (O *AL-AMIN*) art in no wise a compeller over them. But warn by THIS QUR'AN him who feareth My threat.

46. Bism'illah Ar-Rahman Ar-Rahim! al-Buruj: THE CONSTELLATIONS.

By the heaven, holding Mansions of the Stars,
And by the Promised Day.

And by the witness and that whereunto he beareth testimony,
Self-destroyed were the owners of the ditch
Of the fuel-fed fire,
When they sat by it,
And were themselves the witnesses of what they did to the believers.

They had naught against them save that they believed in Allah, the Mighty, the Owner of Praise, Him unto Whom belongeth the Sovereignty of the heavens and the earth; and Allah is of all things the Witness.

Lo! They who persecute believing men and believing women and repent not, theirs verily will be the doom of hell, and theirs the doom of burning.

Lo! those who believe and do good works, theirs will be Gardens underneath which rivers flow. That is the Great Success.

Lo! The punishment of thy Lord is stern.

Lo! He it is Who produceth, then reproduceth,
And He is the Forgiving, the Loving,
Lord of the Throne of Glory,
Doer of what He will.

Hath there come unto Thee the story of the hosts
Of Pharaoh and Thamud?

Nay, but those who disbelieve live in denial
And Allah, ALL UNSEEN, surroundeth them.

Nay, but THIS IS A MOST-GLORIOUS QUR'AN.

On a Guarded Tablet.

CHINVAT-SIRAT: Bism'illah Ar-Rahman Ar-Rahim!

When Allah's succour (an-Nasr) and the triumph cometh
And thou seest mankind Entering the religion of Allah in Troops,
Then hymn the praises of thy Lord, and seek forgiveness of Him.
Lo! He is ever ready to show mercy.

-Sadisa

87

JUMU'AH!

JUMU'AH!

---THE GATHERING STORM---
Manzil-i-Shahada va Rakat
Jamál

"__Come__ and __Gather__ yourselves together __unto__ the __Supper__ of the __Great God__
(__Allah-Hu Akbar__: Magnified Be Thy Name! O Lord!)
(__Allah-Hu Akbar__: May Thy Name be Magnified Through Me! O Lord!)"
---Book of Revelation 19:17 KJV---

Bism'illah Ar-Rahman Ar-Rahim!

__RECITE__ (aq-Qaara): In the name of thy Lord Who createth,
Createth man from a clot (al-'Alaq).
__RECITE:__ And thy Lord is the Most Bounteous,
Who teacheth by the __PEN__,
Teacheth man that which he knew not.

IX. JUZ'UN SIPARA NOVA:

47. Bism'illah Ar-Rahman Ar-Rahim!

"By the snorting courses,
Striking sparks of fire
And scouring to the raid at dawn,
Then, therewith, with their trail of dust,
Cleaving, as one, the centre (of the foe),
Lo! man is an ingrate unto his Lord
And lo! he is a witness unto that;
And lo! in the love of wealth he is violent.
Knoweth he not that, when the contents of the graves are poured forth
And the secrets of the breasts are made known,
On that day will their Lord be perfectly informed concerning them. (Q. al-'Adiyat)

48. Bism'illah Ar-Rahman Ar-Rahim! al-Jumu`ah THE DAY OF CONGREGATION.

All that is in the heavens and all that is in the earth **GLORIFIETH ALLAH**, the Sovereign Lord, the Holy One, the Mighty, the Wise.[*]

---

[*]**Al-Musabbihat** refer to the collective name of the seven surahs that begin with Allah's *__glorification__* 'Subhana,' 'Sabbaha,' and 'Yusabbihu:' *al-Hadid*; *al-Hashr*; *as-Saff*; *al-Jumua*; *at-Taghabun*; *al-Isra*; and *al-Ala*.

He it is Who hath sent among the unlettered ones a messenger of their own, to recite unto them His revelations and **to *make* them grow**, and to teach them the Scripture and wisdom, though heretofore they were indeed in error manifest, along with others of them who have not yet joined them. He is the Mighty, the Wise.

That is the bounty of Allah; which He giveth unto whom He will. Allah is of Infinite Bounty. The likeness of those who are entrusted with the WAY of *MOSES*, yet apply it not, is as the likeness of the ass carrying books. Wretched is the likeness of folk who deny the Revelations of Allah. And Allah guideth not wrongdoing folk.

Say (O AL-MAIN): "O ye who are Jews! If ye claim that ye are favoured of Allah apart from all humankind, then long for death if ye are truthful!" But they will never long for it because of all that their own hands have sent before, and Allah is Aware of evil-doers.

Say (unto them): "Lo! The Death from which ye shrink will surely meet you, and afterward ye will be returned unto the Knower of the Invisible and the Visible, and He will tell you what ye used to do!"

O ye who Believe! When the call is heard for the prayer of the **Day of Congregation**,[*] haste unto Remembrance of Allah and leave your trading. That is better for you if ye did but know.

And when the prayer is ended, then Disperse in **The Land** and seek of Allah's bounty, and remember Allah much, that ye may be successful.

But when they SPY some merchandise or pastime they break away to it and leave Thee standing.

Say: "That which Allah hath is better than pastime and than merchandise, and Allah is the Best of providers!"

49. Bism'illah Ar-Rahman Ar-Rahim! al-Ma'idah: THE OUTSPREAD TABLE OF THE SUPPER OF GOD.

O ye who believe! Fulfil your indentures. The beast of cattle is made lawful unto you for food except that which is announced unto you, game being unlawful when ye are on the pilgrimage. Lo! Allah ordaineth that which pleaseth Him.

O ye who believe! Profane not Allah's monuments nor the Sacred Month nor the offerings nor the garlands, nor those repairing to **The Sacred House**, seeking the grace and pleasure of their Lord. But when ye have left the sacred territory, then go hunting if ye will. And let not your abhorrence of a folk who (once) stopped your going to **The Inviolable Place of Worship** seduce you to transgress; but help ye one another unto righteousness and pious duty. Help not one another unto sin and transgression, but keep your duty to Allah. Lo! Allah is severe in punishment.

---

[*]Abbas Effendi announced--from his dream--that he is "the one whom had made this first call."

Forbidden unto you for food are carrion and blood and swineflesh, and that which hath been dedicated unto any other than Allah, and the strangled, and the dead through beating, and the dead through falling from a height, and that which hath been killed by the goring of horns, and the devoured of wild beasts, saving that which ye make lawful (by the death-stroke), and that which hath been immolated unto idols. And forbidden is it that ye swear by the divining arrows. This is an abomination. This day are those who disbelieve in despair of ever harming your religion; so fear them not, fear Me! This day have I perfected your religion for you and completed My favour unto you, and have chosen for you as religion the Surrender of *al-Islam*. **Whoso is forced by hunger, not by will, to transgression: For him Lo! Allah is Forgiving, Merciful.**

They ask Thee what is made lawful for them. Say: "Good things are made lawful for you." And those beasts and birds of prey which ye have trained as hounds are trained, ye teach them that which Allah taught you; so eat of that which they catch for you and mention Allah's name upon it, and observe your duty to Allah. Lo! Allah is swift to take account.

This day are good things made lawful for you. The food of those who have received the Scripture is lawful for you, and your food is lawful for them. And so are the virtuous women of the believers and the virtuous women of those who received the Scripture before you lawful for you when ye give them their marriage portions and live with them in honour, not in fornication, nor taking them as secret concubines. Whoso denieth the faith, his work is vain and he will be among the losers in the Hereafter.

O ye who believe! When ye rise up for prayer, wash you faces, and your hands up to the elbows, and lightly rub your heads and wash your feet up to the ankles. And if ye are unclean, PURIFY YOUSELVES. And if ye are sick or on a journey, or one of you cometh from the closet, or ye have had contact with women, and ye find not water, then go to clean, high ground and rub your faces and your hands with some of it. Allah would not place a burden on you, but He would PURIFY YOU and would perfect His grace upon you, that ye may give thanks. Remember Allah's grace upon you and **His Covenant** by which He bound you when ye said: "We hear and we obey!" And keep your duty to Allah. Lo! He knoweth what is in the breasts of persons.

O ye who believe! Be steadfast witnesses for Allah in equity, and let not hatred of any people seduce you that ye deal not justly. Deal justly, that is nearer to your duty. Observe your duty to Allah. Lo! Allah is Informed of what ye do. Allah hath promised those who believe and do good works: "Theirs will be forgiveness and immense reward." And they who disbelieve and deny Our Revelations, such are rightful owners of hell.

O ye who believe! Remember Allah's favour unto you, how a people were minded to stretch out their hands against you but He withheld their hands from you; and keep your duty to Allah. In Allah let believers put their trust.

Allah made a **Covenant of Old** with the Children of Israel and We raised among them twelve chieftains, and Allah said: "Lo! I am with you. If ye establish worship and pay the poor-due (*zakat*), and believe in My messengers and support them, **and lend unto Allah a kindly loan,** surely I shall remit your sins, and surely I shall bring you into Gardens underneath which rivers flow. Whoso among you disbelieveth after this will go astray from a plain road."

And **because of their breaking their Covenant**, We have **cursed them** and made hard their hearts.* They change words from their context and forget a part of that whereof they were admonished. Thou wilt not cease to discover treachery from all save a few of them. **But bear with them and pardon them**. Lo! Allah loveth the kindly.

And with those who say: "Lo! We are Christians," We made **a Covenant**, but they forgot a part of that whereof they were admonished. Therefore We have stirred up enmity and hatred among them till the Day of Resurrection, when Allah will inform them of their handiwork.

O People of the Scripture! Now hath Our messenger come unto you, **expounding unto you much of that which ye used to hide in the Scripture**, and forgiving much. now hath come unto you light from Allah and plain Scripture, whereby Allah guideth him who seeketh His good pleasure unto paths of peace. He bringeth them out of darkness unto light by His decree, and guideth them unto a straight path.

They indeed have disbelieved who say: "Lo! Allah is the Messiah, son of Miriam." Say: "Who then can do aught against Allah, if He had willed to destroy the Messiah son of Miriam, and his mother and everyone on earth? Allah's is the Sovereignty of the heavens and the earth and all that is between them. He createth what He will. And Allah is Able to do all things."

The Jews and Christians say: "We are sons of Allah and His loved ones." Say: "Why then doth He chastise you for your sins? Nay, ye are but mortals of His creating. He forgiveth whom He will, and chastiseth whom He will. Allah's is the Sovereignty of the heavens and the earth and all that is between them, and **unto Him is the journeying**."

O People of the Scripture! Now hath Our messenger come unto you to make things plain unto you after an interval of the messengers, lest ye should say: "There came not unto us a messenger of cheer nor any warner." Now hath a messenger of cheer and a warner come unto you. Allah is Able to do all things.

And remember when *MOSES* said unto his people: "O My People! Remember Allah's favour unto you, how He placed among you prophets, and He made you kings, and gave you that which

---

*Three-Part Covenant of the Blessing, the Curse and the Re-Gathering: "And if you obey the voice of the LORD your God, being careful to do all his commandments which I command you this day, the LORD your God will set you high above all the nations of the earth. And all these blessings shall come upon you and overtake you, if you obey the voice of the LORD your God... But if you will not obey the voice of the LORD your God or be careful to do all his commandments and his statutes which I command you this day, then **all these curses shall come upon you** and overtake you... The LORD will send upon you **curses, confusion, and frustration,** in all that you undertake to do, until you are destroyed and perish quickly, on account of the evil of your doings, because you have forsaken Me... And when all these things come upon you, **the Blessing and the Curse**, which I have set before you, and you call them to mind among all the nations where the LORD your God has driven you, and **Return** to the LORD your God, you and your children, and obey his voice in all that I command you this day, with all your heart and with all your soul; then the LORD your God **will restore your fortunes**, and have compassion upon you, and he will **Gather you again** from all the peoples where the LORD your God has scattered you" (Deut. 28:1-2, 15, 20; 30:1-3 RSV).

He gave not to any other of the creatures. O My People! Go into the holy land which Allah hath ordained for you. Turn not in flight, for surely ye turn back as losers."

They said: "O *MOSES*! Lo! A giant people dwell therein and Lo! We go not in till they go forth from thence. When they go forth from thence, then we will enter."

Then out spake two of those who feared for God, unto whom Allah had been gracious: "Enter in upon them by the GATE, for if ye enter by *it*, Lo! Ye will be Victorious. So put your trust in the LORD if ye are indeed believers."

They said: "O *MOSES*! We will never enter while they are in it. So go Thou and Thy Lord and fight! We will sit here."

He said: "My Lord! I have control of none but myself and my brother, so distinguish between us and the wrong-doing folk." He said: "For this **the land** will surely be forbidden them for forty years that they will wander in the earth, bewildered. So grieve not over the wrongdoing folk. But recite unto them with truth the tale of the two sons of Adam, how they offered each a sacrifice, and it was accepted from the one of them and it was not accepted from the other."

The one said: "I will surely kill Thee." The other answered: "Allah accepteth only from those who ward off evil. Even if thou stretch out thy hand against me to kill me, I shall not stretch out my hand against thee to kill Thee, Lo! I fear Allah, the Lord of the Worlds. Lo! I would rather thou shouldst bear the punishment of the sin against me and Thine own sin and become one of the owners of the fire. That is the reward of evil-doers." But his mind imposed on him the killing of his brother, so he slew him and became one of the losers.

Then Allah sent a raven scratching up the ground, to show him how to hide his brother's naked corpse. He said: "Woe unto me! Am I not able to be as this raven and so hide my brother's naked corpse?" And he became repentant.

For that Cause We decreed for the Children of Israel that **whosoever killeth a human being** for other than manslaughter or corruption in the earth, **it shall be as if he had killed all mankind, and whoso saveth the life of one, it shall be as if he had saved the life of all mankind.**

Our messengers came unto them of old with THIS RIGHTEOUS BOOK, but afterwards Lo! Many of them became prodigals in the earth.

The only **reward** (*karma*) of those who make war upon Allah and His messenger and strive after corruption in the land will be that they **kill or crucify**[*] themselves **on their own account**, or

---

[*]"For it is impossible to restore again to repentance those who have once been enlightened, who have tasted the heavenly gift, and have become partakers of the Holy Spirit, and have tasted the goodness of the word of God and the powers of the age to come, if they then commit apostasy, since they **Crucify the Son of God on their own account** and hold him up to contempt. For land which has drunk the rain that often falls upon it, and brings forth vegetation useful to those for whose sake it is cultivated, receives a blessing from God. But if it bears thorns and thistles, it is worthless and near to being cursed; **its end is to be burned**. Though we speak thus, yet in your case, beloved, we feel sure of better things that belong to salvation" (Hebrews 6:4-9 RSV).

have their hands and feet on alternate sides cut off, or be expelled out of the land. Such will be their degradation in the world, and in the Hereafter theirs will be an awful doom; **Save those who repent** *before* **ye overpower them**. For know that Allah is Forgiving, Merciful.

O ye who believe! Be mindful of your duty to Allah, and seek the way of approach unto Him, and strive in His way in order that ye may succeed. As for those who disbelieve, Lo! If all that is in the earth were theirs, and as much again therewith, to ransom them from the DOOM on the Day of Resurrection, it would not be accepted from them. Theirs will be a painful DOOM. They will wish to come forth from **the Fire**, but they will not come forth from it. Theirs will be a lasting DOOM.

As for the thief, both male and female, they cut off their own hands. It is the **reward** (*karma*) of their own deeds, an exemplary punishment from Allah. Allah is Mighty, Wise. But whoso repenteth after his wrongdoing and amendeth, Lo! Allah will relent toward him. Lo! Allah is Forgiving, Merciful. Knowest Thou not that unto Allah belongeth the Sovereignty of the heavens and the earth? **He punisheth whom He will, and forgiveth whom He will**. Allah is Able to do all things.

O Messenger! Let not them grieve Thee who vie one with another in the race to disbelief, of such as say with their mouths: "We believe," but their hearts believe not, and among the Jews are they who are litigant: listeners for the sake of falsehood, listeners on behalf of other folk who come not unto Thee, **changing words from their context** and saying: "If this be given unto you, receive it, but if this be not given unto you, then Beware! He whom Allah doometh unto sin, Thou (by Thine efforts) wilt avail him naught against Allah. Those are they for whom the Will of Allah is that He cleanse not their hearts. Theirs in the world will be ignominy, and in the Hereafter an awful doom!" Listeners for the sake of falsehood! Greedy for illicit gain! If then they have recourse unto Thee judge between them or disclaim jurisdiction. If Thou **disclaimest jurisdiction**, then they cannot harm Thee at all. But if Thou judgest, judge between them with equity. Lo! Allah loveth the equitable.

How come they unto Thee for judgment when **they have the Torah**, wherein Allah hath delivered judgment for them? Yet even after that they turn away. Such folk are not believers. Lo! We did reveal **the Torah**, wherein is guidance and a light, by which the prophets who surrendered unto Allah **judged the Jews**, and the rabbis and the priests judged by such of Allah's Scripture as they were bidden to observe, and thereunto were they witnesses. So fear not humankind, but fear Me. And My revelations for a little gain. Whoso judgeth not by that which Allah hath revealed: such are disbelievers.

And We prescribed for them therein: "The life for the life, and the eye for the eye, and the nose for the nose, and the ear for the ear, and the tooth for the tooth, and for wounds retaliation." But if any one remits the retaliation by way of charity, it **is an act of atonement for himself**.[*] Whoso judgeth not by that which Allah hath revealed: such are wrong-doers.

And We caused *JESUS*, son of Miriam, to follow in their footsteps, confirming that which was revealed before him in the **Torah**, and We bestowed on him **the Gospel** wherein is guidance and

---

[*]Here Muhammad abrogates and overturns the ruthless interpretations and wrong customs of the people.

a light, confirming that which was before it in the **Torah**--a guidance and an admonition unto those who ward off adversaries. Let the People of the Gospel judge by that which Allah hath revealed therein. Whoso judgeth not by that which Allah hath revealed: such are evil-livers.

And unto Thee have We revealed the Scripture with the truth, **confirming whatever Scripture was before it**, and a watcher over it. So judge between them by that which Allah hath revealed, and follow not their desires away from the truth which hath come unto thee. For each We have appointed a Divine Law and a Traced-Out WAY. Had Allah willed He could have **made you one community**. But that He may try you by that which He hath given you He hath made you as ye are. **So vie one with another in good works**. Unto Allah ye will all return, and He will then inform you of that wherein ye differ.

So judge between them by that which Allah hath revealed, and **follow not their desires**,[*] but beware of them lest they seduce Thee from some part of that which Allah hath revealed unto Thee. And if they turn away, then know that Allah's Will is to smite them for some sin of theirs. Lo! many of mankind are evil-livers. Is it a judgment of **The Time of Ignorance** that they are seeking? Who is better than Allah for judgment to a people who have Certitude in God?

O ye who believe! Take not *the wayward* of the Jews and the Christians for friends. They are friends one to another. He among you who taketh them for friends is of them. Lo! Allah guideth not wrongdoing folk. And Thou seest those in whose heart is a disease race toward them, saying: "We fear lest a change of fortune befall us. And it may happen that Allah will vouchsafe unto Thee the victory, or a commandment from His presence." Then will they repent them of their secret thoughts. Then will the believers reply: "Are these they who swore by Allah their most binding oaths that they were surely with you? Their works have failed, and they have become the losers."

O ye who believe! Whoso of you becometh a renegade from his religion--know that in his stead-- Allah will bring a people whom He loveth and who love Him, humble toward believers, stern toward disbelievers, striving in the way of Allah, and fearing not the blame of any blamer. Such is the grace of Allah which He giveth unto whom He will. Allah is All-Embracing, All-Knowing.

Your Guardian can be only Allah; and His messenger and those who believe, who establish worship and pay the poordue (*zakat*), and bow down. And whoso taketh Allah and His messenger and those who believe for Guardian will know that, Lo! The **Party of Allah**, they are the victorious.

O Ye who believe! Choose not for Guardians such of those who received the Scripture before you, and of the disbelievers, as make a jest and sport of your religion. But keep your duty to Allah if ye are true believers.

And when ye call to prayer they take it for a jest and sport. That is because they are a folk who understand not.

---

[*]For revenge: "an eye for an eye, etc."

Say: "O People of the Scripture! Do ye blame us for aught else than that we believe in Allah and that which is revealed unto us and that which was revealed aforetime, and because most of you are evil-livers?"

Shall I tell Thee of a worse case than theirs for retribution with Allah? Worse is the case of him whom Allah hath cursed, him on whom His wrath hath fallen and of whose sort Allah hath turned some to apes and swine, and who serveth idols. Such are in worse plight and further astray from the plain road. When they come unto you, they say: "We believe!" But they came in unbelief and they went out in the same; and Allah knoweth best what they were hiding. And Thou seest many of them vying one with another in sin and transgression and **their devouring of illicit gain**. Verily evil is what they do.

Why do not the rabbis and the priests forbid their evil-speaking and their devouring of illicit gain? Verily evil is their handiwork. Among the Jews they say: "Allah's hand is fettered." Their hands are fettered and they are accursed for saying so. Nay, but both His hands are spread out wide in bounty. He bestoweth as He will. That which hath been revealed unto Thee from Thy Lord is certain to increase the contumacy and disbelief of many of them, and We have cast among them enmity and hatred till the Day of Resurrection. As often as they light a fire for war, Allah extinguisheth it. Their effort is for corruption in the land, and Allah loveth not corrupters.

If only the People of the Scripture would believe and ward off evil, surely We should remit their sins from them and surely We should bring them into **Gardens of Na'im** (Heb. *Nahum*).

If they had observed the Torah and the Gospel and that which was revealed unto them from their Lord, they would surely have been nourished from above them and from beneath their feet. **Among them there are people who are moderate**, but many of them are of evil conduct.

O Messenger! Make known that which hath been revealed unto Thee from thy Lord, for if Thou do it not, Thou wilt not have conveyed His message. Allah will protect Thee from mankind. Lo! Allah guideth not the disbelieving folk. Say: "O People of the Scripture! Ye have naught of guidance till ye observe the Torah and the Gospel and that which was revealed unto you from your Lord!" That which is revealed unto Thee from thy Lord is certain to increase the contumacy and disbelief of many of them. But grieve not for the disbelieving folk.

Lo! Those who believe, and those who are Jews, and Sabaeans, and Christians[*]--Whosoever believeth in Allah and the Last Day and doeth right--there shall no fear come upon them neither shall they grieve.

We made a **Covenant of Old** with the Children of Israel and We sent unto them messengers. As often as a messenger came unto them with that which their souls desired not they became rebellious. Some of them they denied and some they slew.[†] They thought no harm would come

_____

[*]The "Jews, Sabeans, and Christians" refer to the peoples of the previous Revelations, the Major Independent Prophets that (including *MUHAMMAD*) are SEVEN: The Sabaeans: *ADAM, KRISHNA, ZOROASTER, BUDDHA*; Jewish: *MOSES*; and Christian: *JESUS*.
[†]These are the blood of the martyrs from A to Z: Able to Zechariah, who was slain between the altar and the sanctuary (see Luke 11:51).

of it, so they were wilfully blind and deaf. And afterward Allah turned toward them. Now are many of them wilfully blind and deaf. Allah is Seer of what they do.

They surely disbelieve who say: "Lo! Allah is the Messiah, son of Miriam. The Messiah himself said: "O Children of Israel, worship Allah, my Lord and your Lord. Lo! whoso ascribeth partners unto Allah, for him Allah hath forbidden paradise. His abode is the Fire. For evil-doers there will be no helpers." They surely disbelieve who say: "Lo! Allah is **the third of three**!" When there is no God save the One God. If they desist not from so saying a painful doom will fall on those of them who disbelieve. Will they not rather turn unto Allah and seek forgiveness of Him? For Allah is Forgiving, Merciful.

The Messiah, son of Miriam, was no other than a messenger, messengers the like of whom had passed on before him. And his mother was a saintly woman. And they both used to eat earthly food. See how We make the Revelations clear for them, and see how they are turned away! Say: "Serve ye in place of Allah that which possesseth for you neither hurt nor use? Allah it is Who is the Hearer, the Knower." Say: "O People of the Scripture! Stress not in your religion other than the truth, and follow not the vain desires of folk who erred of old and led many astray, and erred from a plain road."

Those of the Children of Israel who went astray were cursed by the **Tongue of David**, and of *JESUS*, son of Miriam. That was because they rebelled and used to transgress. They restrained not one another from the wickedness they did. Verily evil was that they used to do! Thou seest many of them making friends with those who disbelieve. Surely ill for them is that which they themselves send on before them: that Allah will be wroth with them and in the DOOM they will abide. If they believed in Allah and the Prophet and that which is revealed unto him, they would not choose them for their friends. But many of them are of evil conduct.

Thou wilt find the most vehement of humankind in hostility to those who believe to be amongst the Jews and the Idolaters. And Thou wilt find the nearest of them in affection to those who believe to be those who say: "Lo! We are Christians." That is because there are among them priests and monks, and because they are not proud. When they listen to that which hath been revealed unto the messengers, Thou seest their eyes overflow with tears because of their recognition of the Truth. They say: "Our Lord, we believe. Inscribe us as among the witnesses. How should we not believe in Allah and that which hath come unto us of the Truth. And how should we not hope that our Lord will bring us in along with righteous folk?"

Allah hath rewarded them for that their saying--Gardens underneath which rivers flow, wherein they will abide for ever. That is the reward of the good. But those who disbelieve and deny Our Revelations, they are owners of hell-fire. O ye who believe! Forbid not the good things which Allah hath made lawful for you, and transgress not, Lo! Allah loveth not transgressors.

Eat of that which Allah hath bestowed on you as food lawful and good, and keep your duty to Allah in Whom ye are believers. Allah will not take you to task for that which is unintentional in your oaths, but He will take you to task for the oaths which ye swear in earnest. The expiation thereof is the feeding of ten of the needy with the average of that wherewith ye feed your own folk, or the clothing of them, or the liberation of a slave, and for him who findeth not the wherewithal to do so then a three days' fast. This is the expiation of your oaths when ye have sworn; and keep your oaths. Thus Allah expoundeth unto you His revelations in order that ye may give thanks.

O ye who believe! Strong drink and games of chance and idols and divining arrows are only an infamy of Satan's handiwork. Leave it aside in order that ye may succeed. Satan seeketh only to cast among you enmity and hatred by means of strong drink and games of chance, and to turn you from remembrance of Allah and from worship. Will ye then have done? Obey Allah and obey the messenger, and Beware! But if ye turn away, then know that the duty of Our messenger is only plain conveyance of the message.

There shall be no transgression imputed unto those who believe and do good works for what they may have eaten in the past. So be mindful of your duty, and believe, and do good works; and again: be mindful of your duty, and believe; and once again: be mindful of your duty, and do right. Allah loveth the good.

O ye who believe! Allah will surely **try you somewhat** in the matter **of the game** which ye take with your hands and your spears, that Allah may know him who feareth Him in secret. Whoso transgresseth after this, for him there is a painful doom.

O ye who believe! Kill no wild game while ye are on the pilgrimage. Whoso of you killeth it of set purpose he shall pay its forfeit in the equivalent of that which he hath killed, of domestic animals, the judge to be two men among you known for justice, the forfeit to be brought as an offering to the Ka'bah (Lit. **The Cube**); or, for expiation, he shall feed poor persons, or the equivalent thereof in fasting, that he may taste the evil consequences of his deed. Allah forgiveth whatever of this kind may have happened in the past, but whoso relapseth, Allah will take retribution from him. Allah is Mighty, Able to Requite. To hunt and to eat the fish of the sea is made lawful for you, a provision for you and for seafarers; but to hunt on land is forbidden you so long as ye are on the pilgrimage. Be mindful of your duty to Allah, unto Whom ye will be gathered.

Allah hath appointed the Ka'bah[*], **The Sacred House**, a standard for humankind, and the Sacred Month and the offerings and the garlands. That is so that ye may know that Allah knoweth whatsoever is in the heavens and whatsoever is in the earth, and that Allah is Knower of all things. Know that Allah is severe in punishment, but that Allah is Forgiving, Merciful. The duty of the messenger is only to convey the message. Allah knoweth what ye proclaim and what ye hide. Say: "The evil and the good are not alike even though the plenty of the evil attract Thee. So be mindful of your duty to Allah, O men of understanding, that ye may succeed."

O ye who believe! Ask not of things which, if they were made known unto you, would trouble you; but if ye ask of them when THIS QUR'AN is being revealed, they will be made known unto you. Allah pardoneth this, for Allah is Forgiving, Clement. A folk before you asked for such disclosures and then disbelieved therein. Allah hath not appointed anything in the nature of a Bahirah or a Sa'ibah or a Wasilah or a Hami, but those who disbelieve invent a lie against Allah. Most of them have no sense. And when it is said unto them: "Come unto that which Allah hath

---

[*]Point of Adoration: "Qiblih" as in Qabalah, Kabbalah, Cabala and Ka'ba.

98

revealed and unto the messenger!" They say: "Enough for us is that wherein we found our fathers." What! Even though their fathers had no knowledge whatsoever, and no guidance?

O ye who believe! **Ye have charge of your own souls**. He who erreth cannot injure you if ye are rightly guided. Unto Allah ye will all return; and then He will inform you of what ye used to do.

O ye who believe! Let there be witnesses between you when death draweth nigh unto one of you, at the time of bequest--two witnesses--just folk from among you, or two others from another tribe, in case ye are campaigning in the land and the calamity of death befall you. Ye shall empanel them both after the prayer, and, if ye doubt, they shall be made to swear by Allah saying: "We will not take a bribe, even though it were on behalf of a near kinsman nor will we hide the testimony of Allah, for then indeed we should be of the sinful." But then, if it is afterwards ascertained that both of them merit sin, let two others take their place of those nearly concerned, and let them swear by Allah, saying: "Verily our testimony is truer than their testimony and we have not transgressed the bounds of duty, for them indeed we should be of the evil-doers." Thus it is more likely that they will bear true witness or fear that after their oaths the oaths of others will be taken. So be mindful of your duty and hearken. Allah guideth not the froward folk.

In the day when Allah gathereth together the messengers, and saith: "What was your response from humankind?" They say: "We have no knowledge. Lo! Thou, only Thou art the Knower of Things Hidden." When Allah saith: "O *JESUS*, son of Miriam! Remember My favour unto Thee and unto Thy mother; how I strengthened Thee with the holy Spirit, so that Thou spakest unto mankind in the cradle as in maturity; and how I taught Thee the Scripture and Wisdom (*hikmat/chokhmah*) and the Torah and the Gospel; and how thou didst shape of clay as it were the likeness of a bird by My permission, and didst **blow upon it and it was a bird by My permission**,[*] and thou didst heal him who was born blind and the leper by My permission; and how thou didst raise the dead by My permission; and how I restrained the Children of Israel from harming Thee when thou camest unto them with THIS RIGHTEOUS BOOK, and those of them who disbelieved exclaimed: 'This is naught else than mere magic!'"

And when I inspired the disciples, saying: "Believe in Me and in My messenger." They said: "We believe. Bear witness that we have surrendered: 'We are in submission!'" When the disciples said: "O *JESUS*, son of Miriam! Is thy Lord able to send down for us a **Table Spread** with food from heaven?" He said: "Observe your duty to Allah, if ye are true believers." They said: "We wish to eat thereof, that we may satisfy our hearts and know that thou hast spoken truth to us, and that thereof we may be witnesses."

JESUS, son of Miriam, said: "O Allah, Lord of us! Send down for us a Table Spread with food from heaven, that it may be a feast for Us, for the first of Us and for the last of Us, and a sign from Thee. Give us sustenance, for Thou art the Best of Sustainers."

Allah said: "Lo! I send it down for you. And whoso disbelieveth of you afterward, him surely will I punish with a punishment wherewith I have not punished any of the creatures."

---

[*]This refers to the airplane: and "the four birds" to the four planes at the 9-11.

99

And when Allah saith: "O *JESUS*, son of Miriam! Didst thou say unto mankind: 'Take me and my mother for two gods beside Allah?'" He saith: "Be glorified! It was not mine to utter that to which I had no right. If I used to say it, then Thou knewest it. Thou knowest what is in my mind, and I know not what is in Thy Mind. Lo! Thou, only Thou, art the Knower of Things Hidden? I spake unto them only that which Thou commandedst me, saying: 'Worship Allah, my Lord and your Lord. I was a witness of them while I dwelt among them, and when Thou tookest me Thou wast the Watcher over them. Thou art Witness over all things.' If Thou punish them, Lo! They are Thy slaves, and if Thou forgive them: Lo! They are Thy slaves! Lo! Thou, only Thou, art the Mighty, the Wise.'"

Allah saith: "This is A DAY in which their truthfulness profiteth the truthful, for theirs are Gardens underneath which rivers flow, wherein they are secure for ever, **Allah taking pleasure in them and they in Him**. That is the great triumph!" Unto Allah belongeth the Sovereignty of the heavens and the earth and whatsoever is therein, and He is Able to do all things!

X. JUZ'UN SIPARA DECIMO:

50. Bism'illah Ar-Rahman Ar-Rahim! al-Mu'minun: THE BELIEVERS.

Successful indeed are the believers who are humble in their prayers, and who shun vain conversation, and who are payers of the poor-due (*zakat*); And who guard their modesty--Save from their wives or that which their right hands possess, for then they are not blameworthy, but whoso craveth beyond that, such are transgressors--And who are shepherds of their pledge and **their Covenant**, and who pay heed to their prayers. These are the heirs who will inherit paradise. There they will abide.

Verily We created man from a product of wet earth; Then placed him as a drop of goo in a safe lodging; then fashioned We the drop a clot, then fashioned We the clot a little lump, then fashioned We the little lump bones, then clothed the bones with flesh, and then produced it as another creation. So blessed be Allah, the Best of creators!

Then Lo! Aafter that ye surely die. Then Lo! On the Day of Resurrection ye are raised again. And We have created above you seven paths,[*] and We are never unmindful of creation. And we send down from the sky water in measure, and We give it lodging in the earth, and Lo! We are Able to withdraw it. Then We produce for you therewith gardens of date-palms and grapes, wherein is much fruit for you and whereof ye eat; and **A TREE that springeth forth from Mount Sinai** that groweth oil and relish for the eaters. And Lo! In the cattle there is verily a lesson for you. We give you to drink of that which is in their bellies, and many uses have ye in them, and of them do ye eat; and on them and on the ship ye are carried.

And We verily sent Noah unto his folk, and he said: "O My People! Serve Allah. Ye have no other God save Him. Will ye not ward off?" But the Chieftains of his folk, who disbelieved, said: "This is only a mortal like you who would make himself superior to you. Had Allah willed, He

---

[*]*ADAM*, the Primordial, the Indigenous, the Great Pyramid; *MOSES*, the Torah; *KRISHNA*, the Gita; *ZOROASTER*, the Avestan; *BUDDHA*, the Tripitakan; *JESUS*, the Gospel; and *MUHAMMAD*, the Qur'anic.

surely could have sent down angels. We heard not of this in the case of our fathers of old. He is only a man in whom is a madness, so watch him for a while."

He said: "My Lord! Help me because they deny me."

Then We inspired in him, saying: "Make the ship under Our eyes and Our inspiration. Then, when Our command cometh and the oven gusheth water, introduce therein of every kind two spouses, and Thy household save him thereof against whom the Word hath already gone forth. And plead not with Me on behalf of those who have done wrong. Lo! They will be drowned. And when Thou art on board the ship, Thou and whoso is with Thee, then say: 'Praise be to Allah Who hath saved us from the wrongdoing folk!' And say: 'My Lord! Cause me to land at a blessed landing-place, for Thou art Best of all who bring to land.'"

Lo! Herein verily are portents, for Lo! We are ever putting souls to the TEST.

Then, after them, We brought forth another generation; and we sent among them a messenger of their own--Shem who is Melchizedec who built Jersualem the walled City--saying: "Serve Allah, Ye have no other God save Him. Will ye not ward off evil?" And the Chieftains of his folk, who disbelieved and denied the meeting of the Hereafter, and whom We had made soft in the life of the world--who took pleasures in the Tower of Babel--said: "This is only a mortal like you, who eateth of that whereof ye eat and drinketh of that ye drink. If ye were to obey a mortal like yourselves, then, Lo! Ye surely would be losers. Doth he promise you that you, when ye are dead and have become dust and bones, will again be brought forth? Begone, begone, with that which ye are promised! There is naught but our life of the world; we die and we live, and we shall not be raised again. He is only a man who hath invented a lie about Allah. We are not going to put faith in him."

He said: "My Lord! Help me because they deny me." He said: "In a little while they surely will become repentant."

So the Awful Cry overtook them rightfully, and We made them like as wreckage that a torrent hurleth. A far removal for wrongdoing folk!

Then after them We brought forth other generations.[*] No nation can outstrip its term, nor yet postpone it. Then We sent our messengers one after another. Whenever its messenger came unto a nation they denied him; so We caused them to follow one another to disaster and We made them bywords. A far removal for folk who believe not!

Then We sent *MOSES* and his brother Aaron with Our tokens and a clear warrant unto Pharaoh and his Chiefs, but they scorned them and they were despotic folk. And they said: "Shall we put faith in two mortals like ourselves, and whose folk are servile unto us?" So they denied them, and became of those who were destroyed.

---

[*]See the Table of the Nations: Gen. chapter 10.

101

And We verily gave *MOSES* the Scripture, that haply they might go aright. And We made the Son of Miriam and his mother a portent, and We gave them refuge on a height, a place of flocks and watersprings.

O ye messengers! Eat of the good things, and do right. Lo! I am Aware of what ye do. And Lo! **This your religion is one religion** and I am your Lord, so keep your duty unto Me. But they have broken (*furqan*) their religion among them into sects, each group rejoicing in its tenets. So leave them in their error till a time. Think they that in the wealth and sons wherewith We provide them We hasten unto them with good things? Nay, but they perceive not.

Lo! Those who go in awe for fear of their Lord, and those who believe in the Revelations of their Lord, and those who ascribe not partners unto their Lord, and those who give that which they give with hearts afraid because they are about to return unto their Lord, these race for the good things, and they shall win them in the race.[*]

And we task not any soul beyond its scope, and with Us is a Record which speaketh the truth, and they will not be wronged. Nay, but their hearts are in ignorance of THIS, and they have other works, besides, which they are doing; Till when We grasp their luxurious ones with the punishment, Behold! They supplicate.

Supplicate not this day! Assuredly ye will not be helped by Us.

My Revelations were recited unto you, but ye used to turn back on your heels, in scorn thereof. Nightly did ye RAVE together. Have they not pondered the Word, or hath that come unto them which came not unto their fathers of old? Or know they not their messenger, and so reject him? Or say they: "There is a madness in him?" NAY! But he bringeth them the Truth; and most of them are haters of the Truth.

And if the Truth had followed their desires, verily the heavens and the earth and whosoever is therein had been corrupted. Nay, We have brought them their Reminder, but from their Reminder they now turn away. Or dost Thou ask of them any tribute? But the bounty of thy Lord is better, for He is Best of all who make provision. And Lo! Thou summonest them indeed unto a straight path. And Lo! Those who believe not in the Hereafter are indeed astray from the path. Though We had mercy on them and relieved them of the harm afflicting them, they still would wander blindly on in their contumacy. Already have We grasped them with punishment, but they humble not themselves unto their Lord, nor do they pray, **until, when We open for them the GATE OF EXTREME PUNISHMENT: Behold! they are aghast thereat.** He it is Who hath created for you ears and eyes and hearts. Small thanks give ye!

And He it is Who hath sown you broadcast in the earth, and unto Him ye will be gathered.

And He it is Who giveth life and causeth death, and His is the difference of night and day. Have ye then no sense?

---

[*]"I have fought the good fight, **I have finished the race**, I have kept the faith" (Paul: 1 Tim. 4:7 NIV).

Nay! But they say the like of that which said the men of old. They say: "When we are dead and have become dust and bones, shall we then, forsooth, be raised again? We were already promised this, we and our forefathers. Lo! This is naught but fables of the Old Ones." Say: "Unto Whom belongeth the earth and whosoever is therein, if ye have knowledge?" They will say: "Unto Allah." Say: Will ye not then remember?" Say: "**Who is Lord of the seven heavens, and Lord of the Tremendous Throne**?"[*]

They will say: "Unto Allah (all that belongeth)." Say: "Will ye not then keep duty unto Him?" Say: "In Whose hand is **The Dominion** over all things and He protecteth, while against Him there is no protection, if ye have knowledge?" They will say: "Unto Allah (all that belongeth)." Say: "How then are ye bewitched?" Nay, but We have brought them the Truth, and Lo! They are liars.

Allah hath not chosen any Son, nor is there any god along with Him; else would each god have assuredly championed that which he created, and some of them would assuredly have overcome others. Glorified be Allah above all that they allege.

Knower of the Invisible and the Visible!--Exalted be He over all that they ascribe as partners!

Say: "My Lord! If Thou shouldst show me that which they are promised. My Lord! Then set me not among the wrongdoing folk." And verily We are Able to show thee that which We have promised them. **Repel evil with that which is better**. We are Best Aware of that which they allege. And say: "My Lord! I seek refuge in Thee from suggestions of the evil ones, and I seek refuge in Thee, my Lord, lest they be present with me, until, when death cometh unto one of them, he saith: 'My Lord! Send me back, that I may do right in that which I have left behind!' But Nay! It is but a word that he speaketh; and behind them is **a barrier** until the day when they are raised."

And when the Trumpet is blown (Rev. 11:15) there will be no kinship among them that day, nor will they ask of one another. Then those whose scales are heavy, they are the successful. And those whose scales are light are those who lose their souls, in hell abiding. The fire burneth their faces, and they are glum therein. It will be said: "Were not My Revelations recited unto you, and then ye used to deny them?" They will say: "Our Lord! Our evil fortune conquered us, and we were erring folk. Our Lord! Oh, bring us forth from hence! If we return then indeed we shall be wrong-doers." He saith: "Begone therein, and speak not unto Me."

Lo! There was a party of My slaves who said: "Our Lord! We believe, therefore forgive us and have mercy on us for Thou art Best of all who show mercy!" But ye chose them for a laughing-stock until they caused you to forget remembrance of Me, while ye laughed at them. Lo! I have rewarded them this day forasmuch as they were steadfast in that they, even they, are the triumphant. He will say: "How long tarried ye in the earth, counting by years?" They will say: "We tarried by a day or part of a day." Ask of those who keep count! He will say: "Ye tarried but a little if ye only knew."

---

[*]Seven Major Revelations that testify before the throne of David is made known to them is the year al-Mustaghath: 2001 AD.

Deemed ye then that We had created you for naught, and that ye would not be returned unto Us? Now Allah be Exalted, the True King! There is no God save Him, the **Lord of the Throne** of Grace.

He who crieth unto any other god along with Allah hath no proof thereof. His reckoning is only with his Lord. Lo! Disbelievers will not be successful.

And say: "My Lord! Forgive and have Mercy, for Thou art Best of all who show Mercy!"

51. Bism'illah Ar-Rahman Ar-Rahim! ar-Rum: THE AMERICANS, RUSSIANS, FRENCH AND ENGLAND.

Alif. Lam. Mim.

The Romans (America) have been defeated in **the Nearer Land**,[*] and they, after their defeat will be victorious within ten years--Allah's is the command in the former case and in the latter--and in that day believers will rejoice! In Allah's help to victory. He helpeth to victory whom He will. He is the Mighty, the Merciful.

It is a promise of Allah. Allah faileth not His promise, but most of mankind know not. They know only **some appearance** of the life of the world, and are heedless of the Hereafter. Have they not pondered upon themselves? Allah created not the heavens and the earth, and that which is between them, save with truth and for a destined end. But truly many of mankind are disbelievers in the meeting with their Lord. Have they not travelled in the land and seen the nature of the consequence for those who were before them? They were stronger than these in power, and they dug the earth and built upon it more than these have built. Messengers of their own came unto them with THIS RIGHTEOUS BOOK. Surely Allah wronged them not, but they did wrong themselves. Then evil was the consequence to those who dealt in evil, because they denied the revelations of Allah and made a mock of them. Allah produceth creation, then He reproduceth it, then unto Him ye will be returned.

And in the day when the HOUR riseth the unrighteous will despair. There will be none to intercede for them of those whom they made equal with Allah. And they will reject their partners whom they ascribed unto Him. In the day when the HOUR cometh, in that day they will be sundered. As for those who believed and did good works, they will be made happy in a Garden. But as for those who disbelieved and denied Our Revelations, and denied the meeting of the Hereafter, such will be brought to DOOM. So glory be to Allah when ye enter the night and when ye enter the morning--unto Him be praise in the heavens and the earth!--and at the sun's decline and in the noonday. He bringeth forth the living from the dead, and He bringeth forth the dead from the living, and He reviveth the earth after her death. And even so will ye be brought forth.

And of His signs is this: He created you of dust, and behold you human beings, ranging widely! And of His signs is this: He created for you helpmeets from yourselves that ye might find rest in them, and He ordained between you love and mercy. Lo! herein indeed are portents for folk who

---

[*]Syria, Turkey, Iraq and Kuwait: the path of the Great River Euphrates.

reflect. And of His signs is the creation of the heavens and the earth, and the difference of your languages and colours. Lo! herein indeed are portents for men of knowledge. And of His signs is your slumber by night and by day, and your seeking of His bounty. Lo! herein indeed are portents for folk who heed. And of His signs is this: He showeth you the lightning for a fear and for a hope, and sendeth down water from the sky, and thereby quickeneth the earth after her death. Lo! herein indeed are portents for folk who understand. And of His signs is this: The heavens and the earth stand fast by His command, and afterward, when He calleth you, Lo! From the earth ye will emerge.

Unto Him belongeth whosoever is in the heavens and the earth. All are obedient unto Him. He it is Who produceth creation, then reproduceth it, and it is easier for Him. His is the Sublime Similitude in the heavens and the earth. He is the Mighty, the Wise.

He coineth for you a similitude of yourselves. Have ye, from among those whom your right hands possess, partners in the wealth We have bestowed upon you, equal with you in respect thereof, so that ye fear them as ye fear each other--that ye ascribe unto Us partners out of that which We created? Thus We display the revelations for people who have sense.

Nay, but those who do wrong follow their own lusts without knowledge. Who is able to guide him whom Allah hath sent astray? For such there are no helpers.

So set Thy purpose for religion as a man by nature upright--the nature of Allah, in which He hath created man. There is no altering Allah's creation. That is the right religion, but most men know not--Turning unto Him only; and be careful of your duty unto Him and establish worship, and be not of those who ascribe partners--of those who split up their religion and became schismatics, each sect exulting in its tenets.

And when harm toucheth men they cry unto their Lord, turning to Him in repentance; then, when they have tasted of His mercy, Behold! Some of them attribute partners to their Lord so as to disbelieve in that which We have given them. Unto such it is said: "Enjoy yourselves awhile, but ye will come to know." Or have We revealed unto them any warrant which speaketh of that which they associate with Him?

And when We cause mankind to taste of Mercy they rejoice therein; but if an evil thing befall them as the consequence of their own deeds, Lo! They are in despair! See they not that Allah enlargeth the provision for whom He will, and straiteneth it for whom He will. Lo! Herein indeed are portents for folk who believe.

So give to the kinsman his due, and to the needy, and to the wayfarer. That is best for those who seek Allah's Countenance. And such are they who are successful. That which ye give in usury in order that it may increase on other people's property hath no increase with Allah; but that which ye give in charity, seeking Allah's Countenance, hath increase manifold. Allah is He Who created you and then sustained you, then causeth you to die, then giveth life to you again. Is there any of your so-called partners of Allah that doeth aught of that? Praised and Exalted be He above what they associate with Him!

Corruption doth appear on land and sea because of the evil which men's **Hands have done**, that He may make them taste a part of that which they have done, in order that they may return. Say: "Travel in the land, and see the nature of the consequence for those who were before you! Most of them were Idolaters."

So set Thy purpose resolutely for the right religion, before the inevitable DAY cometh from Allah. On that day mankind will be sundered--whoso disbelieveth must bear the consequences of his disbelief, while those who do right make provision for themselves--that He may reward out of His bounty those who believe and do good works. Lo! He loveth not the disbelievers (who practice harm upon the peoples).

And of His signs is this: He sendeth herald winds to make you taste His mercy, and that the ships may sail at His command, and that ye may seek his favour, and that haply ye may be thankful. Verily We sent before Thee (O *AL-AMIN*) messengers to their own folk. Then we took vengeance upon those who were guilty in regard to them. To help believers is ever incumbent upon Us.

Allah is He Who sendeth the winds so that they raise clouds, and spreadeth them along the sky as pleaseth Him, and causeth them to break and thou seest the rain downpouring from within them. And when He maketh it to fall on whom He will of His bondmen, Lo! They rejoice; though before that, even before it was sent down upon them, they were in despair. Look, therefore, at the prints of Allah's mercy: how He quickeneth the earth after her death. Lo! He verily is the **Quickener of the Dead**, and He is Able to do all things.

And if We sent a wind and they beheld it yellow, they verily would still continue in their disbelief. For verily Thou canst not make the dead to hear, nor canst thou make the deaf to hear the call when they have turned to flee. Nor canst Thou guide the blind out of their error. Thou canst make none to hear save those who believe in Our Revelations so that they surrender. Allah is He Who shaped you out of weakness, then appointed after weakness strength, then, after strength, appointed weakness and grey hair. He createth what He will. He is the Knower, the Mighty.

And on the day when the HOUR riseth the guilty will vow that they did tarry but an HOUR - thus were they ever deceived. But those to whom knowledge and faith are given will say: The truth is, ye have tarried, by Allah's decree, until the Day of Resurrection. This is the Day of Resurrection, but ye used not to know. In THAT DAY their excuses will not profit those who did injustice, nor will they be allowed to make amends. Verily We have coined for humankind in THIS QUR'AN all kinds of similitudes; and indeed if thou camest unto them with a miracle, those who disbelieve would verily exclaim: "Ye are but tricksters!" Thus doth Allah seal the hearts of those who know not.

So have patience! Allah's promise is **the very truth**, and let not those who have no certainty make thee impatient.

O Prophet! Keep thy duty to Allah and obey not the disbelievers and the hypocrites. Lo! Allah is Knower, the All-Wise. And follow that **which is inspired in Thee** from thy Lord. Lo! Allah is Aware of what ye do. And put thy trust in Allah, for Allah is sufficient as Trustee. Allah hath not assigned unto any man two hearts within his body, nor hath He made your wives whom ye declare (to be your mothers) your mothers, nor hath He made those whom ye claim (to be your sons) your sons. This is but a saying of your mouths. But Allah saith the truth and He showeth the way.

Proclaim their real parentage. That will be more equitable in the sight of Allah. And if ye know not their fathers, then they are your brethren in the faith, and your clients. And there is no transgression for you in the mistakes that ye make unintentionally, but what your hearts purpose (that will be a sin for you). Allah is ever Forgiving, Merciful.

The Prophet is closer to the believers than their selves, and **his wives are their mothers** (the Mother of the Belivers). And the owners of kinship are closer one to another in the ordinance of Allah than other believers and the fugitives (who fled from Mecca), except that **ye should do kindness to your friends**. This is written in the Book.

And when We exacted a **Covenant** from the prophets, and from Thee and from Noah and Abraham and *MOSES* and *JESUS* son of Miriam. We took from them **a solemn Covenant**; That He may ask the loyal of their loyalty. And He hath prepared a painful doom for the unfaithful.

O ye who believe! Remember Allah's favour unto you when there came against you hosts, and We sent against them a great wind and hosts ye could not see. And Allah is ever Seer of what ye do. When they came upon you from above you and from below you, and when eyes grew wild and hearts reached to the throats, and ye were imagining vain thoughts concerning Allah. There were the believers sorely tried, and shaken with a mighty shock. And when the hypocrites, and **those in whose hearts is a disease**, were saying: "Allah and His messenger promised us naught but delusion." And when a party of them said: "O folk of Yathrib! There is no standing for you, therefore turn back." And certain of them sought permission of the Prophet, saying: "Our homes lie open (to the enemy)." And they lay not open. They but wished to flee. If the enemy had entered from all sides and they had been exhorted to treachery, they would have committed it, and would have hesitated thereupon but little. And verily they had already sworn unto Allah that they would not turn their backs to the foe. An oath to Allah must be answered for.

Say: "Flight will not avail you if ye flee from death or killing, and then ye dwell in comfort but a little while." Say: "Who is he who can preserve you from Allah if He intendeth harm for you, or intendeth mercy for you." They will not find that they have any friend or helper other than Allah. Allah already knoweth those of you who hinder, and those who say unto their brethren: "Come ye hither unto us!" and they come not to the stress of battle save a little, being sparing of their help to you. But when the fear cometh, then Thou seest them regarding Thee with rolling eyes like one who fainteth unto death. Then, when the fear departeth, they scald you with sharp tongues in their greed for wealth from the spoil. Such have not believed. Therefore Allah maketh their deeds fruitless. And that is easy for Allah.

They hold that the clans have not retired; and if the clans should advance, they would fain be in the desert with the wandering Arabs, asking for the news of you; and if they were among you, they would not give battle, save a little. **Verily in the messenger of Allah ye have a good example** for him who looketh unto Allah and the Last Day, and remembereth Allah much. And when the true believers saw the clans, they said: "This is that which Allah and His messenger promised us. Allah and His messenger are true." It did but confirm them in their faith and resignation.

Of the believers are those who are **true to that which they covenanted** with Allah. Some of them have paid their vow by death, and some of them still are waiting; and they have not altered in the least; that Allah may reward the true men for their truth, and punish the hypocrites if He will, or relent toward them if He will. Lo! Allah is Forgiving, Merciful. And Allah repulsed the disbelievers in their wrath; they gained no good. Allah averted their attack from the believers. Allah is ever Strong, Mighty.

And He brought those of the People of the Scripture who supported them down from their strongholds, and cast panic into their hearts. Some ye slew, and ye made captive some. And He caused you to inherit their land and their houses and their wealth, and land ye have not trodden. Allah is ever Able to do all things.

O Prophet! Say unto thy wives: "If ye desire the world's life and its adornment, come! I will content you and will release you with a fair release. But if ye desire Allah and His messenger and the abode of the Hereafter, then Lo! Allah hath prepared for the good among you an immense reward."

O ye wives of the Prophet! Whosoever of you committeth manifest that which is forbidden, the punishment for her will be doubled, and that is easy for Allah. And whosoever of you is submissive unto Allah and His messenger and doeth right, We shall give her her reward twice over, and We have prepared for her a rich provision.

O ye wives of the Prophet! Ye are not like any other women. If ye keep your duty to Allah, then be not soft of speech, lest he in whose heart is a disease aspire to you, but utter customary speech. And stay in your houses. Bedizen not yourselves with the bedizenment of the **Time of Ignorance**. Be regular in prayer, and pay the poor-due (*zakat*), and obey Allah and His messenger. Allah's wish is but to remove uncleanness far from you, O Folk of the Household, and cleanse you with a thorough cleansing. And bear in mind that which is recited in your houses of the Revelations of Allah and Wisdom. Lo! Allah is Subtile, Aware.

Lo! Men who surrender unto Allah, and women who surrender, and men who believe and women who believe, and men who obey and women who obey, and men who speak the truth and women who speak the truth, and men who persevere in righteousness and women who persevere, and men who are humble and women who are humble, and men who give alms and women who give alms, and men who fast and women who fast, and men who guard their modesty and women who guard their modesty, and men who remember Allah much and women who remember--Allah hath prepared for them forgiveness and a vast reward.

And it becometh not a believing man or a believing woman, when Allah and His messenger have decided an affair, that they should claim any say in their affair; and whoso is rebellious to Allah and His messenger, he verily goeth astray in error manifest. And when thou saidst unto him on whom Allah hath conferred favour and thou hast conferred favour: "Keep thy wife to Thyself, and fear Allah." And Thou didst hide in Thy mind that which Allah was to bring to light, and Thou didst fear mankind whereas Allah hath a better right that Thou shouldst fear Him. So when Zayd had performed that necessary formality of divorce from her, We gave her unto Thee in marriage, so that henceforth there may be no transgression for believers in respect of wives of their adopted sons, when the latter have performed the necessary formality of release from them. The commandment of Allah must be fulfilled.

There is no reproach for the Prophet in that which Allah maketh his due. That was Allah's way with those who passed away of old--and the commandment of Allah is certain destiny--who delivered the messages of Allah and feared Him, and feared none save Allah. Allah keepeth good account. *MUHAMMAD* is not the father of any man among you, but he is the messenger of Allah and **The Seal of the Prophets**; and Allah is ever Aware of all things.

O ye who believe! Remember Allah with much remembrance. And glorify Him early and late. He it is Who blesseth you, and His angels (bless you), that He may bring you forth from darkness unto light; and He is ever Merciful to the believers. Their salutation on the day when they shall meet Him will be: "Salem!" And He hath prepared for them a goodly recompense.

O Prophet! Lo! We have sent Thee as a witness and a bringer of good tidings and a warner. And as a summoner unto Allah by His permission, and as a lamp that giveth light. And announce unto the believers the good tidings that they will have great bounty from Allah. And incline not to the disbelievers and the hypocrites. Disregard their noxious talk, and put thy trust in Allah. Allah is sufficient as Trustee.

O ye who believe! If ye wed believing women and divorce them before ye have touched them, then there is no period that ye should reckon. But content them and release them handsomely.

O Prophet! Lo! We have made lawful unto Thee Thy wives unto whomThou hast paid their dowries, and those whom Thy right hand possesseth of those whom Allah hath given Thee as spoils of war, and the daughters of Thine uncle on the father's side and the daughters of Thine aunts on the father's side, and the daughters of Thine uncle on the mother's side and the daughters of Thine aunts on the mother's side who emigrated with Thee, and a believing woman if she give herself unto the Prophet and the Prophet desire to ask her in marriage--**a privilege for Thee only**, not for the believers--We are Aware of that which We enjoined upon them concerning their wives and those whom their right hands possess--that Thou mayst be free from blame, for Allah is ever Forgiving, Merciful.

Thou canst defer whom Thou wilt of them and receive unto Thee whom Thou wilt, and whomsoever Thou desirest of those whom Thou hast set aside, it is no transgression for Thee to receive her again; that is better; that they may be comforted and not grieve, and may all be pleased with what Thou givest them. Allah knoweth what is in your hearts, and Allah is ever Forgiving, Clement. It is not allowed Thee to take other women henceforth, nor that Thou shouldst change them for other wives even though their beauty pleased thee, save those whom Thy right hand possesseth. And Allah is ever Watcher over all things.

O Ye who believe! Enter not the dwellings of the Prophet for a meal without waiting for the proper time, unless permission be granted you. But if ye are invited, enter, and, when your meal is ended, then disperse. Linger not for conversation. Lo! That would cause annoyance to the Prophet, and he would be shy of asking you to go; but Allah is not shy of the truth. And when ye ask of them (the wives of the Prophet) anything, ask it of them from behind a curtain. That is purer for your hearts and for their hearts. And it is not for you to cause annoyance to the messenger of Allah, nor that ye should ever marry his wives after him. Lo! That in Allah's sight would be an enormity. Whether ye divulge a thing or keep it hidden, Lo! Allah is ever Knower of all things.

It is no transgression for them (Thy wives) to converse freely with their fathers, or their sons, or their brothers, or their brothers' sons, or the sons of their sisters or of their own women, or their slaves. O women! Keep your duty to Allah. Lo! Allah is ever Witness over all things. Lo! Allah and His angels shower blessings on the Prophet. O ye who believe! Ask blessings on him and salute him with a worthy salutation. Lo! those who malign Allah and His messenger, Allah hath cursed them in the world and the Hereafter, and hath prepared for them the doom of the disdained. And those who malign believing men and believing women undeservedly, they bear the guilt of slander and manifest sin.

O Prophet! Tell thy wives and thy daughters and the women of the believers to **draw their cloaks close round them** when they go abroad. That will be better, so that they may be recognised and not annoyed. Allah is ever Forgiving, Merciful. If the hypocrites, and those in whose hearts is a disease, and the alarmists in the city do not cease, We verily shall urge Thee on against them, then they will be your neighbours in it but a little while. Accursed, they will be seized wherever found and slain with a fierce slaughter. That was the way of Allah in the case of those who passed away of old; Thou wilt not find for the way of Allah aught of power to change.

Men ask Thee of the HOUR. Say: "The knowledge of it is with Allah only. What can convey (the knowledge) unto Thee ? It may be that the HOUR is nigh." Lo! Allah hath **cursed** the disbelievers, and hath prepared for them a flaming fire, wherein they will abide for ever. They will find no protecting friend nor helper. On the day when their faces are turned over in the Fire, they say: "Oh, would that we had obeyed Allah and had obeyed His messenger!" And they say: "Our Lord! Lo! We obeyed our princes and great men, and they misled us from THE WAY. Our Lord! Oh, give them double torment and curse them with a mighty curse!"

O ye who believe! Be not as those who slandered *MOSES*, but Allah proved his innocence of that which they alleged, and he was well esteemed in Allah's sight.

O ye who believe! Guard your duty to Allah, and speak words straight to the point. He will adjust your works for you and will forgive you your sins. Whosoever obeyeth Allah and His messenger, he verily hath gained a signal victory.

Lo! We offered the trust unto the heavens and the earth and the hills, but they shrank from bearing it and were afraid of it. And Man assumed it. Lo! He hath proved a tyrant and a fool.

So Allah punisheth hypocritical men and hypocritical women, and idolatrous men and idolatrous women. But Allah pardoneth believing men and believing women, and Allah is ever Forgiving, Merciful.

XI. JUZ'UN SIPARA UNDICI:

53. Bism'illah Ar-Rahman Ar-Rahim! az-Zumar: THE COMPANIES.

The Revelation of the Scripture is from Allah, the Mighty, the Wise!

Lo! We have revealed the Scripture unto Thee with truth; so worship Allah, making religion PURE for Him. Surely PURE religion is for Allah only. And those who choose protecting friends beside Him say: "We worship them only that they may bring us near unto Allah." Lo! Allah will judge between them concerning that wherein they differ. Lo! Allah guideth not him who is a liar, an ingrate. If Allah had willed to choose a Son, He could have chosen what He would of that which He hath created. Be He Glorified! He is Allah, the One, the Absolute.

He hath created the heavens and the earth with truth. He maketh night to succeed day, and He maketh day to succeed night, and He constraineth the sun and the moon to give service, each running on for an appointed term. Is not He the Mighty, the Forgiver?

He created you from ONE BEING, then from that He made its mate; and He hath provided for you of cattle eight kinds. He created you in the wombs of your mothers, creation after creation, in a TRIPLE VEIL of shadows. Such is Allah, your Lord. His is the Sovereignty. There is no God save Him. How then are ye turned away?

If ye are thankless, yet Allah is Independent of you, though He is not pleased with thanklessness for His bondmen; and if ye are thankful He is pleased therewith for you. No laden soul will bear another's load. Then unto your Lord is your return; and He will tell you what ye used to do. Lo! He knoweth what is in the breasts! And when some hurt toucheth man, he crieth unto his Lord, turning unto Him. Then, when He granteth him a boon from Him he forgetteth that for which he cried unto Him before, and setteth up rivals to Allah that he may beguile souls from his way. Say: "Take pleasure in Thy disbelief a while. Lo! Thou art of the owners of the Fire."

Is he who payeth adoration in the watches of the night, prostrate and standing, bewaring of the Hereafter and hoping for the mercy of his Lord, to be accounted equal with a disbeliever? Say: "Are those who know equal with those who know not?" But only those of understanding will pay heed.

Say: "O My bondmen who believe! Observe your duty to your Lord. For those who do good in this world there is good, and Allah's earth is spacious." Verily the steadfast will be paid their wages without stint. Say: "Lo! I am commanded to worship Allah, making religion PURE for Him!" And I am commanded to be the **first of those** who surrender unto Him." Say: "Lo! if I should disobey my Lord, I fear the doom of a tremendous Day." Say: "Allah I worship, making my religion PURE for Him. Then worship what ye will beside Him."

Say: "The losers will be those who lose themselves and their housefolk on the Day of Resurrection. Ah, that will be the manifest loss! They have an awning of fire above them and beneath them a dais of fire." With this doth Allah appal His bondmen. "O My bondmen, therefore fear Me!"
And those who put away false gods lest they should worship them and turn to Allah in repentance, for them there are glad tidings. Therefore give good tidings to My bondmen Who hear advice and follow the best thereof. Such are those whom Allah guideth, and such are men of understanding. Is he on whom the word of doom is fulfilled to be helped, and canst Thou (O *AL-AMIN*) rescue him who is in the Fire? But those who keep their duty to their Lord, for them are lofty halls with lofty halls above them, built, beneath which rivers flow: A promise of Allah. Allah faileth not His promise.

Hast thou not seen how Allah hath sent down water from the sky and hath caused it to penetrate the earth as watersprings, and afterward thereby produceth crops of divers hues; and afterward they wither and thou seest them turn yellow; then He maketh them chaff. Lo! Herein verily is a reminder for men of understanding. Is the one whose bosom Allah hath expanded for Al-Islam, so that they followeth a light from their Lord, as the one who disbelieveth? Then woe unto those whose hearts are hardened against remembrance of Allah. Such are in plain error.

Allah hath revealed the fairest of statements, a Scripture consistent, paired (with reward and punishments), whereat doth creep the flesh of those who fear their Lord, so that their flesh and their hearts soften to Allah's reminder. Such is Allah's guidance, wherewith He guideth whom He will. And him whom Allah sendeth astray, for him there is no guide.

Is he then, who will strike his face against the awful doom upon the Day of Resurrection (equal as he who doeth right)? And it will be said unto the wrong-doers: "Taste what ye used to earn." Those before them denied, and so the DOOM came on them whence they knew not. Thus Allah made them taste humiliation in the life of the world, and verily the doom of the Hereafter will be greater if they did but know.

And verily We have coined for humankind in THIS QUR'AN all kinds of similitudes, that haply they may reflect; A Lecture in Arabic, containing no crookedness, that haply they may ward off contention and strife a rigid prohibition in the Book.

Allah coineth a similitude: "A man in relation to whom are several part-owners, quarrelling, and a man belonging wholly to one man. Are the two equal in similitude?" Praise be to Allah! But most of them know not.

Lo! Thou wilt die, and Lo! They will die; Then Lo! On the Day of Resurrection, before your Lord ye will dispute. And who doth greater wrong than he who telleth a lie against Allah, and denieth the truth when it reacheth him? Will not the home of disbelievers be in hell? And whoso bringeth the truth and believeth therein--Such are the dutiful. They shall have what they will of their Lord's bounty. That is the reward of the good: "That Allah will remit from them the worst of what they did, and will pay them for reward the best they used to do." Will not Allah defend His slave? Yet they would frighten Thee with those beside Him. He whom Allah sendeth astray, for him there is no guide.

And he whom Allah guideth, for him there can be no misleader. Is not Allah Mighty, Able to Requite all? And verily, if thou shouldst ask them: "Who created the heavens and the earth?" They will say: "Allah." Say: "Bethink you then of those ye worship beside Allah, if Allah willed some hurt for me, could they remove from me His hurt; or if He willed some mercy for me, could they restrain His mercy?" Say: "Allah is my all. **He is God! In Him the trusting trust**!" Say: "O My People! Act in your manner. Lo! I too am acting." Thus ye will come to know who it is unto whom cometh a doom that will abase him, and on whom there falleth everlasting doom.

Lo! We have revealed unto Thee the Scripture for humankind with Truth. Then whosoever goeth right it is for his soul, and whosoever strayeth, strayeth only to its hurt. And Thou art not a warder over them. Allah receiveth souls at the time of their death, and that soul which dieth not yet in its sleep. He keepeth that soul for which He hath ordained death and dismisseth the rest till an appointed term. Lo! Herein verily are portents for people who take thought. Or choose they intercessors other than Allah? Say: "What! Even though they have power over nothing and have no intelligence?" Say: "Unto Allah belongeth all intercession. His is the Sovereignty of the heavens and the earth. And afterward unto Him ye will be brought back."

And when Allah alone is mentioned, the hearts of those who believe not in the Hereafter are repelled, and when those beside Him are mentioned, Behold! They are glad. Say: "O Allah! Creator of the heavens and the earth! Knower of the Invisible and the Visible! Thou wilt judge between Thy slaves concerning that wherein they used to differ." And though those who do wrong possess all that is in the earth, and therewith as much again, they verily will seek to ransom themselves therewith on the Day of Resurrection from the awful doom; and there will appear unto them, from their Lord, that wherewith they never reckoned. And the evils that they earned will appear unto them, and that whereat they used to scoff will surround them.

Now when hurt toucheth a man he crieth unto Us, and afterward when We have granted him a boon from Us, he saith: "Only by force of knowledge I obtained it." Nay, but it is a TEST. But most of them know not. Those before them said it, yet all that they had earned availed them not; But the evils that they earned smote them; and such of these as do wrong, the evils that they earn will smite them; they cannot escape.

Know they not that Allah enlargeth providence for whom He will, and straiteneth it for whom He will. Lo! Herein verily are portents for people who believe. Say: "O My slaves who have been prodigal to their own hurt! Despair not of the mercy of Allah, Who forgiveth all sins. Lo! He is the Forgiving, the Merciful!" Turn unto your Lord repentant, and surrender unto Him, before there come unto you the doom, when ye cannot be helped. And follow the better guidance of that which is revealed unto you from your Lord, before the doom cometh on you suddenly when ye know not, lest any soul should say: "Alas, my grief that I was unmindful of Allah, and I was indeed among the scoffers!" Or should say: "If Allah had but guided me I should have been among the dutiful!" Or should say, when it seeth the doom: "Oh, that I had but a second chance that I might be among the righteous!"For them: "Nay! For My revelations came unto Thee, but Thou didst deny them and wast scornful and wast among the disbelievers."

And on the Day of Resurrection Thou seest those who lied concerning Allah with their faces blackened. Is not the home of the scorners in hell? And Allah delivereth those who ward off evil because of their deserts. Evil toucheth them not, nor do they grieve. Allah is Creator of all things, and He is Guardian over all things. His are the KEYS (Rev. 3:7; Is. 22:22; Psalm 89; 2 Sam. 7:1-29) of the heavens and the earth, and they who disbelieve the revelations of Allah--such are they who are the losers.

Say: "Do ye bid me serve other than Allah? O ye fools!" And verily it hath been revealed unto Thee as unto those before Thee: "If thou ascribe a partner to Allah Thy work will fail and Thou indeed wilt be among the losers. Nay! But Allah must Thou serve, and be among the thankful!" And they esteem not Allah as He hath the right to be esteemed, when the whole earth is His handful on the Day of Resurrection, and the heavens are rolled in His right hand. Glorified is He and High Exalted from all that they ascribe as partner.

And the Trumpet is blown (Rev. 11-15), and all who are in the heavens and all who are in the earth swoon away, save him whom Allah willeth. Then **it is blown a second time**, and behold them standing waiting! And the earth shineth with the light of her Lord, and **the Book is set up**, and the prophets and the witnesses are brought, and it is judged between them with truth, and they are not wronged. And each soul is paid in full for what it did. And He is Best Aware of what they do.

And those who disbelieve are driven **unto hell in troops** till, when they reach it and the GATES thereof are opened, and the warders thereof say unto them: "Came there not unto you messengers of your own, reciting unto you the Revelations of your Lord and warning you of the meeting of this your Day?" They say: "Yea, verily!" But the word of doom of disbelievers is fulfilled. It is said unto them: "Enter ye the GATES OF HELL to dwell therein." Thus hapless is the journey's end of the scorners.

And those who keep their duty to their Lord are **driven unto the Garden in troops** till, when they reach it, and the GATES thereof are opened, and the warders thereof say unto them: "Blessings be unto you! Ye are good, so enter ye, to dwell therein." They say: "Praise be to Allah, Who hath fulfilled His promise unto Us and hath made Us inherit **the land**, sojourning in the Garden where we will! So bounteous is the wage of workers. And Thou seest the angels thronging round the Throne, hymning the praises of their Lord. And they are judged aright. And it is said: "Praise be to Allah, the Lord of the Worlds!"

54. Bism'illah Ar-Rahman Ar-Rahim! ash-Shura: THE COUNSEL.

Ha. Mim. A'in. Sin. Qaf.

Thus Allah the Mighty, the Knower inspireth Thee as those before Thee. Unto Him belongeth all that is in the heavens and all that is in the earth, and He is the Sublime, the Tremendous.

Almost might the heavens above be rent asunder while the angels hymn the praise of their Lord and ask forgiveness for those on the earth. Lo! Allah, He is the Forgiver, the Merciful. And as for those who choose protecting friends beside Him, Allah is Warden over them, and Thou art in no wise a Guardian over them.

And thus We have inspired in Thee a Lecture in Arabic, that Thou mayst warn the mother-town and those around it, and mayst warn of a day of assembling whereof there is no doubt. A host will be in the Garden, and a host of them in the Flame.

Had Allah willed, He could have made them one community, but Allah bringeth whom He will into His mercy. And the wrong-doers have no friend nor helper. Or have they chosen protecting friends besides Him? But Allah, He alone is the Protecting Friend. He quickeneth the dead, and He is Able to do all things. And in whatsoever ye differ, the verdict therein belongeth to Allah. Such is my Lord, in Whom I put my trust, and unto Whom I turn--The Creator of the heavens and the earth. He hath made for you pairs of yourselves, and of the cattle also pairs, whereby He multiplieth you. Naught is as His likeness; and He is the Hearer, the Seer.

His are **The Keys** (Rev. 3:7; Is. 22:22; Psalm 89; 2 Sam. 7:1-29) of the heavens and the earth. He enlargeth providence for whom He will and straiteneth (it for whom He will). Lo! He is Knower of all things. He hath ordained for you that religion which He commended unto Noah, and that which We inspire in Thee, and that which We commended unto Abraham and *MOSES* and *JESUS*, saying: "Establish the religion, and be not divided therein." Dreadful for the idolaters is that unto which Thou callest them. Allah chooseth for Himself whom He will, and guideth unto Himself him who turneth toward Him. And they were not divided until after the knowledge came unto them, through rivalry among themselves; and had it not been for a Word that had already gone forth from thy Lord for an appointed term, it surely had been judged between them. And those who were made to inherit the Scripture after them are verily in hopeless doubt concerning it.

Unto this, then, summon (O *AL-AMIN*). And be Thou upright as Thou art commanded, and follow not their lusts, but say: "I believe in whatever Scripture Allah hath sent down, and I am commanded to be just among you. Allah is Our Lord and your Lord. Unto Us our works and unto you your works; no argument between Us and you. Allah will bring us together, and unto Him is the journeying."

And those who argue concerning Allah after He hath been acknowledged, their argument hath no weight with their Lord, and wrath is upon them and theirs will be an awful doom. Allah it is Who hath revealed the Scripture with truth, and the Balance. How canst thou know? It may be that the HOUR is nigh. Those who believe not therein seek to hasten it, while those who believe are fearful of it and know that it is the Truth. Are not they who dispute, in doubt concerning the HOUR, far astray? Allah is gracious unto His slaves. He provideth for whom He will. And He is the Strong, the Mighty.

Whoso desireth the harvest of the Hereafter, We give him increase in its harvest. And whoso desireth the harvest of the world, We give him thereof, and he hath no portion in the Hereafter. Or have they partners who have made lawful for them in religion that which Allah allowed not? And but for a decisive word gone forth already, it would have been judged between them. Lo! for wrong-doers is a painful doom.

Thou seest the wrong-doers fearful of that which they have earned, and it will surely befall them, while those who believe and do good works will be in **flowering meadows of the Gardens**, having what they wish from their Lord. This is the great preferment. This it is which Allah announceth unto His bondmen who believe and do good works. Say: "I ask of you no fee therefore, save lovingkindness among kinsfolk. And whoso scoreth a good deed We add unto its good for him. Lo! Allah is Forgiving, Responsive."

Or say they: "He hath invented a lie concerning Allah?" If Allah willed, He could have sealed Thy heart against them. And Allah will wipe out the lie and will vindicate the truth by His words. Lo! He is Aware of what is hidden in the breasts. And He it is Who accepteth repentance from His bondmen, and pardoneth the evil deeds, and knoweth what ye do, and accepteth those who do good works, and giveth increase unto them of His bounty. And as for disbelievers, theirs will be an awful doom.

And if Allah were to enlarge the provision for His slaves they would surely rebel in the earth, but He sendeth down by measure as He willeth. Lo! He is Informed, a Seer of His bondmen. And He it is Who sendeth down the saving rain after they have despaired, and spreadeth out His mercy. He is the Protecting Friend, the Praiseworthy. And of His portents is the creation of the heaven and the earth, and of whatever beasts He hath dispersed therein. And He is Able to gather them when He will.

Whatever of misfortune striketh you, it is what your right hands have earned. And He forgiveth much. Ye cannot escape in the earth, for beside Allah ye have no protecting friend nor any helper. And of His portents are the ships, like banners on the sea; If He will He calmeth the wind so that they keep still upon its surface--Lo! Herein verily are signs for every steadfast grateful heart--Or He causeth them to perish on account of that which they have earned--And He forgiveth much--And that those who argue concerning Our revelations may know they have no refuge.

Now whatever ye have been given is but a passing comfort for the life of the world, and that which Allah hath is better and more lasting for those who believe and put their trust in their Lord, and those who shun the worst of sins and indecencies and, when they are wroth, forgive, and those who answer the call of their Lord and establish worship, and whose affairs are a matter of counsel, and who spend of what We have bestowed on them, and those who, when great wrong is done to them, defend themselves, the guerdon of an ill-deed is an ill the like thereof. But whosoever pardoneth and amendeth, his wage is the affair of Allah. Lo! He loveth not wrong-doers. And whoso defendeth himself after he hath suffered wrong--for such, there is no way against them. The way of blame is only against those who oppress mankind, and wrongfully rebel in the earth. For such there is a painful doom. And verily whoso is patient and forgiveth-- Lo! That, verily, is of the steadfast heart of things. He whom Allah sendeth astray, for him there is no protecting friend after Him. And Thou wilt see the evil-doers when they see the doom, say: "Is there any way of return?"

And Thou wilt see them exposed, made humble by disgrace, and looking with veiled eyes. And those who believe will say: "Lo! The losers are they who lose themselves and their housefolk on the Day of Resurrection. Lo! are not the wrong-doers in perpetual torment?" And they will have no protecting friends to help them instead of Allah. He whom Allah sendeth astray, for him there is no road.

Answer the call of your Lord before there cometh unto you from Allah a Day which there is no averting. Ye have no refuge on that Day, nor have a ye any power of refusal. But if they are averse, We have not sent Thee as a warder over them. Thine is only to convey the message.

And Lo! When We cause man to taste of mercy from Us he exulteth therefore. And if some evil striketh them because of that which their own hands have sent before, then Lo! Man is an ingrate. Unto Allah belongeth the Sovereignty of the heavens and the earth. He createth what He will. He bestoweth female offspring upon whom He will, and bestoweth male offspring upon whom He will; or He mingleth them, males and females, and He maketh barren whom He will. Lo! He is Knower, Powerful.

And it was not vouchsafed to any mortal that Allah should speak to him unless it be by Revelation or from behind a veil, or that He sendeth a messenger to reveal what He will by His leave. Lo! He is Exalted, Wise.

And thus have We inspired in Thee (O *AL-AMIN*) a Spirit of Our command. Thou knewest not what the Scripture was, nor what the Faith. But We have made it a light whereby We guide whom We will of Our bondmen. And Lo! Thou verily dost guide unto a right path, **The path of Allah**, unto Whom belongeth whatsoever is in the heavens and whatsoever is in the earth. Do not all things reach Allah at last?

55. Bism'illah Ar-Rahman Ar-Rahim! adh-Dhariyat: THE SCATTERERS.

By those that winnow with a winnowing
And those that bear the burden of the rain
And those that glide with ease upon the sea
And those who distribute blessings by command,
Lo! That wherewith ye are threatened is indeed true,
And Lo! The judgment will indeed befall.

By the heaven full of paths, Lo! Ye, forsooth, are of various opinion. He is made to turn away from it who is averse. Accursed be the conjecturers who are careless in an abyss! They ask:

"When is the Day of Judgment?" It is the day when they will be tormented at the Fire: "Taste your torment which ye inflicted. This is what ye sought to hasten."

Lo! Those who keep from evil will dwell amid gardens and watersprings, taking that which their Lord giveth them; For Lo! Aforetime they were doers of good; They used to sleep but little of the night, and ere the dawning of each day would seek forgiveness, and in their wealth the beggar and the outcast had due share.

And in the earth are portents for those whose faith is sure and also in yourselves. Can ye then not see?

And in the heaven is your providence and that which ye are promised; And by the Lord of the heavens and the earth, it is the truth, even as it is true that ye speak.
Hath the story of Abraham's honoured guests reached Thee? When they came in unto him and said: "Salem!" He answered, "Salem!" and thought: "Folk unknown to me." Then he went apart unto his housefolk so that they brought a fatted calf; And he set it before them, saying: "Will ye not eat?" Then he conceived a fear of them. They said: "Fear not!" And gave him tidings of the birth of a wise Son. Then his wife came forward, making moan, and smote her face, and cried: "A barren old woman!" They said: "Even so saith thy Lord. Lo! He is the Wise, the Knower."

Abraham said: "And what is your errand, O ye sent?" They said: "Lo! We are sent unto a guilty folk, that we may send upon them stones of clay, marked by thy Lord for the destruction of the wanton." Then we brought forth such believers as were there. But We found there but one house of those surrendered. And We left behind therein a portent for those who fear a painful doom.

And in *MOSES* (too, there is a portent) when We sent him unto Pharaoh with clear warrant, but he withdrew confiding in his might, and said: "A wizard or a madman." So We seized him and his hosts and flung them in the sea, for he was reprobate. And in A'ad (there is a portent) when we sent the fatal wind[*] against them. It spared naught that it reached, but made it all as dust. And in Thamud (there is a portent) when it was told them: "Take your ease awhile." But they rebelled against their Lord's decree, and so the thunderbolt overtook them even while they gazed; and they were unable to rise up, nor could they help themselves. And the folk of Noah aforetime. Lo! They were licentious folk.

We have built the heaven with might, and We it is Who make the vast extent thereof. And the earth have We laid out, how gracious is the Spreader thereof! And **all things We have created by pairs, that haply ye may reflect.** Therefore flee unto Allah; Lo! I am a plain warner unto you from him. And set not any other god along with Allah; Lo! I am a plain warner unto you from Him.

Even so there came no messenger unto those before them but they said: "A wizard or a madman!" Have they handed down the byword as an heirloom one unto another? Nay, but they are froward folk. So withdraw from them (O *AL-AMIN*), for Thou art in no wise blameworthy, and warn, for warning profiteth believers.

---

[*] Agnia fire-weapon.

I created the jinn and humankind only that they might worship Me. I seek no livelihood from them, nor do I ask that they should feed Me.

Lo! Allah! He it is that giveth livelihood, the Lord of unbreakable might. And Lo! for those who do wrong there is an evil day like unto the evil day which came for their likes of old; so let them not ask Me to hasten on that day. And woe unto those who disbelieve, from that their day which they are promised.

56. Bism'illah Ar-Rahman Ar-Rahim! al-Munafiqun: THE HYPOCRITES.

When the hypocrites come unto Thee, they say: "We bear witness that Thou art indeed Allah's messenger." And Allah knoweth that Thou art indeed His messenger, and Allah beareth witness that the hypocrites indeed are speaking falsely.

They make their faith a pretext so that they may turn souls from the way of Allah. Verily evil is that which they are wont to do, **that is because they believed, then disbelieved**, therefore their hearts are sealed so that they understand not. And when Thou seest them their figures please Thee; and if they speak Thou givest ear unto their speech. They are as though they were blocks of wood in striped cloaks. They deem every shout to be against them. They are the enemy, so beware of them. Allah confound them! How they are perverted!

And when it is said unto them: "Come! The messenger of Allah will ask forgiveness for you!" They avert their faces and thou seest them turning away, disdainful. Whether Thou ask forgiveness for them or ask not forgiveness for them is all one for them; Allah will not forgive them. Lo! Allah guideth not the evil-living folk. They it is who say: "Spend not on behalf of those who dwell with Allah's messenger that they may disperse and go away from you; when Allah's are the treasures of the heavens and the earth; but the hypocrites comprehend not.

They say: "Surely, if we return to THE CITY the mightier will soon drive out the weaker" when might belongeth to Allah and to His messenger and to the believers; but the hypocrites know not.

O ye who believe! Let not your wealth nor your children distract you from remembrance of Allah. Those who do so, they are the losers. And spend of that wherewith We have provided you before death cometh unto one of you and he saith: "My Lord! If only Thou wouldst reprieve me for a little while, then I would give alms and be among the righteous." But Allah reprieveth no soul when its term cometh, and Allah is Informed of what ye do.

57. Bism'illah Ar-Rahman Ar-Rahim! al-Mursalat: THE EMISSARIES.

By the emissary winds,[*] coming one after another,

---

[*]"After this I saw **four angels** standing at the four corners of the earth, **holding back the four winds** of the earth to prevent any wind from blowing on the land or on the sea or on any tree. Then I saw another angel coming up from the east, having **the seal** of the living God. He called out in a loud voice to **the four angels** who had been given power to harm the land and the sea: 'Do not harm the land or the sea or the trees until we put **a seal on the foreheads** of the servants of our God.' Then I heard the number of those who were sealed: 144,000... It said to the sixth angel who had the trumpet, 'Release **the four angels** who are bound at **the great river Euphrates.**' And the

By the raging hurricanes,
By those which cause earth's vegetation to revive;
By those who winnow with a winnowing,
By those who bring down the Reminder,
To excuse or to warn,
Surely that which ye are promised will befall.

So when the stars are put out, and when the sky is riven asunder, and when the mountains are blown away, and when the messengers are brought unto their time appointed--For what day is the time appointed? For the **Day of Decision.** And what will convey unto thee what the **Day of Decision** is!--
Woe unto the repudiators on **that Day**! Destroyed We not the former folk, then caused the latter folk to follow after? Thus deal We ever with the guilty.

Woe unto the repudiators on **that Day**! Did We not create you from an insignificant drop of goo which We laid up in a safe abode for a known term? Thus We arranged. How excellent is Our arranging!

Woe unto the repudiators on **that Day**! Have We not made the earth a receptacle both for the living and the dead, and placed therein high mountains and given you to drink sweet water therein?

Woe unto the repudiators on **that Day**! "Depart unto that which ye used to deny; Depart unto the shadow falling threefold, no relief nor shelter from the flame." Lo! It throweth up sparks like the castles, as it might be camels of bright yellow hue.

Woe unto the repudiators on **that Day**! This is a day wherein they speak not, nor are they suffered to put forth excuses.

Woe unto the repudiators on **that Day**! This is the **Day of Decision**, We have brought you and the men of old together. If now ye have any wit, outwit Me.

Woe unto the repudiators on **that Day**! Lo! Those who kept their duty are amid shade and fountains, and fruits such as they desire. "Eat, drink and welcome, O ye blessed, in return for what ye did!" Thus do We reward the good.

Woe unto the repudiators on **that Day**! Eat and take your ease a little while. Lo! Ye are guilty.

Woe unto the repudiators on **that Day**! When it is said unto them: "Bow down, they bow not down!"

Woe unto the repudiators on **that Day**! In what statement, after this, will they believe?

---

four angels who had been kept ready for this very HOUR and day and month and year were released to kill a third of mankind" (Rev.7:1-4; 9:14-15 NIV).

Woe unto the defrauders: Those who when they take the measure from humankind demand it full, but if they measure unto them or weight for them, they cause them loss. Do such not consider that they will be raised again unto an Awful Day, the day when all humankind stand before the Lord of the Worlds? Nay! But the record of the vile is in Sijjin--Ah! what will convey unto thee what Sijjin is: **A written record**.

Woe unto the repudiators on **that Day**! Those who deny the Day of Judgment which none denieth save each criminal transgressor, who, when Thou readest unto him Our Revelations, saith: "Mere fables of the men of old." Nay! But that which they have earned is rust upon their hearts. Nay, but surely on that day they will be covered from their Lord. Then Lo! They verily will burn in hell,

And it will be said unto them: "This is that which ye used to deny." Nay! But the record of the righteous is in 'Illiyin--Ah, what will convey unto thee what 'Illiyin is: **A written record** attested by those who are brought near unto their Lord.

Lo! The righteous verily are in delight, on couches, gazing, Thou wilt know in their faces the radiance of delight. They are given to drink of A PURE WINE, sealed, **whose seal is musk**--for this **let all those strive who strive for BLISS**--and mixed with water of Tasnim, a spring whence those brought near drink.

Lo! the guilty used to laugh at those who believed, and wink one to another when they passed them; and when they returned to their own folk, they returned jesting; and when they saw them they said: "Lo! these have gone astray." Yet they were not sent as Guardians over them. **This Day** it is those who believe who have the laugh of disbelievers, on high couches, gazing.

Are not the disbelievers paid for what they used to do ?

XII. JUZ'UN SIPARA DODICI:

59. at-Taubah: REPENTANCE.

Freedom from obligation is proclaimed from Allah and His messenger toward those of the idolater-Arabs with whom ye made a treaty. Travel freely in the land four months, and know that ye cannot escape Allah and that Allah will confound the disbelievers. And a proclamation from Allah and His messenger to all men **on the day of the Greater Pilgrimage** (The Great Hajj) that Allah is free from obligation to the idolaters, and so is His messenger. So, if ye repent, it will be better for you; but if ye are averse, then know that ye cannot escape Allah.

Give tidings (O *AL-AMIN*) of a painful doom to those who disbelieve, excepting those of the idolaters with whom ye have a treaty, and who have since abated nothing of your right nor have supported anyone against you. As for these, fulfill their treaty to them till their term. Lo! Allah loveth those who keep their duty.

Then, when the sacred months have passed, slay the idolater-Arabs wherever ye find them, and take them captive, and besiege them, and prepare for them each ambush--but **if they repent** and establish worship and pay the poor-due (*zakat*), **then leave their way free**. Lo! Allah is Forgiving, Merciful.

And if anyone of the idolaters seeketh Thy protection, then protect him so that he may hear the Word of Allah, and afterward convey him to his place of safety. That is because they are a folk who know not. How can there be a treaty with Allah and with His messenger for the idolaters save those with whom ye made a treaty at the **Inviolable Place of Worship**? So long as they are true to you, be true to them. Lo! Allah loveth those who keep their duty.

How (can there be any treaty for the others) when, if they have the upper hand of you, they regard not pact nor honour in respect of you? They satisfy you with their mouths the while their hearts refuse. And most of them are wrongdoers.

They have purchased with the Revelations of Allah a little gain, so they debar souls from His way. Lo! Evil is that which they are wont to do. And they observe toward a believer neither pact nor honour. These are they who are transgressors. But **if they repent** and establish worship and pay the poor-due (*zakat*), then are they your brethren in religion. We detail Our Revelations for a people who have knowledge.

And if they break their pledges after their treaty hath been made with you and assail your religion, then fight the heads of disbelief--Lo! They have no binding oaths-- in order that they may desist. Will ye not fight a folk who **broke their solemn pledges**, and purposed to drive out the messenger and did attack you first? What! Fear ye them? Now Allah hath more right that ye should fear Him, if ye are believers fight them! Allah will chastise them at your hands, and He will lay them low and give you victory over them, and He will heal the breasts of folk who are believers. And He will remove the anger of their hearts. Allah relenteth toward whom He will. Allah is Knower, Wise.

Or deemed ye that ye would be let alone when Allah yet knoweth not those of you who strive, choosing for familiar none save Allah and His messenger and the believers? Allah is Informed of what ye do. It is not for the idolaters to tend Allah's sanctuaries, bearing witness against themselves of disbelief. As for such, their works are vain and in the Fire they will abide. He only shall tend Allah's Sanctuaries who believeth in Allah and the Last Day and observeth proper worship and payeth the poor-due (*zakat*) and feareth none save Allah. For such only is it possible that they can be of the rightly guided.

Count ye the slaking of a pilgrim's thirst and tendance of the **Inviolable Place of Worship** as equal to the worth of him who believeth in Allah and the Last Day, and striveth in the way of Allah? They are not equal in the sight of Allah. Allah guideth not wrongdoing folk. Those who believe, and have left their homes and striven with their wealth and their lives in Allah's way are of much greater worth in Allah's sight. These are they who are triumphant. Their Lord giveth them good tidings of mercy from Him, and acceptance, and Gardens where enduring pleasure will be theirs; There they will abide for ever. Lo! with Allah there is immense reward.

O ye who believe! Choose not your fathers nor your brethren for friends if they **take pleasure** in disbelief rather than faith. Whoso of you taketh them for friends, such are wrong-doers. Say: "If your fathers, and your sons, and your brethren, and your wives, and your tribe, and the wealth ye have acquired, and merchandise for which ye fear that there will no sale, and dwellings ye desire are dearer to you than Allah and His messenger and striving in His way: then wait till Allah bringeth His command to pass." Allah guideth not wrongdoing folk.

Allah hath given you victory on many fields and on the day of Huneyn, when ye exulted in your multitude but it availed you naught, and the earth, vast as it is, was straitened for you; then ye turned back in flight; Then Allah sent His peace of reassurance down upon His messenger and upon the believers, and sent down hosts ye could not see, and punished those who disbelieved. Such is the reward of disbelievers. Then afterward Allah will relent toward whom He will; for Allah is Forgiving, Merciful.

O ye who believe! The idolaters only are unclean. So let them not come near the **Inviolable Place of Worship** after this their year. If ye fear poverty--from the loss of their merchandise--Allah shall preserve you of His bounty if He will. Lo! Allah is Knower, Wise.

Fight against such of those who have been given the Scripture as believe not in Allah nor the Last Day, and forbid not that which Allah hath forbidden by His messenger, and follow not the Religion of Truth, **until they pay the tribute readily**, being brought low. And the Jews say: "Ezra is the Son of Allah," and the Christians say: "The Messiah is the Son of Allah." That is their saying with their mouths. They imitate the saying of those who disbelieved of old. Allah fighteth against them. How perverse are they! They have taken as lords beside Allah their rabbis and their monks and the Messiah son of Miriam, when they were bidden to worship only One God. There is no God save Him. Be He Glorified from all that they ascribe as partner!

Fain would they put out God's light with their mouths: But God hath willed to perfect His light, albeit the infidels abhor it. He it is Who hath sent His messenger with the guidance and the Religion of Truth, that He may cause it to prevail over all religion, however much the idolaters may be averse.

O ye who believe! Lo! many of the clergy (rabbis, mullas, mujtahids, and the monks) devour the wealth of humankind wantonly and debar souls from the way of Allah. They who hoard up gold and silver and spend it not in the way of Allah, unto them give tidings of a painful DOOM. On the day when it will all be heated in the fire of hell, and their foreheads and their flanks and their backs will be branded therewith, it will be said unto them: "Here is that which ye hoarded for yourselves. Now taste of what ye used to hoard."

Lo! The number of the months with Allah is twelve months by Allah's ordinance in the day that He created the heavens and the earth. **Four of them are sacred**: that is the right religion. So wrong not yourselves in them. And wage war on all of the idolaters as they are waging war on all of you. And know that Allah is with those who keep their duty. Postponement (of a sacred month) is only an excess of disbelief whereby those who disbelieve are misled; they allow it one year and forbid it another year, that they may make up the number of the months which Allah hath hallowed, so that they allow that which Allah hath forbidden. The evil of their deeds is made fairseeming unto them. Allah guideth not the disbelieving folk.

O ye who believe! What aileth you that when it is said unto you: "Go forth in the way of Allah," ye are bowed down to the ground with heaviness. Take ye pleasure in the life of the world rather than in the Hereafter? The comfort of the life of the world is but little in the Hereafter. If ye go not forth He will afflict you with a painful doom, and will choose instead of you a folk other than you. Ye cannot harm Him at all. Allah is Able to do all things. If ye help him not, still Allah helped him when those who disbelieve drove him forth, the second of two; when they two were in the cave, when he said unto his comrade: Grieve not. Lo! Allah is with us. Then Allah caused His peace of reassurance to descend upon him and supported him with hosts ye cannot see, and made the word of those who disbelieved the nethermost, while Allah's Word it was that became the uppermost. Allah is Mighty, Wise.

Go forth, light-armed and heavy-armed, and strive with your wealth and your lives in the way of Allah! That is best for you if ye but knew. Had it been a near adventure and an easy journey they had followed Thee, but the distance seemed too far for them. Yet will they swear by Allah saying: "If we had been able we would surely have set out with you." They destroy their souls, and Allah knoweth that they verily are liars.

Allah forgive Thee (O *AL-AMIN*)! Wherefor didst Thou grant them leave ere those who told the truth were manifest to Thee and Thou didst know the liars? Those who believe in Allah and the Last Day ask no leave of Thee lest they should strive with their wealth and their lives. Allah is Aware of those who keep their duty. They alone ask leave of Thee who believe not in Allah and the Last Day, and whose hearts feel doubt, so in their doubt they waver. And if they had wished to go forth they would assuredly have made ready some equipment, but Allah was averse to their being sent forth and held them back and it was said: "Sit ye with the sedentary!" Had they gone forth among you they had added to you naught save trouble and had hurried to and fro among you, seeking to cause sedition among you; and among you there are some who would have listened to them. Allah is Aware of evil- doers. Aforetime they sought to cause sedition and raised difficulties for Thee till the Truth came and the decree of Allah was made manifest, though they were loth. Of them is he who saith: "Grant me leave to stay at home and tempt me not. Surely it is into temptation that they have fallen. Lo! hell verily is all around the disbelievers.

If good befalleth Thee it afflicteth them, and if calamity befalleth Thee, they say: "We took precaution, and they turn away well pleased." Say: "Naught befalleth Us save that which Allah hath decreed for us. He is our Protecting Friend. In Allah let believers put their trust! Say: "Can ye await for us aught save one of two good things (death or victory in Allah's way)? While we await for you that Allah will afflict you with a DOOM from Him or at Our hands. Await then! Lo! We are awaiting with you. Say: "Pay your contribution (*zakat*), willingly or unwillingly, it will not be accepted from you. Lo! Ye were ever froward folk. And naught preventeth that their contributions should be accepted from them save that they have disbelieved in Allah and in His messenger, and they come not to worship save as idlers, and pay not their contribution save reluctantly.

So let not their riches nor their children please Thee. Allah thereby intendeth but to punish them in the life of the world and that their souls shall pass away while they are disbelievers. And they swear by Allah that they are in truth of you, when they are not of you, but they are folk who are afraid. Had they but found a refuge, or caverns, or a place to enter, they surely had resorted thither swift as runaways. And of them is he who defameth Thee in the matter of the alms. If they are given thereof they are content, and if they are not given thereof, Behold! They are enraged. How much more seemly had they been content with that which Allah and His messenger had given them and had said: "Allah sufficeth us. Allah will give us of His bounty, and also His messenger. Unto Allah we are suppliants." The alms (*zakat*) are only for the poor and the needy, and those who collect them, and those whose hearts are to be reconciled, and to free the captives and the debtors, and for the cause of Allah, and for the wayfarer; a duty imposed by Allah. Allah is Knower, Wise.

And of them are those who vex the Prophet and say: "He is only a hearer." Say: "A hearer of good for you, who believeth in Allah and is true to the believers, and a mercy for such of you as believe." Those who vex the messenger of Allah, for them there is a painful doom. They swear by Allah to you to please you, but Allah, with His messenger, hath more right that they should please Him if they are believers. Know they not that whoso opposeth Allah and His messenger, his verily is fire of hell, to abide therein? That is the extreme abasement.

The hypocrites fear lest a SURAH should be revealed concerning them, proclaiming what is in their hearts. Say: "Scoff your fill! Lo! Allah is disclosing what ye fear." And if thou ask them they will say: "We did but talk and jest." Say: "Was it at Allah and His Revelations and His messenger that ye did scoff?" Make no excuse. Ye have disbelieved after your confession of belief. If We forgive a party of you, a party of you We shall punish because they have been guilty.

The hypocrites, both men and women, proceed one from another. They enjoin the wrong, and they forbid the right, and they withhold their hands (from spending for the cause of Allah). They forget Allah, so He hath forgotten them. Lo! the hypocrites, they are the transgressors. Allah promiseth the hypocrites, both men and women, and the disbelievers fire of hell for their abode. It will suffice them. Allah curseth them, and theirs is lasting torment.

Even as those before you who were mightier than you in strength, and more affluent than you in wealth and children. They enjoyed their lot awhile, so ye enjoy your lot awhile even as those before you did enjoy their lot awhile. And ye prate even as they prated. Such are they whose works have perished in the world and the Hereafter. Such are they who are the losers.

Hath not the fame of those before them reached them--the folk of Noah, A'ad, Thamud, the folk of Abraham, the dwellers of Midian and the disasters? Their messengers came unto them with proofs of Allah's Sovereignty. So Allah surely wronged them not, but they did wrong themselves.

And the believers, men and women, are protecting friends one of another; they enjoin the right and forbid the wrong, and they establish worship and they pay the poor-due (*zakat*), and they obey Allah and His messenger. As for these, Allah will have mercy on them. Lo! Allah is Mighty, Wise.

Allah promiseth to the believers, men and women, Gardens underneath which rivers flow, wherein they will abide--blessed dwellings in Gardens of Eden. And--greater far)!--acceptance from Allah. That is the supreme triumph.

O Prophet! Strive against the disbelievers and the hypocrites! Be harsh with them. Their ultimate abode is hell, a hapless journey's end. They swear by Allah that they said nothing wrong, yet they did say the word of disbelief, **and did disbelieve <u>after</u> their Surrender**. And they purposed that which they could not attain, and they sought revenge only that Allah by His messenger should enrich them of His bounty. If they repent it will be better for them; and if they turn away, Allah will afflict them with a painful doom in the world and the Hereafter, and they have no protecting friend nor helper in the earth. And of them is he who made a covenant with Allah saying: "If He give us of His bounty we will give alms (*zakat*) and become of the righteous." Yet when He gave them of His bounty, they hoarded it and turned away, averse; So He hath made the consequence to be hypocrisy in their hearts until the day when they shall meet Him, because they broke their word to Allah that they promised Him, and because they lied. Know they not that Allah knoweth both their secret and the thought that they confide, and that Allah is the Knower of Things Hidden? Those who point at such of the believers as give the alms (*zakat*) willingly and such as can find naught to give but their endeavours, and deride them--Allah (Himself) derideth them. Theirs will be a painful doom.

Ask forgiveness for them (O *AL-AMIN*), or ask not forgiveness for them; though Thou ask forgiveness for them seventy times Allah will not forgive them. That is because they disbelieved in Allah and His messenger, and Allah guideth not wrongdoing folk. Those who were left behind rejoiced at sitting still behind the messenger of Allah, and were averse to striving with their wealth and their lives in Allah's way. And they said: "Go not forth in the heat!" Say: "The fire of hell is more intense of heat!" if they but understood.

Then let them laugh a little: they will weep much, as the reward of what they used to earn. If Allah bring Thee back (from the campaign) unto a party of them and they ask of Thee leave to go out (to fight), then say unto them: "Ye shall never more go out with me nor fight with me against a foe. Ye were content with sitting still the first time. So sit still, with the useless." And never pray for one of them who dieth, nor stand by his grave. Lo! They disbelieved in Allah and His messenger, and they died while they were evil-doers.

Let not their wealth nor their children please Thee! Allah purposeth only to punish them thereby in the world, and that their souls shall pass away while they are disbelievers. And when a SURAH is revealed: "Believe in Allah and strive along with His messenger," the men of wealth among them still ask leave of Thee and say: "Suffer us to be with those who sit (at home)." They are content that they should be with the useless and their hearts are sealed, so that they apprehend not. But the messenger and those who believe with him strive with their wealth and their lives. Such are they for whom are the good things. Such are they who are the successful. Allah hath made ready for them Gardens underneath which rivers flow, wherein they will abide. That is the supreme triumph.

And those among the wandering Arabs who had an excuse came in order that permission might be granted them. And those who lied to Allah and His messenger sat at home. A painful doom will fall on those of them who disbelieve. Not unto the weak nor unto the sick nor unto those who can find naught to spend is any fault (to be imputed though they stay at home) if they are true to Allah and His messenger. Not unto the good is there any road (of blame). Allah is Forgiving, Merciful. Nor unto those whom, when they came to Thee (asking) that Thou shouldst mount them, Thou didst tell: "I cannot find whereon to mount you." They turned back with eyes flowing with tears, for sorrow that they could not find the means to spend. The road (of blame) is only against those who ask for leave of Thee (to stay at home) when they are rich. They are content to be with the useless. Allah hath sealed their hearts so that they know not.

They will make excuse to you when ye return unto them. Say: "Make no excuse, for we shall not believe you. Allah hath told us tidings of you. Allah and His messenger will see your conduct, and then ye will be brought back unto Him Who knoweth the Invisible as well as the Visible, and He will tell you what ye used to do." They will swear by Allah unto you, when ye return unto them, that ye may let them be. Let them be, for Lo! They are unclean, and their abode is hell as the reward for what they used to earn. They swear unto you, that ye may accept them. Though ye accept them. Allah verily accepteth not wrongdoing folk. The wandering Arabs are more hard in disbelief and hypocrisy, and more likely to be ignorant of the limits which Allah hath revealed unto His messenger. And Allah is Knower, Wise.

And of the wandering Arabs there is he who taketh that which he expendeth (for the cause of Allah) as a loss, and awaiteth (evil) turns of fortune for you (that he may be rid of it). The evil turn of fortune will be theirs. Allah is Hearer, Knower.

And of the wandering Arabs there is he who believeth in Allah and the Last Day, and taketh that which he expendeth and also the prayers of the messenger as acceptable offerings in the sight of Allah. Lo! Verily it is an acceptable offering for them. Allah will bring them into His mercy. Lo! Allah is Forgiving, Merciful.

And the first to lead the way, of the Muhajirin and the Ansar, and those who followed them in goodness--Allah is well pleased with them and they are well pleased with Him, and He hath made ready for them Gardens underneath which rivers flow, wherein they will abide for ever. That is the supreme triumph.

And among those around you of the wandering Arabs there are hypocrites, and among the townspeople of THE CITY (there are some who) persist in hypocrisy whom Thou (O *AL-AMIN*) knowest not. We, We know them, and We shall chastise them twice; then they will be relegated to a painful doom. And (there are) others who have acknowledged their faults. They mixed a righteous action with another that was bad. It may be that Allah will relent toward them. Lo! Allah is Forgiving, Merciful.

Take alms of their wealth, wherewith thou mayst PURIFY them and mayst **make them grow**, and pray for them. Lo! Thy prayer is an assuagement for them. Allah is Hearer, Knower. Know they not that Allah is He Who accepteth repentance from His bondmen and taketh the alms, and that Allah is He Who is the Relenting, the Merciful. And say unto them: "Act! Allah will behold your actions, and so will His messenger and the believers, and ye will be brought back to the Knower of the Invisible and the Visible, and He will tell you what ye used to do. And there are others who await Allah's decree, whether He will punish them or will forgive them. Allah is Knower, Wise. And as for those who chose a place of worship out of opposition and disbelief, and in order to cause dissent among the believers, and as an outpost for those who warred against Allah and His messenger aforetime, they will surely swear: "We purposed naught save good." Allah beareth witness that they verily are liars.

Never stand to pray there. A place of worship which was found upon duty from the first day is more worthy that thou shouldst stand to pray therein, wherein are men who love to purify themselves. Allah loveth the purifiers. Is he who founded his building upon duty to Allah and His good pleasure better; or he who founded his building on the brink of a crumbling, overhanging precipice so that it toppled with him into the fire of hell? Allah guideth not wrongdoing folk. The building which they built will never cease to be a misgiving in their hearts unless their hearts be torn to pieces. Allah is Knower, Wise.

Lo! Allah hath bought from the believers their lives and their wealth because the Garden will be theirs: they shall fight in the way of Allah and shall slay and be slain. It is a promise which is binding on Him in the Torah and the Gospel and the Qur'an. Who fulfilleth His **covenant** better than Allah? Rejoice then in **your bargain that ye have made**, for that is the supreme triumph. Triumphant are those who turn repentant, those who serve, those who praise, those who fast, those who bow down, those who fall prostrate, those who enjoin the right and who forbid the wrong and those who keep the limits of Allah--And give glad tidings to believers!

It is not for the Prophet, and those who believe, to pray for the forgiveness of idolaters even though they may be near of kin to them after it hath become clear that they are people of hell-fire.

The prayer of Abraham for the forgiveness of his father was only because of a promise he had promised him, but when it had become clear unto him that he his father was an enemy to Allah he disowned him. Lo! Abraham was soft of heart, long-suffering. It was never Allah's part that He should send a folk astray after He had guided them until He had made clear unto them what they should avoid. Lo! Allah is Aware of all things. Lo! Allah! Unto Him belongeth the Sovereignty of the heavens and the earth. He quickeneth and He giveth death. And ye have, instead of Allah, no protecting friend nor helper.

Allah hath turned in mercy to the Prophet, and to the Muhajirin and the Ansar who followed him in the HOUR of hardship. After the hearts of a party of them had almost swerved aside, then turned He unto them in mercy. Lo! He is Full of Pity, Merciful for them.And to the three also who were left behind, when the earth, vast as it is, was straitened for them, and their own souls were straitened for them till they bethought them that there is no refuge from Allah save toward Him. Then turned He unto them in mercy that they too might turn repentant unto Him. Lo! Allah! He is the Relenting, the Merciful.

O ye who believe! Be careful of your duty to Allah, and be with the truthful. It is not for the townsfolk of THE CITY and for those around them of the wandering Arabs so stay behind the messenger of Allah and prefer their lives to his life. That is because neither thirst nor toil nor hunger afflicteth them in the way of Allah, nor step they any step that angereth the disbelievers, nor gain they from the enemy a gain, but a good deed is recorded for them therefore. Lo! Allah loseth not the wages of the good. Nor spend they any spending, small or great, nor do they cross a valley, but it is recorded for them, that Allah may repay them the best of what they used to do. And the believers should not all go out to fight. Of every troop of them, a party only should go forth, that they who are left behind may gain sound knowledge in religion, and that they may warn their folk when they return to them, so that they may beware.

O ye who believe! Fight those of the disbelievers who are near to you, and let them find harshness in you, and know that Allah is with those who keep their duty unto Him. And whenever a SURAH is revealed there are some of them who say: "Which one of you hath thus increased in faith?" As for those who believe, it hath increased them in faith and they rejoice! But as for those in whose hearts is disease, it only addeth wickedness to their wickedness, and they die while they are disbelievers.

See they not that they are tested once or twice in every year? Still they turn not in repentance, neither pay they heed. And whenever a SURAH is revealed, they look one at another (as who should say): "Doth anybody see you?" Then they turn away. Allah turneth away their hearts because they are a folk who understand not. There hath come unto you a messenger--of yourselves--unto whom aught that ye are overburdened is grievous, full of concern for you, for the believers full of pity, merciful. Now, if they turn away say: "Allah sufficeth me. There is no God save Him. In Him have I put my trust, and **He is Lord of the Tremendous Throne**."

60. Bism'illah Ar-Rahman Ar-Rahim! an-Nazi'at: THOSE WHO PULL OUT.

By those who drag forth to destruction,
By the meteors rushing,
By the lone stars floating,
By the angels hastening,
And those who govern the event,
On the day when the first trump resoundeth.
And the second followeth it,
On that day hearts beat painfully
While eyes are downcast

Now they are saying: "Shall we really be restored to our first state even after we are crumbled bones?" They say: "Then that would be a vain proceeding." Surely it will need but one shout, and Lo! They will be awakened!"

Hath there come unto Thee the history of *MOSES*? How his Lord called him in the Holy Vale of Tuwa, saying: "Go Thou unto Pharaoh--Lo! He hath rebelled--And say: 'Hast Thou will to grow? Then I will guide Thee to thy Lord and thou shalt fear (Him).'"And he showed him the tremendous token. But he denied and disobeyed, then turned he away in haste, then gathered he and summoned and proclaimed: "I (Pharaoh) am your Lord the Highest!" So Allah seized him (and made him) an example for the after and for the former. Lo! Herein is indeed a lesson for him who feareth.

Are ye the harder to create, or is the heaven that He built? He raised the height thereof and ordered it; and He made dark the night thereof, and He brought forth the morn thereof. And after that He spread the earth, and produced therefrom the water thereof and the pasture thereof, and He made fast the hills, a provision for you and for your cattle.

But when the great disaster cometh, the day when man will call to mind his whole endeavour, and hell will stand forth visible to him who seeth, then, as for him who rebelled and chose the life of the world, Lo! Hell will be his home. But as for him who feared to stand before his Lord and restrained his soul from lust, Lo! The Garden will be his home.

They ask Thee of the HOUR: "When will it come to port?"
Why? What hast Thou to tell thereof? Unto thy Lord belongeth (knowledge of) the term thereof. Thou art but a warner unto him who feareth it. On the day when they behold it, it will be as if they had but tarried for an evening or the morn thereof.

61. Bism'illah Ar-Rahman Ar-Rahim! as-Sajdah: THE ADORATION.

Alif. Lam. Mim

The Revelation of the Scripture whereof there is no doubt is from the Lord of the Worlds. Or say they: "He hath invented it?" Nay, but it is the Truth from thy Lord, that Thou mayst warn a folk to whom no warner came before thee, that haply they may walk aright. **Allah it is Who created the heavens and the earth, and that which is between them, in <u>six Days</u>. Then He mounted the Throne.** Ye have not, beside Him, a protecting friend or mediator. Will ye not then remember? He directeth the ordinance from the heaven unto the earth; then it ascendeth unto **Him in a Day, whereof the measure is a thousand years**[*] of that ye reckon.

Such is the Knower of the Invisible and the Visible, the Mighty, the Merciful, Who made all things good which He created, and He began the creation of man from clay; then He made his seed from a drop of goo; then He fashioned him and breathed into him of His Spirit; and appointed for you hearing and sight and hearts. Small thanks give ye!

And they say: "When we are lost in the earth, how can we then be re-created?" Nay but they are disbelievers in the meeting with their Lord.

---

[*]"But, beloved, be not ignorant of this one thing, that <u>one day</u> *is* with the Lord as **a thousand years**, and **a thousand years as one day**" (2 Pet. 3:8 KJV). This represents 6 "days" of a thousand years each for a total of 6000 years cycle of Adam from Septmeber 21st, 4000 BC until September 21st, 2001 AD ten days after the 9-11 when the identity of the living Davidic King in exile (**exilarch**--*exiled monarch of King David*: Heb. Resh Galutha; Ar. Ras Al-Jalut) was made known (see also Dr. Leland Jensen's *CHILD OF THE EAST*; *EZEKIEL'S TEMPLE IN MONTANA* by Neal Chase, and David Davidson, *The Great Pyramid: Its Divine Message*, for more.)

Say: "The angel of death, who hath charge concerning you, will gather you, and afterward unto your Lord ye will be returned."

Couldst Thou but see when the guilty hang their heads before their Lord, saying: "Our Lord! We have now seen and heard, so send us back; we will do right, now we are sure."

And if We had so willed, We could have given every soul its guidance, but the word from Me concerning evildoers took effect: "That I will fill hell with the jinn and humankind together." So taste the evil of your deeds. **Forasmuch as ye forgot** the meeting of this your Day, Lo! **We forget you.** Taste the doom of immortality because of what ye used to do.

Only those believe in Our Revelations who, when they are reminded of them, fall down prostrate and hymn the praise of their Lord, and they are not scornful, who forsake their beds to cry unto their Lord in fear and hope, and spend of that We have bestowed on them. No soul knoweth what is kept hid for them of joy, as a reward for what they used to do. Is he who is a believer like unto him who is an evil-liver? They are not alike.

But as for those who believe and do good works, for them are the Gardens of Retreat--a welcome reward for what they used to do. And as for those who do evil, their retreat is the Fire. Whenever they desire to issue forth from thence, they are brought back thither. Unto them it is said: "Taste the torment of the Fire which ye used to deny." And verily We make them taste the lower punishment before the greater, that haply they may return.

And who doth greater wrong than he who is reminded of the Revelations of his Lord, then turneth from them. Lo! We shall requite the guilty.

We verily gave *MOSES* the Scripture; so be not ye in doubt of his receiving it; and We appointed it a guidance for the Children of Israel. And when they became steadfast and believed firmly in Our Revelations, We appointed from among them leaders who guided by Our command. Lo! Thy Lord will judge between them on the Day of Resurrection concerning that wherein they used to differ.Is it not a guidance for them to observe how many generations We destroyed before them, amid whose dwelling places they do walk? Lo! Therein verily are portents! Will they not then heed?

Have they not seen how We lead the water to the barren land and therewith bring forth crops whereof their cattle eat, and they themselves? Will they not then see?

And they say: "**When cometh this Victory** of yours if ye are truthful?" Say unto them: "On the **Day of the Victory** the faith of those who disbelieve will not avail them, neither will they be reprieved."

So withdraw from them, and await. Lo! They also are awaiting.

131

62. Bism'illah Ar-Rahman Ar-Rahim! al-Anfal: THE SPOILS OF WAR.

They ask Thee of the spoils of war. Say: "The spoils of war belong to Allah and the messenger, so keep your duty to Allah, and adjust the matter of your difference, and obey Allah and His messenger, if ye are true believers."

They only are the true believers whose hearts feel fear when Allah is mentioned, and when His Revelations are recited unto them they increase their faith, and who trust in their Lord; who establish worship and spend of that We have bestowed on them. Those are they who are in truth believers. For them are grades of honour with their Lord, and pardon, and a bountiful provision. Even as thy Lord caused Thee to go forth from Thy home with the Truth, and Lo! A party of the believers were averse to it. Disputing with Thee of the Truth after it had been made manifest, as if they were being driven to death visible.

And when Allah promised you one of the two bands (of the enemy) that it should be yours, and ye longed that other than the armed one might be yours. And Allah willed that He should cause the Truth to triumph by His words, and cut the root of the disbelievers; that He might cause the Truth to triumph and bring vanity to naught, however much the guilty might oppose; When ye sought help of your Lord and He answered you saying: **"I will help you with a thousand of the angels, rank on rank."** Allah appointed it only as good tidings, and that your hearts thereby might be at rest. **Victory cometh only by the help of Allah**. Lo! Allah is Mighty, Wise.

When He made the slumber fall upon you as a reassurance from him and sent down water from the sky upon you, that thereby He might purify you, and remove from you the fear of Satan, and make strong your hearts and firm your feet thereby. When thy Lord inspired the angels, saying: "I am with you. So make those who believe stand firm. I will throw fear into the hearts of those who disbelieve. Then smite the necks and smite of them each finger." That is because they opposed Allah and His messenger. Whoso opposeth Allah and His messenger, for him Lo! Allah is severe in punishment. That is the award, so taste it, and know that for disbelievers is the torment of the Fire.

O ye who believe! When ye meet those who disbelieve in battle, turn not your backs to them. Whoso on that day turneth his back to them, unless manoeuvring for battle or intent to join a company, he truly hath incurred wrath from Allah, and his habitation will be hell, a hapless journey's end. Ye slew them not, but Allah slew them. And Thou threwest not when Thou didst throw, but Allah threw, that He might test the believers by a fair test from Him. Lo! Allah is Hearer, Knower. That is the case; and know that Allah it is Who maketh weak the plan of disbelievers. If ye sought a judgment, now hath the judgment come unto you. And if ye cease (from persecuting the believers) it will be better for you, but if ye return (to the attack) We also shall return. And your host will avail you naught, however numerous it be, and know that Allah is with the believers.

O ye who believe! Obey Allah and His messenger, and turn not away from him when ye hear him speak. Be not as those who say, we hear, and they hear not. Lo! the worst of beasts in Allah's sight are the deaf, the dumb, who have no sense. Had Allah known of any good in them

He would have made them hear, but had He made them hear they would have turned away, averse.

O ye who believe! Obey Allah, and the messenger when He calleth you to that which quickeneth you, and know that Allah cometh in between the man and his own heart, and that He it is unto Whom ye will be gathered. And **guard yourselves against a chastisement** which cannot fall **exclusively** on those of you who are wrong-doers, and know that Allah is severe in punishment. And remember, when ye were few and reckoned feeble in the land, and were in fear lest men should extirpate you, how He gave you refuge, and strengthened you with His help, and made provision of good things for you, that haply ye might be thankful.

O ye who believe! Betray not Allah and His messenger, nor knowingly betray your trusts. And know that your possessions and your children are a test, and that with Allah is immense reward.

O ye who believe! If ye keep your duty to Allah, He will give you discrimination and will rid you of your evil thoughts and deeds, and will forgive you. Allah is of Infinite Bounty. And when those who disbelieve plot against Thee to wound Thee fatally, or to kill Thee or to drive Thee forth; **They plot, but Allah also plotteth; and Allah is the best of plotters.**

And when Our Revelations are recited unto them they say: "We have heard. If we wish we can speak the like of this. Lo! this is naught but fables of the men of old." And when they said: "O Allah! If this be indeed the truth from Thee, then rain down stones on us or bring on us some painful doom!" But Allah would not punish them while thou wast with them, nor will He punish them while they seek forgiveness. What have they that Allah should not punish them, when they debar souls from the **Inviolable Place of Worship**, though they are not its fitting guardians. Its fitting guardians are those only who keep their duty to Allah. But most of them know not.

And their worship at the HOLY HOUSE is naught but whistling and hand-clapping. Therefore (it is said unto them): "Taste of the doom because ye disbelieve." Lo! those who disbelieve spend their wealth in order that they may debar souls from the way of Allah. They will spend it, then it will become an anguish for them, then they will be conquered. And those who disbelieve will be gathered unto hell, that Allah may separate the wicked from the good, The wicked will He place piece upon piece, and heap them all together, and consign them unto hell. Such verily are the losers.

Tell those who disbelieve that if they cease (from persecution of believers) that which is past will be forgiven them; but if they return (thereto) then the example of the men of old hath already gone (before them, for a warning). And fight them **until persecution is no more**, and religion is all for Allah. But if they cease, then lo! Allah is Seer of what they do. And if they turn away, then know that Allah is your Befriender - a Transcendent Patron, a Transcendent Helper!

And know that whatever ye take as spoils of war, Lo! A fifth thereof is for Allah, and for the messenger and for the kinsman who hath need and orphans and the needy and the wayfarer, if ye believe in Allah and that which We revealed unto Our slave on the **Day of Discrimination**, the **Day when the two armies met**. And Allah is Able to do all things.

133

When ye were on the near bank (of the valley) and they were on the yonder bank, and the caravan was below you (on the coast plain). And had ye trysted to meet one another ye surely would have failed to keep the tryst, but (it happened, as it did, without the forethought of either of you) that Allah might conclude a thing that must be done; that he who perished on that day might perish by THIS RIGHTEOUS BOOK and he who survived might survive by THIS RIGHTEOUS BOOK. Lo! Allah in truth is Hearer, Knower.

When Allah showed them unto Thee in Thy dream as few in number, and if He had shown them to Thee as many, ye would have faltered and would have quarrelled over the affair. But Allah saved you. Lo! He knoweth what is in the breasts. And when He made you, when ye met them, see them with your eyes as few, and lessened you in their eyes, it was that Allah might conclude a thing that must be done. Unto Allah all things are brought back.

O ye who believe! When ye meet an army, hold firm and think of Allah much, that ye may be successful. And obey Allah and His messenger, and dispute not one with another lest ye falter and your strength depart from you; but be steadfast! Lo! Allah is with the steadfast. Be not as those who came forth from their dwellings boastfully and to be seen of men, and debar souls from the way of Allah, while Allah is surrounding all they do.

And when Satan made their deeds seem fair to them and said: "No-one of humankind can conquer you this day, for I am your protector." But when the armies came in sight of one another, he took flight, saying: "Lo! I am guiltless of you. Lo! I see that which ye see not. Lo! I fear Allah. And Allah is severe in punishment." When the hypocrites and those in whose hearts is a disease said: "Their religion hath deluded these." Whoso putteth his trust in Allah will find that Lo! Allah is Mighty, Wise.

If thou couldst see how the angels receive those who disbelieve, smiting faces and their backs and saying: "Taste the punishment of burning!" This is for that which your own hands have sent before, and know that Allah is not a tyrant to His slaves. Their way is as the way of Pharaoh's folk and those before them; they disbelieved the Revelations of Allah, and Allah took them in their sins. Lo! Allah is Strong, severe in punishment. That is because Allah never changeth the grace He hath bestowed on any people until they first change that which is in their hearts, and that is because Allah is Hearer, Knower. Their way is as the way of Pharaoh's folk and those before them; they denied the Revelations of their Lord, so We destroyed them in their sins. And We drowned the folk of Pharaoh. All were evil-doers. Lo! the worst of beasts in Allah's sight are the ungrateful who will not believe.

Those of them with whom Thou madest a treaty, and then at every opportunity they break their treaty, and they keep not duty. If Thou comest on them in the war, deal with them so as to strike fear in those who are behind them, that haply they may remember. And if thou fearest treachery from any folk, then throw back to them (their treaty) fairly. Lo! Allah loveth not the treacherous. And let not those who disbelieve suppose that they can outstrip Allah's Purpose. Lo! They cannot escape.

Make ready for them all Thou canst of (armed) force and of horses tethered, that thereby ye may dismay the enemy of Allah and your enemy, and others beside them whom ye know not. Allah knoweth them. Whatsoever ye spend in the way of Allah it will be repaid to you in full, and ye will not be wronged. And if they incline to peace, incline Thou also to it, and trust in Allah. Lo! He, even He, is the Hearer, the Knower. And if they would deceive Thee, then lo! Allah is Sufficient for Thee. He it is Who supporteth Thee with His help and with the believers who hath attuned their hearts. If thou hadst spent all that is in the earth Thou couldst not have attuned their hearts, but Allah hath attuned them. Lo! He is Mighty, Wise.

O Prophet! Allah is Sufficient for Thee and those who follow Thee of the believers.

O Prophet! Exhort the believers to fight. If there be of you twenty steadfast they shall overcome two hundred, and if there be of you a hundred (steadfast) they shall overcome a thousand of those who disbelieve, because they are a folk without intelligence. Now hath Allah lightened your burden, for He knoweth that there is weakness in you. So if there be of you a steadfast hundred they shall overcome two hundred, and if there be of you a thousand (steadfast) they shall overcome two thousand by permission of Allah. Allah is with the steadfast. It is not for any prophet to have captives until he hath made slaughter in the land. Ye desire the lure of this world and Allah desireth the Hereafter, and Allah is Mighty, Wise.

Had it not been for an ordinance of Allah which had gone before, an awful doom had come upon you on account of what ye took. Now enjoy what ye have won, as lawful and good, and keep your duty to Allah. Lo! Allah is Forgiving, Merciful.

O Prophet! Say unto those captives who are in your hands: "If Allah knoweth any good in your hearts He will give you better than that which hath been taken from you, and will forgive you. Lo! Allah is Forgiving, Merciful." And if they would betray Thee, they betrayed Allah before, and He gave Thee power over them. Allah is Knower, Wise.

Lo! those who believed and left their homes and strove with their wealth and their lives for the cause of Allah, and those who took them in and helped them: these are protecting friends one of another. And those who believed but did not leave their homes, ye have no duty to protect them till they leave their homes; but if they seek help from you in the matter of religion then it is your duty to help them except against a folk between whom and you there is a treaty. Allah is Seer of what ye do.

And those who disbelieve are protectors one of another--If ye do not so, there will be confusion in the land, and great corruption. Those who believed and left their homes and strove for the cause of Allah, and those who took them in and helped them--these are the believers in truth. For them is pardon, and bountiful provision. And those who afterwards believed and left their homes and strove along with you, they are of you; and those who are akin are nearer one to another in the ordinance of Allah. Lo! Allah is Knower of all things.

63. Bism'illah Ar-Rahman Ar-Rahim! al-Fath: THE VICTORY

-- The Treaty of Hudaybiyyah 628 AD--

"Bism'illah Ar-Rahman Ar-Rahim! In your Name, O God!
This is the treaty of peace between MUHAMMAD Ibn Abdullah and Suhayl ibn Amr.
They have agreed to allow their arms to rest for ten years.
During this time each party shall be secure, and neither shall injure the other; no secret damage
shall be inflicted, but honesty and honour shall prevail between them.
Whoever in Arabia wishes to enter into a Treaty or Covenant with MUHAMMAD can do so, and
whoever wishes to enter into a treaty or covenant with the Quraysh can do so.
And if a Qurayshite comes without the permission of his guardian to MUHAMMAD, he shall be
delivered up to the Quraysh; but if, on the other hand, one of MUHAMMAD's people comes to
the Quraysh, he shall not be delivered up to MUHAMMAD.
This year, MUHAMMAD, with his companions, must withdraw from Mecca,
but next year, he may come to Mecca and remain for three days,
yet without their weapons except those of a traveler,
the swords remaining in their sheaths."

--The Haramization of Yathrib as The City (Medina) September 16th, 628 AD--
(After the Expedition to Khaybar)

"Bism'illah Ar-Rahman Ar-Rahim! In the Name of God. the Compassionate, the Merciful! This
is a document from MUHAMMAD the Prophet of God (concerning the relations) between the
believers and Muslims of the Quraysh and Yathrib, and those who followed them and joined
them and labored with them. They are one community (umma) tot he exclusion of all men..."

"The center of Yathrib is sacred for the people of this document."

" Yathrib shall be a sanctuary for the people of this document."
"A stranger under protection shall be as his host doing no harm and committing no crime. A
woman shall only be given protection with the consent of her family."
whenever among the people of this document there occurs any dispute or controversy likely to
cause trouble, it should be referred to God and to MUHAMMAD, the Messenger of God. God is
the most scrupulous and trues (guarantor) of what is in this document.
(Articles 39-42)

--The Victory Surah Revealed on April 21st, 628 AD--

Lo! We have given Thee a signal Victory, that Allah may forgive Thee of Thy sin that which is
past and that which is to come, and may perfect His favour unto Thee, and may guide Thee on a
right path, and that Allah may help Thee with strong help--He it is Who sent down peace of
reassurance into the hearts of the believers that they might add faith unto their faith. Allah's are
the hosts of the heavens and the earth, and Allah is ever Knower, Wise--that He may bring the
believing men and the believing women into Gardens underneath which rivers flow, wherein

they will abide, and may remit from them their evil deeds--that, in the sight of Allah, is the supreme triumph--and may punish the hypocritical men and the hypocritical women, and the idolatrous men and the idolatrous women, who think an evil thought concerning Allah. For them is the evil turn of fortune, and Allah is wroth against them and hath cursed them, and hath made ready for them hell, a hapless journey's end. Allah's are the hosts of the heavens and the earth, and Allah is ever Mighty, Wise.

Lo! We have sent Thee as a witness and a bearer of good tidings and a warner, that ye may believe in Allah and His messenger, and may honour Him, and may revere Him, and may glorify Him at early dawn and at the close of day.

Lo! Those who swear allegiance unto Thee, swear allegiance only unto Allah. The Hand of Allah is above their hands. So whosoever breaketh his oath, breaketh it only to his soul's hurt; while whosoever keepeth his **covenant** with Allah, on him will He bestow immense reward. Those of the wandering Arabs who were left behind will tell thee: "Our possessions and our households occupied us, so ask forgiveness for us!" They speak with their tongues that which is not in their hearts. Say: "Who can avail you aught against Allah, if He intend you hurt or intend you profit? Nay, but Allah is ever Aware of what ye do. Nay, but ye deemed that the messenger and the believers would never return to their own folk, and that was made fairseeming in your hearts, and ye did think an evil thought, and ye were worthless folk. And so for him who believeth not in Allah and His messenger--Lo! We have prepared a flame for disbelievers." And Allah's is the Sovereignty of the heavens and the earth. He forgiveth whom He will, and punisheth whom He will. And Allah is ever Forgiving, Merciful.

Those who were left behind will say, when ye set forth to capture booty: "Let us go with you." They fain would change the verdict of Allah. Say: "Ye shall not go with us." Thus hath Allah said beforehand. Then they will say: "Ye are envious of us." Nay, but they understand not, save a little. Say unto those of the wandering Arabs who were left behind: "Ye will be called against a folk of mighty prowess, to fight them until they surrender; and if ye obey, Allah will give you a fair reward; but if ye turn away as ye did turn away before, He will punish you with a painful doom." There is no blame for the blind, nor is there blame for the lame, nor is there blame for the sick (that they go not forth to war). And whoso obeyeth Allah and His messenger, He will make him enter Gardens underneath which rivers flow; and whoso turneth back, him will He punish with a painful doom.

Allah was well pleased with the believers when they swore allegiance unto Thee beneath the tree, and He knew what was in their hearts, and He sent down peace of reassurance on them, and hath rewarded them with a near victory; and much booty that they will capture. Allah is ever Mighty, Wise.

Allah promiseth you much booty that ye will capture, and hath given you this in advance, and hath withheld men's hands from you, that it may be a token for the believers, and that He may guide you on a right path. And other gain, which ye have not been able to achieve, Allah will compass it, Allah is Able to do all things. And if those who disbelieve join battle with you they will take to flight, and afterward they will find no protecting friend nor helper. It is the law of Allah which hath taken course aforetime. Thou wilt not find for the law of Allah aught of power to change. And He it is Who hath withheld men's hands from you, and hath withheld your hands from them, in the **Valley of Mecca**, after He had made you **victors** over them. Allah is Seer of what ye do.

These it was who disbelieved and debarred you from the **Inviolable Place of Worship**, and debarred the offering from reaching its goal. And if it had not been for believing men and believing women, whom ye know not--lest ye should tread them under foot and thus incur guilt for them unknowingly; that Allah might bring into His mercy whom He will--If ye had been clearly separated We verily had punished those of them who disbelieved with painful punishment. When those who disbelieve had set up in their hearts zealotry, the zealotry of the **Age of Ignorance**, then Allah sent down His peace of reassurance upon His messenger and upon the believers and imposed on them the word of self-restraint, for they were worthy of it and meet for it. And Allah is Aware of all things.

Allah hath fulfilled the vision for His messenger in very truth. Ye shall indeed enter the **Inviolable Place of Worship**, if Allah will, secure, (having your hair) shaven and cut, not fearing. But He knoweth that which ye know not, and hath given you a near victory beforehand. He it is Who hath sent His messenger with the guidance and the religion of truth, that He may cause it to prevail over all religion. And Allah sufficeth as a Witness.

MUHAMMAD is the messenger of Allah. And those with him are hard against the disbelievers and merciful among themselves. Thou seest them bowing and falling prostrate, seeking bounty from Allah and Acceptance. The **mark of them is on their foreheads** from the traces of prostration. Such is their likeness in the Torah and their likeness in the Gospel (Rev. 13:16-17; 16:2; 19:20)--like as sown corn that sendeth forth its shoot and strengtheneth it and riseth firm upon its stalk, delighting the sowers--that He may enrage the disbelievers with them. Allah hath promised, unto such of them as believe and do good works, forgiveness and immense reward.

CHINVAT-SIRAT: Bism'illah Ar-Rahman Ar-Rahim!

When Allah's succour (an-Nasr) and the triumph cometh
And thou seest mankind Entering the religion of Allah in Troops,
Then hymn the praises of thy Lord, and seek forgiveness of Him.
Lo! He is ever ready to show mercy.

-Thania

138

JINN!

JINN!

---MAGIC, ENCHANTMENT, SPELL, & CHARMS OF THE UNSEEN---
---THE HEAT OF FASTING & THE JINN---
Manzil-i-Ruzah va Siyam va Sujud
Jalál

Bism'illah Ar-Rahman Ar-Rahim!

RECITE *(aq-Qaara): In the name of thy Lord Who createth,*
Createth man from a clot (al-'Alaq).
RECITE: *And thy Lord is the Most Bounteous,*
Who teacheth by the **PEN**,
Teacheth man that which he knew not.

XIII. JUZ'UN SIPARA TREDICI:

64. Bism'illah Ar-Rahman Ar-Rahim! al-Hashr: THE EXILE.

All that is in the heavens and all that is in the earth **GLORIFIETH ALLAH,** and He is the Mighty, the Wise.[*]

He it is Who hath caused those of the People of the Scripture who disbelieved to go forth from their homes unto the first exile. Ye deemed not that they would go forth, while they deemed that their strongholds would protect them from Allah. But Allah reached them from a place whereof they recked not, and cast terror in their hearts so that **they ruined their houses** with their own **hands** and **the hands** of the believers. So learn a lesson, O ye who have eyes! And if Allah had not decreed migration for them, He verily would have punished them in the world, and theirs in the Hereafter is the punishment of the Fire. That is because they were opposed to Allah and His messenger; and whoso is opposed to Allah, for them verily Allah is stern in reprisal.

Whatsoever palm-trees ye cut down or left standing on their roots, it was by Allah's leave, in order that He might confound the evil-livers. And that which Allah gave as spoil unto His messenger from them, ye urged not any horse or riding-camel for the sake thereof, but Allah giveth His messenger lordship over whom He will. Allah is Able to do all things.

That which Allah giveth as spoil unto His messenger from the people of the townships, it is for Allah and His messenger and for the near of kin and the orphans and the needy and the wayfarer, that it become not a commodity between the rich among you. And whatsoever the messenger giveth you, take it. And whatsoever he forbiddeth, abstain from it. And keep your duty to Allah. Lo! Allah is stern in reprisal.

And it is for the poor fugitives who have been driven out from their homes and their belongings, who seek bounty from Allah and help Allah and His messenger. They are the loyal. Those who entered the city and the faith before them love those who flee unto them for refuge, and find in their breasts no need for that which hath been given them, but prefer the fugitives above themselves though poverty become their lot. And whoso is **saved from his own avarice**--such are they who are successful. And those who came in after them say: "Our Lord! Forgive us and our brethren who were before us in the faith, and place not in our hearts any rancour toward those who believe. Our Lord! Thou art Full of Pity, Merciful!"

Hast Thou not observed those who are hypocrites, how they tell their brethren who disbelieve among the People of the Scripture: "If ye are driven out, we surely will go out with you, and we will never obey anyone against you, and if ye are attacked we verily will help you." And Allah beareth witness that they verily are liars. Becuase indeed if they are driven out they go not out with them, and indeed if they are attacked they help them not, and indeed if they had helped them they would have turned and fled, and then they would not have been victorious.

---

[*]**Al-Musabbihat** refer to the collective name of the seven surahs that begin with Allah's *glorification* 'Subhana,' 'Sabbaha,' and 'Yusabbihu:' *al-Hadid*; *al-Hashr*; *as-Saff*; *al-Jumua*; *at-Taghabun*; *al-Isra*; and *al-Ala*.

Ye are more awful as a fear in their bosoms than Allah. That is because they are a folk who understand not. They will not fight against you in a body save in fortified villages or from behind walls. **Their adversity among themselves is very great.**[*] Ye think of them as a whole whereas their hearts are divers. That is because they are a folk who have no sense. On the likeness of those who suffered a short time before them, they taste the ill-effects of their own conduct, and theirs is painful punishment. And the hypocrites are on the likeness of the devil when he telleth man to disbelieve, then, when he disbelieveth saith: "Lo! I am quit of Thee. Lo! I fear Allah, the Lord of the Worlds." And the consequence for both will be that they are in the Fire, therein abiding. Such is the reward of evil-doers.

O ye who believe! Observe your duty to Allah. And let every soul look to that which it sendeth on before for the morrow. And observe your duty to Allah. Lo! Allah is Informed of what ye do. **And be not ye as those who forgot Allah, therefore He caused them to forget their souls.** Such are the evil-doers. Not equal are the owners of the Fire and the owners of the Garden. The owners of the Garden, they are the victorious.

If We had caused THIS QUR'AN to descend upon a mountain, Thou verily hadst seen it humbled, rent asunder by the fear of Allah. Such similitudes coin We for mankind that haply they may reflect.

He is Allah, than Whom there is no other God, the Knower of the Invisible and the Visible. He is the Beneficent, Merciful.

He is Allah, than Whom there is no other God, the Sovereign Lord, the Holy One, Peace, the Keeper of Faith, the Guardian, the Majestic, the Compeller, the Superb. Glorified be Allah from all that they ascribe as partner unto Him. He is Allah, the Creator, the Shaper out of naught, the Fashioner. His are the most Beautiful Names. All that is in the heavens and the earth glorifieth Him, and He is the Mighty, the Wise.

---

[*] Intrapsychic conflict.

65. Bism'illah Ar-Rahman Ar-Rahim! (al-Falaq): THE DAYBREAK.

Say: I seek refuge in the Lord of the Daybreak[*]
From the evil of that which He created;
From the evil of the darkness when it is intense,
And from the evil of malignant witchcraft (of those who blow on knots),
And from the evil of the envier when he envieth.

66. Bism'illah Ar-Rahman Ar-Rahim! an-Nas: HUMANITY.

Say: I seek refuge in the Lord of mankind,
The King of mankind,
The God of mankind,
From the evil of the sneaking whisperer,
Who whispereth in the hearts of mankind,
Of the jinn and of mankind.

67. Bism'illah Ar-Rahman Ar-Rahim! al-Jinn: THE JINN.

Say: "It is revealed unto me that a company of the Jinn gave ear, and they said: "Lo! we have heard THIS MARVELOUS QUR'AN, which guideth unto righteousness, so we believe in it and we ascribe no partner unto our Lord. And we believe that He--exalted be **the Glory of our**

---

[*]Lord of the Dawn Prayer: "O my God and my Master! I am Thy servant and the son of Thy servant. I have risen from my couch at this dawntide when the Daystar of Thy oneness hath shone forth from the Dayspring of Thy will, and hath shed its radiance upon the whole world, according to what had been ordained in the Books of Thy Decree. Praise be unto Thee, O my God, that we have wakened to the splendors of the light of Thy knowledge. **Send down, then, upon us, O my Lord, what will enable us to <u>dispense with anyone but Thee</u>, and will rid us of all attachment to aught except Thyself.** Write down, moreover, for me, and for such as are dear to me, and for my kindred, man and woman alike, the good of this world and the world to come. Keep us safe, then, through Thine unfailing protection, O Thou the Beloved of the entire creation and the Desire of the whole universe, from them whom Thou hast made to be the manifestations of the Evil Whisperer, who whisper in men's breasts. Potent art Thou to do Thy pleasure. Thou art, verily, the Almighty, the Help in Peril, the Self-Subsisting. Bless Thou, O Lord my God, Him Whom Thou hast set over Thy most excellent Titles, and through Whom Thou hast divided between the godly and the wicked, and graciously aid us to do what Thou lovest and desirest. Bless Thou, moreover, O my God, them Who are Thy Words and Thy Letters, and them who have set their faces towards Thee, and turned unto Thy face, and hearkened to Thy Call. Thou art, truly, the Lord and King of all men, and art potent over all things."

142

Lord!--hath taken neither wife nor son, and that the foolish one among us used to speak concerning Allah an atrocious lie."

And Lo! We had supposed that humankind and jinn would not speak a lie concerning Allah--and indeed individuals of humankind used to invoke the protection of individuals of the jinn, so that they increased them in revolt against Allah; and indeed they supposed, even as ye suppose, that Allah would not raise anyone--and (the Jinn who had listened to the Qur'an said): "We had sought the heaven but had found it filled with strong warders and meteors. And we used to sit on places therein to listen. But he who listeneth now findeth a flame in wait for him; and we know not whether harm is boded unto all who are in the earth, or whether their Lord intendeth guidance for them. And among us there are righteous folk and among us there are far from that. **We are sects having different rules.** And we know that we cannot escape from Allah in the earth, nor can we escape by flight. And when we heard the guidance, we believed therein, and whoso believeth in his Lord, he feareth neither loss nor oppression. And there are among us some who have surrendered and there are among us some who are unjust. And whoso hath surrendered to Allah, such have taken the right path purposefully. And as for those who are unjust, they are firewood for hell."

If they tread the right path, We shall give them to drink of water in abundance that We may test them thereby, and whoso turneth away from the remembrance of his Lord; He will thrust him into ever-growing torment. And the places of worship are only for Allah, so pray not unto anyone along with Allah.

And when the slave of Allah stood up in prayer to Him, they crowded on him, almost stifling. Say: "I pray unto Allah only, and ascribe unto Him no partner." Say: "Lo! I control not hurt nor benefit for you." Say: "Lo! None can protect me from Allah, nor can I find any refuge beside Him. Mine is but conveyance of the Truth from Allah, and His messages; and whoso disobeyeth Allah and His messenger, Lo! His is fire of hell, wherein such dwell for ever. Till when they shall behold that which they are promised; but then they will know for certain who is weaker in allies and less in multitude."

Say: "I know not whether that which ye are promised is nigh, or if my Lord hath set a distant term for it. He is the Knower of the Unseen, and He revealeth unto none His secret, save unto every messenger whom He hath chosen, and then He maketh a guard to go before him and a guard behind him[*] that He may know that they have indeed conveyed the messages of their Lord. He surroundeth all their doings, and He keepeth count of all things.

68. Bism'illah Ar-Rahman Ar-Rahim! al-Hijr: THE ROCK.

Alif. Lam. Ra.

These are verses of the Scripture and a plain Reading.

It may be that those who disbelieve wish ardently that they were Muslims. Let them eat and enjoy life, and let (false) hope beguile them. They will come to know!

---

[*]Forerunners and Establishers.

And We destroyed no township but there was a known decree for it. No nation can outstrip its term nor can they lag behind. And they say: "O Thou unto whom THE REMINDER is revealed, Lo! Thou art indeed a madman! Why bringest Thou not angels unto us, if Thou art of the truthful?" We send not down the angels save with the Fact, and in that case the disbelievers would not be tolerated. Lo! We, even We, reveal the Reminder, and Lo! **We verily are its Guardian**.

We verily sent messengers before Thee among the factions of the Old Ones. And never came there unto them a messenger but they did mock him. Thus do We make it traverse the hearts of the guilty: they believe not therein, though the example of the men of old hath gone before. And even if We opened unto them a GATE of Heaven and they kept mounting through it, they would say: "Our sight is wrong--nay, but we are folk bewitched."

And verily in the heaven we have set mansions of the stars, and We have beautified it for beholders. And We have guarded it from every outcast devil, save him who stealeth the hearing, and them doth a clear flame pursue. And the earth have We spread out, and placed therein firm hills, and caused each seemly thing to grow therein. And we have given unto you livelihoods therein, and unto those for whom ye provide not. And there is not a thing but with Us are the stores thereof. And we send it not down save in appointed measure. And We send the winds fertilizing, and cause water to descend from the sky, and give it you to drink. It is not ye who are the holders of the store thereof.

Lo! And it is We, even We, Who quicken and give death, and We are the Inheritor. And verily We know the eager among you and verily We know the laggards. Lo! Thy Lord will gather them together. Lo! He is Wise, Aware.

Verily We created man of potter's clay of black mud altered, and the jinn did We create aforetime of essential fire. And when thy Lord said unto the angels: "Lo! I am creating a mortal out of potter's clay of black mud altered, so, when I have made him and have breathed into him of My Spirit, do ye fall down, prostrating yourselves unto him. So the angels fell prostrate, all of them together save Iblis. He refused to be among the prostrate.

He said: "O Iblis! What aileth Thee that thou art not among the prostrate?"

He said: "I am not one to prostrate myself unto a mortal whom Thou hast created out of potter's clay of black mud altered!"

He said: "Then go thou forth from hence, for Lo! Thou art outcast. And Lo! The curse shall be upon Thee till the Day of Judgment."

He said: "My Lord! Reprieve me till the day when they are raised."

He said: "Then Lo! Thou art of those reprieved till the Day of appointed time."

144

He said: "My Lord! Because Thou hast sent me astray, I verily shall adorn the path of error for them in the earth, and shall mislead them every one, save such of them as are Thy perfectly devoted slaves."

He said: "This is a right course incumbent upon Me: Lo! as for My slaves, Thou hast no power over any of them save such of the froward as follow Thee, and Lo! For all such, hell will be the promised place. It hath SEVEN GATES, and each GATE hath an appointed portion. Lo! Those who ward off evil are among gardens and watersprings: 'Enter them in peace, secure.' And We remove whatever rancour may be in their breasts. As brethren, face to face, they rest on couches raised. Toil cometh not unto them there, nor will they be expelled from thence."

Announce, (O *AL-AMIN*) unto My slaves that verily I am the Forgiving, the Merciful, and that My doom is the dolorous doom. And tell them of Abraham's guests, how when they came in unto him, and said: "Salem!" He said: "Lo! We are afraid of you." They said: "Be not afraid! Lo! We bring thee good tidings of a boy possessing wisdom."

He said: "Bring ye me good tidings (of a son) when old age hath overtaken me? Of what then can ye bring good tidings?"

They said: "We bring Thee good tidings in truth. So be not Thou of the despairing."
He said: "And who despaireth of the mercy of his Lord save those who are astray?" He said: "And afterward what is your business, O ye messengers?"

They said: "We have been sent unto a guilty folk, all save the family of Lot. Them we shall deliver every one, except his wife (*Anna*), of whom We had decreed that she should be of those who stay behind."

And when the messengers came unto the family of Lot, He said: "Lo! Ye are folk unknown to me."

They said: "Nay, but we bring Thee that concerning which they keep disputing, and bring Thee the Truth, and Lo! we are truth-tellers! So travel with thy household in a portion of the night, and follow Thou their backs. Let none of you turn round, but go whither ye are commanded." And We made plain the case to him, that the root of them (who did wrong) was to be cut at early morn.

And the people of the city came, rejoicing at the news of new arrivals. He said: "Lo! They are my guests. Affront me not! And keep your duty to Allah, and shame me not!"

They said: "Have we not forbidden you from entertaining anyone?"

He said: "Here are my daughters, if ye must be doing so."

By Thy life (O *AL-AMIN*) they moved blindly in the frenzy of approaching death. Then the Awful Cry overtook them at the sunrise. And We utterly confounded them, and We rained upon them stones of heated clay. Lo! therein verily are portents for those who read the signs.

And Lo! It is upon a road still uneffaced. Lo! Therein is indeed a portent for believers. And the dwellers in the wood indeed were evil-doers. So we took vengeance on them; and Lo! They both are on a high-road plain to see. And the dwellers in Al-Hijr denied Our messengers. And we gave them Our Revelations, but they were averse to them. And they used to hew out dwellings from the hills, (wherein they dwelt) secure. But the Awful Cry overtook them at the morning *hour*, and that which they were wont to count as gain availed them not.

We created not the heavens and the earth and all that is between them save with truth, and Lo! the HOUR is surely coming. So forgive, with a gracious forgiveness.

Lo! Thy Lord! He is the All-Wise Creator.

We have given Thee **seven** of the oft-repeated (verses) and THIS GREAT QUR'AN. Strain not Thine eyes toward that which We cause some wedded pairs among them to enjoin, and be not grieved on their account, and lower Thy wing (in tenderness) for the believers. And say: Lo! I, even I, am a plain warner,

Such as We send down for those who make division,
Those who break the Qur'an into parts.
Them, by thy Lord, We shall question, every one,
Of what they used to do.

So proclaim that which Thou art commanded, and withdraw from the idolaters. Lo! We defend Thee from the scoffers, who set some other god along with Allah. But they will come to know. Well know We that thy bosom is oppressed by what they say, but hymn the praise of thy Lord, and be of those who make prostration. And serve thy Lord till the Inevitable cometh unto Thee.

XIV. JUZ'UN SIPARA QUATTORZICI:

69. Bism'illah Ar-Rahman Ar-Rahim! al-Furqan: THE BROKEN PIECES.[*]

---

[*]This comes from the Aramaic *farraqo* that means to **"break up"** "to separate." and refers to those who divide their religion, split their own selves, create sects and divisions; separated the people; scattered the gatherings; and who have cut up the Qur'an into broken up little pieces out of order--thus ruining the message, perverting the song, misleading the people, disrupting the tale and the story from God! Thus have they *broken up* (**al-Firkin**) the Revelation of the Holy Koran into parts, mis-assembled them (from longest fragment and part to shortest) out of their correct order--the Order of Imam Ali, and ABANDONED the true "Statute Book." As it is written: "On that Day, the wrongdoer will bite his hands, and say, 'If only I had followed the way [the true of Order of the Holy Koran as compiled by Imam Ali and presented by him in person to Exilarch Bostanai]... If only I had followed the way with the Messenger [the true order of the Koran of Muhammad, PBUH]. Oh, woe to me; I wish I never took so-and-so [who dissembled both the book, their faith, and their own souls] for a friend. He led me away from the Message [true order of the Holy Koran] after it had come to me; for Satan has always been a betrayer [abandoner; forsaker; Ar. *Khadhulu*] of human kind.' And the Messenger will say, 'My Lord, my people have abandoned (*Khadhulu*) this Quran [as given by Muhammad to Ali in the correct order].' Likewise, to every prophet We assign enemies from among the wicked. But your Lord suffices as a Guide and Savior. Those who disbelieve say, 'Why was the Quran not revealed to him at once?' Thus in order to strengthen your heart thereby, and *We Revealed it in Stages*. Whatever argument they come to you with, We provide you with the truth, and a better exposition" (*al-Furqan: The BROKEN PIECES*). Thus have the quibbled over the order of the book and dissembled and broken it

Blessed is He Who hath revealed unto His slave THE CRITERIA, that he may be a warner to the peoples. He unto Whom belongeth the Sovereignty of the heavens and the earth, He hath chosen no son nor hath He any partner in the Sovereignty. He hath created everything and hath meted out for it a measure. Yet they choose beside Him other gods who create naught but are themselves created, and possess not hurt nor profit for themselves, and possess not death nor life, nor power to raise the dead. Those who disbelieve say: "This is naught but a lie that he hath invented, and other folk have helped him with it, so that they have produced a slander and a lie." And they say: "Fables of the men of old which he hath had written down so that they are dictated to him morn and evening."

Say: "He who knoweth the secret of the heavens and the earth hath revealed it. Lo! He ever is Forgiving, Merciful."

And they say: "What aileth this messenger that he eateth food and walketh in the markets? Why is not an angel sent down unto him, to be a warner with him. Or why is not treasure thrown down unto him, or why hath he not a paradise from whence to eat?" And the evil-doers say: "Ye are but following a man bewitched." See how they coin similitudes for thee, so that they are all astray and cannot find a road!

Blessed is He Who, if He will, will assign Thee better than all that--Gardens underneath which rivers flow--and will assign Thee mansions. Nay, but they deny the HOUR, and for those who deny) the HOUR We have prepared a flame. When it seeth them from afar, they hear the crackling and the roar thereof. And when they are flung into a narrow place thereof, chained together, they pray for destruction there. Pray not that day for one destruction, but pray for many destructions!

Say: "Is that better or the Garden of Immortality which is promised unto those who ward off evil?" It will be their reward and journey's end. Therein abiding, they have all that they desire. It is for thy Lord a promise that must be fulfilled. And on the day when He will assemble them and that which they worship instead of Allah and will say: "Was it ye who misled these my slaves or did they themselves wander from the way?"

They will say: "Be Thou Glorified! It was not for us to choose any protecting friends beside Thee; but Thou didst give them and their fathers ease till they forgot the warning and became

---

up into pieces. "The Arabic word FURQAN (Arabic: فرقان) is the criterion or the standard to distinguish between good and bad. The name "The Criterion" refers to the Qur'an itself as the decisive (Key) factor between the Good and the Evil... The Furqan [also] means the Criterion which separates the truth (Haqq) from falsehood (Baatil) and through it Allah made the truth known to mankind. According to Dr. Sobhy as-Salih, this word is also not Arabic but Aramaic, the original language in which Gospel/ Injil was revealed in. From the language the word Furqan describes something which separates a thing into different parts. In the above ayat Allah used the word Faraqna in describing how He separated the water of the sea into two parts so as to allow *MOSES* (Musa) and his followers to cross the dry path. Verily, those who divide [*Farraqo (break up)*] their religion and break up into sects (all kinds of religious sects), you (O Muhammad) have no concern in them in the least. Their affair is only with Allah" *(al-An'am: THE LIVESTOCK).* Similarly Allah uses the word Farraqo to describe the evil act of breaking up the religion into separate sects. So again the word is used in reference to **that which separates something into parts.**"

lost folk." Thus they will give you the lie regarding what ye say, then ye can neither avert the doom nor obtain help. And whoso among you doeth wrong, We shall make him taste great torment.

We never sent before Thee any messengers but Lo! They verily ate food and walked in the markets. **And We have appointed some of you a test for others** ("the greatest test is each other"): "Will ye be steadfast?" And Thy Lord is ever Seer.

And those who look not for a meeting with Us say: "Why are angels not sent down unto us and why do we not see our Lord!" Assuredly they think too highly of themselves and are scornful with great pride. On the day when they behold the angels, on that day there will be no good tidings for the guilty; and they will cry: "A forbidding ban!" And We shall turn unto the work they did and make it scattered motes.

Those who have earned the Garden on that day will be better in their home and happier in their place of noonday rest; a day when the heaven with the clouds will be rent asunder and the angels will be sent down, a grand descent. **The Sovereignty (Government) on that day will be the True Government belonging to the Beneficent One, and** <u>**it will be a hard day for disbelievers.**</u> On the day when the wrong-doer gnaweth his hands, he will say: "Ah, would that I had chosen a way together with the messenger! Alas for me! Ah, would that I had never taken such an one for friend! He verily led me astray from the Reminder after it had reached me. **Satan was ever man's deserter in the *hour* of need.**"

And the messenger saith: "O my Lord! Lo! Mine own folk make THIS QUR'AN of no account."

Even so have We appointed unto every prophet an opponent from among the guilty; but Allah sufficeth for a Guide and Helper.

And those who disbelieve say: "**Why is THIS QUR'AN not revealed unto him all at once?**" It is revealed thus that We may strengthen thy heart therewith; and **We have arranged it in RIGHT ORDER!**

And they bring Thee no similitude but We bring Thee the Truth, and better as argument. Those who will be gathered on their faces unto hell: such are worse in plight and further from the right road.

We verily gave *MOSES* the Scripture and placed with him his brother Aaron as henchman. Then We said: "Go together unto the folk who have denied Our Revelations." Then We destroyed them, a complete destruction. And Noah's folk, when they denied the messengers, We drowned them and made of them a portent for mankind. We have prepared a painful doom for evil-doers. And A'ad and Thamud, and the dwellers in Ar-Rass, and many generations in between. Each We warned by examples, and each We brought to utter ruin. And indeed they have passed by the township whereon was rained the fatal rain. Can it be that they have not seen it? Nay, but they hope for no resurrection.

And when they see Thee they treat Thee only as a jest: "Is this he whom Allah sendeth as a messenger? He would have led us far away from our gods if we had not been staunch to them." They will know, when they behold the doom, who is more astray as to the road. Hast Thou seen him who chooseth for his god his own lust? Wouldst Thou then be guardian over him? Or deemest Thou that most of them hear or understand? They are but as the cattle--Nay, but they are farther astray? Hast Thou not seen how thy Lord hath spread the shade--And if He willed He could have made it still--then We have made the sun its pilot; then We withdraw it unto Us, a gradual withdrawal?

And He it is Who maketh night a covering for you, and sleep repose, and maketh day a resurrection. And He it is Who sendeth the winds, glad tidings heralding His mercy, and We send down purifying water from the sky, that We may give life thereby to a dead land, and We give many beasts and men that We have created to drink thereof. And verily We have repeated it among them that they may remember, but most of humankind begrudge aught save ingratitude.

If We willed, We could raise up a warner in every village.

So obey not the disbelievers, but strive against them herewith with a great endeavour.

And He it is Who hath given independence to the two seas; one palatable, sweet, and the other saltish, bitter; and hath set a bar and a forbidding ban (*barzakh*) between them. And He it is Who hath created man from water, and hath appointed for him kindred by blood and kindred by marriage; for thy Lord is ever Powerful. Yet they worship instead of Allah that which can neither benefit them nor hurt them. The disbeliever was ever a partisan against his Lord.

And We have sent Thee only as a bearer of good tidings and a warner. Say: "I ask of you no reward for this, save that whoso will may choose a way unto his Lord." And trust Thou in the Living One Who dieth not, and hymn His praise. He sufficeth as the Knower of His bondmen's sins, who created the heavens and the earth and all that is between them **in six Days, then He mounted the Throne**.[*] **The Beneficent**!

Ask anyone informed concerning Him!

And when it is said unto them: "Adore the Beneficent!" they say: "And what is the Beneficent? Are we to adore whatever Thou biddest us?" And it increaseth aversion in them.

Blessed be He Who hath placed in the heaven mansions of the stars, and hath placed therein a great lamp and a moon giving light! And He it is Who hath appointed night and day in succession, for him who desireth to remember, or desireth thankfulness.

---

[*]"But, beloved, be not ignorant of this one thing, that **one day** *is* with the Lord as **a thousand years**, and **a thousand years as one day**" (2 Pet. 3:8 KJV; see also 61st *Basmala as-Sajdah*). This represents 6 "days" of a thousand years each for a total of 6000 years cycle of Adam from Septmeber 21st, 4000 BC until September 21st, 2001 AD ten days after the 9-11 when the identity of the living Davidic King in exile (**exilarch**--*exiled monarch of King David*: Heb. Resh Galutha; Ar. Ras Al-Jalut) was made known (see also Dr. Leland Jensen's *CHILD OF THE EAST*; *EZEKIEL'S TEMPLE IN MONTANA* by Neal Chase, and David Davidson, *The Great Pyramid: Its Divine Message*, for more.)

The loyal slaves of the Beneficent are they who walk upon the earth modestly, and when the foolish ones address them answer: "Salem!" And who spend the night before their Lord, prostrate and standing, and who say: "Our Lord! Avert from us the doom of hell!" Lo! The doom thereof is anguish; Lo! It is wretched as abode and station; and those who, when they spend, are neither prodigal nor grudging; and there is ever a firm station between the two; and those who cry not unto any other god along with Allah, nor take the life which Allah hath forbidden save in (course of) justice, nor commit adultery--and whoso doeth this shall pay the penalty. The doom will be doubled for him on the Day of Resurrection, and he will abide therein disdained for ever; save him who repenteth and believeth and doth righteous work; as for such, Allah will change their evil deeds to good deeds. Allah is ever Forgiving, Merciful.

And whosoever repenteth and doeth good, he verily repenteth toward Allah with true repentance --and those who will not witness vanity, but when they pass near senseless play, pass by with dignity. And those who, when they are reminded of the Revelations of their Lord, fall not deaf and blind thereat. And who say: "Our Lord! Vouchsafe us comfort of our wives and of our offspring, and make us patterns for those who ward off evil." They will be awarded the high place forasmuch as they were steadfast, and they will meet therein with welcome and the ward of peace, abiding there for ever. Happy is it as abode and station!

Say: "My Lord would not concern Himself with you but for your prayer. But now ye have denied the Truth, therefore there will be judgment."

70. Bism'illah Ar-Rahman Ar-Rahim! al-Fajr: THE DAYBREAK.

By the Daybreak
And ten nights,
And the Even and the Odd,
And the night when it departeth,
There surely is an oath for thinking man.

Dost thou not consider how Thy Lord dealt with A'ad (whose regions extended from Hyderabad, Hadhramut, Shambhala, Bamiyan, *al-Rub' al Khali* and adjacent lands), with many-columned Iram (*Iram dhat al-'Imad*) who were very tall like lofty pillars (Persian: بت های بامیان the Buddhas of Bamiyan) the like of which was not created in the lands; And with Thamud, who clove the rocks in the valley; And with Pharaoh, firm of might, who all were rebellious in these lands, and multiplied iniquity therein? Therefore thy Lord poured on them the disaster of His punishment. Lo! thy Lord is ever watchful.

As for man, whenever his Lord trieth him by honouring him, and is gracious unto him, he saith: "My Lord honoureth me." But whenever He trieth him by straitening his means of life, he saith: "My Lord despiseth me."

Nay, but ye honour not the orphan and urge not on the feeding of the poor. And ye devour heritages with devouring greed. And love wealth with abounding love.

150

Nay, but when the earth is ground to atoms, grinding, grinding, and thy Lord shall come with angels, rank on rank, and hell is brought near that day; on that day man will remember, but how will the remembrance then avail him?

He will say: "Ah, would that I had sent before me some provision for my life!"

None punisheth as He will punish on that day! None bindeth as He then will bind. But ah! Thou soul at calm! Return unto thy Lord, content in His good pleasure! Enter thou among My bondmen! Enter thou My Garden!

71. Bism'illah Ar-Rahman Ar-Rahim! ash-Shu`ara': THE POETS.

Ta. Sin. Mim.

These are revelations of the Scripture that maketh plain. **It may be that Thou tormentest Thyself** (*O AL-AMIN*) because they believe not. If We will, We can send down on them from the sky a portent so that their necks would remain bowed before it. Never cometh there unto them a fresh reminder from the **Beneficent One**, but they turn away from it. Now they have denied the Truth; but there will come unto them tidings of that whereat they used to scoff. Have they not seen the earth, how much of every fruitful kind We make to grow therein? Lo! Herein is indeed a portent; yet most of them are not believers. And Lo! Thy Lord! He is indeed the Mighty, the Merciful.

And when thy Lord called *MOSES*, saying: "Go unto the wrongdoing folk, the folk of Pharaoh. Will they not ward off evil?"

He said: "My Lord! Lo! I fear that they will deny me, and I shall be embarrassed, and my tongue will not speak plainly, therefore send for Aaron to help me. And they have a crime against me, so I fear that they will kill me."

He said: "Nay, verily. So go ye TWAIN with Our tokens. Lo! We shall be with you, Hearing. And come together unto Pharaoh and say: 'Lo! We bear a message of the Lord of the Worlds: Let the Children of Israel GO with Us.'"

Pharaoh said: "Did we not rear Thee among us as a child? And Thou didst dwell many years of thy life among us, and Thou didst that Thy deed which Thou didst, and Thou wast one of the ingrates."

He said: "I did it then, when I was of those who are astray. Then I fled from you when I feared you, and my Lord vouchsafed me a command and appointed me of those sent by Him. And is this a favor of which you remind me--that you have enslaved the Children of Israel?"

Pharaoh said: "And what is the Lord of the Worlds?

MOSES said: "Lord of the heavens and the earth and all that is between them, if ye had but sure belief."

Pharaoh said unto those around him: "Hear ye not?"

He said: "Your Lord and the Lord of your fathers."

Pharaoh said: "Lo! Your messenger who hath been sent unto you is indeed a madman!"

He said: "Lord of the East and the West and all that is between them, if ye did but understand."

Pharaoh said: "If Thou choosest a god other than me, I assuredly shall place Thee among the prisoners."

He said: "Even though I show Thee something plain?"

Pharaoh said: "Produce it then, if Thou art of the truthful!"

Then he flung down his staff and it became a serpent manifest, and he drew forth his hand and Lo! It was white to the beholders. Pharaoh said unto the chiefs about him: "Lo! This is verily a knowing wizard, who would drive you out of your land by his magic. Now what counsel ye?"

They said: "Put him off, and his brother, and send into the cities summoners who shall bring unto Thee every knowing wizard." So the wizards were gathered together at a set time on a day appointed. And it was said unto the people: "Are ye gathering?"
They said: "Aye, so that we may follow the wizards if they are the winners." And when the wizards came they said unto Pharaoh: "Will there surely be a reward for us if we are the winners?"

He said: "Aye, and ye will then surely be of those brought near (to me)."

MOSES said unto them: "Throw what ye are going to throw!" Then they threw down their cords and their staves and said: "By Pharaoh's might, Lo! We verily are the winners."

Then *MOSES* threw his staff and Lo! "It swallowed that which they did falsely show." And the wizards were flung prostrate, Crying: "We believe in the Lord of the Worlds, the Lord of *MOSES* and Aaron."

Pharaoh said: "Ye put your faith in him before I give you leave. Lo! He doubtless is your chief who taught you magic! But verily ye shall come to know. Verily I will cut off your hands and your feet alternately, and verily I will crucify you every one."

They said: "It is no hurt, for Lo! Unto our Lord we shall return. Lo! We ardently hope that our Lord will forgive us our sins because we are the first of the believers."

And We inspired *MOSES*, saying: "Take away My slaves by night, for ye will be pursued."

Then Pharaoh sent into the cities summoners, who said: "Lo! These indeed are but a little troop, and Lo! They are offenders against us. And Lo! We are a ready host." Thus did We take them away from gardens and watersprings, and treasures and a fair estate. Thus were those things taken from them and We caused the Children of Israel to inherit them.

And they overtook them at sunrise. And when the two hosts saw each other, those with *MOSES* said: "Lo! we are indeed caught."

He said: "Nay, verily! for Lo! My Lord is with me. He will guide me." Then We inspired *MOSES*, saying: "Smite the sea with thy staff." And it parted, and each part was as a mountain vast. Then brought We near the others to that place. And We saved *MOSES* and those with him, every one; and We drowned the others. Lo! Herein is indeed a portent, yet most of them are not believers. And Lo, Thy Lord! He is indeed the Mighty, the Merciful.

Recite unto them the story of Abraham: When he said unto his father and his folk: "What worship ye?"

They said: "We worship idols, and are ever devoted unto them."

He said: "Do they hear you when ye cry? Or do they benefit or harm you?"

They said: "Nay, but we found our fathers acting on this wise."

He said: "See now that which ye worship, ye and your forefathers! Lo! they are an enemy unto me, save the Lord of the Worlds, Who created me, and He doth guide me, and Who feedeth me and watereth me. And when I sicken, then He healeth me, and Who causeth me to die, then giveth me life again, and Who, I ardently hope, will forgive me my sin on the Day of Judgment. My Lord! Vouchsafe me wisdom and unite me to the righteous. And give unto me a good report in later generations. And place me among the inheritors of the Garden of Na'im (Heb. Nahum). And forgive my father. Lo! He is of those who err. And abase me not on the day when they are raised, the day when wealth and sons avail not save him who bringeth unto Allah a whole heart.

And the Garden will be brought nigh for those who ward off evil. And hell will appear plainly to the erring. And it will be said unto them: "Where is all that ye used to worship instead of Allah? Can they help you or help themselves?" Then will they be hurled therein, they and the seducers And the hosts of Iblis, together. And they will say, when they are quarrelling therein: "By Allah, of a truth we were in error manifest when we made you equal with the Lord of the Worlds. It was but the guilty who misled us. Now we have no intercessors nor any loving friend. Oh, that we had another turn on earth, that we might be of the believers!" Lo! herein is indeed a portent, yet most of them are not believers! And lo, thy Lord! He is indeed the Mighty, the Merciful.

Noah's folk denied the messengers of Allah, when their brother Noah said unto them: "Will ye not ward off evil? Lo! I am a faithful messenger unto you, so keep your duty to Allah, and obey me. And I ask of you no wage therefore; my wage is the concern only of the Lord of the Worlds. So keep your duty to Allah, and obey me."

153

They said: "Shall we put faith in Thee, when the lowest of the people follow Thee?"

He said: "And what knowledge have I of what they may have been doing in the past? Lo! Their reckoning is my Lord's concern, if ye but knew; and I am not here to repulse believers. I am only a plain warner."

They said: "If Thou cease not, O Noah, Thou wilt surely be among those stoned (to death)."

He said: "My Lord! Lo! My own folk deny me. Therefore judge Thou between us, a (conclusive) judgment, and save me and those believers who are with me." And We saved him and those with him in the laden ship. Then afterward We drowned the others. Lo! Herein is indeed a portent, yet most of them are not believers. And lo, thy Lord, He is indeed the Mighty, the Merciful.

A'ad denied the messengers of Allah. When their brother *KRISHNA* (*Hud*) *MADHUSUDAN* said unto them: "Will ye not ward off evil?" Lo! I am a faithful messenger unto you, so keep your duty to Allah and obey me. And I ask of you no wage therefore; my wage is the concern only of the Lord of the Worlds. Build ye on every high place a monument for vain delight? And seek ye out strongholds, that haply ye may last for ever? And if ye seize by force, seize ye as tyrants? Rather keep your duty to Allah, and obey me. Keep your duty toward Him Who hath aided you with the good things that ye know, hath aided you with cattle and sons. And gardens and watersprings. Lo! I fear for you the retribution of an awful day."

They said: "It is all one to us whether Thou preachest or art not of those who preach; This is but a fable of the Old Ones, and we shall not be doomed." And they denied him; therefore We destroyed them. Lo! Herein is indeed a portent, yet most of them are not believers. And Lo! Thy Lord, He is indeed the Mighty, the Merciful.

Thamud denied the messengers of Allah when their brother *SIDDHARTHA* (*Salih*) *THE BUDDHA* said unto them: "Will ye not ward off evil? Lo! I am a faithful messenger unto you, so keep your duty to Allah and obey me. And I ask of you no wage therefore; my wage is the concern only of the Lord of the Worlds. Will ye be left secure in that which is here before us, in gardens and watersprings. And tilled fields and heavy-sheathed palm-trees, though ye hew out dwellings in the mountain, being skilful? Therefore keep your duty to Allah and obey me, and obey not the command of the prodigal, who spread corruption in the earth, and reform not."

They said: "Thou art but one of the bewitched; Thou art but a mortal like us. So bring some token if thou art of the truthful."

He said: "Behold this she-camel.* She hath the right to drink at the well, and ye have the right to drink, each on an appointed day. And touch her not with ill lest there come on you the retribution of an awful day." But they hamstrung her, and then were penitent. So the retribution came on

---

*The Avestan "Hustra" literally means "camel" and refers to the Pure Revelation of *ZOROASTER* (*zarathustra*) that immediately preceded the Revelation (vehicle: *Vahana*) of *THE BUDDHA* and immediately followed the Revelation of *KRISHNA*.

them. Lo! Herein is indeed a portent, yet most of them are not believers. And Lo! Thy Lord! He is indeed the Mighty, the Merciful.

The folk of Lot denied the messengers of Allah, when their brother Lot said unto them: "Will ye not ward off evil? Lo! I am a faithful messenger unto you, so keep your duty to Allah and obey me. And I ask of you no wage therefore; my wage is the concern only of the Lord of the Worlds. What! Of all creatures do ye come unto the males, and leave the wives your Lord created for you? Nay, but ye are froward folk."

They said: "If Thou cease not, O Lot, Thou wilt soon be of the outcast."

He said: "I am in truth of those who hate your conduct. My Lord! Save me and my household from what they do." So We saved him and his household, every one, save an old woman among those who stayed behind. Then afterward We destroyed the others. And We rained on them a rain. And dreadful is the rain of those who have been warned. Lo! Herein is indeed a portent, yet most of them are not believers. And Lo! Thy Lord, He is indeed the Mighty, the Merciful.

The **Dwellers in the Wood** (the Persians) denied the messengers of Allah, when *ZOROASTER* (*Shu'ayb*) *SPENTA MANIYUSH* said unto them: "Will ye not ward off evil?" Lo! I am a faithful messenger unto you, so keep your duty to Allah and obey me. And I ask of you no wage for it; my wage is the concern only of the Lord of the Worlds. Give full measure, and be not of those who give less than the due. And weigh with the true balance. Wrong not mankind in their goods, and do not evil, making mischief, in the earth. And keep your duty unto Him Who created you and the generations of the men of old."
They said: "Thou art but one of the bewitched; Thou art but a mortal like us, and Lo! We deem Thee of the liars. Then make fragments of the heaven fall upon us, if Thou art of the truthful."

He said: "My Lord is Best Aware of what ye do." But they denied him, so there came on them the retribution of the **Day of Gloom**. Lo! It was the retribution of an awful day. Lo! Herein is indeed a portent; yet most of them are not believers. And Lo! Thy Lord! He is indeed the Mighty, the Merciful.

And Lo! it is a Revelation of the Lord of the Worlds, which the True Spirit hath brought down upon thy heart, that Thou mayst be of the warners, in plain Arabic speech. And Lo! it is in the Scriptures of the Old Ones. Is it not a token for them that the doctors of the Children of Israel know it? And if We had revealed it unto one of any other nation than the Arabs, and he had read it unto them, they would not have believed in it.

Thus do We make it traverse the hearts of the guilty. **They will not believe in it** till they behold the painful doom, so that it will come upon them suddenly, when they perceive not. Then they will say: "Are we to be reprieved? Would they hasten on Our doom?"

Hast Thou then seen, if We content them for long years, and then cometh that which they were promised, how that wherewith they were contented naught availeth them? And We destroyed no township but it had its warners for reminder, for We never were oppressors.

155

The devils did not bring it down. It is not meet for them, nor is it in their power, Lo! Verily they are banished from the hearing. Therefore invoke not with Allah another god, lest thou be one of the doomed.

And warn Thy tribe of near kindred, and lower Thy wing (in kindness) unto those believers who follow Thee. And if they (Thy kinsfolk) disobey thee, say: "Lo! I am innocent of what they do." And put Thy trust in the Mighty, the Merciful. Who seeth Thee when Thou standest up (to pray) And (seeth) Thine abasement among those who fall prostrate (in adoration). Lo! He, only He, is the Hearer, the Knower.

Shall I inform you upon whom the devils descend? They descend on every sinful, false one. They listen eagerly, but most of them are liars.

As for poets, the erring follow them. Hast thou not seen how they stray in every valley, and how they say that which they do not? Save those who believe and do good works, and remember Allah much, and vindicate themselves after they have been wronged. Those who do wrong will come to know by what a **Great Reversal** they will be overturned!

XV. JUZ'UN SIPARA QUINTICI:

72. Bism'illah Ar-Rahman Ar-Rahim! al-Baqarah I: HARUT AND MARUT.

Alif. Lam. Mim.

This is the Scripture whereof there is no doubt, a guidance unto those who ward off evil, who believe in the Unseen, and establish worship, and spend of that We have bestowed upon them; And who believe in that which is revealed unto Thee and that which was revealed before Thee, and are certain of the Hereafter. These depend on guidance from their Lord. These are the successful.

As for the Disbelievers, Whether Thou warn them or Thou warn them not it is all one for them; they believe not. Allah hath sealed their hearing and their hearts, and on their eyes there is a covering. Theirs will be an awful doom. And of humankind are some who say: "We believe in Allah and the Last Day, when they believe not." They think to beguile Allah and those who believe, and they beguile none save themselves; but they perceive not. **In their hearts is a disease, and Allah increaseth their disease**. A painful doom is theirs because they lie. And when it is said unto them: "Make not mischief in the earth," they say: "We are peacemakers only." Are not they indeed the mischief-makers? But they perceive not.

And when it is said unto them: "Believe as the people believe," they say: "Shall we believe as the foolish believe?" Are not they indeed the foolish? But they know not. And when they fall in with those who believe, they say: "We believe;" but when they go apart to their devils they declare: "Lo! we are with you; verily we did but mock." Allah Himself doth mock them, leaving them to wander blindly on in their contumacy. These are they who purchase error at the price of guidance, so their commerce doth not prosper, neither are they guided. Their likeness is as the likeness of one who kindleth fire, and when it sheddeth its light around him Allah taketh away their light and leaveth them in darkness, where they cannot see, deaf, dumb and blind; and they return not.

Or like a rainstorm from the sky, wherein is darkness, thunder and the flash of lightning. They thrust their fingers in their ears by reason of the thunder-claps, for fear of death, Allah encompasseth the disbelievers. The lightning almost snatcheth away their sight from them. As often as it flasheth forth for them they walk therein, and when it darkeneth against them they stand still. If Allah willed, He could destroy their hearing and their sight. Lo! Allah is able to do all things.

O Humankind! Worship your Lord, Who hath created you and those before you, so that ye may ward off evil. Who hath appointed the earth a resting-place for you, and the sky a canopy; and causeth water to pour down from the sky, thereby producing fruits as food for you. And do not set up rivals to Allah when ye know better. And if ye are in doubt concerning that which We reveal unto Our slave (AL-AMIN), then produce a SURAH of the like thereof, and call your witness beside Allah if ye are truthful. And if ye do it not--and ye can never do it--then guard yourselves against the Fire prepared for disbelievers, whose fuel is of men and stones.

And give glad tidings (O AL-AMIN) unto those who believe and do good works; that theirs are Gardens underneath which rivers flow; as often as they are regaled with food of the fruit thereof, they say: "This is what was given us aforetime;" and it is given to them in resemblance. There for them are PURE companions; there for ever they abide.

Lo! Allah disdaineth not to coin the similitude even of a gnat. Those who believe know that it is the truth from their Lord; but those who disbelieve say: "What doth Allah wish to teach by such a similitude? He misleadeth many thereby, and He guideth many thereby; and He misleadeth thereby only miscreants.

Those who break THE COVENANT OF ALLAH after ratifying it, and sever that which Allah ordered to be joined, and who make mischief in the earth: Those are they who are the losers.

How disbelieve ye in Allah when ye were dead and He gave life to you! Then He will give you death, then life again, and then unto Him ye will return. He it is Who created for you all that is in the earth. Then turned He to the heaven, and fashioned it as **seven heavens**. And He is knower of all things. And when thy Lord said unto the angels: "Lo! I am about to place **A VICEROY** (Khalifah) in the earth--a successive authority[*]--they said: "Wilt thou place therein one who will do harm therein and will shed blood, while we, we hymn Thy praise and sanctify Thee?" He said: "Surely I know that which ye know not!"

---

[*]The Khalifah is the the bloodline (of the Throne) from Adam to Abraham, Isaac, and Jacob, unto Judah and unto David and Solomon: the throne-line of Davidic Kingship (Khalifah: exilarchate--exiled monarchs of King David: Ar. Ras al-Jalut; Heb. Resh Galutha) that comes down to this day. "O David! Lo! We have set Thee as the Government (**Khalifah**) of God in the earth; Therefore judge aright between humankind, and follow not desire that it beguile Thee from the way of Allah. Lo! Those who wander from the way of Allah have an awful doom, forasmuch as they forgot the Day of Reckoning!" (ANUBIS: basmala 106: Sad of Samad).

And He taught *ADAM* all the names, then showed them to the angels, saying: "Inform Me of the names of these, if ye are truthful." They said: "Be glorified! We have no knowledge saving that which Thou hast taught us. Lo! Thou, only Thou, art the Knower, the Wise."

He said: "O *ADAM*! Inform them of their names," and when he had informed them of their names, He said: "Did I not tell you that I know **The Secret** of the heavens and the earth? And I know that which ye disclose and which ye hide." And when We said unto the angels: "Prostrate yourselves before *ADAM*," they fell prostrate, all save Iblis. He demurred through pride, and so became a disbeliever.

And We said: "O *ADAM*! Dwell Thou and Thy wife in the Garden, and eat ye freely thereof where ye will; but come not nigh this tree lest ye become wrong-doers." But Satan caused them to deflect therefrom and expelled them from the happy state in which they were; and We said: "Fall down, one of you a foe unto the other! There shall be for you on earth a habitation and provision for a time."

Then *ADAM* received from his Lord words of revelation, and He relented toward him. Lo! He is the relenting, the Merciful. We said: "Go down, all of you, from hence;" but verily there cometh unto you from Me a guidance; and whoso followeth My guidance, there shall no fear come upon them neither shall they grieve. But they who disbelieve, and deny Our revelations, such are rightful Peoples of the Fire. They will abide therein.

O Children of Israel! Remember My favor wherewith I favored you, and fulfil your (part of the) covenant, **I shall fulfill My Covenant**,* and fear Me. And believe in that which I reveal, confirming that which ye possess already of the Scripture, and be not first to disbelieve therein, and part not with My Revelations for a trifling price, and keep your duty unto Me. Confound not truth with falsehood, nor knowingly conceal the truth. Establish worship, pay the poor-due (*zakat*), and bow your heads with those who bow. Enjoin ye righteousness upon humanity while ye yourselves forget to practise it? And ye are readers of the Scripture! Have ye then no sense? Seek help in patience and prayer; and truly it is hard save for the humble- minded, who know that they will have to meet their Lord, and that unto Him they are returning.

O Children of Israel! Remember My favor wherewith I favored you and how I preferred you to all creatures. And guard yourselves against a day when no soul will in aught avail another, nor will intercession be accepted from it, nor will compensation be received from it, nor will they be helped. And remember when We did deliver you from Pharaoh's folk, who were afflicting you with dreadful torment, slaying your sons and sparing your women: that was a tremendous trial from your Lord. And when We brought you through the sea and rescued you, and drowned the folk of Pharaoh in your sight. And when We did appoint for *MOSES* forty nights (of solitude), and then ye chose the calf, when he had gone from you, and were wrong-doers. Then, even after that, We pardoned you in order that ye might give thanks.

And when We gave unto *MOSES* the Scripture and THE GOLDEN CRITERIA, that ye might be led aright. And when *MOSES* said unto his people: "O my people! Ye have wronged yourselves

---

*See Pslams 89, etc.

158

by your choosing of the calf* so turn in penitence to your Creator, and slay the guilty yourselves. That will be best for you with your Creator and He will relent toward you. Lo! He is the Relenting, the Merciful."

And when ye said: "O *MOSES*! We will not believe in Thee till we see Allah plainly;" and even while ye gazed the lightning seized you. Then We revived you after your extinction, that ye might give thanks. And We caused the white cloud to overshadow you and sent down on you the manna and the quails, (saying): "Eat of the good things wherewith We have provided you"--they wronged Us not, but they did wrong themselves.

And when We said: "Go into this township and eat freely of that which is therein, and enter the GATE *prostrate!* and Say: "Repentance." We will forgive you your sins and will increase reward for the right-doers. But those who did wrong changed the word which had been told them for another saying, and We sent down upon the evil-doers wrath from heaven for their evil-doing.

And when *MOSES* asked for water for his people, We said: "Smite with thy staff the rock." And there gushed out therefrom twelve springs so that each tribe knew their drinking-place. Eat and drink of that which Allah hath provided, and do not act corruptly, making mischief in the earth.

And when ye said: "O *MOSES*! We are weary of one kind of food; so call upon thy Lord for us that He bring forth for us of that which the earth groweth--of its herbs and its cucumbers and its corn and its lentils and its onions." He said: "Would ye exchange that which is higher for that which is lower? Go down to settled country, thus ye shall get that which ye demand." And humiliation and wretchedness were stamped upon them and they were visited with wrath from Allah. That was because they disbelieved in Allah's Revelations and slew the prophets wrongfully. That was for their disobedience and transgression.

Lo! Those who believe and those who are Jews, and Christians, and Sabaeans[†]--whoever believeth in Allah and the Last Day and doeth right--surely their reward is with their Lord, and there shall no fear come upon them neither shall they grieve. And when We made **a covenant** with you and caused the mount to tower above you, (saying): "Hold fast that which We have given you, and remember that which is therein, that ye may ward off evil. Then, even after that, ye turned away, and if it had not been for the grace of Allah and His mercy ye had been among the losers.

And ye know of those of you who broke the Sabbath, how We said unto them: "Be ye apes, despised and hated!" And We made it an example to their own and to succeeding generations, and an admonition to the God-fearing.

---

[*]Exodus 32:20, 27-28 NIV: "And he took the calf the people had made and burned it in the fire; then he ground it to powder, scattered it on the water and made the Israelites drink it... Then he said to them, "This is what the LORD, the God of Israel, says: 'Each man strap a sword to his side. Go back and forth through the camp from one end to the other, each killing his brother and friend and neighbor.'" The Levites did as Moses commanded, and that day about three thousand of the people died."

[†]The "Jews, Sabeans, and Christians" refer to the peoples of the previous Revelations, the Major Independent Prophets that (including *MUHAMMAD*) are SEVEN: The Sabaeans: *ADAM, KRISHNA, ZOROASTER, BUDDHA*; Jewish: *MOSES*; and Christian: *JESUS*.

And when *MOSES* said unto his people: "**Lo! Allah commandeth you that ye sacrifice a cow**," they said: "Dost thou make game of us?" He answered: "Allah forbid that I should be among the foolish!"

They said: "Pray for us unto thy Lord that He make clear to us what she is."

He answered: "Lo! He saith, Verily she is a cow neither with calf nor immature; she is between the two conditions; so do that which ye are commanded."

They said: "Pray for us unto thy Lord that He make clear to us of what color she is."

He answered: "Lo! He saith: Verily she is a yellow cow. Bright is her color, gladdening beholders."

They said: "Pray for us unto Thy Lord that He make clear to us what she is. Lo! Cows are much alike to us; and Lo! if Allah wills, we may be led aright."

He answered: "Lo!" He saith: "Verily she is a cow unyoked; she plougheth not the soil nor watereth the tilth; whole and without mark." They said: "Now Thou bringest the truth." So they sacrificed her, though almost they did not.

And (remember) when ye slew a man and disagreed concerning it and Allah brought forth that which ye were hiding. And We said: "Smite him with some of it." Thus Allah bringeth the dead to life and showeth you His portents so that ye may understand.

Then, even after that, your hearts were hardened and became as rocks, or worse than rocks, for hardness. For indeed there are rocks from out which rivers gush, and indeed there are rocks which split asunder so that water floweth from them. And indeed there are rocks which fall down for the fear of Allah. Allah is not unaware of what ye do.

Have ye any hope that they will be true to you when a party of them used to listen to the word of Allah, then used to change it, after they had understood it, knowingly?

And when they fall in with those who believe, they say: "We believe." But when they go apart one with another they say: "Prate ye to them of that which Allah hath disclosed to you that they may contend with you before your Lord concerning it?" Have ye then no sense?

Are they then unaware that Allah knoweth that which they keep hidden and that which they proclaim?

Among them are unlettered folk who know the Scripture not except from hearsay. They but guess. Therefore woe be unto those who write the Scripture with their hands and then say, "This is from Allah," that they may purchase a small gain therewith. Woe unto them for that their hands have written, and woe unto them for that they earn thereby.

And they say: "The Fire will not touch us save for a certain number of days." Say: "Have ye received **a covenant** from Allah--truly **Allah will not break His covenant**--or tell ye concerning Allah that which ye know not? Nay, but whosoever hath done evil and his sin surroundeth him; such are rightful owners of the Fire; they will abide therein. And those who believe and do good works: such are rightful owners of the Garden. They will abide therein."

And remember when We made **a covenant** with the Children of Israel, (saying): "Worship none save Allah, and be good to parents and to kindred and to orphans and the needy, and speak kindly to mankind; and establish worship and pay the poor-due (*zakat*)." Then, after that, ye slid back, save a few of you, being averse.

And when We made with you **a covenant** (saying): "Shed not the blood of your people nor turn a party of your people out of your dwellings. Then **ye ratified Our covenant** and ye were witnesses thereto.

Yet ye it is who slay each other and drive out a party of your people from their homes, supporting one another against them by sin and transgression?--and if they came to you as captives ye would ransom them, whereas their expulsion was itself unlawful for you--Believe ye in part of the Scripture and disbelieve ye in part thereof? And what is the reward of those who do so save ignominy in the life of the world, and on the Day of Resurrection they will be consigned to the most grievous doom. For Allah is not unaware of what ye do. Such are those who buy the life of the world at the price of the Hereafter. Their punishment will not be lightened, neither will they have support.

And verily We gave unto *MOSES* the Scripture and We caused a train of messengers to follow after him, and We gave unto *JESUS*, son of Miriam, THIS RIGHTEOUS BOOK, and We supported him with the Holy Spirit. Is it ever so, that, when there cometh unto you a messenger with that which ye yourselves desire not, ye grow arrogant, and some ye disbelieve and some ye slay?

And they say: "Our hearts are hardened." Nay, but Allah hath cursed them for their unbelief. Little is that which they believe.

And when there cometh unto them a Scripture from Allah, confirming that in their possession-- though before that they were asking for a signal triumph over those who disbelieved--and when there cometh unto them that which they know (to be the truth) they disbelieve therein. The curse of Allah is on disbelievers.

Evil is that for which they sell their souls: that they should disbelieve in that which Allah hath revealed, grudging that Allah should reveal of His bounty unto whom He will of His slaves. They have incurred anger upon anger. For disbelievers is a shameful doom.

And when it is said unto them: "Believe in that which Allah hath revealed," they say: "We believe in that which was revealed unto us." And they disbelieve in that which cometh after it, though it is the truth confirming that which they possess. Say: "Why then slew ye the prophets of Allah aforetime, if ye are indeed believers?"

And *MOSES* came unto you with THIS RIGHTEOUS BOOK, yet, while he was away, ye chose the calf (and ye were wrong-doers.

And when We made with you **a covenant** and caused the Mount to tower above you, (saying): "Hold fast by that which We have given you, and hear!" they said: "We hear and we rebel." And the calf was made to sink into their hearts **because of their rejection of the Covenant**. Say: "Evil is that which your belief enjoineth on you, if ye are believers." Say: "If the abode of the Hereafter in the providence of Allah is indeed for you alone and not for others of mankind (as ye pretend), then long for death (for ye must long for death) if ye are truthful." But they will never long for it, because of that which their own hands have sent before them. Allah is aware of evil-doers.

And Thou wilt find amongst them the greediest of mankind for life and (greedier) than the idolaters. **Each one of them would like to be allowed to live a thousand years**. And to live (a thousand years) would be no means remove him from the doom. Allah is Seer of what they do.

Say: "Who is an enemy to Gabriel!" For he it is who hath revealed to Thy heart by Allah's leave, confirming that which was before it, and a guidance and glad tidings to believers; "Who is an enemy to Allah, and His angels and His messengers, and Gabriel and Michael!" Then, Lo! Allah Himself is an enemy to the disbelievers. Verily We have revealed unto Thee clear tokens, and only miscreants will disbelieve in them. Is it ever so that when they make **a covenant** a party of them set it aside? The truth is, most of them believe not.

And when there cometh unto them a messenger from Allah, confirming that which they possess, a party of those who have received the Scripture fling the Scripture of Allah behind their backs as if they knew not, and follow that which the devils falsely related against the kingdom of Solomon. Solomon disbelieved not; but the devils disbelieved, teaching mankind magic and that which was revealed to the two angels in Babel, Harut and Marut. Nor did they teach it to anyone till they had said: "We are only a temptation, therefore disbelieve not!" And from these two people learn that by which they cause division between man and wife; but they injure thereby no-one save by Allah's leave. And they learn that which harmeth them and profiteth them not. And surely they do know that he who trafficketh therein will have no happy portion in the Hereafter; and surely evil is the price for which they sell their souls, if they but knew. And if they had believed and kept from evil, a recompense from Allah would be better, if they only knew.

O ye who believe, say not (unto *AL-AMIN*): "Listen to us" but say "Look upon us," and be ye listeners. For disbelievers is a painful doom. Neither those who disbelieve among the people of the Scripture nor the idolaters love that there should be sent down unto you any good thing from your Lord. But Allah chooseth for His mercy whom He will, and Allah is of Infinite Bounty. Nothing of our Revelation do we abrogate or cause be forgotten, but we bring in place **one better or the like thereof.** Knowest Thou not that Allah is Able to do all things? Knowest Thou not that it is Allah unto Whom belongeth the Sovereignty of the heavens and the earth; and ye have not, beside Allah, any guardian or helper?

Or would ye question your messenger as *MOSES* was questioned aforetime? He who chooseth disbelief instead of faith, verily he hath gone astray from a plain road.

Many of the people of the Scripture long to make you disbelievers after your belief, through envy on their own account, after the truth hath become manifest unto them. Forgive and be indulgent toward them until Allah give command. Lo! Allah is Able to do all things. Establish worship, and pay the poor-due (*zakat*); and whatever of good ye send before you for your souls, ye will find it with Allah. Lo! Allah is Seer of what ye do.

And they say: "None entereth paradise unless he be a Jew or a Christian (or a Muslim)." These are their own desires. Say: "Bring your proof of what ye state if ye are truthful!" Nay, but whosoever surrendereth his purpose to Allah while doing good, his reward is with his Lord; and there shall no fear come upon them neither shall they grieve.

And the Jews say the Christians follow nothing, and the Christians say the Jews follow nothing; yet both are readers of the Scripture (like readers of the Furqan). Even thus speak those who know not. Allah will judge between them on the Day of Resurrection concerning that wherein they differ.

And who doth greater wrong than he who forbiddeth the approach to the Sanctuaries of Allah lest His name should be mentioned therein, and striveth for their ruin. As for such, it was never meant that they should enter them except in fear. Theirs in the world is ignominy and theirs in the Hereafter is an awful doom.

Unto Allah belong the East and the West, and whithersoever ye turn, there is Allah's Countenance. Lo! Allah is All-Embracing, All-Knowing.

And they say: "Allah hath taken unto Himself a Son." Be He glorified! Nay, but whatsoever is in the heavens and the earth is His. All are subservient unto Him.

73. Bism'illah Ar-Rahman Ar-Rahim! Ya Sin: ONE SHOUT!

Ya Sin.

BY THIS WISE QUR'AN: Lo! Thou art of those sent on a straight path, a Revelation of the Mighty, the Merciful, that Thou mayst warn a folk whose fathers were not warned, so they are heedless. Already hath the judgment, proved true of most of them, for they believe not.

Lo! We have put on their necks carcans reaching unto the chins, so that they are made stiff-necked. And We have set a bar before them and a bar behind them, and thus have covered them so that they see not. Whether Thou warn them or Thou warn them not, it is alike for them, for they believe not. Thou warnest only him who followeth the Reminder and **feareth the Beneficent in secret**. To him bear tidings of forgiveness and a rich reward.

Lo! We it is Who bring the dead to life. We record that which they send before them, and their footprints. And all things We have kept in a clear Register. Coin for them a similitude: The people of the city when those sent came unto them; when We sent unto them TWAIN, and they denied them both, so **We reinforced them with a third**, and they said: "Lo! we have been sent unto you."

They said: "Ye are but mortals like unto us. The Beneficent hath naught revealed. Ye do but lie!"

They answered: "Our Lord knoweth that we are indeed sent unto you, and our duty is but plain conveyance of the message.

They said: "We augur ill of you. If ye desist not, we shall surely stone you, and grievous torture will befall you at our hands."

They said: "Your evil augury be with you! Is it because ye are reminded of the truth? Nay, but ye are froward folk!"

And there came from the uttermost part of the city a man running (the fourth one). He cried: "O my people! Follow those who have been sent! Follow those who ask of you no fee, and who are rightly guided. For what cause should I not serve Him Who hath created me, and unto Whom ye will be brought back? Shall I take other gods in place of Him when, if the Beneficent should wish me any harm, their intercession will avail me naught, nor can they save? Then truly I should be in error manifest. Lo! I have believed in your Lord, so hear me!"

It was said (unto him): "Enter paradise." He said: "Would that my people knew with what munificence my Lord hath pardoned me and made me of the honored ones!"

We sent not down against his people after him a host from heaven, nor do We ever send. It was but ONE SHOUT, and Lo! They were extinct.

Ah, the anguish for the bondmen! Never came there unto them a messenger but they did mock him! Have they not seen how many generations We destroyed before them, which indeed returned not unto them; But all, without exception, will be brought before Us.

A token unto them is the dead earth. We revive it, and We bring forth from it grain so that they eat thereof; And We have placed therein gardens of the date-palm and grapes, and We have caused springs of water to gush forth therein, that they may eat of the fruit thereof, and their hands made it not. Will they not, then, give thanks?

Glory be to Him Who created all the sexual pairs, of that which the earth groweth, and of themselves, and of that which they know not! A token unto them is night. We strip it of the day, and Lo! They are in darkness. And the sun runneth on unto a resting-place for him. That is the measuring of the Mighty, the Wise. And for the moon We have appointed mansions till she return like an old shrivelled palm-leaf. It is not for the sun to overtake the moon, nor doth the night outstrip the day. They float each in an orbit.

And a token unto them is that We bear their offspring in the laden ship, and have created for them of the like thereof whereon they ride. And if We will, We drown them, and there is no help for them, neither can they be saved; unless by mercy from Us and as comfort for a while. When it is said unto them: "Beware of that which is before you and that which is behind you, that haply ye may find mercy" they are heedless. Never came **a token of the tokens** of their Lord to them, but they did turn away from it!

And when it is said unto them: "Spend of that wherewith Allah hath provided you, those who disbelieve say unto those who believe: Shall we feed those whom Allah, if He willed, would feed? Ye are in naught else than error manifest."

And they say: "When will this promise be fulfilled, if ye are truthful?" They await but ONE SHOUT, which will surprise them while they are disputing. Then they cannot make bequest, nor can they return to their own folk.

And the trumpet is blown and Lo! From the graves they hie unto their Lord, crying: "Woe upon us! Who hath raised us from our place of sleep? This is that which the Beneficent did promise, and the messengers spoke truth."

It is but ONE SHOUT, and behold them brought together before Us!

This day no soul is wronged in aught; nor are ye requited aught save what ye used to do.Lo! those who merit paradise this day are happily employed, they and their wives, in pleasant shade, on thrones reclining; theirs the fruit (of their good deeds) and theirs (all) that they ask; the word from a Merciful Lord (for them) is: "Salem!" But avaunt ye, O ye guilty, this day!

Did I not charge you, O ye sons of *ADAM*, that ye worship not the devil --Lo! He is your open foe!

But that ye worship Me ? That was the right path.

Yet he hath led astray of you a great multitude. Had ye then no sense?

This is hell which ye were promised if ye followed him. Burn therein this day for that ye disbelieved.

This day We seal up their mouths, and their hands speak out to Us and their feet bear witness as to what they used to earn. And had We willed, We verily could have quenched their eyesight so that they should struggle for the way. Then how could they have seen? And had We willed, We verily could have fixed them in their place, making them powerless to go forward or turn back. He whom we bring unto old age, We reverse him in creation (making him go back to weakness after strength). Have ye then no sense?

And We have not taught him (*MUHAMMAD*) poetry, nor is it meet for him. This is naught else than a Reminder and a Lecture making plain, to warn whosoever liveth, and that the word may be fulfilled against the disbelievers. Have they not seen how We have created for them of Our handiwork the cattle, so that they are their owners, and have subdued them unto them, so that some of them they have for riding, some for food? Benefits and divers drinks have they from them. Will they not then give thanks? And they have taken gods beside Allah, in order that they may be helped. It is not in their power to help them; but they are unto them a host in arms.

So let not their speech grieve Thee (*AL-AMIN*). Lo! We know what they conceal and what they proclaim. Hath not man seen that We have created him from a drop of goo? Yet Lo! He is an open opponent.

And he hath coined for Us a similitude, and hath forgotten the fact of his creation, saying: "Who will revive these bones when they have rotted away?"

Say: "He will revive them Who produced them at the first, for He is Knower of every creation, Who hath appointed for you fire from the green tree, and behold! Ye kindle from it. Is not He Who created the heavens and the earth Able to create the like of them? Aye, that He is! for He is the All-Wise Creator, but His command, when He intendeth a thing, is only that He saith unto it: 'Be! and it is.' Therefore Glory be to Him in Whose hand is the dominion over all things! Unto Him ye will be brought back."

XVI. JUZ'UN SIPARA DECIMO-SEXTO:

74. Bism'illah Ar-Rahman Ar-Rahim! al-Hijr: *al-Kahf: THE CAVE.*

Praise be to Allah Who hath revealed the Scripture unto His slave, and hath not placed therein any crookedness, but hath made it straight, to give warning of stern punishment from Him, and to bring unto the believers who do good works the news that theirs will be a fair reward, wherein they will abide for ever; and to warn those who say: "Allah hath chosen a Son," whereof they have no knowledge, nor do their fathers, **Dreadful is the word** that cometh out of their mouths. They speak naught but a lie. Yet it **may be**, if they believe not in this statement, that Thou **wilt torment Thy soul with grief** over their footsteps.

Lo! We have placed all that is on the earth as an ornament thereof that We may try them: which of them is best in conduct. And Lo! We shall make all that is thereon a barren mound. Or deemest Thou that the **People of the Cave** and **the Inscription** are a wonder among Our portents?

When the young men fled for refuge to the Cave and said: "Our Lord! Give us mercy from Thy presence, and shape for us right conduct in our plight." Then We sealed up their hearing in the Cave for a number of years. And afterward We raised them up that We might know which of the two parties would best calculate the time that they had tarried. We narrate unto Thee their story with truth. Lo! They were young men who believed in their Lord, and We increased them in guidance. And We made firm their hearts when they stood forth and said: "Our Lord is the Lord of the heavens and the earth. We cry unto no God beside Him, for then should we utter an enormity. These, our people, have chosen gods beside Him though they bring no clear warrant vouchsafed to them. And who doth greater wrong than he who inventeth a lie concerning Allah? And when ye withdraw from them and that which they worship except Allah, then seek refuge in the Cave; your Lord will spread for you of His mercy and will prepare for you a pillow in your plight."

And Thou mightest have seen the sun when it rose move away from their cave to the right, and when it set go past them on the left, and they were in the cleft thereof. That was of the portents of Allah. He whom Allah guideth, he indeed is led aright, and he whom He sendeth astray, for him thou wilt not find a guiding friend. And Thou wouldst have deemed them waking though they were asleep, and We caused them to turn over to the right and the left, and **their dog** stretching out his paws on the threshold.

If thou hadst observed them closely Thou hadst assuredly turned away from them in flight, and hadst been filled with awe of them. And in like manner We awakened them that they might question one another. A speaker from among them said: "How long have ye tarried?" They said: "We have tarried a day or some part of a day, others said: "Your Lord best knoweth what ye have tarried. Now send one of you with this your silver coin unto the city, and let him see what food is purest there and bring you a supply thereof. Let him be courteous and let no man know of you. For they, if they should come to know of you, will stone you or turn you back to their religion; then ye will never prosper."

And in like manner We disclosed them (to the people of the city) that they might know that the promise of Allah is true, and that, as for the HOUR, there is no doubt concerning it. When (the people of the city) disputed of their case among themselves, they said: "Build over them a building; their Lord knoweth best concerning them." Those who won their point said: "We verily shall build a place of worship over them." Some will say: "They were three, **their dog** the fourth," and some say: "Five, their dog the sixth," guessing at random; and some say: "Seven, and their dog the eighth." Say: "My Lord is Best Aware of their number. None knoweth them save a few." So contend not concerning them except with an outward contending, and ask not any of them to pronounce concerning them. And say not of anything: "Lo! I shall do that tomorrow," except if Allah will. And remember thy Lord when Thou forgettest, and say: "It may be that my Lord guideth me unto a nearer way of truth than this."

And it is said they tarried in their Cave three hundred years and add nine. Say: "Allah is Best Aware how long they tarried. His is the Invisible of the heavens and the earth. How clear of sight is He and keen of hearing! They have no protecting friend beside Him, and He maketh none to share in His Government."

And recite that which hath been revealed unto Thee of the Scripture of Thy Lord. There is none who can change His words, and Thou wilt find no refuge beside Him. Restrain Thyself along with those who cry unto their Lord at morn and evening, seeking His Countenance; and let not Thine eyes overlook them, desiring the pomp of the life of the world; and obey not him whose heart We have made heedless of Our remembrance, who followeth his own lust and whose case hath been abandoned.

Say: "It is the truth from the Lord of you all. Then whosoever will, let him believe, and whosoever will, let him disbelieve." Lo! We have prepared for disbelievers Fire. Its tent encloseth them. If they ask for showers, they will be showered with water like to molten lead which burneth the faces. Calamitous the drink and ill the resting-place!

Lo! As for those who believe and do good works--Lo! We suffer not the reward of one whose work is goodly to be lost. As for such, theirs will be Gardens of Eden, wherein rivers flow beneath them; therein they will be given **armlets of gold** and will wear **green robes of finest silk** and gold embroidery, reclining upon throne therein. Blest the reward, and fair the resting-place!

Coin for them a similitude: Two men, unto one of whom We had assigned two gardens of grapes, and We had surrounded both with date-palms and had put between them tillage. Each of the gardens gave its fruit and withheld naught thereof. And We caused a river to gush forth therein. And he had fruit. And he said unto his comrade, when he spake with him: "I am more than Thee in wealth, and stronger in respect of men." And he went into his garden, while he wronged himself. He said: "I think not that all this will ever perish. I think not that the HOUR will ever come, and if indeed I am brought back unto my Lord I surely shall find better than this as a resort."

His comrade, when he spake with him, exclaimed: "Disbelievest Thou in Him Who created Thee of dust, then of a drop of goo, and then fashioned Thee a man? But He is Allah, my Lord, and I ascribe unto my Lord no partner. If only, when Thou enteredst Thy garden, Thou hadst said: 'That which Allah willeth (will come to pass)!' There is no strength save in Allah! Though Thou seest me as less than Thee in wealth and children, yet it may be that my Lord will give me better than Thy garden, and will send on it a bolt from heaven, and some morning it will be a smooth hillside, or some morning the water thereof will be lost in the earth so that Thou canst not make search for it."

And his fruit was beset with destruction. Then began he to wring his hands for all that he had spent upon it, when now it was all ruined on its trellises, and to say: "Would that I had ascribed no partner to my Lord!" And he had no troop of men to help him as against Allah, nor could he save himself. In this case is protection only from Allah, the True, He is Best for reward, and best for consequence.

And coin for them the similitude of the life of the world as water which We send down from the sky, and the vegetation of the earth mingleth with it and then becometh dry twigs that the winds scatter. Allah is able to do all things. Wealth and children are **an ornament** of the life of the world. But the good deeds which endure are better in thy Lord's sight for reward, and better in respect of hope.

And bethink you of the Day when we remove the hills and ye see the earth emerging, and We gather them together so as to leave not one of them behind. And they are set before thy Lord in ranks: "Now verily have ye come unto Us as We created you at the first. But ye thought that We had set no tryst for you." And **the Book** is placed, and Thou seest the guilty fearful of that which is therein, and they say: "What kind of **a Book is this** that leaveth not a small thing nor a great thing but hath counted it!" And they find all that they did confronting them, and thy Lord wrongeth no-one.

And when We said unto the angels: "Fall prostrate before *ADAM*," and they fell prostrate, all save Iblis. He was of the jinn, so he rebelled against his Lord's command. Will ye choose him and his seed for your protecting friends instead of Me, when they are an enemy unto you? Calamitous is the exchange for evil-doers.

I made them not to witness the creation of the heavens and the earth, nor their own creation; nor choose I misleaders for My helpers. And (be mindful of) the Day when He will say: "Call those partners of Mine whom ye pretended." Then they will cry unto them, but they will not hear their prayer, and We shall set **a gulf of doom** between them. And the guilty behold the Fire and know that they are about to fall therein, and they find no way of escape thence. And verily We have displayed for mankind in THIS QUR'AN all manner of similitudes, but man is more than anything contentious.

And naught hindereth mankind from believing when the guidance cometh unto them, and from asking forgiveness of their Lord unless it be that they wish that the judgment of the Old Ones should come upon them or that they should be confronted with the Doom. We send not the messengers save as bearers of good news and warners. Those who disbelieve contend with falsehood in order to refute the Truth thereby. And they take Our Revelations and that wherewith they are threatened as a jest. And who doth greater wrong than he who hath been reminded of the revelations of his Lord, yet turneth away from them and forgetteth what his hands send forward? Lo! On their **hearts We have placed coverings** so that they understand not, and in their ears a deafness. And though Thou call them to the guidance, in that case they can never be led aright. Thy Lord is the Forgiver, Full of Mercy. If He took them to task for what they earn, He would hasten on the doom for them; but theirs is an appointed term from which they will find no escape.

And all those townships! We destroyed them when they did wrong, and We appointed a fixed time for their destruction. And when *MOSES* said unto his servant: "I will not give up until I reach the point where the two rivers meet, though I march on for ages." And when they reached the point where the two met, they forgot **their fish**, and it took its way into the waters, being free. And when they had gone further, he said unto his servant: "Bring us our breakfast. Verily we have found fatigue in this our journey."

He said: "Didst Thou see, when we took refuge on the rock, and I forgot the fish--and none but Satan caused me to forget to mention it--it took its way into the waters by a marvel."

He said: "This is that which we have been seeking." So they retraced their steps again. Then found they one of Our slaves, unto whom We had given mercy from Us, and had taught him knowledge from Our presence. *MOSES* said unto him: "May I follow Thee, to the end that Thou mayst teach me right conduct of that which Thou hast been taught?"

He said: "Lo! Thou canst not bear with me. How canst Thou bear with that whereof Thou canst not compass any knowledge?"

He said: "Allah willing, Thou shalt find me patient and I shall not in aught gainsay Thee."

He said: "Well, if Thou go with me, **ask me not concerning aught** till I myself make mention of it unto Thee." So they TWAIN set out till, when they were in the ship, he made a hole therein.

MOSES said: "Hast Thou made a hole therein to drown the folk thereof? Thou verily hast done a dreadful thing."

He said: "Did I not tell Thee that Thou couldst not bear with me?"

He said: "Be not wroth with me that I forgot, and be not hard upon me for my fault." So they TWAIN journeyed on till, when they met a lad, he slew him. *MOSES* said: "What! Hast Thou slain an innocent soul who hath slain no man? Verily Thou hast done a horrid thing."

He said: "Did I not tell Thee that Thou couldst not bear with me?"

MOSES said: "If I ask Thee after this concerning aught, keep not company with me. Thou hast received an excuse from me." So they TWAIN journeyed on till, when they came unto the folk of a certain township, they asked its folk for food, but they refused to make them guests. And they found therein a wall upon the point of falling into ruin, and he repaired it. *MOSES* said: "If Thou hadst wished, Thou couldst have taken payment for it."

He said: "This is the parting between Thee and me! I will announce unto Thee the interpretation of that Thou couldst not bear with patience. As for the ship, it belonged to poor people working on the river, and I wished to mar it, for there was a king behind them who is taking every ship by force. And as for the lad, his parents were believers and we feared lest he should oppress them by rebellion and disbelief. And we intended that their Lord should change him for them for one better in purity and nearer to mercy. And as for the wall, it belonged to two orphan boys in the city, and there was beneath it a treasure belonging to them, and their father had been righteous, and thy Lord intended that they should come to their full strength and should bring forth their treasure as a mercy from their Lord; and I did it not upon my own command. Such is the interpretation of that wherewith thou couldst not bear."

They will ask Thee of Dhu'l-Qarneyn. Say: "I shall recite unto you a remembrance of him."

Lo! We made him strong in the land and gave him unto every thing a road. And he followed a road till, when he reached the setting-place of the sun, he found it setting in a muddy spring, and found a people thereabout. We said: "O Dhu'l-Qarneyn! Either punish or show them kindness."

He said: "As for him who doeth wrong, we shall punish him, and then he will be brought back unto his Lord, Who will punish him with awful punishment! But as for him who believeth and doeth right, good will be his reward, and We shall speak unto him a mild command."

Then he followed a road till, when he reached the rising-place of the sun, he found it rising on a people for whom We had appointed no shelter therefrom. So it was. And We knew all concerning him. Then he followed a road till, when he came between the two mountains, he found upon their hither side a folk that scarce could understand a saying. They said: "O Dhu'l-Qarneyn! Lo! Gog and Magog are spoiling the land. So may we pay Thee tribute on condition that **Thou set a barrier**[*] between us and them?"

---

[*] Qin Shi Huang builder of the Great Wall of China united the early Walls built by King Xuan of Zhou. The Great Wall of Gorgan was built-up circa the same time, that includes the Gates of Alexander, the Caspian Gates and that

He said: "That wherein my Lord hath established me is better than your tribute. Do but help me with strength of men, I will set between you and them a bank. Give me pieces of iron--till, when he had levelled up (the gap) between the cliffs, he said: "Blow!" till, when he had made it a fire, he said: "Bring me molten copper to pour thereon." And (Gog and Magog) were not able to surmount, nor could they pierce it.

He said: "This is a mercy from my Lord; but when the promise of my Lord cometh to pass, He will lay it low, for the promise of my Lord is true."

And on that day we shall let some of them surge against others, and the Trumpet will be blown. Then We shall gather them together in one gathering. On that day we shall present hell to the disbelievers, plain to view, those whose eyes were hoodwinked from MY REMINDER, and who could not bear to hear.
Do the disbelievers reckon that they can choose My bondmen as protecting friends beside Me? Lo! We have prepared hell as a welcome for the disbelievers. Say: "Shall We inform you who will be the greatest losers by their works?" Those whose effort goeth astray in the life of the world, and yet they reckon that they do good work. Those are they who disbelieve in the Revelations of their Lord and in the meeting with Him. Therefore their works are vain, and on the Day of Resurrection We assign no weight to them.

That is their reward: hell, because they disbelieved, and made a jest of Our Revelations and Our messengers. Lo! Those who believe and do good works, theirs are the Gardens of Paradise for welcome, wherein they will abide, with no desire to be removed from thence.

Say: "Though the sea became ink for the Words of my Lord, verily the sea would be used up before the words of my Lord were exhausted, even though We brought the like thereof to help."

Say: "I am only a mortal like you. **My Lord inspireth in me that your God is only One God**. And whoever hopeth for the meeting with his Lord, let him do righteous work, and make none sharer of the worship due unto his Lord."

75. Bism'illah Ar-Rahman Ar-Rahim! ar-Rahman: ARRAMAN (THE MERCIFUL).

The Beneficent
Hath made known THIS QUR'AN.
He hath created man.
He hath taught him utterance.
The sun and the moon are made punctual.
The stars and the trees adore.
And the sky He hath uplifted; and He hath set the measure,
That ye exceed not the measure,
But observe the measure strictly, nor fall short thereof.

---

of Cyrus the Great and Anushurvan the Just. In Meso-America we have also the Great Walls of the Maya Snake-Kings (*Kaanul*) uncovered from beneath the trees of the remote Guatemalan jungle. Gog and Magog are identified with Russia and Moscow (see Hal Lindsey, ***The Late Great Planet Earth***, chapter 5: 'Russia is a Gog' for more).

And the earth hath He appointed for (His) creatures,
Wherein are fruit and sheathed palm-trees,
Husked grain and scented herb.
Which is it, of the favors of your Lord, that ye deny?

He created man of clay like the potter's,
And the jinn did He create of smokeless fire.
Which is it, of the favors of your Lord, that ye deny?

Lord of the two Easts, and Lord of the two Wests!
Which is it, of the favors of your Lord, that ye deny?

He hath loosed the two seas. They meet.
There is a barrier (*barzakh*) between them. They encroach not one upon the other.
Which is it, of the favors of your Lord, that ye deny?

There cometh forth from both of them the pearl and coral-stone.
Which is it, of the favors of your Lord, that ye deny?

His are the ships displayed upon the sea, like banners.
Which is it, of the favors of your Lord, that ye deny?

Everyone that is thereon will pass away;
There remaineth but the Countenance of thy Lord of Might and Glory.
Which is it, of the favors of your Lord, that ye deny?

All that are in the heavens and the earth entreat Him. Every day He exerciseth (universal) power.
Which is it, of the favors of your Lord, that ye deny?

We shall dispose of you, O ye two dependents (man and jinn).
Which is it, of the favors of your Lord, that ye deny?

O company of jinn and men, if ye have power to penetrate (all) regions of the heavens and the
earth, then penetrate (them)! Ye will never penetrate them save with (Our) sanction.
Which is it, of the favors of your Lord, that ye deny?

There will be sent, against you both, heat of fire and flash of brass, and ye will not escape.
Which is it, of the favors of your Lord, that ye deny?

And when the heaven splitteth asunder and becometh rosy like red hide--
Which is it, of the favors of your Lord, that ye deny?

On that day neither man nor jinni will be questioned of his sin.
Which is it, of the favors of your Lord, that ye deny?

The guilty will be known by their marks, and will be taken by the forelocks and the feet.
Which is it, of the favors of your Lord, that ye deny ?

This is hell which the guilty deny.
They go circling round between it and fierce, boiling water.
Which is it, of the favors of your Lord, that ye deny?

But for him who feareth the standing before his Lord there are two gardens.
Which is it, of the favors of your Lord, that ye deny?

Of spreading branches.
Which is it, of the favors of your Lord, that ye deny?

Wherein are two fountains flowing.
Which is it, of the favors of your Lord, that ye deny?

Wherein is every kind of fruit in pairs.
Which is it, of the favors of your Lord, that ye deny?

Reclining upon couches lined with silk brocade,
the fruit of both the gardens near to hand.
Which is it, of the favors of your Lord, that ye deny?

Therein are those of modest gaze, whom neither man nor jinni
will have touched before them.
Which is it, of the favors of your Lord, that ye deny?

(In beauty) like the jacynth and the coral-stone.
Which is it, of the favors of your Lord, that ye deny?

Is the reward of goodness aught save goodness?
Which is it, of the favors of your Lord, that ye deny?

And beside them are two other gardens,
Which is it, of the favors of your Lord, that ye deny?

Dark green with foliage.
Which is it, of the favors of your Lord, that ye deny?

Wherein are two abundant springs.
Which is it, of the favors of your Lord, that ye deny?

Wherein is fruit, the date-palm and pomegranate.
Which is it, of the favors of your Lord, that ye deny?

Wherein (are found) the good and beautiful--

Which is it, of the favors of your Lord, that ye deny?

Fair ones, close-guarded in pavilion--
Which is it, of the favors of your Lord, that ye deny?

Whom neither man nor jinni will have touched before them--
Which is it, of the favors of your Lord, that ye deny?

Reclining on green cushions and fair carpets.
Which is it, of the favors of your Lord, that ye deny?

Blessed be the name of thy Lord, Mighty and Glorious!

CHINVAT-SIRAT: Bism'illah Ar-Rahman Ar-Rahim!

When Allah's succour (an-Nasr) and the triumph cometh
And thou seest mankind Entering the religion of Allah in Troops,
Then hymn the praises of thy Lord, and seek forgiveness of Him.
Lo! He is ever ready to show mercy.

Thaleth

174

HOURIS!

HOURIS!

---THE WOMEN*---
Manzil-i-Zakat va Qiblih
Istiqlál

Bism'illah Ar-Rahman Ar-Rahim!

RECITE *(aq-Qaara): In the name of thy Lord Who createth,*
Createth man from a clot (al-'Alaq).
RECITE: *And thy Lord is the Most Bounteous,*
*Who teacheth by the **PEN**,*
Teacheth man that which he knew not.

XVII. JUZ'UN SIPARA DICIASSETTE:

76. Bism'illah Ar-Rahman Ar-Rahim! at-Taghabun: THE CHEATING.

All that is in the heavens and all that is in the earth **GLORIFIETH ALLAH;**[†] unto Him belongeth the Sovereignty and unto Him belongeth the Praise, and He is Able to do All Things!

He it is Who created you, but one of you is a disbeliever and one of you is a believer, and Allah is Seer of what ye do.

He created the heavens and the earth with truth, and He shaped you and made good your shapes, and **unto Him is the journeying**. He knoweth all that is in the heavens and the earth, and He knoweth what ye conceal and what ye publish. And Allah is Aware of what is in the breasts.

Hath not the story reached you of those who disbelieved of old and so did taste the ill-effects of their conduct, and theirs will be a painful doom. That was because their messengers kept coming unto them with THIS RIGHTEOUS BOOK, but they said: "Shall mere mortals guide us?" So they disbelieved and turned away, and Allah was independent of them. Allah is Absolute, Owner of Praise.

Those who disbelieve assert that they will not be raised again. Say: "Yea, verily, by my Lord! Ye will be raised again and then ye will be informed of what ye did; and that is easy for Allah. So believe in Allah and His messenger and the light which We have revealed. And Allah is Informed of what ye do."

---

[*]Islamic tradition signalizes four "Ladies of Heaven" (*Houris*) Aiyah, Miriam, Khadijih, and Fatima as human exemplars of true faith. See Shahda Sharelle Haqq (2012) ***Nobel Women of Faith: Asiya, Miriam, Khadijih, Fatima*** for more.

[†]**Al-Musabbihat** refer to the collective name of the seven surahs that begin with Allah's ***glorification*** 'Subhana,' 'Sabbaha,' and 'Yusabbihu:' *al-Hadid*; *al-Hashr*; *as-Saff*; *al-Jumua*; *at-Taghabun*; *al-Isra*; and *al-Ala*.

The day when He shall gather you unto **the Day of Assembling**, that will be a day of mutual disillusion. And whoso believeth in Allah and doeth right, He will remit from him his evil deeds and will bring him unto Gardens underneath which rivers flow, therein to abide for ever. That is the supreme triumph.

But those who disbelieve and deny Our Revelations, such are owners of the Fire; they will abide therein--a hapless journey's end! No calamity befalleth save by Allah's leave. And whosoever believeth in Allah, He guideth his heart. And Allah is Knower of all things.

Obey Allah and obey His messenger; but if ye turn away, then the duty of Our messenger is only to convey the message plainly.

Allah! There is no God save Him. In Allah, therefore, let believers put their trust.

O ye who believe! Lo! among your wives and your children there are enemies for you, therefore beware of them. And if ye efface and overlook and forgive, then Lo! Allah is Forgiving, Merciful. **Your wealth and your children are only a temptation**, whereas Allah! with Him is an immense reward.

So keep your duty to Allah as best ye can, and listen, and obey, and spend; that is better for your souls. And whoso is saved from his own greed, such are the successful.

If ye lend unto Allah a goodly loan, He will double it for you and will forgive you, for Allah is Responsive, Clement, Knower of the Invisible and the Visible, the Mighty, the Wise.

77. Bism'illah Ar-Rahman Ar-Rahim! az-Zukhruf: THE EMBELLISHMENT OF THE GOLDEN ORNAMENTS!

Ha. Mim.

By the Scripture which maketh plain, Lo! We have appointed it a Lecture, in Arabic that haply ye may understand.

And Lo! In the Source of Decrees, which We possess, it is indeed sublime, decisive. Shall We utterly ignore you because ye are a wanton folk? How many a prophet did We send among the Old Ones! And never came there unto them a prophet but they used to mock him. Then We destroyed men mightier than these in prowess; and the example of the Old Ones hath gone before them. And if Thou ask them: "Who created the heavens and the earth," they will surely answer: "The Mighty, the Knower created them; who made the earth a resting-place for you, and placed roads for you therein, that haply ye may find your way; and Who sendeth down water from the sky in due measure, and We revive a dead land therewith. Even so will ye be brought forth; He Who created all the pairs, and appointed for you ships and cattle whereupon ye ride. That ye may mount upon their backs, and may remember your Lord's favor when ye mount thereon, and may say: "Glorified be He Who hath subdued these unto us, and we were not capable of subduing them; And Lo! unto our Lord we surely are returning."

And they allot to Him a portion of His bondmen! Lo! Man is verily a mere ingrate. Or chooseth He daughters of all that He hath created, and honoureth He you with sons? And if one of them hath tidings of that **which he likeneth to the Beneficent One**, his countenance becometh black and he is full of inward rage. Liken they then to Allah that which is bred up in outward show, and in dispute cannot make itself plain?

And they make the angels, who are the slaves of the Beneficent, females. Did they witness their creation? Their testimony will be recorded and they will be questioned.

And they say: "If the Beneficent One had so willed, we should not have worshipped them." They have no knowledge whatsoever of that. They do but guess.

Or have We given them any scripture before so that they are holding fast thereto? Nay, for they say only: "Lo! We found our fathers following a religion, and we are guided by their footprints." And even so We sent not a warner before Thee into any township but its luxurious ones said: "Lo! We found our fathers following a religion, and we are following their footprints."

And the warner said: "What! Even though I bring you better guidance than that ye found your fathers following?" They answered: "Lo! In what ye bring we are disbelievers." So We requited them. Then see the nature of the consequence for the rejecters!

And when Abraham said unto his father and his folk: "Lo! I am innocent of what ye worship save Him Who did create me, for He will surely guide me." And he made it a word enduring among his seed, that haply they might return.

Nay, but I let these and their fathers enjoy life only till there should come unto them the Truth and a messenger making plain. And now that the Truth hath come unto them they say: "This is mere magic," and "Lo! We are disbelievers therein."

And they say: "If only THIS QUR'AN had been revealed to some great man of the two towns?" Is it they who apportion thy Lord's mercy? We have apportioned among them their livelihood in the life of the world, and raised some of them above others in rank that some of them may take labor from others; and the mercy of thy Lord is better than the wealth that they amass.

And were it not that humankind would have become one community, We might well have appointed, for those who disbelieve in **the Beneficent**, roofs of silver for their houses and stairs of silver whereby to mount, and for their houses doors of silver and couches of silver whereon to recline, **and ornaments of gold**.

Yet all that would have been but a provision of the life of the world. And the Hereafter with your Lord would have been for those who keep from evil. And he whose sight is dim to the **remembrance of the Beneficent**, We assign unto him a devil who becometh his comrade; And Lo! They surely turn them from the way of Allah, and yet they deem that they are rightly guided; till, when he cometh unto Us, he saith unto his comrade: "Ah, would that between me and Thee there were the distance of the two horizons"--an evil comrade!--"And it profiteth you not this day, because ye did wrong, that ye will be sharers in the doom."

Canst Thou make the deaf to hear, or canst Thou guide the blind or him who is in error manifest? And if We take Thee away, We surely shall take vengeance on them, or if We show Thee that wherewith We threaten them; for Lo! We have complete command of them. So hold Thou fast to that which is inspired in Thee. Lo! Thou art on a RIGHT PATH. And Lo! It is in truth a Reminder for Thee and for Thy folk; and ye will be questioned. And ask those of Our messengers whom We sent before Thee: "Did We ever appoint gods to be worshipped beside **the Beneficent**?"

And verily We sent *MOSES* with Our Revelations unto Pharaoh and his Chiefs, and he said: "I am a messenger of the Lord of the Worlds." But when he brought them Our tokens, Behold! they laughed at them. And every token that We showed them was greater than its sister (token), and We grasped them with **the torment** (COVID-19), that haply they might turn again.

And they said: "O wizard! Entreat thy Lord for us by the pact that He hath made with Thee. Lo! we verily will walk aright." But when We eased them of the torment, Behold! They broke their word.

And Pharaoh caused a proclamation to be made among his people saying: "O my people! Is not mine the sovereignty of Egypt and these rivers flowing under me? Can ye not then discern? I am surely better than this fellow, who is despicable and can hardly make his meaning plain! Why, then, have armlets of gold not been set upon him, or angels sent along with him?" Thus he persuaded his people to make light of *MOSES*, and they obeyed him. Lo! They were a wanton folk.

So, when they angered Us, We punished them and drowned them every one. And We made them a thing past, and an example for those after them. And when *THE SON* of Miriam is quoted as an example, Behold! The folk laugh out, and say: "Are our gods better, or is he?" They raise not the objection save for argument. Nay! but they are a contentious folk. He is nothing but a slave on whom We bestowed favor, and We made **him a pattern** for the Children of Israel.

And had We willed We could have set among you angels to be viceroys in the earth. And Lo! Verily there is knowledge of the HOUR. So doubt ye not concerning it, but follow Me. This is the right path. And let not Satan turn you aside. Lo! He is an open enemy for you.

When *JESUS* came with THIS RIGHTEOUS BOOK (*al-Bayan*), he said: "I have come unto you with wisdom, and to make plain some of that concerning which ye differ. So keep your duty to Allah, and obey me. Lo! Allah, He is my Lord and your Lord. So worship Him. This is a right path."

But the factions among them differed. Then woe unto those who do wrong from the doom of a painful day. Await they aught save the HOUR, that it shall come upon them suddenly, when they know not? Friends on that day will be foes one to another, save those who kept their duty to Allah. "O My slaves! For you there is no fear this day, nor is it ye who grieve! Ye who believed Our Revelations and were **self-surrendered**, enter the Garden, ye and your wives, to be made glad. Therein are brought round for them trays of gold and goblets, and therein is all that souls desire and eyes find sweet. And ye are immortal therein. This is the Garden which ye are made to inherit because of what ye used to do. Therein for you is fruit in plenty whence to eat."

Lo! The guilty are immortal in hell's torment. It is not relaxed for them, and they despair therein. We wronged them not, but they it was who did the wrong. And they cry: "O Master! Let Thy Lord make an end of us." He saith: "Lo! Here ye must remain. We verily brought the Truth unto you, but ye were, most of you, averse to the Truth."

Or do they determine any thing (against the Prophet)? Lo! We also are determining. Or deem they that We cannot hear their secret thoughts and private confidences? Nay, but Our envoys, present with them, do record. Say: "If **the Beneficent One** hath a Son, then, I shall be first among the worshippers. Glorified be the Lord of the heavens and the earth, the Lord of the Throne, from that which they ascribe unto Him!"

So let them flounder in their talk and play until they meet the Day which they are promised. And He it is Who in the heaven is God, and in the earth God. He is the Wise, the Knower. And **blessed be He** unto Whom belongeth the Sovereignty of the heavens and the earth and all that is between them, and with Whom is knowledge of the HOUR, and unto Whom ye will be returned.

And those unto whom they cry instead of Him possess no power of intercession, saving him who beareth witness unto the Truth knowingly. And if Thou ask them who created them, they will surely say: "Allah." How then are they turned away?

And he saith: "O my Lord! Lo! These are a folk who believe not." Then bear with them (*O Al-AMIN*) and say: "Salem!" But they will come to know.

78. Bism'illah Ar-Rahman Ar-Rahim! at-Taghabun: al-Hujurat: THE CHAMBERS.

O ye who believe! <u>Be not forward</u> in the presence of Allah and His messenger, and keep your duty to Allah. Lo! Allah is Hearer, Knower.

O ye who believe! <u>Lift not up your voices above the voice</u> of the Prophet, nor shout when speaking to him as ye shout one to another, lest your works be rendered vain while ye perceive not. Lo! They who subdue their voices in the presence of the messenger of Allah, those are they whose hearts Allah hath proven unto righteousness. Theirs will be forgiveness and immense reward.

Lo! those who call Thee from behind the private apartments, most of them have no sense. And if they had had patience till Thou camest forth unto them, it had been better for them. And Allah is Forgiving, Merciful.

O ye who believe! If an evil-liver bring you tidings, verify it, lest ye smite some folk in ignorance and afterward repent of what ye did. And know that the messenger of Allah is among you. If he were to obey you in much of the government, ye would surely be in trouble; but Allah hath endeared the faith to you and hath beautified it in your hearts, and hath made disbelief and forbidden acts and rebellion hateful unto you. Such are they who are the rightly guided. It is a bounty and a grace from Allah; and Allah is Knower, Wise.

And if two parties of believers fall to fighting, then make peace between them. And if one party of them doeth wrong to the other, fight ye that which doeth wrong till it return unto the ordinance of Allah; then, if it return, make peace between them justly, and act equitably. Lo! Allah loveth the equitable. The believers are naught else than brothers. Therefore make peace between your brethren and observe your duty to Allah that haply ye may obtain mercy.

O ye who believe! Let not a folk deride a folk who may be better than they are, not let women deride women who may be better than they are; neither defame one another, nor insult one another by nicknames. Bad is the name of disobedience after faith. And whoso turneth not in repentance, such are evil-doers.

O ye who believe! Shun much suspicion; for Lo! Some suspicion is a crime. And spy not, **neither backbite one another**. **Would one of you love to eat the flesh** of his dead brother? Ye abhor that so abhor the other! And keep your duty to Allah. Lo! Allah is Relenting, Merciful.

O Humankind! Lo! We have created you male and female, and have made you nations and tribes that ye may know one another. Lo! The noblest of you, in the sight of Allah, is the best in conduct. Lo! Allah is Knower, Aware.

The wandering Arabs say: "We believe." Say: "Ye believe not, but rather say 'We submit,' for **the faith hath not yet entered into your hearts.**

Yet, if ye obey Allah and His messenger, He will not withhold from you aught of the reward of your deeds. Lo! Allah is Forgiving, Merciful.

The believers are those only who believe in Allah and His messenger and afterward doubt not, but strive with their wealth and their lives for the cause of Allah. Such are the sincere. Say: "Would ye teach Allah your religion, when Allah knoweth all that is in the heavens and all that is in the earth, and Allah is Aware of all things?"

They make it a favor unto Thee that they have surrendered. Say: "Deem not your Surrender a favor unto me; but Allah doth confer a favor on you, inasmuch as He hath led you to the Faith, if ye are earnest."

Lo! Allah knoweth the Unseen of the heavens and the earth. And Allah is Seer of what ye do.

XVIII. JUZ'UN SIPARA DICIOTTO:

79. Bism'illah Ar-Rahman Ar-Rahim! an-Nisa: WOMEN.

O Humanity! Be careful of your duty to your Lord *Who created you from a single soul* and from it created its mate and from them TWAIN hath spread abroad a multitude of men and women. Be careful of your duty toward Allah in Whom ye claim your rights of one another, and toward the wombs that bare you. Lo! Allah hath been a watcher over you.

Give unto orphans their wealth. Exchange not the good for the bad in your management thereof nor absorb their wealth into your own wealth. Lo! that would be a great sin. And if ye fear that ye will not deal fairly by the orphans, marry of the women, who seem good to you, two or three or four; and if ye fear **that ye cannot do justice** then **one only** or that your right hands possess. **Thus it is more likely that ye will not do injustice**.[*]

And give unto the women whom ye marry free gift of their marriage portions; but if they of their own accord remit unto you a part thereof, then ye are welcome to absorb it in your wealth. Give not unto the foolish what is in your keeping of their wealth, which Allah hath given you to maintain; but feed and clothe them from it, and speak kindly unto them.

Prove orphans till they reach the marriageable age; then, if ye find them of sound judgment, deliver over unto them their fortune; and devour it not by squandering and in haste lest they should grow up Whoso is rich, let him abstain generously from taking of the property of orphans; and whoso is poor let him take thereof in reason. And when ye deliver up their fortune unto orphans, have the transaction witnessed in their presence. Allah sufficeth as a Reckoner.

Unto the men (of a family) belongeth a share of that which parents and near kindred leave, and unto the women a share of that which parents and near kindred leave, whether it be little or much--a legal share. And when kinsfolk and orphans and the needy are present at the division (of the heritage), bestow on them therefrom and speak kindly unto them. And let those fear (in their behavior toward orphans) who if they left behind them weak offspring would be afraid for them. So let them mind their duty to Allah, and speak justly. Lo! Those who devour the wealth of orphans wrongfully, they do but swallow fire into their bellies, and they will be exposed to burning flame.

Allah chargeth you concerning the provision for your children: to the male the equivalent of the portion of two females, and if there be women more than two, then theirs is two-thirds of the inheritance, and if there be one only then the half. And to each of his parents a sixth of the inheritance, if he have a son; and if he have no son and his parents are his heirs, then to his mother appertaineth the third; and if he have brethren, then to his mother appertaineth the sixth, after any legacy he may have bequeathed, or debt hath been paid. Your parents and your children: Ye know not which of them is nearer unto you in usefulness. It is an injunction from Allah. Lo! Allah is Knower, Wise.

And unto you belongeth a half of that which your wives leave, if they have no child; but if they have a child then unto you the fourth of that which they leave, after any legacy they may have bequeathed, or debt (they may have contracted, hath been paid). And unto them belongeth the fourth of that which ye leave if ye have no child, but if ye have a child then the eighth of that which ye leave, after any legacy ye may have bequeathed, or debt (ye may have contracted, hath

---

[*]Exodus 21:10-11 NIV contingent upon JUSTICE: "If he marries another woman, he **must not deprive the first one** of her food, clothing and (her sexual) marital rights. If he does not provide her with these three things, she is to go free, without any payment of money (to you)."

181

been paid). And if a man or a woman have a distant heir (having left neither parent nor child), and he (or she) have a brother or a sister (only on the mother's side) then to each of them twain (the brother and the sister) the sixth, and if they be more than two, then they shall be sharers in the third, after any legacy that may have been bequeathed or debt (contracted) not injuring (the heirs by willing away more than a third of the heritage) hath been paid. A commandment from Allah. Allah is Knower, Indulgent.

These are the limits (imposed by) Allah. Whoso obeyeth Allah and His messenger, He will make him enter Gardens underneath which rivers flow, where such will dwell for ever. That will be the great success. And whoso disobeyeth Allah and His messenger and transgresseth His limits, He will make him enter Fire, where he will dwell for ever; his will be a shameful doom.

As for those of your women who are guilty of that which is forbidden, call to witness four of you against them. And if they testify (to the truth of the allegation) then confine them to the houses until death take them or until Allah provides for them a way for their freedom through new legislation. And as for the two of you who are guilty thereof, punish them both. And if they repent and improve, then let them be. Lo! Allah is ever relenting, Merciful.

Forgiveness is only incumbent on Allah toward those who do evil in ignorance and then turn quickly in repentance to Allah. These are they toward whom Allah relenteth. Allah is ever Knower, Wise. The forgiveness is not for those who do ill-deeds until, when death attendeth upon one of them, he saith: "Lo! I repent now;" nor yet for those who die while they are disbelievers. For such We have prepared a painful doom.

O ye who believe! It is **not lawful for you** forcibly to inherit the women (of your deceased kinsmen), nor (that) ye should put constraint upon them that ye may take away a part of that which ye have given them, unless they be guilty of flagrant acts that are forbidden. But consort with them in kindness, for if ye hate them it may happen that ye hate a thing wherein Allah hath placed much good. And if ye wish to exchange one wife for another and ye have given unto one of them a sum of money (however great), take nothing from it.[*] Would ye take it by the way of calumny and open wrong? How can ye take it back after one of you hath gone in unto the other, and they have taken a strong pledge from you?

And marry not those women whom your fathers married, except what hath already happened (of that nature) in the past. Lo! It was ever forbidden and abomination, and an evil way. Forbidden unto you are your mothers, and your daughters, and your sisters, and your father's sisters, and your mother's sisters, and your brother's daughters and your sister's daughters, and your foster-mothers, and your foster-sisters, and your mothers-in-law, and your step-daughters who are under your protection (born) of your women unto whom ye have gone in--but if ye have not gone in unto them, then it is no sin for you (to marry their daughters) --and the wives of your sons who (spring) from your own loins. And (it is forbidden unto you) that ye should have two sisters together, except what hath already happened (of that nature) in the past. Lo! Allah is ever Forgiving, Merciful.

---

[*] Exodus 21:11 NIV: "She is to go free, without any payment of money (to you)."

And all married women (are forbidden unto you) save those whom your right hands possess. It is a decree of Allah for you. Lawful unto you are all beyond those mentioned, so that ye seek them with your wealth in honest wedlock, not debauchery. And those of whom ye seek content (by marrying them), give unto them their portions as a duty. And there is no sin for you in what ye do by mutual agreement after the duty (hath been done). Lo! Allah is ever Knower, Wise.

And whoso is not able to afford to marry free, believing women, let them marry from the believing maids whom your right hands possess. Allah knoweth best (concerning) your faith. Ye (proceed) one from another; so **wed them by permission of their folk**, and give unto them their portions in kindness, they being honest, not debauched nor of loose conduct. And if when they are honourably married they commit lewdness they shall incur the half of the punishment (prescribed) for free women (in that case). This is for him among you who feareth to commit sin. But to have patience would be better for you. Allah is Forgiving, Merciful.

Allah would explain to you and guide you by the examples of those who were before you, and would turn to you in mercy. Allah is Knower, Wise. And Allah would turn to you in mercy; but those who follow vain desires would have you go tremendously astray. Allah would make the burden light for you, for man was created weak.

O ye who believe! Squander not your wealth among yourselves in vanity, except it be a trade by mutual consent, and kill not one another. Lo! Allah is ever Merciful unto you. Whoso doeth that through aggression and injustice, we shall cast him into Fire, and that is ever easy for Allah.

If ye avoid the great things which ye are forbidden, We will remit from you your evil deeds and make you enter at a NOBLE GATE.

And covet not the thing in which Allah hath made some of you excel others. Unto men a fortune from that which they have earned, and unto women a fortune from that which they have earned. Envy not one another but ask Allah of His bounty. Lo! Allah is ever Knower of all things.

And unto each We have appointed heirs of that which parents and near kindred leave; and as for those with whom your right hands have made a covenant, give them their due. Lo! Allah is ever Witness over all things.

Men are supporters of women because God has given some of them an advantage over others and because they spend of their wealth. Therefore righteous women are pure, devoutly obedient (unto Allah), the ones who guard the unseen of what God has kept safe. As for those from whom ye preceive disloyalty, ill-conduct and resistence first reprove and admionish them; and (if they do not amend) separate them (from yourselves) in beds; and (if they still do not improve) turn away from them, striking a temporary parting. But if they return to you seek not a way against them. Lo! Allah is ever High, Exalted, Great.[*]

---

[*] "Admonish them and abandon them in their sleeping place, then go away from them" "Then if they become cooperative with you, do not seek any way against them. Surely, Allah is Most High, Most Great" (Lahleh Bakhtiar & Muhammad Tahir-ul-Qadri translations).

And if ye fear a breach between them TWAIN (the man and wife), appoint an arbiter from his folk and an arbiter from her folk. If they desire amendment Allah will make them of one mind. Lo! Allah is ever Knower, Aware.

And serve Allah. Ascribe no thing as partner unto Him. Show kindness unto parents, and unto near kindred, and orphans, and the needy, and unto the neighbor who is of kin (unto you) and the neighbor who is not of kin, and the fellow-traveler and the wayfarer and (the slaves) whom your right hands possess. Lo! Allah loveth not such as are proud and boastful, who hoard their wealth and enjoin avarice on others, and hide that which Allah hath bestowed upon them of His bounty.

For disbelievers We prepare a shameful doom; and (also) those who spend their wealth in order to be seen of men, and believe not in Allah nor the Last Day. Whoso taketh Satan for a comrade, a bad comrade hath he. What have they (to fear) if they believe in Allah and the Last Day and spend (aright) of that which Allah hath bestowed upon them, when Allah is ever Aware of them (and all they do)?

Lo! Allah wrongeth not even of the weight of an ant; and if there is a good deed, He will double it and will give (the doer) from His presence an immense reward. But how (will it be with them) **when We bring of every people a witness**, and We bring Thee a witness against these? On that day those who disbelieved and disobeyed the messenger will wish that they were level with the ground, and they can hide no fact from Allah.

O ye who believe! Draw not near unto prayer **when ye are drunken**, till ye know that which ye utter, nor when ye are polluted, save when journeying upon the road, till ye have bathed. And if ye be ill, or on a journey, or one of you cometh from the closet, or ye have touched women, and ye find not water, then go to high clean soil and rub your faces and your hands (therewith). Lo! Allah is Benign, Forgiving.

Seest Thou not those unto whom a portion of the Scripture hath been given, how they purchase error, and seek to make you err from the right way? Allah knoweth best (who are) your enemies. Allah is sufficient as a Guardian, and Allah is sufficient as a Supporter.

Some of those who are Jews change words from their context and say: "We hear and disobey; hear Thou as one who heareth not" and "Listen to us!" distorting with their tongues and slandering religion. If they had said: "We hear and we obey: hear Thou, and look at us" it had been better for them, and more upright. But Allah hath cursed them for their disbelief, so they believe not, save a few.

O ye unto whom the Scripture hath been given! Believe in what We have revealed confirming that which ye possess, before We destroy countenances so as to confound them, or curse them as We cursed the Sabbath-breakers (of old time). The commandment of Allah is always executed.

Lo! Allah forgiveth not that a partner should be ascribed unto Him. He forgiveth (all) save that to whom He will. Whoso ascribeth partners to Allah, he hath indeed invented a tremendous sin. Hast thou not seen those who praise themselves for purity? Nay, Allah purifieth whom He will, and they will not be wronged even the hair upon a date- stone.

See, how they invent lies about Allah! That of itself is flagrant sin. Hast Thou not seen those unto whom a portion of the Scripture hath been given, how they believe in idols and false deities, and how they say of those (idolaters) who disbelieve: "These are more rightly guided than those who believe?" Those are they whom Allah hath cursed, and he whom Allah hath cursed, Thou wilt find for him no helper. Or have they even a share in the Sovereignty? Then in that case, they would not give humankind even the speck on a date-stone.

Or are they jealous of humankind because of that which Allah of His bounty hath bestowed upon them? For We bestowed upon **the House of Abraham** the Scripture and wisdom, and We bestowed on them a mighty Kingdom. And of them were (some) who believed therein and of them were (some) who turned away from it. Hell is sufficient for (their) burning.

Lo! Those who disbelieve Our Revelations, We shall expose them to the Fire. As often as their skins are consumed We shall exchange them for fresh skins that they may taste the torment. Lo! Allah is ever Mighty, Wise.

And as for those who believe and do good works, We shall make them enter Gardens underneath which rivers flow--to dwell therein for ever; there for them are pure companions--and We shall make them enter plenteous shade.

Lo! Allah commandeth you that ye restore deposits to their owners, and, if ye judge between mankind, that ye judge justly. Lo! Comely is this which Allah admonisheth you. Lo! Allah is ever Hearer, Seer.

O ye who believe! Obey Allah, and obey the messenger and those of you who are in authority; and if ye have a dispute concerning any matter, refer it to Allah and the messenger if ye are (in truth) believers in Allah and the Last Day. That is better and more seemly in the end.

Hast Thou not seen those who pretend that they believe in that which is revealed unto Thee and that which was revealed before Thee, how they would go for judgment (in their disputes) to false deities when they have been ordered to abjure them? Satan would mislead them far astray.

And when it is said unto them: "Come unto that which Allah hath revealed and unto the messenger," Thou seest the hypocrites turn from Thee with aversion. How would it be if a misfortune smote them because of that which their own hands have sent before (them)? Then would they come unto Thee, swearing by Allah that they were seeking naught but harmony and kindness. Those are they, the secrets of whose hearts Allah knoweth. So oppose them and admonish them, and address them in plain terms about their souls.

We sent no messenger save that he should be obeyed by Allah's leave. And if, when they had wronged themselves, they had but come unto thee and asked forgiveness of Allah, and asked forgiveness of the messenger, they would have found Allah Forgiving, Merciful.

But nay, by thy Lord, they will not believe (in truth) until they make Thee judge of what is in dispute between them and find within themselves no dislike of that which Thou decidest, and submit with full submission. And if We had decreed for them: "Lay down your lives or go forth from your dwellings," but few of them would have done it; though if they did what they are exhorted to do it would be better for them, and more strengthening; and then We should bestow upon them from Our Presence an immense reward, and should guide them unto a straight path. Whoso obeyeth Allah and the messenger, they are with those unto whom Allah hath shown favor, of the prophets and the saints and the martyrs and the righteous. The best of company are they! That is bounty from Allah, and Allah sufficeth as Knower.

O ye who believe! Take your precautions, then advance the proven ones, or advance all together. Lo! Among you there is he who loitereth; and if disaster overtook you, he would say: "Allah hath been gracious unto me since I was not present with them." And if a bounty from Allah befell you, he would surely cry, as if there had been no love between you and him: "Oh, would that I had been with them, then should I have achieved a great success!"

Let those fight in the way of Allah who sell the life of this world for the other. Whoso fighteth in the way of Allah, be he slain or be he victorious, on him We shall bestow a vast reward. How should ye not fight (greater and lesser *jihad*) for **the Cause of Allah** and of the feeble among men and of the women and the children who are crying: "Our Lord! Bring us forth from out this town of which the people are oppressors! Oh, give us from thy presence some protecting friend! Oh, give us from Thy presence some defender!"

Those who believe do battle for the Cause of Allah; and those who disbelieve do battle for the cause of idols. So fight the minions of the devil. Lo! the devil's strategy is ever weak. Hast Thou not seen those unto whom it was said: "Withhold your hands, establish worship and pay the poordue (*zakat*)," but when fighting was prescribed for them Behold! a party of them fear mankind even as their fear of Allah or with greater fear, and say: "Our Lord! Why hast Thou ordained *jihad* for us?" If only Thou wouldst give us respite yet a while!" Say: "The comfort of this world is scant; the Hereafter will be better for him who wardeth off; and ye will not be wronged the down upon a date-stone."

Wheresoever ye may be, death will overtake you, even though ye were in lofty towers. Yet if a happy thing befalleth them they say: "This is from Allah;" and if an evil thing befalleth them they say: "This is of Thy doing (O *AL-AMIN*)." Say: "All is from Allah." What is amiss with these people that they come not nigh to understand a happening? Whatever of good befalleth Thee (O man) it is from Allah, and whatever of ill befalleth Thee it is from Thyself. We have sent Thee as a messenger unto humankind and Allah is sufficient as Witness. Whoso obeyeth the messenger hath obeyed Allah, and whoso turneth away: We have not sent Thee as a warder over them.

And they say: "It is obedience;" but when they have gone forth from Thee a party of them spend the night in planning other than what Thou sayest. Allah recordeth what they plan by night. So oppose them and put thy trust in Allah. Allah is sufficient as Trustee.

Will they not then ponder on THIS QUR'AN? If it had been from other than Allah they would have found therein much incongruity. And if any tidings, whether of safety or fear, come unto them, they noise it abroad, whereas if they had referred it to the messenger and to such of them as are in authority, those among them who are able to think out the matter would have known it. If it had not been for the grace of Allah upon you and His mercy ye would have followed Satan, save a few.

So strive in the way of Allah Thou art not taxed (with the responsibility for anyone) except Thyself--and urge on the believers. Peradventure Allah will restrain the might of those who disbelieve. Allah is stronger in might and stronger in inflicting punishment. Whoso interveneth in a good cause will have the reward thereof, and whoso interveneth in an evil cause will bear the consequence thereof. Allah overseeth all things.

When ye are greeted with a greeting, greet ye with a better than it or return it. Lo! Allah taketh count of all things.

Allah! There is no God save Him. He gathereth you all unto a Day of Resurrection whereof there is no doubt. Who is more true in statement than Allah? What aileth you that ye are become two parties regarding the hypocrites, when Allah cast them back (to disbelief) because of what they earned? Seek ye to guide him whom Allah hath sent astray? He whom Allah sendeth astray, for him Thou canst not find a road.

They long that ye should disbelieve even as they disbelieve, that ye may be upon a level (with them). So choose not friends from them till they forsake their homes in the way of Allah; if they turn back as renegades or terrorists (to kill you) then take them and execute them (by rule by law) wherever ye find them, and choose no friend nor helper from among them, except those who seek refuge with a people between whom and you there is **a covenant**, or (those who) come unto you because **their hearts forbid them to make war on you or make war on their own folk**. Had Allah willed He could have given them power over you so that assuredly they would have fought you. So, if they hold aloof from you and wage not war against you and offer you peace, Allah alloweth you no way against them.

Ye will find others who desire that they should have security from you, and security from their own folk. So often as they are returned to hostility they are plunged therein. If they keep not aloof from you nor offer you peace nor hold their hands, then take them and execute them (by rule by law) wherever ye find them. Against such We have given you clear warrant.

It is not for a believer to kill a believer unless (it be) by mistake. He who hath killed a believer by mistake must set free a believing slave, and pay the blood-money to the family of the slain, unless they remit it as a charity. If he (the victim) be of a people hostile unto you, and he is a believer, then (the penance is) to set free a believing slave. And if he cometh of a folk between whom and you there is **a covenant**, then the blood-money must be paid unto his folk and (also) a believing slave must be set free. And whoso hath not the wherewithal must fast two consecutive months. A penance from Allah. Allah is Knower, Wise.

Whoso slayeth a believer of set purpose, his reward is hell for ever. Allah is wroth against him and He hath cursed him and prepared for him an awful doom.

O ye who believe! When ye go forth (to fight) in the way of Allah, be careful to discriminate, and say not unto one who offereth you peace: "Thou art not a believer," seeking the chance profits of this life (so that ye may despoil him). With Allah are plenteous spoils. Even thus (as he now is) were ye before; but Allah hath since then been gracious unto you. Therefore take care to discriminate. Allah is ever Informed of what ye do.

Those of the believers who sit still, other than those who have a (disabling) hurt, are not on an equality with those who strive in the way of Allah with their wealth and lives. Allah hath conferred on those who strive with their wealth and lives a rank above the sedentary. Unto each Allah hath promised good, but He hath bestowed on those who strive a great reward above the sedentary; degrees of rank from Him, and forgiveness and mercy. Allah is ever Forgiving, Merciful.

Lo! As for those whom the angels take (in death) while they wrong themselves, (the angels) will ask: "In what were ye engaged?" They will say: "We were oppressed in the land." (The angels) will say: "Was not Allah's earth spacious that ye could have migrated therein?" As for such, their habitation will be hell, an evil journey's end; except the feeble among men, and the women, and the children, who are unable to devise a plan and are not shown a way. **As for such, it may be that Allah will pardon them.** Allah is ever Clement, Forgiving.

Whoso migrateth for the **Cause of Allah** will find much refuge and abundance in the earth, and whoso forsaketh his home, a fugitive unto Allah and His messenger, and death overtaketh him, his reward is then incumbent on Allah. Allah is ever Forgiving, Merciful.

And when ye go forth in the land, it is no sin for you to curtail your worship if ye fear that those who disbelieve may attack you. In truth the disbelievers are an open enemy to you. And when Thou (O *AL-AMIN*) art among them and arrangest their worship for them, let only a party of them stand with Thee to worshi) and let them take their arms. Then when they have performed their prostrations let them fall to the rear and let another party come that hath not worshipped and let them worship with Thee, and let them take their precaution and their arms. Those who disbelieve long for you to neglect your arms and your baggage that they may attack you once for all. It is no sin for you to lay aside your arms, if rain impedeth you or ye are sick. But take your precaution. Lo! Allah prepareth for the disbelievers shameful punishment.

When ye have performed the act of worship, remember Allah, standing, sitting and reclining. And when ye are in safety, observe proper worship. **Worship at fixed times hath been enjoined on the believers.** Relent not in pursuit of the enemy. If ye are suffering, Lo! They suffer even as ye suffer and ye hope from Allah that for which they cannot hope. Allah is ever Knower, Wise.

Lo! We reveal unto Thee the Scripture with the truth, that Thou mayst judge between humankind by that which Allah showeth Thee. And be not Thou a pleader for the treacherous; And seek forgiveness of Allah. Lo! Allah is ever Forgiving, Merciful.

And plead not on behalf of people who deceive themselves. Lo! Allah loveth not one who is treacherous and sinful. They seek to hide from men and seek not to hide from Allah. He is with them when by night they hold discourse displeasing unto Him. Allah ever surroundeth what they do. Ho! Ye are they who pleaded for them in the life of the world. But who will plead with Allah for them on the Day of Resurrection, or who will then be their defender? Yet whoso doeth evil or wrongeth his own soul, then seeketh pardon of Allah, will find Allah Forgiving, Merciful. **Whoso committeth sin committeth it only against himself**. Allah is ever Knower, Wise.

And whoso committeth a delinquency or crime, then throweth (the blame) thereof upon the innocent, hath burdened himself with falsehood and a flagrant crime. But for the grace of Allah upon Thee, and His mercy, a party of them had resolved to mislead Thee, but they will mislead only themselves and they will hurt Thee not at all. Allah revealeth unto Thee the Scripture and wisdom, and teacheth Thee that which Thou knewest not. The grace of Allah toward Thee hath been infinite.

There is no good in much of their secret conferences save (in) him who enjoineth almsgiving and kindness and peace-making among the people. Whoso doeth that, seeking the good pleasure of Allah, We shall bestow on him a vast reward. And **whoso opposeth** the messenger **after the guidance (of Allah) hath been manifested** unto him, **and followeth other than the believer's way**, We appoint for him **that unto which he himself hath turned**[*], and expose him unto hell-- a hapless journey's end!

Lo! Allah pardoneth not that partners should be ascribed unto Him. He pardoneth all save that to whom He will. Whoso ascribeth partners unto Allah hath wandered far astray. They invoke in His stead only females; they pray to none else than Satan, a rebel Whom Allah cursed, and he said: "Surely I will take of Thy bondmen an appointed portion, and surely I will lead them astray, and surely **I will arouse desires in them**, and surely I will command them and they will cut the cattle's ears, and surely I will command them and they will change Allah's creation."

Whoso chooseth Satan for a patron instead of Allah is verily a loser and his loss is manifest. He promiseth them and stirreth up desires in them, and Satan promiseth them only to beguile. For such, their habitation will be hell, and they will find no refuge therefrom. But as for those who believe and do good works We shall bring them into Gardens underneath which rivers flow, wherein they will abide for ever. It is a promise from Allah in truth; and who can be more truthful than Allah in utterance?

It will not be in accordance with your desires, nor the desires of the People of the Scripture. He who doeth wrong will have the recompense thereof, and will not find against Allah any protecting friend or helper. And whoso doeth good works, whether of male or female, and he (or she) is a believer, such will enter paradise and they will not be wronged the dint in a date-stone.

Who is better in religion than he who surrendereth his purpose to Allah while doing good (to others) and followeth the tradition of Abraham, the upright? Allah Himself chose Abraham for friend. Unto Allah belongeth whatsoever is in the heavens and whatsoever is in the earth. Allah ever surroundeth all things.

They consult thee concerning women. Say: "Allah giveth you decree concerning them, and the Scripture which hath been recited unto you (giveth decree), concerning female orphans and those

---

[*] Personal hell.

unto whom ye give not that which is ordained for them though ye desire to marry them, and (concerning) the weak among children, and that ye should deal justly with orphans. Whatever good ye do, Lo! Allah is ever Aware of it."

If a woman feareth ill treatment from her husband, or desertion, it is no sin for them TWAIN if they make terms of peace between themselves. Peace is better. But greed hath been made present in the minds (of men). If ye do good and keep from evil, Lo! Allah is ever Informed of what ye do. **Ye will not be able to deal equally** between your wives, however much ye wish (to do so). But turn not altogether away (from one), leaving her as in suspense. If ye do good and keep from evil, Lo! Allah is ever Forgiving, Merciful. But if they separate, Allah will compensate each out of His abundance. Allah is ever All-Embracing, All-Knowing. Unto Allah belongeth whatsoever is in the heavens and whatsoever is in the earth.

And We charged those who received the Scripture before you, and We charge you, that ye keep your duty toward Allah. And if ye disbelieve, Lo! Unto Allah belongeth whatsoever is in the heavens and whatsoever is in the earth, and Allah is ever Absolute, Owner of Praise. Unto Allah belongeth whatsoever is in the heavens and whatsoever is in the earth. And Allah is sufficient as Defender. If He will, He can remove you, O people, and produce others (in your stead). Allah is Able to do that. Whoso desireth the reward of the world, (let him know that) with Allah is the reward of the world and the Hereafter. Allah is ever Hearer, Seer.

O ye who believe! Be ye staunch in justice, witnesses for Allah, even though it be against yourselves or (your) parents or (your) kindred, whether (the case be of) a rich man or a poor man, for Allah is nearer unto both (them ye are). So follow not passion lest ye lapse (from truth) and if ye lapse or fall away, then Lo! Allah is ever Informed of what ye do.

O ye who believe! Believe in Allah and His messenger and the Scripture which He hath revealed unto His messenger, and the Scripture which He revealed aforetime. Whoso disbelieveth in Allah and His angels and His scriptures and His messengers and the Last Day, he verily hath wandered far astray.

Lo! Those who believe, then disbelieve and then again believe, then disbelieve, and then increase in disbelief, Allah will never pardon them, nor will He guide them unto a way. Bear unto the hypocrites the tidings that for them there is a painful doom; Those who chose disbelievers for their friends instead of believers! Do they look for power at their hands? Lo! All power appertaineth to Allah.

He hath already revealed unto you in the Scripture that, when ye hear the Revelations of Allah rejected and derided, ye sit not with them (who disbelieve and mock) until they engage in some other conversation. Lo! in that case (if ye stayed) ye would be like unto them. Lo! Allah will gather hypocrites and disbelievers, all together, into hell; Those who wait upon occasion in regard to you and, if a victory cometh unto you from Allah, say: "Are we not with you?" and if the disbelievers meet with a success say: "Had we not the mastery of you, and did we not protect you from the believers?"--Allah will judge between you at the Day of Resurrection, and Allah will not give the disbelievers any way (of success) against the believers.

Lo! The hypocrites seek to beguile Allah, but it is He Who beguileth them. When they stand up to worship they perform it **languidly and to be seen of men**, and are mindful of Allah but little; Swaying between this and that, belonging neither to these nor to those. He whom Allah causeth to go astray, Thou wilt not find a way for him: "O ye who believe! Choose not disbelievers for your friends in place of believers." Would ye give Allah a clear warrant against you?

Lo! The hypocrites (will be) in the lowest deep of the Fire, and Thou wilt find no helper for them; save those who repent and amend and hold fast to Allah and make their religion PURE for Allah only. Those are with the believers. And Allah will bestow on the believers an immense reward. What concern hath Allah for your punishment if ye are thankful for His mercies and believe in Him? Allah was ever Responsive, Aware. Allah loveth not the utterance of harsh speech save by one who hath been wronged. Allah is ever Hearer, Knower. If ye do good openly or keep it secret, or forgive evil, Lo! Allah is ever Forgiving, Powerful.

Lo! Those who disbelieve in Allah and His messengers, and seek to make distinction between Allah and His messengers, and say: "We believe in some and disbelieve in others, and seek to choose a way in between;" such are disbelievers in truth; and for disbelievers We prepare a shameful doom. But those who believe in Allah and His messengers and **make no distinction between any of them**, unto them Allah will give their wages; and Allah was ever Forgiving, Merciful.

The people of the Scripture ask of Thee that thou shouldst cause an **actual Book to descend upon them from heaven**. They asked a greater thing of *MOSES* aforetime, for they said: "Show us Allah plainly." The storm of lightning seized them for their wickedness. Then even after that they chose the calf after THIS RIGHTEOUS BOOK had come unto them. And We forgave them that! And We bestowed on *MOSES* evident authority. And We caused the Mount to tower above them at the taking of their **Covenant**: and We bade them: "Enter the GATE, *prostrate!*" and We bode them: "Transgress not the Sabbath!" and We took from them **a Firm Covenant**.

Then because of their breaking of their Covenant, and their disbelieving in the Revelations of Allah, and their slaying of the prophets wrongfully, and their saying: "Our hearts are hardened"-- Nay, but Allah set a seal upon them for their disbelief, so that they believe not save a few--and because of their disbelief and of their speaking against Miriam a tremendous calumny; and because of their saying: "We slew the Messiah, *JESUS* son of Miriam, Allah's messenger"--they slew him not nor crucified him, but it appeared so unto them; and Lo! Those who disagree concerning it are in doubt thereof; they have no knowledge thereof save pursuit of a conjecture; they slew him not for certain. But Allah took him up unto Himself. Allah was ever Mighty, Wise.

There is not one of the People of the Scripture but will believe in him before his death, and on the Day of Resurrection he will be a witness against them--because of the wrongdoing of the clergy of the Jews We forbade them good things which were before made lawful unto them, and because of their much hindering from Allah's way, and of their taking usury when they were forbidden it, and of their devouring people's wealth by false pretenses, We have prepared for those of them who disbelieve a painful doom. But **those of them who are firm in knowledge** and the believers believe in that which is revealed unto Thee, and that which was revealed before

Thee, especially the diligent in prayer and those who pay the poor-due (*zakat*), the believers in Allah and the Last Day. Upon these We shall bestow immense reward.

Lo! We inspire Thee as We inspired Noah and the prophets after him, as We inspired Abraham and Ishmael and Isaac and Jacob and the tribes, and *JESUS* and Job and Jonah and Aaron and Solomon, and as We imparted unto David the Psalms;[*] and messengers We have mentioned unto Thee before and messengers We have not mentioned unto Thee; and Allah spake directly unto *MOSES*; Messengers of good cheer and of warning, in order that humankind might have no argument against Allah after the messengers. Allah was ever Mighty, Wise.

But Allah Himself testifieth concerning that which He hath revealeth unto Thee; in His knowledge hath He revealed it; and the angels also testify. And Allah is sufficient Witness. Lo! Those who disbelieve and hinder others from the way of Allah, they verily have wandered far astray. Lo! Those who disbelieve and deal in wrong, Allah will never forgive them, neither will He guide them unto a road, except the road of hell, wherein they will abide for ever. And that is ever easy for Allah.

O Humankind! The messenger hath come unto you with the Truth from your Lord. Therefore believe; it is better for you. But if ye disbelieve, still, Lo! Unto Allah belongeth whatsoever is in the heavens and the earth. Allah is ever Knower, Wise.

O People of the Scripture! Do not exaggerate in your religion nor utter aught concerning Allah save the truth. The Messiah, *JESUS* son of Miriam, was only a messenger of Allah, and His word which He conveyed unto Miriam, and a spirit from Him. So believe in Allah and His messengers, and say not "Three"--Cease! It is better for you!--Allah is only One God.[†] Far is it removed from His Transcendent Majesty that He should have a Son. His is all that is in the heavens and all that is in the earth. And Allah is sufficient as Defender.

The Messiah will never scorn to be a slave unto Allah, nor will the favored angels. Whoso scorneth His service and is proud, all such will He assemble unto Him; Then, as for those who believed and did good works, unto them will He pay their wages in full, adding unto them of His bounty; and as for those who were scornful and proud, them will He punish with a painful doom. And they will not find for them, against Allah, any protecting friend or helper.

O Humankind! Now hath a proof from your Lord come unto you, and We have sent down unto you a clear light (ABHA); As for those who believe in Allah, and hold fast unto Him, them He will cause to enter into His mercy and grace, and will guide them unto Him by a straight road.

---

[*]Psalm 89:1-4; 26-29; 35-37 KJV: "I will sing of the mercies of the LORD for ever: with my mouth will I make known Thy faithfulness to all generations. For I have said, Mercy shall be built up for ever: Thy faithfulness shalt Thou establish in the very heavens. **I have made a Covenant with my chosen, I have sworn unto David my servant, Thy seed will I establish for ever, and build up Thy throne to all generations. Selah**... He shall cry unto me, Thou art my Father, my God, and the Rock of my Salvation. Also I will make him my firstborn, higher than the kings of the earth. My mercy will I keep for him for evermore, and **my covenant shall stand fast with him**. His seed also will I make to endure for ever, and his throne as the days of heaven... Once have I sworn by my holiness that **I will not lie unto David**. His seed shall endure for ever, and his **throne** as the sun before me. **It shall be established for ever** as the moon, and as a faithful witness in heaven. Selah."
[†] "Hear, O Israel: The LORD our God, the LORD is ONE" (Deut. 6:4 NIV).

They ask Thee for a pronouncement. Say: "Allah hath pronounced for you concerning distant kindred." If a man die childless and he have a sister, hers is half the heritage, and he would have inherited from her had she died childless. And if there be two sisters, then theirs are two-thirds of the heritage, and if they be brethren, men and women, unto the male is the equivalent of the share of two females. Allah expoundeth unto you, so that ye err not. Allah is Knower of all things.

80. Bism'illah Ar-Rahman Ar-Rahim! at-Talaq: THE DIVORCE.

O Prophet! When ye put away women, put them away for their (legal) period and reckon the period, and keep your duty to Allah, your Lord. Expel them not from their houses nor let them go forth unless they commit open immorality. Such are the limits (imposed by) Allah; and whoso transgresseth Allah's limits, he verily wrongeth his soul. Thou knowest not: it may be that Allah will afterward bring some new thing to pass.

Then, when they have reached their term, take them back **in kindness** or part from them **in kindness**, and call to witness two just men among you, and keep your testimony upright for Allah. Whoso believeth in Allah and the Last Day is exhorted to act thus. And whosoever keepeth his duty to Allah, Allah will appoint a way out for him, and will provide for him from (a quarter) whence he hath no expectation. And whosoever putteth his trust in Allah, He will suffice him. Lo! Allah bringeth His command to pass. Allah hath set a measure for all things.

And for such of your women as despair of menstruation, if ye doubt, their period (of waiting) shall be three months, along with those who have it not. And for those with child, their period shall be till they bring forth their burden. And whosoever keepeth his duty to Allah, He maketh his course easy for him. That is the commandment of Allah which He revealeth unto you. And whoso keepeth his duty to Allah, He will remit from him his evil deeds and magnify reward for him.

Lodge them where ye dwell, according to your wealth, and **harass them not** so as to straiten life for them. And if they are with child, then spend for them till they bring forth their burden. Then, if they give suck for you, give them their due payment and consult together in kindness; but if ye make difficulties for one another, then let some other woman give suck for him (the father of the child).

Let him who hath abundance spend of his abundance, and he whose provision is measured, let him spend of that which Allah hath given him. Allah asketh naught of any soul save that which He hath given it. Allah will vouchsafe, after hardship, ease.

And how many a community revolted against the ordinance of its Lord and His messengers, and We called it to a stern account and punished it with dire punishment, so that it tasted the ill-effects of its conduct, and the consequence of its conduct was loss. Allah hath prepared for them stern punishment; so keep your duty to Allah, O men of understanding! O ye who believe! Now Allah hath sent down unto you THE REMINDER, a messenger reciting unto you the Revelations of Allah made plain, that He may bring forth those who believe and do good works from darkness unto light. And whosoever believeth in Allah and doeth right, He will bring him into

Gardens underneath which rivers flow, therein to abide for ever. Allah hath made good provision for him.

Allah it is who hath created **seven heavens**, and of the earth the like thereof. The commandment cometh down among them slowly, that ye may know that Allah is Able to do all things, and that Allah surroundeth all things in knowledge.

XIX. JUZ'UN SIPARA DICIANNOVA:

81. Bism'illah Ar-Rahman Ar-Rahim! al-Ikhlas va al-Baqarah!!: THE UNITY.

Say: "He alone is Allah, the One!
Allah, the eternally Besought of all!
He begetteth not nor was begotten.
And there is none comparable unto Him."

The Originator of the heavens and the earth! When He decreeth a thing, He saith unto it only: "Be! and it is."

And those who have no knowledge say: "Why doth not Allah speak unto us, or some sign come unto us?" Even thus, as they now speak, spake those (who were) before them. Their hearts are all alike. We have made clear the Revelations for people who are sure.

Lo! We have sent Thee with the truth, a bringer of glad tidings and a warner. And Thou wilt not be asked about the owners of hell-fire. And the Jews will not be pleased with Thee, nor will the Christians, till Thou follow their creed. Say: "Lo! The guidance of Allah Himself is Guidance." And if Thou shouldst follow their desires after the knowledge which hath come unto Thee, then wouldst Thou have from Allah no protecting guardian nor helper. Those unto whom We have given the Scripture, who read it with the right reading, those believe in it. And whoso disbelieveth in it, those are they who are the losers.

O Children of Israel! Remember My favor wherewith I favored you and how I preferred you to all creatures. And guard yourselves against a day when no soul will in aught avail another, nor will compensation be accepted from it, nor will intercession be of use to it; nor will they be helped.

And when his Lord tried Abraham with His commands, and he fulfilled them, He said: "Lo! I have appointed Thee a leader for humankind." Abraham said: "And of my offspring will there be leaders?" He said: "My covenant includeth not wrong-doers."

And when We made the House A RESORT for humankind and Sanctuary, saying: "Take as your place of worship the place where Abraham stood to pray." And We imposed a duty upon Abraham and Ishmael, saying: "Purify My house for those who go around and those who meditate therein and those who bow down and prostrate themselves in adoration."

194

And when Abraham prayed: "My Lord! Make this a region of security and bestow upon its people fruits, such of them as believe in Allah and the Last Day," He answered: "As for him who disbelieveth, I shall leave him in contentment for a while, then I shall compel him to the doom of Fire--a hapless journey's end!"

And when Abraham and Ishmael were raising the foundations of the House, Abraham prayed: "Our Lord! Accept from us this duty. Lo! Thou, only Thou, art the Hearer, the Knower. Our Lord! And make us submissive unto Thee and of our seed a nation submissive unto Thee, and show us our ways of worship, and relent toward us. Lo! Thou, only Thou, art the Relenting, the Merciful. Our Lord! And raise up in their midst **a messenger from among them** who shall recite unto them Thy revelations, and shall instruct them in the Scripture and in Wisdom (*hikmat/chokhmah*) and **shall make them grow**. Lo! Thou, only Thou, art the Mighty, Wise!"

And who forsaketh the religion of Abraham save him who befooleth himself? Verily We chose him in the world, and Lo! In the Hereafter he is among the righteous. When his Lord said unto him: "Surrender!" he said: "I have surrendered to the Lord of the Worlds."

The same did Abraham enjoin upon his sons, and also Jacob, saying: "O my Sons! Lo! Allah hath chosen for you the true religion; therefore die not save as men who have surrendered unto Him." Or were ye present when death came to Jacob, when he said unto his Sons: "What will ye worship after me?" They said: "We shall worship Thy God, the God of Thy fathers, Abraham and Ishmael and Isaac, One God, and unto Him we have surrendered."

Those are a people who have passed on. Theirs is that which they earned, and yours is that which ye earn. And ye will not be asked of what they used to do. And they say: "Be Jews or Christians, then ye will be rightly guided." Say: "Nay, but we follow the religion of Abraham, the upright, and he was not of the idolaters."

Say: "We believe in Allah and that which is revealed unto us and that which was revealed unto Abraham, and Ishmael, and Isaac, and Jacob, and the tribes, and that which *MOSES* and *JESUS* received, and that which the prophets received from their Lord. We make no distinction between any of them, and unto Him we have surrendered." And if they believe in the like of that which ye believe, then are they rightly guided. But if they turn away, then are they in schism, and Allah will suffice Thee (for defense) against them. He is the Hearer, the Knower.

We take our color from Allah, and who is better than Allah at coloring. We are His worshippers. Say (unto the People of the Scripture): "Dispute ye with us concerning Allah when He is our Lord and your Lord? Ours are our works and yours your works. We look to Him alone. Or say ye that Abraham, and Ishmael, and Isaac, and Jacob, and the tribes were Jews or Christians?" Say: "Do ye know best, or doth Allah?" And who is more unjust than he who hideth a testimony which he hath received from Allah? Allah is not unaware of what ye do. Those are a people who have passed on; theirs is that which they earned and yours that which ye earn. And ye will not be asked of what they used to do.

The foolish of the people will say: "What hath turned them from *__the qiblih__* which they formerly observed? Say: "Unto Allah belong the East and the West. He guideth whom He will unto a straight path." **Thus We have appointed you a middle nation**, that ye may be witnesses against mankind, and that the messenger may be a witness against you. And We appointed *the qiblih* which ye formerly observed **only that We might know him who followeth the messenger, from him who turneth on his heels**. In truth it was a hard (test) save for those whom Allah guided. But it was not Allah's purpose that your faith should be in vain, for Allah is Full of Pity, Merciful toward mankind.

We have seen the turning of Thy face to heaven. And now verily We shall make Thee turn (in prayer) toward *a qiblih* which is dear to Thee. So turn thy face toward the **Inviolable Place of Worship**, and ye, wheresoever ye may be, turn your faces (when ye pray) toward it. Lo! Those who have received the Scripture know that is the Truth from their Lord. And Allah is not unaware of what they do.

And even if Thou broughtest unto those who have received the Scripture all kinds of portents, they would not follow *thy qiblih*, nor canst thou be a follower of *their qiblih*; nor are some of them followers of *the qiblah* of others. And if Thou shouldst follow their desires after the knowledge which hath come unto Thee, then surely wert Thou of the evil-doers.

Those unto whom We gave the Scripture recognize this Revelation as they recognize their sons. But Lo! A party of them knowingly conceal the truth. It is the Truth from Thy Lord, so be not Thou of those who waver. And each one hath a goal toward which he turneth; so vie with one another in good works. **Wheresoever ye may be, Allah will bring you all together**. Lo! Allah is Able to do all things. And whencesoever Thou comest forth for prayer turn thy face toward the **Inviolable Place of Worship**. Lo! It is the Truth from thy Lord. Allah is not unaware of what ye do.

Whencesoever Thou comest forth turn Thy face toward the **Inviolable Place of Worship**; and wheresoever ye may be turn your faces toward it when ye pray so that men may have no argument against you, save such of them as do injustice--Fear them not, but fear Me!--and so that I may complete My grace upon you, and that ye may be guided. Even as We have sent unto you a messenger from among you, who reciteth unto you Our Revelations and **causeth you to grow**, and teacheth you the Scripture and Wisdom (*hikmat/chokhmah*), and teacheth you that which ye knew not.

Therefore remember Me, I will remember you. Give thanks to Me, and reject not Me. O ye who believe! Seek help in steadfastness and prayer. Lo! Allah is with the steadfast. **And call not those who are slain in the way of Allah "dead." Nay, they are living**, only ye perceive not. And surely We shall try you with something of fear and hunger, and loss of wealth and lives and crops; but give glad tidings to the steadfast, who say, when a misfortune striketh them: "Lo! We are Allah's" and "Lo! unto Him we are returning." Such are they on whom are blessings from their Lord, and mercy. Such are the rightly guided.

Lo! The mountains As-Safa and Al-Marwah are among the indications of Allah. It is therefore no sin for him who is on pilgrimage to the HOUSE or visiteth it, to go around them (as the pagan custom is). And he who doeth good of his own accord, for him Lo! Allah is Responsive, Aware.

Lo! Those who hide the proofs and the guidance which We revealed, after We had made it clear to mankind in the Scripture: such are accursed of Allah and accursed of those who have the power to curse. Except those who repent and amend and make manifest the truth. These it is toward whom I relent. I am the Relenting, the Merciful.

Lo! Those who disbelieve, and die while they are disbelievers; on them is the curse of Allah and of angels and of men combined. They ever dwell therein. The doom will not be lightened for them, neither will they be reprieved.
Your God is One God; there is no God save Him, the Beneficent, the Merciful!

Lo! In the creation of the heavens and the earth, and the difference of night and day, and the ships which run upon the sea with that which is of use to men, and the water which Allah sendeth down from the sky, thereby reviving the earth after its death, and dispersing all kinds of beasts therein, and (in) the ordinance of the winds, and the clouds obedient between heaven and earth: are signs (of Allah's Sovereignty) for people who have sense.

Yet of mankind are some who take unto themselves (objects of worship which they set as) rivals to Allah, loving them with a love like (that which is the due) of Allah (only)--those who believe are stauncher in their love for Allah--Oh, that those who do evil had but known, (on the day) when they behold the doom, that power belongeth wholly to Allah, and that Allah is severe in punishment!

On the day when those who were followed disown those who followed (them), and they behold the doom, and all their aims collapse with them. And those who were but followers will say: "If a return were possible for us, we would disown them even as they have disowned us." Thus will Allah show them their own deeds as anguish for them, and they will not emerge from the Fire.

O Humankind! Eat of that which is lawful and wholesome in the earth, and follow not the footsteps of the devil. Lo! he is an open enemy for you. He enjoineth upon you only the evil and the foul, and that ye should tell concerning Allah that which ye know not. And when it is said unto them: "Follow that which Allah hath revealed," they say: "We follow that wherein we found our fathers." What! Even though their fathers were **wholly unintelligent** and had **no guidance**? The likeness of those who disbelieve (in relation to the messenger) is as the likeness of one who calleth unto that which heareth naught except a shout and cry. Deaf, dumb, blind, therefore they have no sense.

O ye who believe! Eat of the good things wherewith We have provided you, and render thanks to Allah if it is (indeed) He Whom ye worship. He hath forbidden you only carrion, and blood, and swineflesh, and that which hath been immolated to (the name of) any other than Allah. But he who is driven by necessity, neither craving nor transgressing, it is no sin for him. Lo! Allah is Forgiving, Merciful.

Lo! Those who hide aught of the Scripture which Allah hath revealed and purchase a small gain therewith, they eat into their bellies nothing else than fire. Allah will not speak to them on the Day of Resurrection, nor will He make them grow. Theirs will be a painful doom. Those are they who purchase error at the price of guidance, and torment at the price of pardon. How constant are they in their strife to reach the Fire!

That is because Allah hath revealed the Scripture with the truth. Lo! Those who find (a cause of) disagreement in the Scripture are in open schism. It is not righteousness that ye turn your faces to the East and the West; but righteous is he who believeth in Allah and the Last Day and the angels and the Scripture and the prophets; and giveth wealth, for love of Him, to kinsfolk and to orphans and the needy and the wayfarer and to those who ask, and to set slaves free; and observeth proper worship and payeth the poor-due (*zakat*). And those who keep their treaty when they make one, and the patient in tribulation and adversity and time of stress. Such are they who are sincere. Such are the God-fearing.

O ye who believe! Retaliation is prescribed for you in the matter of the murdered; the freeman for the freeman, and the slave for the slave, and the female for the female. And for him who is forgiven somewhat by his (injured) brother, prosecution according to usage and payment unto him in kindness. This is an alleviation and a mercy from your Lord. He who transgresseth after this will have a painful doom.

And there is life for you in retaliation, O men of understanding, that ye may ward off evil. It is prescribed for you, when death approacheth one of you, if he leave wealth, that he bequeath unto parents and near relatives in kindness. This is a duty for all those who ward off. And whoso changeth THE WILL after he hath heard it--the sin thereof is only upon those who change it. Lo! Allah is Hearer, Knower. But he who feareth from a testator some unjust or sinful clause, and maketh peace between the parties, (it shall be) no sin for him. Lo! Allah is Forgiving, Merciful.

O ye who believe! **Fasting is prescribed for you**, even as it was prescribed for those before you, that ye may ward off; Fast a certain number of days; and for him who is sick among you, or on a journey, the same number of other days; and for those who can afford it there is a ransom: the feeding of a man in need--but whoso doeth good of his own accord, it is better for him: and that ye fast is better for you if ye did but know!

The month of Ramadan in which was revealed THIS QUR'AN, a guidance for mankind, and THIS RIGHTEOUS BOOK of Guidance, and the GOLDEN CRITERIA. And whosoever of you is present, let him fast the month, and whosoever of you is sick or on a journey, (let him fast the same) number of other days. Allah desireth for you ease; He desireth not hardship for you; and (He desireth) that ye should complete the period, and that ye should magnify Allah for having guided you, and that peradventure ye may be thankful.

And when My servants question Thee concerning Me, then surely I am nigh. I answer the prayer of the suppliant when he crieth unto Me. So let them hear My call and let them trust in Me, in order that they may be led aright. It is made lawful for you to go in unto your wives on the night of the fast. **They are raiment for you and ye are raiment for them**. Allah is Aware that ye were deceiving yourselves in this respect and He hath turned in mercy toward you and relieved you**. So hold intercourse with them** and seek that which Allah hath ordained for you, and eat and drink until the white thread becometh distinct to you from the black thread of the dawn. Then strictly observe the fast till nightfall and touch them not, but be at your devotions in the mosques. These are the limits imposed by Allah, so approach them not. Thus Allah expoundeth His Revelation to mankind that they may ward off.

And eat not up your property among yourselves in vanity, nor seek by it to gain the hearing of the judges that ye may knowingly devour a portion of the property of others wrongfully. They ask Thee, of new moons, say: "They are fixed seasons for mankind and for the pilgrimage." It is not righteousness that ye go to houses by the backs thereof (as do the idolaters at certain seasons), but the righteous man is he who wardeth off. So go to Houses by the GATES thereof, and observe your duty to Allah, that ye may be successful.
Fight in the way of Allah against those (terrorists) who fight against you, but begin not hostilities. Lo! Allah loveth not aggressors. And execute them (the terrorists by rule of law) wherever ye find them, and drive them out of the places whence they drove you out, for persecution is worse than slaughter. And fight not with them at the **Inviolable Place of Worship** until they **first attack you** there, but if they attack you (there) then slay them. Such is the reward of disbelievers. But if they desist, then lo! Allah is Forgiving, Merciful. And fight them until persecution is no more, and religion is for Allah. But if they desist, then let there be no hostility except against wrong-doers.

The forbidden month for the forbidden month, and forbidden things in retaliation. And one who attacketh you, respond to him with proportional force as he attacked you. Observe your duty to Allah, and know that Allah is with those who ward off (evil). Spend your wealth for the cause of Allah, and be not cast by your own hands to ruin; and do good. Lo! Allah loveth the beneficent.

Perform the pilgrimage and the visit for Allah. And if ye are prevented, then send such gifts as can be obtained with ease, and shave not your heads until the gifts have reached their destination. And whoever among you is sick or hath an ailment of the head must pay a ransom of fasting or almsgiving or offering. And if ye are in safety, then whosoever contenteth himself with the visit for the pilgrimage (shall give) such gifts as can be had with ease. And whosoever cannot find (such gifts), then a fast of three days while on the pilgrimage, and of seven when ye have returned; that is, ten in all. That is for him whoso folk are not present at the **Inviolable Place of Worship**. Observe your duty to Allah, and know that Allah is severe in punishment.

The pilgrimage is in the well-known months, and whoever is minded to perform the pilgrimage therein there is no forbidden acts nor abuse nor angry conversation on the pilgrimage. And whatsoever good ye do Allah knoweth it. So make provision for yourselves; for the best provision is to ward off evil. Therefore keep your duty unto Me, O men of understanding. It is no sin for you that ye seek the bounty of your Lord (by trading). But, when ye press on in the multitude from 'Arafat, remember Allah by the sacred monument. Remember Him as He hath guided you, although before ye were of those astray. Then hasten onward from the place whence the multitude hasteneth onward, and ask forgiveness of Allah. Lo! Allah is Forgiving, Merciful.

And when ye have completed your devotions, then remember Allah as ye remember your fathers or with a more lively remembrance. But of mankind is he who saith: "Our Lord! Give unto us in the world," and he hath no portion in the Hereafter. And of them (also) is he who saith: "Our Lord! Give unto us in the world that which is good and in the Hereafter that which is good, and guard us from the doom of Fire." For them there is in store a goodly portion out of that which they have earned. Allah is swift at reckoning.

Remember Allah through the appointed days. Then whoso hasteneth (his departure) by two days, it is no sin for him, and whoso delayeth, it is no sin for him; that is for him who wardeth off (evil). Be careful of your duty to Allah, and know that unto Him ye will be gathered.

And of mankind there is he whoso conversation on the life of this world pleaseth Thee, and he calleth Allah to witness as to that which is in his heart; yet he is the most rigid of opponents. And when he turneth away his effort in the land is to make mischief therein and to destroy the crops and the cattle; and Allah loveth not mischief. And when it is said unto him: "Be careful of Thy duty to Allah, pride taketh him to sin." Hell will settle his account, an evil resting-place. And of mankind is he who would sell himself, seeking the pleasure of Allah; and Allah hath compassion on (His) bondmen.

O ye who believe! Come, all of you, into submission unto Him; and follow not the footsteps of the devil. Lo! he is an open enemy for you. And if ye slide back after THIS RIGHTEOUS BOOK has come unto you, then know that Allah is Mighty, Wise.

Wait they for naught else than that Allah should come unto them in the shadows of the clouds with the angels? Then the case would be already judged. All cases go back to Allah for judgment.

Ask of the Children of Israel how many a clear Revelation We gave them! He who altereth the grace of Allah after it hath come unto him for him, Lo! Allah is severe in punishment.

Beautified is the life of the world for those who disbelieve; they make a jest of the believers. But those who keep their duty to Allah will be above them on the Day of Resurrection. Allah giveth without stint to whom He will.

Humankind is one community, and Allah sent (unto them) prophets as bearers of good tidings and as warners, and revealed therewith the Scripture with the truth that it might judge between mankind concerning that wherein they differed. And only those unto whom (the Scripture) was given differed concerning it, after THIS RIGHTEOUS BOOK had come unto them, through hatred one of another. And Allah by His Will guided those who believe unto the truth of that concerning which they differed. Allah guideth whom He will unto a straight path.

Or think ye that ye will enter paradise while yet there hath not come unto you the like of (that which came to) those who passed away before you? Affliction and adversity befell them, they were shaken as with earthquake, till the messenger (of Allah) and those who believed along with him said: "When cometh Allah's help?" Now surely Allah's help is nigh.

They ask Thee, what they shall spend. Say: "That which ye spend for good (must go) to parents and near kindred and orphans and the needy and the wayfarer. And whatsoever good ye do, Lo! Allah is Aware of it."

Jihad (the greater and the lesser) is ordained for you, though it is hateful unto you; but it may happen that ye hate a thing which is good for you, and it may happen that ye love a thing which is bad for you. Allah knoweth, ye know not.

They question Thee with regard to warfare (the lesser *jihad*) in the sacred month. Say: "Warfare therein is a great (transgression), but to turn souls from the way of Allah, and to disbelieve in Him and in the **Inviolable Place of Worship**, and to expel His people thence, is a greater with Allah;" for persecution is worse than killing. And they will not cease from fighting against you till they have made you renegades from your religion, if they can. And whoso becometh a renegade and dieth in his disbelief: such are they whose works have fallen both in the world and the Hereafter. Such are rightful owners of the Fire: they will abide therein.

Lo! Those who believe, and those who emigrate (to escape the persecution) and strive in the way of Allah, these have hope of Allah's mercy. Allah is Forgiving, Merciful.

They question thee about strong drink and games of chance. Say: "In both is great harm, and some utility for people; but the harm of them is greater than their usefulness." And they ask Thee what they ought to spend. Say: "That which is superfluous." Thus Allah maketh plain to you His Revelations, that haply ye may reflect upon the world and the Hereafter.

And they question Thee concerning orphans. Say: "To improve their lot is best. And if ye mingle your affairs with theirs, then (they are) your brothers." Allah knoweth him who spoileth from him who improveth. Had Allah willed He could have overburdened you. Allah is Mighty, Wise.

Wed not idolatresses **till they believe**; for Lo! A believing bondwoman is better than an idolatress though she please you; and give not your daughters in marriage to idolaters till they believe, for Lo! A believing slave is better than an idolater though he please you. These invite unto the Fire, and Allah inviteth unto the Garden, and unto forgiveness by His grace, and expoundeth His revelations to humankind that haply they may remember.

They question Thee concerning menstruation. Say: "It is a sacrament (Ar. *adha*: a sacrifice), so let women alone at such times and go not in unto them till they are cleansed. And when they have purified themselves, then go in unto them as Allah hath enjoined upon you. Truly Allah loveth those who turn unto Him, and loveth those who have a care for cleanness. Your women are a tilth for you (to cultivate) so go to your tilth as ye will, and send (good deeds) before you for your souls, and fear Allah, and know that ye will (one day) meet Him. Give glad tidings to believers.

And make not Allah, by your oaths, a hindrance to your being righteous and observing your duty unto Him and making peace among mankind. Allah is Hearer, Knower. Allah will not take you to task for that which is unintentional in your oaths. But He will take you to task for that which your hearts have garnered. Allah is Forgiving, Clement.

Those who forswear their wives must wait four months; then, if they change their mind, lo! Allah is Forgiving, Merciful. And if they decide upon divorce (let them remember that) Allah is Hearer, Knower.

Women who are divorced shall wait, keeping themselves apart, three (monthly) courses. And it is not lawful for them that they should conceal that which Allah hath created in their wombs if they are believers in Allah and the Last Day. And their husbands would **do better to take them back** in that case if they desire a reconciliation. **And they (women) have rights similar to those (of men) over them in kindness**, even though men had a degree of worldly advantage above them. Allah is Mighty, Wise.

Divorce must be pronounced twice and then (a woman) must be retained in honor or **released in kindness.** And it is not lawful for you that ye take from women aught of that which ye have given them; except (in the case) when both fear that they may not be able to keep within the limits (imposed by) Allah. And if ye fear that they may not be able to keep the limits of Allah, in that case there is no blame on them for what she gives up to become free thereby. These are the limits (imposed by) Allah. Transgress them not. For whoso transgresseth Allah's limits: such are wrong-doers.

And if he hath divorced her (the third time), **then she is not lawful unto him thereafter until she hath wedded another husband.** Then if he (the other husband) divorce her **it is no sin for both of them that they come together again if they consider that they are able to observe the limits of Allah.** These are the limits of Allah. He manifesteth them for people who have knowledge.

When ye have divorced women, and they have reached their term, then retain them in kindness or release them in kindness. Retain them not to their hurt so that ye transgress (the limits). He who doeth that **hath wronged his soul**. Make not the Revelations of Allah a laughing-stock (by your behavior), but remember Allah's grace upon you and that which He hath revealed unto you of the Scripture and of wisdom, whereby He doth exhort you. Observe your duty to Allah and know that Allah is Aware of all things.

And when ye have divorced women and they reach their term, place not difficulties in the way of their marrying their husbands if it is agreed between them in kindness. This is an admonition for him among you who believeth in Allah and the Last Day. That is more virtuous for you, and cleaner. Allah knoweth; ye know not.

Mothers shall suckle their children for two whole years; (that is) for those who wish to complete the suckling. **The duty of feeding and clothing nursing mothers in a seemly manner is upon the father of the child.** No-one should be charged beyond his capacity. A mother should not be made to suffer because of her child, nor should he to whom the child is born (be made to suffer) because of his child. And on the (father's) heir is incumbent the like of that (which was incumbent on the father). If they desire to wean the child by mutual consent and (after) consultation, it is no sin for them; and if ye wish to give your children out to nurse, it is no sin for you, provide that ye pay what is due from you in kindness. Observe your duty to Allah, and know that Allah is Seer of what ye do.

Such of you as die and leave behind them wives, they (the wives) shall wait, keeping themselves apart, four months and ten days. And when they reach the term (prescribed for them) then there is no sin for you in aught that they may do with themselves in decency. Allah is informed of what ye do.

There is no sin for you in that which ye proclaim or hide in your minds concerning your troth with women. Allah knoweth that ye will remember them. But plight not your troth with women except by uttering a recognized form of words. And do not consummate the marriage until (the term) prescribed is run. Know that Allah knoweth what is in your minds, so beware of Him; and know that Allah is Forgiving, Clement.
It is no sin for you if ye divorce women while yet ye have not touched them, nor appointed unto them a portion. Provide for them, the rich according to his means, and the straitened according to his means, a fair provision. (This is) a bounden duty for those who do good. If ye divorce them before ye have touched them and ye have appointed unto them a portion, then (pay the) half of that which ye appointed, unless they (the women) agree to forgo it, or he agreeth to forgo it in whose hand is the marriage tie. To forgo is nearer to piety. And forget not kindness among yourselves. Allah is Seer of what ye do.

Be guardians of your prayers, and of the midmost prayer, and stand up with devotion to Allah. And if ye go in fear, then (pray) standing or on horseback. And when ye are again in safety, remember Allah, as He hath taught you that which (heretofore) ye knew not. In the case of those of you who are about to die and leave behind them wives, they should bequeath unto their wives a provision for the year without turning them out, but if they go out (of their own accord) there is no sin for you in that which they do of themselves within their rights. Allah is Mighty, Wise. For divorced women a provision in kindness: a duty for those who ward off (evil). Thus Allah expoundeth unto you His revelations so that ye may understand.

Bethink Thee of those of old, who went forth from their habitations in their thousands, fearing death, and Allah said unto them: Die; and then He brought them back to life. Lo! Allah is a Lord of Kindness to mankind, but most of mankind give not thanks. Fight (*jihad*) in the way of Allah, and know that Allah is Hearer, Knower.

Who is it that will <u>lend unto Allah a goodly loan</u>, so that He may give it increase manifold? Allah straiteneth and enlargeth. Unto Him ye will return.

Bethink Thee of the leaders of the Children of Israel after *MOSES*, how they said unto a prophet (Samuel) whom they had: "Set up for us a king and we will fight in Allah's way." He said: "Would ye then refrain from fighting if fighting were prescribed for you?" They said: "Why should we not fight in Allah's way when we have been driven from our dwellings with our children?" Yet, when fighting was prescribed for them, they turned away, all save a few of them. Allah is aware of evil-doers.

Their Prophet said unto them: "Lo! Allah hath raised up Saul to be a king for you." They said: "How can he have kingdom over us when we are more deserving of the kingdom than he is, since he hath not been given wealth enough?" Samuel said: "Lo! Allah hath chosen him above you, and hath increased him abundantly in wisdom and stature!" Allah bestoweth His Sovereignty on whom He will. Allah is All-Embracing, All-Knowing.

And their Prophet said unto them: "Lo! The token of his kingdom is that there shall come unto you the ark wherein is peace of reassurance from your Lord, and a remnant of that which the house of *MOSES* and the house of Aaron left behind, the angels bearing it. Lo! herein shall be a token for you if (in truth) ye are believers."

And when Saul set out with the army, he said: "Lo! Allah will try you by (the ordeal of) a river. Whosoever therefore drinketh thereof he is not of me, and whosoever tasteth it not he is of me, save him who taketh (thereof) in the hollow of his hand." But they drank thereof, all save a few of them. And after he had crossed (the river), he and those who believed with him, they said: "We have no power this day against Goliath and his hosts." But those who knew that they would meet Allah exclaimed: "How many a little company hath overcome a mighty host by Allah's leave! Allah is with the steadfast."

And when they went into the field against Goliath and his hosts they said: "Our Lord! Bestow on us endurance, make our foothold sure, and give us help against the disbelieving folk." So they routed them by Allah's leave and David slew Goliath; and Allah gave him the Kingdom and Wisdom (*hikmat/chokhmah*), and taught him of that which He willeth. And if Allah had not repelled some men by others the earth would have been corrupted. But Allah is a Lord of Kindness to His creatures. These are the portents of Allah which We recite unto Thee with truth, and Lo! Thou *art* of the number of Our messengers.

Of those messengers, some of whom We have caused to excel others, and of whom there are some unto whom Allah spake, while some of them He exalted above others in degree; and We gave *JESUS*, son of Miriam, THIS RIGHTEOUS BOOK and We supported him with the Holy Spirit. And if Allah had so willed it, those who followed after them would not have fought one with another after THIS RIGHTEOUS BOOK had come unto them. But they differed, some of them believing and some disbelieving. And if Allah had so willed it, they would not have fought one with another; but Allah doeth what He will.

O ye who believe! Spend of that wherewith We have provided you ere a day come when there will be no trafficking, nor friendship, nor intercession. The disbelievers, they are the wrong-doers. Allah! There is no God save Him, the Alive, the Eternal. Neither slumber nor sleep overtaketh Him. Unto Him belongeth whatsoever is in the heavens and whatsoever is in the earth. Who is he that intercedeth with Him save by His leave? He knoweth that which is in front of them and that which is behind them, while they encompass nothing of His knowledge save what He will. **His throne includeth the heavens and the earth**, and He is never weary of preserving them. He is the Sublime, the Tremendous.

There is no compulsion in religion. The right direction is henceforth distinct from error. And he who rejecteth false deities and believeth in Allah hath grasped a firm handhold which will never break. Allah is Hearer, Knower.

Allah is the Protecting Guardian of those who believe. He bringeth them out of darkness into light. As for those who disbelieve, their patrons are false deities. They bring them out of light into darkness. Such are rightful owners of the Fire. They will abide therein.

Bethink Thee of him who had an argument with Abraham about his Lord, because Allah had given him the kingdom; how, when Abraham said: "My Lord is He Who giveth life and causeth death," he answered: "I give life and cause death." Abraham said: "Lo! Allah causeth the sun to rise in the East, so do Thou cause it to come up from the West." Thus was the disbeliever abashed. And Allah guideth not wrongdoing folk.

Or the like of him who, passing by a township which had fallen into utter ruin, exclaimed: "How shall Allah give this township life after its death?" And Allah made him die a hundred years, then brought him back to life. He said: "How long hast thou tarried?" The man said: "I have tarried a day or part of a day." He said: "Nay, but Thou hast tarried for a hundred years. Just look at Thy food and drink which have not rotted! Look at Thine ass! And, that We may make Thee a token unto mankind, look at the bones, how We adjust them and then cover them with flesh!" And when the matter became clear unto him, he said: "I know now that Allah is Able to do all things."

And when Abraham said: "My Lord! Show me how Thou givest life to the dead," He said: "Dost Thou not believe?" Abraham said: "Yea, but I ask in order that my heart may be at ease." His Lord said: "Take four of the birds* and cause them to incline unto Thee, then place a part of them on each hill, then call them, they will come to Thee in haste, and know that Allah is Mighty, Wise."

The likeness of those who spend their wealth in Allah's way is as the likeness of a grain which groweth seven ears, in every ear a hundred grains. Allah giveth increase manifold to whom He will. Allah is All-Embracing, All-Knowing.

Those who spend their wealth for the cause of Allah and afterward make not reproach and injury to follow that which they have spent; their reward is with their Lord, and there shall no fear come upon them, neither shall they grieve. A kind word with forgiveness is better than almsgiving followed by injury. Allah is Absolute, Clement.

O ye who believe! Render not vain your almsgiving by reproach and injury, like him who spendeth his wealth only to be seen of men and believeth not in Allah and the Last Day. His likeness is as the likeness of a rock whereon is dust of earth; a rainstorm smiteth it, leaving it smooth and bare. They have no control of aught of that which they have gained. Allah guideth not the disbelieving folk.

And the likeness of those who spend their wealth in search of Allah's pleasure, and for the strengthening of their souls, is as the likeness of **a Garden on a Height**. The rainstorm smiteth it and it bringeth forth its fruit twofold. And if the rainstorm smite it not, then the shower. Allah is Seer of what ye do. Would any of you like to have a garden of palm-trees and vines, with rivers flowing underneath it, with all kinds of fruit for him therein; and old age hath stricken him and he hath feeble offspring; and a fiery whirlwind striketh it and it is all consumed by fire. Thus Allah maketh plain His Revelations unto you, in order that ye may give thought.

---

*Four planes at the 9-11.

O ye who believe! Spend of the good things which ye have earned, and of that which We bring forth from the earth for you, and seek not the bad (with intent) to spend thereof (in charity) when ye would not take it for yourselves save with disdain; and know that Allah is Absolute, Owner of Praise.

The devil promiseth you destitution and enjoineth on you what is forbidden. But Allah promiseth you forgiveness from Himself with bounty. Allah is All-Embracing, All-knowing.
He giveth Wisdom unto whom He will, and he unto whom Wisdom is given, he truly hath received abundant good. But none remember except men of understanding.
 Whatever alms ye spend or vow ye vow, Lo! Allah knoweth it. Wrong-doers have no helpers.
If ye publish your almsgiving, it is well, **but if ye hide it** (*mitzvah*) and give it to the poor, it will be better for you, and will atone for some of your ill-deeds. Allah is Informed of what ye do.

The guiding of them is not Thy duty, but Allah guideth whom He will. And whatsoever good thing ye spend, it is for yourselves, when ye spend not save in search of Allah's Countenance; and whatsoever good thing ye spend, it will be repaid to you in full, and ye will not be wronged. Alms are for the poor who are straitened for the cause of Allah, who cannot travel in the land (for trade). The unthinking man accounteth them wealthy because of their restraint. Thou shalt know them by their mark: They do not beg of men with importunity. And whatsoever good thing ye spend, Lo! Allah knoweth it.

Those who spend their wealth by night and day, by stealth and openly, verily their reward is with their Lord, and their shall no fear come upon them neither shall they grieve. Those who swallow usury cannot rise up save as he ariseth whom the devil hath prostrated by (his) touch. That is because they say: "Trade is just like usury;" whereas Allah permitteth trading and forbiddeth usury. He unto whom an admonition from his Lord cometh, and (he) refraineth (in obedience thereto), he shall keep (the profits of) that which is past, and his affair (henceforth) is with Allah. As for him who returneth (to usury)--Such are rightful owners of the Fire. They will abide therein.

Allah hath blighted usury and made almsgiving fruitful. Allah loveth not the impious and guilty. Lo! Those who believe and do good works and establish worship and pay the poor-due (*zakat*), their reward is with their Lord and there shall no fear come upon them neither shall they grieve.

O ye who believe! Observe your duty to Allah, and give up what remaineth (due to you) from usury, if ye are (in truth) believers. And if ye do not, then be warned of war (against you) from Allah and His messenger. And if ye repent, then ye have your principal. Wrong not, and ye shall not be wronged.

And if the debtor is in straitened circumstances, then (let there be) postponement to (the time of) ease; and that ye remit the debt as almsgiving would be better for you if ye did but know. And guard yourselves against a day in which ye will be brought back to Allah. Then every soul will be paid in full that which it hath earned, and they will not be wronged.

O ye who believe! When ye contract a debt for a fixed term, record it in writing. Let a scribe record it in writing between you in (terms of) equity. No scribe should refuse to write as Allah hath taught him, so let him write, and let him who incurreth the debt dictate, and let him observe his duty to Allah his Lord, and diminish naught thereof. But if he who oweth the debt is of low understanding, or weak, or unable himself to dictate, then let the guardian of his interests dictate in (terms of) equity. And call to witness, from among your men, two witnesses. And if two men be not (at hand) then a man and two women, of such as ye approve as witnesses, so that if the one erreth (through forgetfulness) the other will remember. And the witnesses must not refuse when they are summoned. Be not averse to writing down (the contract) whether it be small or great, with (record of) the term thereof. That is more equitable in the sight of Allah and more sure for testimony, and the best way of avoiding doubt between you; save only in the case when it is actual merchandise which ye transfer among yourselves from hand to hand. In that case it is no sin for you if ye write it not. And have witnesses when ye sell one to another, and let no harm be done to scribe or witness. If ye do (harm to them) Lo! It is a sin in you. Observe your duty to Allah. Allah is teaching you. And Allah is knower of all things.

If ye be on a journey and cannot find a scribe, then a pledge in hand (shall suffice). And if one of you entrusteth to another let him who is trusted deliver up that which is entrusted to him (according to the pact between them) and let him observe his duty to Allah his Lord. Hide not testimony. He who hideth it, verily his heart is sinful. Allah is Aware of what ye do.

Unto Allah belongeth whatsoever is in the heavens and whatsoever is in the earth; and whether ye make known what is in your minds or hide it, Allah will bring you to account for it. **He will forgive whom He will and He will punish whom He will.** Allah is Able to do all things.

85. Bism'illah Ar-Rahman Ar-Rahim! an-Nur: THE LIGHT.

A SURAH which We have revealed and enjoined, and wherein We have revealed plain tokens, that haply ye may take heed.

The adulterer and the adulteress, scourge ye each one of them a hundred stripes. And let not pity for the TWAIN withhold you from obedience to Allah, if ye believe in Allah and the Last Day. And let a party of believers witness their punishment.

The adulterer shall not marry save an adulteress or an idolatress, and the adulteress none shall marry save an adulterer or an idolater. All that is forbidden unto believers.

And those who accuse honorable women but bring not four witnesses, scourge them eighty stripes and never (afterward) accept their testimony--They indeed are evil-doers--save those who afterward repent and make amends. Lo! Allah is Forgiving, Merciful.

As for those who accuse their wives but have no witnesses except themselves; let the testimony of one of them be four testimonies--by Allah that he is of those who speak the truth; and yet a fifth, invoking the curse of Allah on him if he is of those who lie.

And it shall avert the punishment from her if she bear witness before Allah four times that the thing he saith is indeed false, and a fifth time that the wrath of Allah be upon her if he speaketh truth. And had it not been for the grace of Allah and His mercy unto you, and that Allah is Clement, Wise, (ye had been undone).

Lo! **They who spread the slander are <u>a gang among you</u>**. Deem it not a bad thing for you; nay, it is good for you. Unto every man of them will be paid that which he hath earned of the sin; and as for him among them who had the greater share therein, his will be an awful doom.

Why did not the believers, men and women, when ye heard it, think good of their own own folk, and say: "It is a manifest untruth?" Why did they not produce four witnesses? Since they produce not witnesses, they verily are liars in the sight of Allah.

Had it not been for the grace of Allah and His mercy unto you in the world and the Hereafter an awful doom had overtaken you for that whereof ye murmured. When ye welcomed it with your tongues, and uttered with your mouths that whereof ye had no knowledge, ye counted it a trifle. In the sight of Allah it is very great.

Wherefore, when ye heard it, said ye not: "It is not for us to speak of this. Glory be to Thee! This is awful calumny!"

Allah admonisheth you that ye repeat not the like thereof ever, if ye are (in truth) believers. And He expoundeth unto you the Revelations. Allah is Knower, Wise. Lo! Those who love that slander should be spread concerning those who believe, theirs will be a painful punishment in the world and the Hereafter. Allah knoweth. Ye know not. Had it not been for the grace of Allah and His mercy unto you, and that Allah is Clement, Merciful, ye had been undone.

O ye who believe! Follow not the footsteps of the devil. Unto whomsoever followeth the footsteps of the devil, Lo! He commandeth filthiness and wrong. Had it not been for the grace of Allah and His mercy unto you, not one of you would ever have grown PURE. But Allah causeth whom He will to grow. And Allah is Hearer, Knower.

And let not those who possess dignity and ease among you swear not to give to the near of kin and to the needy, and to fugitives for the cause of Allah. Let them forgive and show indulgence. Yearn ye not that Allah may forgive you? Allah is Forgiving, Merciful.

Lo! As for **<u>those who traduce</u>** virtuous, believing women (who are) careless, cursed are **<u>they</u>** in the world and the Hereafter. Theirs will be an awful doom on the day when their tongues and their hands and their feet testify against them as to what they used to do, on that day Allah will pay them their just due, and they will know that Allah, He is the Manifest Truth.

Vile women are for vile men, and vile men for vile women. Good women are for good men, and good men for good women; such are innocent of that which people say: For them is pardon and a bountiful provision.

O ye who believe! Enter not houses other than your own without first announcing your presence and invoking blessings upon the folk thereof. That is better for you, that ye may be heedful. And if ye find no-one therein, still enter not until permission hath been given. And if it be said unto you: "Go away again," then go away, for it is PURER for you. Allah knoweth what ye do. It is no sin for you to enter uninhabited houses wherein is comfort for you. Allah knoweth what ye proclaim and what ye hide.

Tell the believing men to lower their gaze and be modest. That is PURER for them. Lo! Allah is aware of what they do.

And tell the believing women to lower their gaze and be modest, and to display of their adornment only that which is apparent, and **to draw their veils over their bosoms**, and not to reveal their adornment save to their own husbands or fathers or husbands' fathers, or their sons or their husbands' sons, or their brothers or their brothers' sons or sisters' sons, or their women, or their slaves, or male attendants who lack vigor, or children who know naught of women's nakedness. And let them not stamp their feet so as to reveal what they hide of their adornment. And turn unto Allah together, O believers, in order that ye may succeed.

And marry such of you as are solitary and the pious of your slaves and maid-servants. If they be poor, Allah will enrich them of His bounty. Allah is of ample means, Aware.

And let those who cannot find a match keep chaste till Allah give them independence by His grace. And such of your slaves as seek a writing (of emancipation), write it for them if ye are aware of aught of good in them, and bestow upon them of the wealth of Allah which He hath bestowed upon you. Force not your slave-girls to whoredom that ye may seek enjoyment of the life of the world, if they would preserve their chastity. And if one force them, then (unto the victim), after their compulsion, Lo! Allah will be Forgiving, Merciful.

And verily We have sent down for you Revelations that make plain, and the example of those who passed away before you. An admonition unto those who ward off.

Allah is the Light of the heavens and the earth. The similitude of His light is as a niche wherein is a lamp. The lamp is in a glass. The glass is as it were a shining star. This lamp is kindled from a Blessed Tree--**an olive neither of the East nor of the West**--whose oil would almost glow forth of itself though no fire touched it. Light upon light. Allah guideth unto His light whom He will. And **Allah speaketh to humankind in allegories**, for Allah is Knower of all things.

This lamp is found in houses which Allah hath allowed to be exalted and that His name shall be remembered therein. Therein do offer praise to Him at morn and evening. **Men whom neither merchandise nor traffic beguileth from remembrance of Allah** and constancy in prayer and paying to the poor their due; who fear a day when **hearts** and **eyeballs** will be overturned; That Allah may reward them with the best of what they did, and increase reward for them of His bounty. Allah giveth blessings without stint to whom He will.

As for those who disbelieve, **their deeds are as a mirage in a desert**. The thirsty one supposeth it to be water till he cometh unto it and findeth it naught, and findeth, in the place thereof, Allah Who payeth him his due; and Allah is swift at reckoning.

Or as darkness on a vast, abysmal sea. There covereth him a wave, above which is a wave, above which is a cloud. Layer upon layer of darkness. When he holdeth out his hand he scarce can see it. And he for whom Allah hath not appointed light, for him there is no light.

Hast Thou not seen that Allah, He it is Whom all who are in the heavens and the earth praise, and the birds in their flight? Of each He knoweth verily the worship and the praise; and Allah is Aware of what they do.

And unto Allah belongeth the Sovereignty of the heavens and the earth, and unto Allah is the journeying.

Hast Thou not seen how Allah wafteth the clouds, then gathereth them, then maketh them layers, and Thou seest the rain come forth from between them; He sendeth down from the heaven mountains wherein is hail, and smiteth therewith whom He will, and averteth it from whom He will. The flashing of His lightning all but snatcheth away the sight. Allah causeth the revolution of the day and the night. Lo! **Herein is indeed <u>a lesson</u> for those who <u>see</u>**.

Allah hath created every animal of water. Of them is a kind that goeth upon its belly and a kind that goeth upon two legs and a kind that goeth upon four. Allah createth what He will. Lo! Allah is Able to do all things.

Verily We have sent down Revelations and explained them. Allah guideth whom He will unto a straight path. And they say: "We believe in Allah and the messenger, and we obey;" then after that a faction of them turn away. Such are not believers. And when they appeal unto Allah and His messenger to judge between them, Lo! A faction of them are averse; But if right had been with them they would have come unto him willingly. Is there in their hearts a disease, or have they doubts, or fear they lest Allah and His messenger should wrong them in judgment? Nay, but such are evil-doers.

The saying of believers when they appeal unto Allah and His messenger to judge between them is only that they say: "We hear and we obey." And such are the successful.

He who obeyeth Allah and His messenger, and feareth Allah, and keepeth duty unto Him: such indeed are the victorious. They swear fealty by Allah solemnly that, if Thou order them, they will go forth. Say: "Swear not! Known obedience is better. Lo! Allah is Informed of what ye do."

Say: "Obey Allah and obey the messenger." But if ye turn away, then it is for him to do only that wherewith he hath been charged, and for you to do only that wherewith ye have been charged. If ye obey him, ye will go aright. But the messenger hath no other charge than to convey the message plainly.

Allah hath promised such of you as believe and do good work that He will surely make them to succeed the present rulers in the earth even as He caused those who were before them to succeed others; and that He will surely establish for them their religion which He hath approved for them, and will give them in exchange safety after their fear. They serve Me. They ascribe no thing as partner unto Me. Those who disbelieve henceforth, they are the miscreants.

Establish worship and pay the poor-due (*zakat*) and obey the messenger, that haply ye may find mercy. Think not that the disbelievers can escape in **the land**. Fire will be their home--a hapless journey's end!

O ye who believe! Let your slaves, and those of you who have not come to puberty, ask leave of you at three times (before they come into your presence): Before the Prayer of Dawn,[*] and when ye lay aside your raiment for the heat of noon, and after the prayer of night. Three times of privacy for you. It is no sin for them or for you at other times, when some of you go round attendant upon others (if they come into your presence without leave). Thus Allah maketh clear the Revelations for you. Allah is Knower, Wise.

And when the children among you come to puberty then let them ask leave even as those before them used to ask it. Thus Allah maketh clear His Revelations for you. Allah is Knower, Wise.

As for women past child-bearing, who have no hope of marriage, it is no sin for them if they discard their (outer) clothing in such a way as not to show adornment. But to refrain is better for them. Allah is Hearer, Knower.

No blame is there upon the blind nor any blame upon the lame nor any blame upon the sick nor on yourselves if ye eat from your houses, or the houses of your fathers, or the houses of your mothers, or the houses of your brothers, or the houses of your sisters, or the houses of your fathers' brothers, or the houses of your fathers' sisters, or the houses of your mothers' brothers, or the houses of your mothers' sisters, or from that whereof ye hold the keys, or from the house of a friend. No sin shall it be for you whether ye eat together or apart. But when ye enter houses, salute one another with a greeting from Allah, blessed and sweet. Thus Allah maketh clear His Revelations for you, that haply ye may understand.

They only are the true believers who believe in Allah and His messenger and, when they are with him on some common errand, go not away until they have asked leave of him. Lo! Those who ask leave of Thee, those are they who believe in Allah and His messenger. So, if they ask Thy leave for some affair of theirs, give leave to whom Thou wilt of them, and ask for them forgiveness of Allah. Lo! Allah is Forgiving, Merciful.

---

[*] The Dawn Prayer: "O my God and my Master! I am Thy servant and the son of Thy servant. I have risen from my couch at this dawntide when the Daystar of Thy oneness hath shone forth from the Dayspring of Thy will, and hath shed its radiance upon the whole world, according to what had been ordained in the Books of Thy Decree. Praise be unto Thee, O my God, that we have wakened to the splendors of the light of Thy knowledge. **Send down, then, upon us, O my Lord, what will enable us to dispense with anyone but Thee, and will rid us of all attachment to aught except Thyself.** Write down, moreover, for me, and for such as are dear to me, and for my kindred, man and woman alike, the good of this world and the world to come. Keep us safe, then, through Thine unfailing protection, O Thou the Beloved of the entire creation and the Desire of the whole universe, from them whom Thou hast made to be the manifestations of the Evil Whisperer, who whisper in men's breasts. Potent art Thou to do Thy pleasure. Thou art, verily, the Almighty, the Help in Peril, the Self-Subsisting. Bless Thou, O Lord my God, Him Whom Thou hast set over Thy most excellent Titles, and through Whom Thou hast divided between the godly and the wicked, and graciously aid us to do what Thou lovest and desirest. Bless Thou, moreover, O my God, them Who are Thy Words and Thy Letters, and them who have set their faces towards Thee, and turned unto Thy face, and hearkened to Thy Call. Thou art, truly, the Lord and King of all men, and art potent over all things."

Make not the calling of the messenger among you as your calling one of another. Allah knoweth those of you who steal away, hiding themselves. And let those who conspire to evade orders beware lest grief or painful punishment befall them.

Lo! Verily unto Allah belongeth whatsoever is in the heavens and the earth. He knoweth your Condition. And He knoweth the Day when they are returned unto Him so that He may inform them of what they did. Allah is Knower of all things.

CHINVAT-SIRAT: Bism'illah Ar-Rahman Ar-Rahim!

When Allah's succour (an-Nasr) and the triumph cometh
And thou seest mankind Entering the religion of Allah in Troops,
Then hymn the praises of thy Lord, and seek forgiveness of Him.
Lo! He is ever ready to show mercy.

Khaames

LUQMAN AL-HAKIM!

LUQMAN AL-HAKIM!

---LAO-TZU THE WISE!---
Manzil-i-Hajj va Ihram
Kamál

Bism'illah Ar-Rahman Ar-Rahim!

RECITE *(aq-Qaara): In the name of thy Lord Who createth,*
Createth man from a clot (al-'Alaq).
RECITE: *And thy Lord is the Most Bounteous,*
*Who teacheth by the **PEN**,*
Teacheth man that which he knew not.

XXI. JUZ'UN SIPARA VENTUNO:

86. Bism'illah Ar-Rahman Ar-Rahim! as-Saff: THE RANKS.

All that is in the heavens and all that is in the earth **GLORIFIETH ALLAH;**[*] and He is the Mighty, the All-Wise.

O ye who believe! Why say ye that which ye do not?

It is most hateful in the sight of Allah that ye say that which ye do not.

Lo! Allah loveth them who battle for His cause in ranks, as if they were a solid structure.

And when *MOSES* said unto his people: "O my people! Why persecute ye me, when ye well know that I am Allah's messenger unto you?" So when they went astray Allah sent their hearts astray. And Allah guideth not the evil-living folk.

And when *JESUS* son of Miriam said: "O Children of Israel! Lo! I am the messenger of Allah unto you, confirming that which was before me in the Torah, and bringing good tidings of a messenger who cometh after me, whose name is *THE PRAISED ONE*.[†] Yet when he hath come unto them with THIS RIGHTEOUS BOOK, they say: "This is mere magic."

And who doeth greater wrong than he who inventeth a lie against Allah when he is summoned unto Al-Islam? And Allah guideth not wrongdoing folk. **Fain would they put out God's light with their mouths: But God hath willed to perfect His light, albeit the infidels abhor it so.**

---

[*]**Al-Musabbihat** refer to the collective name of the seven surahs that begin with Allah's *glorification* 'Subhana,' 'Sabbaha,' and 'Yusabbihu:' *al-Hadid; al-Hashr; as-Saff; al-Jumua; at-Taghabun; al-Isra;* and *al-Ala*.
[†]*JESUS* spoke Aramaic--in his original language he said: "AHMAD" THE PRAISED ONE--that has been translated sometimes as Comforter, Advocate or Counselor, etc. (see John 16:7-11).

He it is Who hath sent His messenger with the guidance and the religion of truth, that He may make it conqueror of all religion however much idolaters may be averse.

O ye who believe! Shall I show you a commerce that will save you from a painful doom? Ye should believe in Allah and His messenger, and should strive for the cause of Allah with your wealth and your lives. That is better for you, if ye did but know.

He will forgive you your sins and bring you into Gardens underneath which rivers flow, and pleasant dwellings in Gardens of Eden. That is the supreme triumph.

And He will give you another blessing which ye love: help from Allah and present **victory**. Give good tidings to believers.

O ye who believe! Be Allah's helpers, even as *JESUS* son of Miriam said unto the disciples: "Who are my helpers for Allah?" They said: "We are Allah's helpers." And a party of the Children of Israel believed, while a party disbelieved.

Then We strengthened those who believed against their foe, and they became the uppermost.

87. Bism'illah Ar-Rahman Ar-Rahim! Luqman: LAO TZU.

Alif. Lam. Mim.

These are revelations of the wise Scripture, a guidance and a mercy for the good, those who establish worship and pay the poor-due (*zakat*) and have sure faith in the Hereafter.

Such have guidance from their Lord. Such are the successful.

And of humankind is he who payeth for mere pastime of discourse, that he may mislead from Allah's way without knowledge, and maketh it the butt of mockery. For such there is a shameful doom. And when Our Revelations are recited unto him he turneth away in pride as if he heard them not, as if there were a deafness in his ears. So give him tidings of a painful doom.

Lo! Those who believe and do good works, for them are the Gardens of Na'im (Heb. Nahum). Wherein they will abide. It is a promise of Allah in truth. He is the Mighty, the Wise.

He hath created the heavens without supports that ye can see, and hath cast into the earth firm hills, so that it quake not with you; and He hath dispersed therein all kinds of beasts. And We send down water from the sky and We cause plants of every goodly kind to grow therein. This is the Creation of Allah. Now show me that which those beside Him have created. Nay, but the wrong-doers are in error manifest!

And verily We gave Lao-Tzu (*Luqman*) wisdom, saying: "Give thanks unto Allah;" and whosoever giveth thanks, he giveth thanks for the good of his soul. And whosoever refuseth--Lo! Allah is Absolute, Owner of Praise.

And when Lao-Tzu (*Luqman*) said unto his son, when he was exhorting him: "O My Dear Son! Ascribe no partners unto Allah. Lo! To ascribe partners unto Him is a tremendous wrong!"

And We have enjoined upon man concerning his partners--his mother beareth him in weakness upon weakness, and his weaning is in two years--Give thanks unto Me and unto Thy parents. Unto Me is the journeying.

But if they strive with Thee to make Thee ascribe unto Me as partner that of which Thou hast no knowledge, then obey them not. Consort with them in the world kindly, and follow the path of him who repenteth unto Me. Then unto Me will be your return, and I shall tell you what ye used to do:

"O My Dear Son! Lo! though it be but the weight of a grain of mustard-seed, and though it be in a rock, or in the heavens, or in the earth, Allah will bring it forth. Lo! Allah is Subtile, Aware."

"O My Dear Son! Establish worship and enjoin kindness and forbid iniquity, and persevere whatever may befall Thee. Lo! That is of the steadfast heart of things. Turn not Thy cheek in scorn toward folk, nor walk with pertness in the land. Lo! Allah loveth not each braggart boaster. Be modest in thy bearing and subdue thy voice. Lo! the harshest of all voices is the voice of the ass."

"O My Dear Son! If you doubt about death, prevent yourself from sleep and surely you cannot and if you doubt resurrection, prevent yourself from waking and surely you cannot. If you think of that, you will know that your Self is in the hand of other than you. In fact (wakening from) sleep is like resurrection after death."[*]

See ye not how Allah hath made serviceable unto you whatsoever is in the skies and whatsoever is in the earth and hath loaded you with His favours both without and within? Yet of mankind is he who disputeth concerning Allah, without knowledge or guidance or a scripture giving light.

And if it be said unto them: "Follow that which Allah hath revealed," they say: "Nay, but we follow that wherein we found our fathers." What! Even though the devil were inviting them unto the doom of flame?

Whosoever surrendereth his purpose to Allah while doing good, he verily hath grasped **the firm hand-hold** (*Urvatu'l-Vuthqa*). Unto Allah belongeth the SEQUEL of all things. And whosoever disbelieveth, let not his disbelief afflict thee. Unto Us is their return, and We shall tell them what they did. Lo! Allah is Aware of what is in the breasts. We give them comfort for a little, and then We drive them to a heavy doom.

If thou shouldst ask them: "Who created the heavens and the earth?" They would answer: "Allah." Say: "Praise be to Allah!" But most of them know not. Unto Allah belongeth whatsoever is in the heavens and the earth. Lo! Allah, He is the Absolute, the Owner of Praise.

---

[*]See *Bihar'ul Anwar*, Vol. 7, p. 42 for more.

And if all the trees in the earth were pens, and the sea, with seven more seas to help it, were ink, the words of Allah could not be exhausted. Lo! Allah is Mighty, Wise.

Your creation and your raising (from the dead) are only as the creation and the raising of a single soul. Lo! Allah is Hearer, Knower.

Hast thou not seen how Allah causeth the night to pass into the day and causeth the day to pass into the night, and hath subdued the sun and the moon, each running unto an appointed term; and that Allah is Informed of what ye do?

That is so because Allah, He is the True, and that which they invoke beside Him is the False, and because Allah, He is the Sublime, the Great.

Hast Thou not seen how the ships glide on the sea by Allah's grace, that He may show you of His wonders? Lo! Therein indeed are portents for every steadfast, grateful soul.

And if a wave **enshroudeth them like awnings**, they cry unto Allah, making their faith PURE for Him only. But when He bringeth them safe to land, some of them compromise. None denieth Our signs save every traitor ingrate.

O Humanity! Keep your duty to your Lord and fear a Day when the parent will not be able to avail the child in aught, nor the child to avail the parent. Lo! Allah's promise is the very truth.

Let not the life of the world beguile you, nor let the deceiver beguile you, in regard to Allah.

Lo! Allah! With Him is knowledge of the HOUR. He sendeth down the rain, and knoweth that which is in the wombs. No soul knoweth what it will earn tomorrow, and no soul knoweth in what land it will die. Lo! Allah is Knower, Aware.

88. Bism'illah Ar-Rahman Ar-Rahim! al-Fil: THE ELEPHANT.

Hast thou not seen how thy Lord dealt with the owners of the Elephant?
Did He not bring their stratagem to naught,
And send against them swarms of flying creatures,
Which pelted them with stones of baked clay,
And made them like green crops devoured?

89. Bism'illah Ar-Rahman Ar-Rahim! an-Naml: THE ANT.

Ta. Sin.

These are Revelations of THIS QUR'AN and a Scripture that maketh plain; a guidance and good tidings for believers who establish worship and pay the poor-due (*zakat*) and are sure of the Hereafter. Lo! As for those who believe not in the Hereafter, We have made their works fairseeming unto them so that they are all astray. Those are they for whom is the worst of punishment, and in the Hereafter they will be the greatest losers.

Lo! As for Thee, Thou verily receivest THIS QUR'AN from the presence of One Wise, Aware.

When *MOSES* said unto his household: "**Lo! I spy afar off a fire; I will bring you tidings thence, or bring to you a borrowed flame that ye may warm yourselves." But when he reached it, he was called, saying: "Blessed is Whosoever is in the fire and Whosoever is round about it! And Glorified be Allah, the Lord of the Worlds!"**

"O *MOSES*! Lo! it is I, Allah, the Mighty, the Wise." And "throw down thy staff!"

But when he saw it writhing as it were a demon, he turned to flee headlong: "O *MOSES*! Fear not! The emissaries fear not in My presence, save him who hath done wrong and afterward hath changed evil for good. And lo! I am Forgiving, Merciful. And put Thy hand into the bosom of Thy robe, it will come forth white but unhurt: among nine tokens unto Pharaoh and his people Lo! they were ever evil-living folk."

But when Our tokens came unto them, plain to see, they said: "This is mere magic," and they denied them, though their souls acknowledged them, for spite and arrogance. Then see the nature of the consequence for the wrong-doers!

And We verily gave knowledge unto David and Solomon, and they said: "Praise be to Allah, Who hath preferred us above many of His believing slaves!"

And Solomon was David's heir. And he said: "O humankind! Lo! We have been taught the **Language of Birds**, and have been given abundance of all things. This surely is evident favor."

And there were gathered together unto Solomon his armies of the jinn and humankind, and of the birds, and they were set in battle order; till, when they reached the **Valley of the Ants**, an ant exclaimed: "O Ants! Enter your dwellings lest Solomon and his armies crush you, unperceiving."

And Solomon smiled, laughing at her speech, and said: "My Lord, arouse me to be thankful for Thy favour wherewith Thou hast favoured me and my parents, and to do good that shall be pleasing unto Thee, and include me in the number of Thy righteous slaves." And he sought among the birds and said: "How is it that I see not the hoopoe, or is he among the absent? I verily will punish him with hard punishment or I verily will slay him, or he verily shall bring me a plain excuse."

But he was not long in coming, and he said: "I have found out a thing that Thou apprehendest not, and **I come unto Thee from Sheba** * **with sure tidings**. Lo! I found a woman ruling over them, and she hath been given abundance of all things, and hers is a mighty throne. I found her and her people worshipping the sun instead of Allah; and Satan maketh their works fairseeming unto them, and debarreth them from THE WAY, so that they go not aright; So that they worship not Allah, Who bringeth forth the hidden in the heavens and the earth, and knoweth what ye hide and what ye proclaim, 'Allah; there is no God save Him, the Lord of the Tremendous Throne!'"

---

*Thebes.

Solomon said: "We shall see whether Thou speakest truth or whether Thou art of the liars. Go with this my letter and throw it down unto them; then turn away and see what answer they return."

 (The Queen of Sheba) said (when she received the letter): "O Chieftains! Lo! There hath been thrown unto me a noble letter. Lo! It is from Solomon, and Lo! It is: 'In the name of Allah, the Beneficent, the Merciful--Exalt not yourselves against me, but come unto me as those who surrender.'"

She said: "O Chieftains! Pronounce for me in my case. I decide no case till ye are present with me."

They said: "We are lords of might and lords of great prowess, but it is for Thee to command; so consider what Thou wilt command."

She said: "Lo! Kings, when they enter a township, ruin it and make the honor of its people shame. Thus will they do. But Lo! I am going to send a present unto them, and to see with what answer the messengers return."

So when the envoy came unto Solomon, he said: "What! Would ye help me with wealth? But that which Allah hath given me is better than that which He hath given you. Nay it is ye who exult in your gift. Return unto them. We verily shall come unto them with hosts that they cannot resist, and we shall drive them out from thence with shame, and they will be abased."

He said: "O Chiefs! Which of you will bring me her throne before they come unto me, surrendering?"

A stalwart of the jinn said: "I will bring it Thee before Thou canst rise from thy place. Lo! I verily am strong and trusty for such work."

One with whom was knowledge of the Scripture said: "I will bring it Thee before thy gaze returneth unto Thee."

And when he saw it set in his presence, he said: "This is of the bounty of my Lord, that He may **try me whether I give thanks or am ungrateful**. Whosoever giveth thanks he only giveth thanks for (the good of) his own soul; and whosoever is ungrateful (is ungrateful only to his own soul's hurt). For Lo! My Lord is Absolute in independence, Bountiful."

He said: "Disguise her throne for her that we may see whether she will go aright or be of those not rightly guided."

So, when she came, it was said unto her: "Is Thy throne like this?" She said: "It is as though it were the very one." And Solomon said: "We were given the knowledge before her and we had surrendered." And all that she was wont to worship instead of Allah hindered her, for she came of disbelieving folk.

It was said unto her: "Enter the hall. And when she saw it she deemed it a pool and bared her legs. Solomon said: "Lo! It is a hall, made smooth, of glass." She said: "My Lord! Lo! I have wronged myself, and I surrender with Solomon unto Allah, the Lord of the Worlds."

And We verily sent unto Thamud their brother *SIDDHARTHA (Salih) THE BUDDHA*, saying: "Worship Allah." And Lo! They then became two parties quarrelling.

He said: "O my people! Why will ye hasten on the evil rather than the good ? Why will ye not ask pardon of Allah, that ye may receive mercy."

They said: "We augur evil of Thee and those with Thee."

He said: "Your evil augury is with Allah. Nay, but ye are folk that are being tested."

And there were in the city nine persons who made mischief in the land and reformed not. They said: "Swear one to another by Allah that we verily will attack him and his household by night, and afterward we will surely say unto his friend: 'We witnessed not the destruction of his household. And Lo! We are truthtellers.'"

So they plotted a plot: and We plotted a plot, while they perceived not.

Then see the nature of the consequence of their plotting, for Lo! We destroyed them and their people, every one. See, yonder are their dwellings empty and in ruins because they did wrong. Lo! Herein is indeed a portent for a people who have knowledge. And we saved those who believed and used to ward off evil.

And Lot! When he said unto his folk: "Will ye commit abomination knowingly? Must ye needs lust after men instead of women? Nay, but ye are folk who act senselessly."

But the answer of his folk was naught save that they said: "Expel the household of Lot from your township, for they (forsooth) are folk who would keep clean!"

Then We saved him and his household save his wife; we destined her to be of those who stayed behind. And We rained a rain upon them. Dreadful is the rain of those who have been warned.

Say: "Praise be to Allah, and peace be on His slaves whom He hath chosen! Is Allah best, or all that ye ascribe as partners unto Him? Is not He best Who created the heavens and the earth, and sendeth down for you water from the sky wherewith We cause to spring forth joyous orchards, whose trees it never hath been yours to cause to grow. Is there any God beside Allah? Nay, but they are folk who ascribe equals unto Him!

Is not He best Who made the earth a fixed abode, and placed rivers in the folds thereof, and placed firm hills therein, and hath set a barrier between the two seas? Is there any God beside Allah? Nay, but most of them know not! Is not He best Who answereth the wronged one when he crieth unto Him and removeth the evil, and hath made you viceroys of the earth? Is there any God beside Allah? Little do they reflect!

Is not He bestWho guideth you in the darkness of the land and the sea, He Who sendeth the winds as heralds of His mercy? Is there any God beside Allah? High Exalted be Allah from all that they ascribe as partner unto Him!

Is not He best Who produceth creation, then reproduceth it, and Who provideth for you from the heaven and the earth? Is there any God beside Allah? Say: "Bring your proof, if ye are truthful!"

Say: "None in the heavens and the earth knoweth the Unseen save Allah; and they know not when they will be raised again. Nay! But doth their knowledge reach to the Hereafter? Nay, for they are in doubt concerning it. Nay, for they cannot see it."

Yet those who disbelieve say: "When we have become dust like our fathers, shall we verily be brought forth again? We were promised this, forsooth, we and our fathers. All this is naught but fables of the Old Ones."

Say unto them: "Travel in the land and see the nature of the sequel for the guilty!" And grieve Thou not for them, nor be in distress because of what they plot against Thee. And they say: "When will this promise be fulfilled, if ye are truthful?"

Say: "It may be that a part of that which ye would hasten on is close behind you." Lo! Thy Lord is full of bounty for humankind, but most of them do not give thanks. Lo! Thy Lord knoweth surely all that their bosoms hide, and all that they proclaim. And there is nothing hidden in the heaven or the earth but it is in a CLEAR RECORD."

Lo! THIS QUR'AN narrateth unto the Children of Israel most of that concerning which they differ. And Lo! It is a guidance and a mercy for believers. Lo! Thy Lord will judge between them of His wisdom, and He is the Mighty, the Wise. Therefore put thy trust in Allah, for Thou standest on the plain Truth.

Lo! Thou canst not make the dead to hear, nor canst Thou make the deaf to hear the call when they have turned to flee; nor canst thou lead the blind out of their error. Thou canst make none to hear, save those who believe Our revelations and who have surrendered.

And when the word is fulfilled concerning them, We shall bring forth **a BEAST**[*] of the earth to speak unto them because mankind had not faith in Our Revelations.

And remind them of the Day when We shall gather out of every nation a host of those who denied Our Revelations, and they will be set in array; till, when they come (before their Lord), He will say: "Did ye deny My Revelations when ye could not compass them in knowledge, or what was it that ye did?" And the Word will be fulfilled concerning them because they have done wrong, and they will not speak. Have they not seen how We have appointed the night that they may rest therein, and the day sight-giving? Lo! Therein verily are portents for a people who believe.

---

[*]See Revelation Chapter 13 for more.

And remind them o) the Day when **the Trumpet** will be blown, and all who are in the heavens and the earth will start in fear, save him whom Allah willeth. And all come unto Him, humbled. And Thou seest the hills Thou deemest solid flying with the flight of clouds: the doing of Allah Who perfecteth all things. Lo! He is Informed of what ye do.

Whoso bringeth a good deed will have better than its worth; and such are safe from fear that Day. And whoso bringeth an ill-deed, such will be flung down on their faces in the Fire. Are ye rewarded aught save what ye did?

"I am commanded only to serve the Lord of this land which He hath hallowed, and unto Whom all things belong. And I am commanded to be of those who surrender unto Him, and to recite THIS QUR'AN. And whoso goeth right, goeth right only for the good of his own soul; and as for him who goeth astray--unto him--say: "Lo! I am only a warner."

And say: "Praise be to Allah Who will show you His portents so that ye shall know them." And thy Lord is not unaware of what ye do.

XXII. JUZ'UN SIPARA VENTIDUO:

90. Bism'illah Ar-Rahman Ar-Rahim! al-An'am: THE LIVESTOCK.

Praise be to Allah, Who hath created the heavens and the earth, and hath appointed darkness and light. Yet those who disbelieve ascribe rivals unto their Lord.

He it is Who hath created you from clay, and hath decreed a term for you. A term is fixed with Him. Yet still ye doubt!

He is Allah in the heavens and in the earth. He knoweth both your secret and your utterance, and He knoweth what ye earn.

Never came there unto them a Revelation of the Revelations of Allah but they did turn away from it. And they denied the truth when it came unto them. But there will come unto them the tidings of that which they used to deride.

See they not how many a generation We destroyed before them, whom We had established in the earth more firmly than We have established you, and We shed on them abundant showers from the sky, and made the rivers flow beneath them. Yet we destroyed them for their sins, and created after them another generation.

Had we sent down unto Thee actual writing upon parchment, so that they could feel it with their hands, those who disbelieve would have said: "This is naught else than mere magic." They say: "Why hath not an angel been sent down unto him?" If We sent down an angel, then the matter would be judged; no further time would be allowed them for reflection. Had we appointed him an angel, We assuredly had made him as a man (that he might speak to men); and thus obscured for them the truth they now obscure.

221

Messengers of Allah have been derided before Thee, but that whereat they scoffed surrounded such of them as did deride. Say (unto the disbelievers): "Travel in the land, and see the nature of the consequence for the rejecters!" Say: "Unto whom belongeth whatsoever is in the heavens and the earth?" Say: "Unto Allah." **He hath prescribed for Himself MERCY**, that He may bring you all together to the Day of Resurrection whereof there is no doubt. Those who ruin their souls will not believe. Unto Him belongeth whatsoever resteth in the night and the day. He is the Hearer, the Knower.

Say: "Shall I choose for a protecting friend other than Allah, the Originator of the heavens and the earth, Who feedeth and is never fed?" Say: "I am ordered to be the first to surrender (unto Him). And be not Thou of the idolaters."

Say: "I fear, if I rebel against my Lord, the retribution of an Awful Day." He from whom such retribution is averted on that Day, Allah hath in truth had mercy on him. That will be the signal triumph.

If Allah touch thee with affliction, there is none that can relieve therefrom save Him, and if He touch thee with good fortune there is none that can impair it; for He is Able to do all things. He is the Omnipotent over His slaves, and He is the Wise, the Knower.

Say: "What thing is of most weight in testimony?" Say: "Allah is Witness between me and you. And THIS QUR'AN hath been inspired in me, that I may warn therewith you and whomsoever it may reach. Do ye in sooth bear witness that there are gods beside Allah?" Say: "I bear no such witness." Say: "He is only One God. Lo! I am innocent of that which ye associate with Him." Those unto whom We gave the Scripture recognize this Revelation of THIS HOLY QUR'AN as they recognize their own sons. Those who ruin their own souls will not believe. Who doth greater wrong than he who inventeth a lie against Allah or denieth His Revelations? Lo! The wrongdoers will not be successful.

And on the Day We gather them together We shall say unto those who ascribed partners unto Allah: "Where are those partners of your make-believe?" Then will they have no contention save that they will say: "By Allah, our Lord, we never were idolaters." See how they lie against themselves, and how the thing which they devised hath failed them!

Of them are some who listen unto Thee, but We have placed upon their hearts veils, lest they should understand, and in their ears a deafness. If they saw every token they would not believe therein; to the point that, when they come unto thee to argue with Thee, the disbelievers say: "This is naught else than fables of the Old Ones." And they forbid souls from it and avoid it, and they ruin none save themselves, though they perceive not.

If Thou couldst see when they are set before the Fire and say: "Oh, would that we might return! Then would we not deny the Revelations of our Lord but we would be of the believers!" Nay, but that hath become clear unto them which before they used to hide. And if they were sent back they would return unto that which they are forbidden. Lo! They are liars.

And they say: "There is naught save our life of the world, and we shall not be raised again." If Thou couldst see when they are set before their Lord! He will say: "Is not this real?" They will say: "Yea, verily, by our Lord!" He will say: "Taste now the retribution for that ye used to disbelieve." They indeed are losers who deny their meeting with Allah until, when the HOUR cometh on them suddenly, they cry: "Alas for us, that we neglected it!" They bear upon their backs their burdens. Ah, evil is that which they bear! **Naught is the life of the world save a pastime and a sport.** Better far is the abode of the Hereafter for those who keep their duty. Have ye then no sense?

We know well how their talk grieveth Thee, though in truth they deny not Thee but evil-doers flout the Revelations of Allah. Messengers indeed have been denied before Thee, and they were patient under the denial and the persecution till Our succour reached them. There is none to alter the decisions of Allah. Already there hath reached Thee of the tidings of the messengers We sent before.

And if their aversion is grievous unto Thee, then, if thou canst, seek a way down into the earth or a ladder unto the sky that Thou mayst bring unto them a portent (to convince them all)!--If Allah willed, He could have brought them all together to the guidance--So be not Thou among the foolish ones.

Only those can accept who hear. As for the dead, Allah will raise them up; then unto Him they will be returned. They say: "Why hath no portent been sent down upon him from his Lord?" Say: "Lo! Allah is Able to send down a portent." But most of them know not. There is not an animal in the earth, nor a flying creature flying on two wings, but they are peoples like unto you. We have neglected nothing in THE BOOK. Then unto their Lord they will be gathered.

Those who deny Our Revelations are deaf and dumb in darkness. Whom Allah will sendeth astray, and whom He will He placeth on a straight path. Say: "Can ye see yourselves, if the punishment of Allah come upon you or the HOUR come upon you? Do ye then call to any other than Allah? Answer that) if ye are truthful!"

Nay, but unto Him ye call, and He removeth that because of which ye call unto Him, if He will, and ye forget whatever partners ye ascribed unto Him. We have sent already unto peoples that were before Thee, and We visited them with tribulation and adversity, **in order that they might grow humble**. If only, when Our disaster came on them, they had been humble! But their hearts were hardened and **the devil made all that they used to do seem fair unto them**! Then, when they forgot that whereof they had been reminded, We opened unto them the GATES OF ALL THINGS *(Kulli-Shay')* till, even as they were rejoicing in that which they were given, We seized them unawares, and Lo! They were dumbfounded. So of the people who did wrong the last remnant was cut off. Praise be to Allah, Lord of the Worlds!

Say: "Have ye imagined, if Allah should take away your hearing and your sight and seal your hearts, Who is the God Who could restore it to you save Allah?" See how We display the revelations unto them! Yet still they turn away.

223

Say: "Can ye see yourselves, if the punishment of Allah come upon you unawares or openly? Would any perish save wrongdoing folk? We send not the messengers save as bearers of good news and warners. Whoso believeth and doeth right, there shall no fear come upon them neither shall they grieve. But as for those who deny Our Revelations, torment will afflict them for that they used to disobey."

Say (O *MUHAMMAD*, to the disbelievers): "I say not unto you that I possess the treasures of Allah, nor that I have knowledge of the Unseen; and I say not unto you: 'Lo! I am an angel.' I follow only that which is inspired in me." Say: "Are the blind man and the seer equal?" Will ye not then take thought?

Warn hereby those who fear because they know that they will be gathered unto their Lord, for whom there is no protecting ally nor intercessor beside Him, that they may ward off. Repel not those who call upon their Lord at morn and evening, seeking His Countenance. Thou art not accountable for them in aught, nor are they accountable for Thee in aught, that Thou shouldst repel them and be of the wrong-doers.

And even so do **We try some of them by others**, that they say: "Are these they whom Allah favoureth among us?" Is not Allah best Aware of the thanksgivers?

And when those who believe in Our Revelations come unto Thee, say: "Peace be unto you! Your Lord hath prescribed for Himself mercy, that whoso of you doeth evil through ignorance and repenteth afterward thereof and doeth right, for him Lo! He is Forgiving, Merciful. Thus do We expound the Revelations that the way of the unrighteous may be manifest.

Say: "I am forbidden to worship those on whom ye call instead of Allah." Say: "I will not follow your desires, for then should I go astray and I should not be of the rightly guided."

Say: "I am relying on THIS RIGHTEOUS BOOK from my Lord, while ye deny Him. I have not that for which ye are impatient. The decision is for Allah only. He telleth the truth and He is the Best of Deciders."

Say: "If I had that for which ye are impatient, then would the case ere this have been decided between me and you. Allah is Best Aware of the wrong-doers."

And with Him are the KEYS (Rev. 3:7; Is. 22:22; Psalm 89; 2 Sam. 7:1-29) of the Invisible. None but He knoweth them. And He knoweth what is in **the land** and **the sea**. Not a leaf falleth but He knoweth it, not a grain amid the darkness of the earth, naught of wet or dry but it is noted in a CLEAR RECORD.

He it is Who gathereth you at night and knoweth that which ye commit by day. Then He raiseth you again to life therein, that the term appointed for you may be accomplished. And afterward unto Him is your return. Then He will proclaim unto you what ye used to do. He is the Omnipotent over His slaves. He sendeth Guardians over you until, when death cometh unto one of you, Our messengers receive him, and they neglect not. Then are they restored unto Allah, their Lord, the Just. Surely His is the judgment. And He is the most swift of reckoners.

Say: "Who delivereth you from the darkness of the land and the sea?" Ye call upon Him humbly and in secret, saying: "If we are delivered from **this fear** we truly will be of the thankful."

Say: "**Allah delivereth you from this and from all affliction**. Yet ye attribute partners unto Him."

Say: "He is able to send punishment upon you from above you or from beneath your feet, or to bewilder you with dissension and make you taste the tyranny one of another." See how **We Display** the Revelations so that they may understand. Thy people (*O AL-AMIN*) have denied it, though it is the Truth. Say: "I am not put in charge of you. For every announcement there is a term, and ye will come to know."

And when Thou seest those who meddle with Our Revelations, withdraw from them until they meddle with another topic. And if the devil cause Thee to forget, sit not, after the remembrance, with the congregation of wrong-doers. Those who ward off are not accountable for them in aught, but THE REMINDER that haply they too may ward off.

And forsake those who take their religion for a pastime and a jest, and whom the life of the world beguileth. Remind humanity hereby lest a soul be destroyed by what it earneth. It hath beside Allah no protecting ally nor intercessor, and though it offer every compensation it will not be accepted from it. Those are they who **perish by their own deserts**. For them is drink of boiling water and a painful doom, because they disbelieved.

Say: "Shall we cry, instead of unto Allah, unto that which neither profiteth us nor hurteth us, and shall we turn back after Allah hath guided us, like one bewildered whom the devils have infatuated in the earth, who hath companions who invite him to the guidance saying: "Come into us?" Say: "Lo! The guidance of Allah is Guidance, and we are ordered to surrender to the Lord of the Worlds, and to establish worship and be dutiful to Him, and He it is unto Whom ye will be gathered. He it is Who created the heavens and the earth in truth. In the day when He saith: 'Be! It is!' His Word is the Truth, and His will be the Sovereignty on the day when the trumpet is blown. Knower of the Invisible and the Visible, He is the Wise, the Aware."

When Abraham said unto his father Terah (*Azar*): "Takest Thou idols for gods? Lo! I see Thee and Thy folk in error manifest." Thus did We show Abraham the Kingdom of the heavens and the earth that he might be of those possessing certainty (*Iqan*): When the night grew dark upon him he beheld a star. He said: "This is my Lord!" But when it set, he said: "I love not things that set." And when he saw the moon uprising, he exclaimed: "This is my Lord!" But when it set, he said: "Unless my Lord guide me, I surely shall become one of the folk who are astray." And when he saw the sun uprising, he cried: "This is my Lord! This is greater!" And when it set he exclaimed: "O my people! Lo! I am free from all that ye associate. Lo! I have turned my face toward Him Who created the heavens and the earth, as one by nature upright, and I am not of the idolaters."

His people argued with him.

He said: "Dispute ye with me concerning Allah when He hath guided me? I fear not at all that which ye set up beside Him unless my Lord willeth aught. My Lord includeth all things in His knowledge. Will ye not then remember? How should I fear **that which ye set up beside Him**, when ye fear not to set up beside Allah that for which He hath revealed unto you no warrant? Which of the two factions hath more right to safety? Answer me that if ye have knowledge."

Those who believe and obscure not their belief by wrongdoing, theirs is safety; and they are rightly guided. That is Our argument. We gave it unto Abraham against his folk. We raise unto Degrees of Wisdom (*hikmat/chokhmah*) whom We will. Lo! Thy Lord is Wise, Aware.

And We bestowed upon him Isaac and Jacob; each of them We guided; and Noah did We guide aforetime; and of his seed We guided David and Solomon and Job and Joseph and *MOSES* and Aaron. Thus do We reward the good. And Zachariah and John and *JESUS* and Elijah. Each one of them was of the righteous. And Ishmael and Elisha and Jonah and Lot. Each one of them did We prefer above Our creatures, with some of their forefathers and their offspring and their brethren; and We chose them and guided them unto a straight path. Such is the guidance of Allah wherewith He guideth whom He will of His bondmen. **But if they had set up** aught beside Him, all that they did would have been vain.

Those are they unto whom We gave the Scripture and command and prophethood. But if these disbelieve therein, then indeed We shall entrust it to a people who will not be disbelievers therein. Those are they whom Allah guideth, so follow their guidance. Say: "I ask of you no fee for it. Lo! It is naught but THE REMINDER to His creatures.

And they measure not the power of Allah its true measure when they say: "Allah hath naught revealed unto a human being." Say: "Who revealed the Book which *MOSES* brought, a light and guidance for mankind, which ye have put on parchments which ye show, but ye hide much thereof, and by which ye were taught that which ye knew not yourselves nor did your fathers know it?" Say: "Allah." Then leave them to their play of cavilling.

And THIS IS A BLESSED SCRIPTURE which We have Revealed, confirming that which was revealed before it, that Thou mayst warn **the Mother of Villages** and those around her. Those who believe in the Hereafter believe herein, and they are careful of their worship.

Who is guilty of more wrong than he who forgeth a lie against Allah, or saith: "I am inspired," when he is not inspired in aught; and who saith: "I will reveal the like of that which Allah hath revealed?" If Thou couldst see, when the wrong-doers reach the pangs of death and the angels stretch their hands out saying: "Deliver up your souls. This day ye are awarded doom of degradation for that ye spake concerning Allah other than the truth, and used to scorn His portents. Now have ye come unto Us solitary as We did create you at the first, and ye have left behind you all that We bestowed upon you, and We behold not with you those your intercessors, of whom ye claimed that they possessed a share in you. Now is the bond between you severed, and that which ye presumed hath failed you."

Lo! Allah it is Who splitteth the grain of corn and the date-stone for sprouting. He bringeth forth the living from the dead, and is the bringer-forth of the dead from the living. Such is Allah. How then are ye perverted?

He is the Cleaver of the Daybreak, and He hath appointed the night for stillness, and the sun and the moon for reckoning. That is the measuring of the Mighty, the Wise.

And He it is Who hath set for you the stars that ye may guide your course by them amid the darkness of the land and the sea. We have detailed Our Revelations for a people who have knowledge.

And He it is Who hath produced you from a single being, and hath given you a habitation and a repository. We have detailed Our Revelations for a people who have understanding.

He it is Who sendeth down water from the sky, and therewith We bring forth buds of every kind; We bring forth the green blade from which We bring forth the thick-clustered grain; and from the date-palm, from the pollen thereof, spring pendant bunches; and We bring forth gardens of grapes, and the olive and the pomegranate, alike and unlike. Look upon the fruit thereof, when they bear fruit, and upon its ripening. Lo! Herein verily are portents for a people who believe.

Yet they ascribe as partners unto Him the jinn, although He did create them, and impute falsely, without knowledge, sons and daughters unto Him. Glorified be He and High Exalted above all that they ascribe unto Him.

The Originator of the heavens and the earth! How can He have a child, when there is for Him no consort, when He created all things and is Aware of all things?

Such is Allah, your Lord. There is no God save Him, the Creator of all things, so worship Him. And **He taketh care of all things**.

Vision comprehendeth Him not, but He comprehendeth all vision. He is the Subtile, the Aware.

Proofs have come unto you from your Lord, so whoso seeth, it is for his own good, and whoso is blind is blind to his own hurt. And I am not a keeper over you. Thus do We display Our Revelations that they may say (unto Thee): "Thou hast studied," and that We may make it clear for people who have knowledge.

Follow that which is inspired in Thee from Thy Lord; there is no God save Him; and turn away from the idolaters. Had Allah willed, they had not been idolatrous. We have not set Thee as a keeper over them, nor art Thou responsible for them. Revile not those unto whom they pray beside Allah lest they wrongfully revile Allah through ignorance. Thus unto every nation have We made their deed seem fair. Then unto their Lord is their return, and He will tell them what they used to do.

And they swear a solemn oath by Allah that if there come unto them a portent they will believe therein. Say: "Portents are with Allah and so is that which telleth you that if such came unto them they would not believe." We confound their hearts and their eyes. As they believed not therein at the first, We let them wander blindly on in their contumacy.

And though We should send down the angels unto them, and the dead should speak unto them, and We should gather against them all things in array, they would not believe unless Allah so willed. Howbeit, most of them are ignorant.

Thus have We appointed unto every prophet an adversary--devils of humankind and jinn who inspire in one another plausible discourse through guile. If thy Lord willed, they would not do so; so leave them alone with their devising; that the hearts of those who believe not in the Hereafter may incline thereto, and that they may take pleasure therein, and that they may earn what they are earning.

"Shall I seek other than Allah for judge, when He it is Who hath revealed unto you THIS SCRIPTURE fully explained?" Those unto whom We give the Scripture know that it is revealed from thy Lord in truth. So be not Thou of the waverers. Perfected is the **Word of Thy Lord** in truth and justice. There is naught that can change His words. He is the Hearer, the Knower.

If Thou obeyedst most of those on earth they would mislead Thee far from Allah's way. They follow naught but an opinion, and they do but guess. Lo! Thy Lord, He knoweth best who erreth from His way; and He knoweth best who are the rightly guided.

Eat of that over which the name of Allah hath been mentioned, if ye are believers in His Revelations. How should ye not eat of that over which the name of Allah hath been mentioned, when He hath explained unto you that which is forbidden unto you unless ye are compelled thereto. But Lo! Many are led astray by their own lusts through ignorance. Lo! Thy Lord, He is Best Aware of the transgressors.

Forsake the outwardness of sin and the inwardness thereof. Lo! Those who garner sin will be awarded that which they have earned.

And eat not of that whereon Allah's name hath not been mentioned, for Lo! It is abomination. Lo! The devils do inspire their minions to dispute with you. But if ye obey them, ye will be in truth idolaters. Is he who was dead and We have raised him unto life, and set for him a light wherein he walketh among men, as him whose similitude is in utter darkness whence he cannot emerge? Thus is their conduct made fairseeming for the disbelievers.

And thus have We made in every city great ones of its wicked ones, that they should plot therein. They do but plot against themselves, though they perceive not. And when a token cometh unto them, they say: "We will not believe till we are given that which Allah's messengers are given." Allah knoweth best with whom to place His message. Humiliation from Allah and heavy punishment will smite the guilty for their scheming.

And whomsoever it is Allah's will to guide, **He expandeth his bosom unto the Surrender**, and whomsoever it is His Will to send astray, He maketh his bosom close and narrow **as if he were engaged in sheer ascent**. Thus Allah layeth ignominy upon those who believe not.

This is the path of thy Lord, a straight path. We have detailed Our Revelations for a people who take heed. For them is the Abode of Peace (Baghdad) with their Lord. He will be their Protecting Friend because of what they used to do. In the day when He will gather them together He will say: "O ye assembly of the jinn! Many of humankind did ye seduce." And their adherents among humankind will say: "Our Lord! We enjoyed one another, but now we have arrived at the appointed term which Thou appointedst for us." He will say: "Fire is your home. Abide therein for ever, save him whom Allah willeth." Lo! Thy Lord is Wise, Aware. Thus We let some of the wrong-doers have power over others because of what they are wont to earn.

O ye assembly of the jinn and humankind! Came there not unto you messengers of your own who recounted unto you My tokens and warned you of the meeting of this your Day? They will say: "We testify against ourselves." And **the life of the world** beguiled them. And they testify against themselves that they were disbelievers. This is because thy Lord destroyeth not the townships arbitrarily while their people are unconscious of the wrong they do.

For all there will be ranks from what they did. Thy Lord is not unaware of what they do. Thy Lord is the Absolute, the Lord of Mercy. If He will, He can remove you and can cause what He will to follow after you, even as He raised you from the seed of other folk. Lo! that which ye are promised will surely come to pass, and ye cannot escape.

Say: "O my people! Work according to your power. Lo! I too am working." Thus ye will come to know for which of us will be the happy SEQUEL. Lo! the wrong-doers will not be successful. They assign unto Allah, of the crops and cattle which He created, a portion, and they say: "This is Allah's"--in their make-believe--"and this is for partners in regard to us." Thus that which they assign unto His partners in them reacheth not Allah and that which they assign unto Allah goeth to their (so-called) partners. Evil is their ordinance.

Thus have their (so-called) partners **made the killing of their children** (**including in war**) to seem fair unto many of the idolaters, that they may ruin them and make their faith obscure for them. Had Allah willed it otherwis), they had not done so. So leave them alone with their devices.

And they say: "Such cattle and crops are forbidden. No-one is to eat of them save whom we will"--in their make-believe--cattle whose backs are forbidden, cattle over which they mention not the name of Allah. All that is a lie against Him. He will repay them for that which they invent.

And they say: "That which is in the bellies of such cattle is reserved for our males and is forbidden to our wives;" but if it be born dead, then they all may be partakers thereof. He will **reward them for their attribution of such ordinances unto Him**. Lo, He is Wise, Aware.

They are losers who **besottedly have slain their children** without knowledge, and have forbidden that which Allah bestowed upon them, inventing a lie against Allah. They indeed have gone astray and are not guided.

He it is Who produceth gardens trellised and untrellised, and the date-palm, and crops of divers flavor, and the olive and the pomegranate, like and unlike. Eat ye of the fruit thereof when it fruiteth, and pay the due thereof upon the harvest day, and be not prodigal. Lo! Allah loveth not the prodigals.

And of the cattle (He produceth) some for burdens, some for food. Eat of that which Allah hath bestowed upon you, and follow not the footsteps of the devil, for Lo! He is an open foe to you. Eight pairs: Of the sheep twain, and of the goats twain. Say: "Hath He forbidden the two males or the two females, or that which the wombs of the two females contain? Expound to me the case with knowledge, if ye are truthful." And of the camels twain and of the oxen twain. Say: "Hath He forbidden the two males or the two females, or that which the wombs of the two females contain; or were ye by to witness when Allah commanded you all this?" Then who doth greater wrong than he who deviseth a lie concerning Allah, that he may lead mankind astray without knowledge. Lo! Allah guideth not wrongdoing folk.

Say: "I find not in that which is revealed unto me aught prohibited to an eater that he eat thereof, except it be carrion, or blood poured forth, or swineflesh--for that verily is foul[*]--or the abomination which was immolated to the name of other than Allah. But whoso is compelled thereto, neither craving nor transgressing, for him Lo! Thy Lord is Forgiving, Merciful.

Unto those who are Jews We forbade every animal with claws. And of the oxen and the sheep forbade We unto them the fat thereof save that upon the backs or the entrails, or that which is mixed with the bone. That we awarded them for their rebellion. And Lo! We verily are truthful.

So if they give the lie to Thee, say: "Your Lord is a Lord of All- Embracing Mercy, and His wrath will never be withdrawn from guilty folk."

They who are idolaters will say: "Had Allah willed, we had not ascribed (unto Him) partners neither had our fathers, nor had we forbidden aught." Thus did those who were before them give the lie till they tasted of the fear of Us. Say: "Have ye any knowledge that ye can adduce for Us? Lo! ye follow naught but an opinion, Lo! ye do but guess."

Say: "For Allah's is the final argument--Had He willed He could indeed have guided all of you."

Say: "Come, bring your witnesses who can bear witness that Allah forbade all this." And if they bear witness, do not thou bear witness with them. **Follow Thou not the whims** of those who deny Our Revelations, those who believe not in the Hereafter and deem others equal with their Lord.

Say: "Come, I will recite unto you that which your Lord hath made a sacred duty for you: That ye ascribe no thing as partner unto Him and that ye do good to parents, and that ye slay not your

---

[*]With Trichanosis.

230

children because of penury--We provide for you and for them--and that ye draw not nigh to lewd things whether open or concealed. And that ye slay not the life which Allah hath made sacred, save in the course of justice. This He hath command you, in order that ye may discern."

"And approach not the wealth of the orphan save with that which is better, till he reach maturity. Give full measure and full weight, in justice. We task not any soul beyond its scope. And if ye give your word, do justice thereunto, even though it be against a kinsman; and fulfill **the covenant of Allah**." This He commandeth you that haply ye may remember.

And (He commandeth you, saying): "This is **My Straight Path**, so follow it. Follow not other ways, lest ye be parted from His WAY. This hath He ordained for you, that ye may ward off."

Again, We gave the Scripture unto *MOSES*, complete for him who would do good, an explanation of all things, a guidance and a mercy, that they might believe in the meeting with their Lord.

And THIS IS A BLESSED SCRIPTURE which We have revealed. So follow it and ward off evil, that ye may find mercy. Lest ye (Muslims) should say: "The Scripture was revealed only to two sects before us,* and we in sooth were unaware of what they read;" Or lest ye should say: "If the Scripture had been revealed unto us, we surely had been better guided than are they." Now hath there come unto you THIS RIGHTEOUS BOOK from your Lord, a guidance and mercy; and who doeth greater wrong than he who denieth the Revelations of Allah, and turneth away from them? We award unto those who turn away from Our Revelations an evil doom because of their aversion.

Wait they, indeed, for nothing less than that the angels should come unto them, or thy Lord should come, or there should come one of the portents from Thy Lord? In the day when one of the portents from thy Lord cometh, its belief availeth naught a soul which theretofore believed not, nor in its belief earned good (by works). Say: "Wait ye! Lo! We too are waiting."

Lo! As for those who sunder their religion and become schismatics, no concern at all hast Thou with them. Their case will go to Allah, Who then will tell them what they used to do. Whoso bringeth a good deed will receive tenfold the like thereof, while whoso bringeth an ill-deed will be awarded but the like thereof; and they will not be wronged.

Say: "Lo! As for me, my Lord hath guided me unto a straight path, a right religion, the **Community of the Covenant Abraham**, the upright, who was no idolater."

Say: "Lo! My worship and my sacrifice and my living and my dying are for Allah, Lord of the Worlds. He hath no partner. This am I commanded, and I am first of those who Surrender unto Him."

Say: "Shall I seek another than Allah for Lord, when He is Lord of all things? Each soul earneth only on its own account, nor doth any laden bear another's load. Then unto your Lord is your return and He will tell you that wherein ye differed."

---

*Jews and Christians.

He it is Who hath placed you as viceroys of the earth and hath exalted some of you in rank above others, that He may try you by that which He hath given you. Lo! Thy Lord is swift in prosecution, and Lo! He verily is Forgiving, Merciful.

XXIII. JUZ'UN SIPARA VENTITERZO:

91. Bism'illah Ar-Rahman Ar-Rahim! an-Nahl: THE BEE.

The commandment of Allah will come to pass, so seek not ye to hasten it. Glorified and Exalted be He above all that they associate. He sendeth down the angels with the Spirit of His command unto whom He will of His bondmen, saying: "Warn mankind that there is no God save Me, so keep your duty unto Me." He hath created the heavens and the earth with truth. High be He Exalted above all that they associate.

He hath created man from a drop of goo, yet Behold! He is an open opponent.

And the cattle hath He created, whence ye have warm clothing and uses, and whereof ye eat; and wherein is beauty for you, when ye bring them home, and when ye take them out to pasture. And they bear your loads for you unto a land ye could not reach save with great trouble to yourselves. Lo! your Lord is Full of Pity, Merciful.

And horses and mules and asses hath He created that ye may ride them, and for ornament. And He createth that which ye know not.

And Allah's is the direction of THE WAY, and some go not straight. And had He willed He would have led you all aright. He it is Who sendeth down water from the sky, whence ye have drink, and whence are trees on which ye send your beasts to pasture. Therewith He causeth crops to grow for you, and the olive and the date-palm and grapes and all kinds of fruit. Lo! Herein is indeed a portent for people who reflect.

And He hath constrained the night and the day and the sun and the moon to be of service unto you, and the stars are made subservient by His command. Lo! Herein indeed are portents for people who have sense.

And whatsoever He hath created for you in the earth of divers hues, Lo! Therein is indeed a portent for people who take heed.

And He it is Who hath constrained the sea to be of service that ye eat fresh meat from thence, and bring forth from thence ornaments which ye wear. And thou seest the ships ploughing it that ye may seek of His bounty and that haply ye may give thanks. And He hath cast into the earth firm hills that it quake not with you, and streams and roads that ye may find a way. And landmarks (*mitzvah*) too, and by the star they find a way. Is He then Who createth as him who createth not? Will ye not then remember? And if ye would count the favor of Allah ye cannot reckon it. Lo! Allah is indeed Forgiving, Merciful.

And Allah knoweth that which ye keep hidden and that which ye proclaim. Those unto whom they cry beside Allah created naught, but are themselves created. They are dead, not living. And they know not when they will be raised.

Your God is One God.[*] But as for those who believe not in the Hereafter their hearts refuse to know, for they are proud. Assuredly Allah knoweth that which they keep hidden and that which they proclaim. Lo! He loveth not the proud. And when it is said unto them: "What hath your Lord revealed?" They say: "Mere fables of the Old Ones." That they may bear their burdens undiminished on the Day of Resurrection, with somewhat of the burdens of those whom they mislead without knowledge. Ah! Evil is that which they bear!

Those before them plotted, so Allah struck at the foundations of their building, and then the roof fell down upon them from above them, and the doom came on them whence they knew not; then on the Day of Resurrection He will disgrace them and will say: "Where are My partners, for whose sake ye opposed My guidance?" Those who have been given knowledge will say: "Disgrace this day and evil are upon the disbelievers, whom the angels cause to die while they are wronging themselves." Then will they make full submission saying: "We used not to do any wrong." Nay! Surely Allah is Knower of what ye used to do.

So enter the GATES of hell (there are at least two HELLGATES) , to dwell therein for ever. Woeful indeed will be the lodging of the arrogant. And it is said unto those who ward off evil: "What hath your Lord revealed?" They say: "Good. For those who do good in this world there is a good reward and the home of the Hereafter will be better. Pleasant indeed will be the home of those who ward off--Gardens of Eden which they enter, underneath which rivers flow, wherein they have what they will. Thus Allah repayeth those who ward off, those whom the angels cause to die when they are good. They say: "Salem be unto you! Enter the Garden because of what ye used to do."

Await they aught say that the angels should come unto them or thy Lord's command should come to pass? Even so did those before them. **Allah wronged them not, but they did wrong themselves**, so that the evils of what they did smote them, and that which they used to mock surrounded them. And the idolaters say: "Had Allah willed, we had not worshipped aught beside Him, we and our fathers, nor had we forbidden aught without command from Him. Even so did those before them. Are the messengers charged with aught save plain conveyance of the message?

And verily We have raised in every nation a messenger, proclaiming: "Serve Allah and shun false gods." Then some of them are whom Allah guided, and some of them upon whom error had just hold. Do but travel in the land and see the nature of the consequence for the deniers! Even if Thou desirest their right guidance, still Allah assuredly will not guide him who misleadeth. Such have no helpers.

And they swear by Allah their most binding oaths that Allah will not raise up him who dieth. Nay, but it is a promise binding upon Him in truth, but most of humankind know not, that He may explain unto them that wherein they differ, and that those who disbelieved may know that

---

[*]"Hear, O Israel: The LORD our God, the LORD is ONE" (Deut. 6:4 NIV).

they were liars. And Our word unto a thing, when We intend it, is only that We say unto it: "Be! and it is."

And those who became fugitives for the cause of Allah after they had been oppressed, We verily shall give them goodly lodging in the world, and surely the reward of the Hereafter is greater, if they but knew; such as are steadfast and put their trust in Allah. And We sent not as Our messengers before Thee other than men whom We inspired--Ask the followers of THE REMEMBRANCE if ye know not!--with THIS RIGHTEOUS BOOK and writings; and We have revealed unto Thee THE REMEMBRANCE that Thou mayst explain to mankind that which hath been revealed for them, and that haply they may reflect.

Are they who plan ill-deeds then secure that Allah will not cause the earth to swallow them, or that the doom will not come on them whence they know not? Or that He will not seize them in their going to and fro so that there be no escape for them? Or that He will not seize them with a gradual wasting? Lo! Thy Lord is indeed Full of Pity, Merciful.

Have they not observed all things that Allah hath created, how their shadows incline to the right and to the left, making prostration unto Allah, and they are lowly? And unto Allah maketh prostration whatsoever is in the heavens and whatsoever is in the earth of living creatures, and the angels also and they are not proud. They fear their Lord above them, and do what they are bidden. Allah hath said: "Choose not two gods. There is only One God. So of Me, Me only, be in awe." Unto Him belongeth whatsoever is in the heavens and the earth, and **religion is His for ever**. Will ye then fear any other than Allah?

And whatever of comfort ye enjoy, it is from Allah. Then, when misfortune reacheth you, unto Him ye cry for help. And afterward, when He hath rid you of the misfortune, Behold! A set of you attribute partners to their Lord, so as to deny that which We have given them. Then enjoy life while ye may, for ye will come to know. And they assign a portion of that which We have given them unto what they know not. By Allah! But ye will indeed be asked concerning all that ye used to invent.

And they assign unto Allah daughters--Be He Glorified!--and unto themselves what they desire; when if one of them receiveth tidings of the birth of a female, his face remaineth darkened, and he is wroth inwardly. He hideth himself from the folk because of the evil of that whereof he hath had tidings, asking himself: "Shall he keep it in contempt, or bury it beneath the dust." Verily evil is their judgment. For those who believe not in the Hereafter is an evil similitude, and Allah's is **the Sublime Similitude**. He is the Mighty, the Wise.

If Allah were to take mankind to task for their wrong-doing, he would not leave hereon a living creature, but He reprieveth them to an appointed term, and when their term cometh they cannot put it off an *hour* nor yet advance it. And they assign unto Allah that which they themselves dislike, and their tongues expound the lie that the better portion will be theirs. Assuredly theirs will be the Fire, and they will be abandoned.

By Allah, We verily sent messengers unto the nations before Thee, but the devil made their deeds fairseeming unto them. So he is their patron this day, and theirs will be a painful doom.

234

And We have revealed the Scripture unto Thee only that Thou mayst explain unto them that wherein they differ, and as a guidance and a mercy for a people who believe. Allah sendeth down water from the sky and therewith reviveth the earth after her death. Lo! herein is indeed a portent for a folk who hear.

And Lo! In the cattle there is a lesson for you. We give you to drink of that which is in their bellies, from betwixt the refuse and the blood, pure milk palatable to the drinkers. And of the fruits of the date-palm, and grapes, whence ye derive strong drink and also good nourishment. Lo! Therein is indeed a portent for people who have sense.

And thy Lord inspired the bee, saying: "Choose Thou habitations in the hills and in the trees and in that which they thatch; then eat of all fruits, and follow the ways of thy Lord, made smooth for Thee. There cometh forth from their bellies a drink divers of hues, wherein is healing for humankind. Lo! herein is indeed a portent for people who reflect.

And Allah createth you, then causeth you to die, and among you is he who is brought back to the most abject stage of life, so that he knoweth nothing after having had knowledge. Lo! Allah is Knower, Powerful. And Allah hath favored some of you above others in provision. Now those who are more favored will by no means hand over their provision to those whom their right hands possess, so that they may be equal with them in respect thereof. Is it then the grace of Allah that they deny?

And Allah hath given you wives of your own kind, and hath given you, from your wives, sons and grandsons, and hath made provision of good things for you. Is it then in vanity that they believe and in the grace of Allah that they disbelieve? And they worship beside Allah that which owneth no provision whatsoever for them from the heavens or the earth, nor have they (whom they worship) any power. So coin not similitudes for Allah. Lo! Allah knoweth; ye know not.

Allah coineth a similitude: on the one hand a chattel slave, who hath control of nothing, and on the other hand one on whom we have bestowed a fair provision from Us, and he spendeth thereof secretly and openly. Are they equal? Praise be to Allah! But most of them know not.

And Allah coineth a similitude: Two men, one of them dumb, having control of nothing, and he is a burden on his owner; whithersoever he directeth him to go, he bringeth no good. Is he equal with one who enjoineth justice and followeth a straight path?

And unto Allah belongeth the Unseen of the heavens and the earth, and the matter of the HOUR is but as a twinkling of the eye, or it is nearer still. Lo! Allah is Able to do all things. And Allah brought you forth from the wombs of your mothers knowing nothing, and gave you hearing and sight and hearts that haply ye might give thanks. Have they not seen the birds obedient in mid-air? None holdeth them save Allah. Lo! Herein, verily, are portents for a people who believe.

And Allah hath given you in your houses an abode, and hath given you also, of the hides of cattle, houses which ye find light to carry on the day of migration and on the day of pitching camp; and of their wool and their fur and their hair, caparison and comfort for a while. And Allah hath given you, of that which He hath created, shelter from the sun; and hath given you places of refuge in the mountains, and hath given you coats to ward off the heat from you, and coats of armor to save you from your own foolhardiness. Thus doth He perfect His favor unto you, in order that ye may Surrender.

Then, if they turn away, Thy duty is but plain conveyance of the message. They know the favor of Allah and then deny it. Most of them are ingrates. And bethink you of the day when we raise up of every nation a witness, then there is no leave for disbelievers, nor are they allowed to make amends. And when those who did wrong behold the doom, it will not be made light for them, nor will they be reprieved. And when those who ascribed partners to Allah behold those partners of theirs, they will say: "Our Lord! These are our partners unto whom we used to cry instead of Thee." But they will fling to them the saying: "Lo! Ye verily are liars!" And they proffer unto Allah submission on that day, and all that they used to invent hath failed them.

For those who disbelieve and debar souls from the way of Allah, We add doom to doom because they wrought corruption, and bethink you of the day when We raise in every nation a witness against them of their own folk, and We bring Thee (*O AL-AMIN*) as a witness against these. And We reveal the Scripture unto Thee as an exposition of all things, and a guidance and a mercy and good tidings for those who have Surrendered.

Lo! Allah enjoineth justice and kindness, and giving to kinsfolk, and forbiddeth illegal acts and abomination and wickedness. He exhorteth you in order that ye may take heed. Fulfill **the Covenant of Allah** when ye have covenanted, and break not your oaths after the asseveration of them, and after ye have made Allah surety over you. Lo! Allah knoweth what ye do.

And be not like unto her who unravelleth the thread, after she hath made it strong, to thin filaments, making your oaths a deceit between you because of a nation being more numerous than another nation. Allah only trieth you thereby, and He verily will explain to you on the Day of Resurrection that wherein ye differed.

Had Allah willed He could have made you all one nation, but He sendeth whom He will astray and guideth whom He will, and ye will indeed be asked of what ye used to do. Make not your oaths a deceit between you, lest a foot should slip after being firmly planted and ye should taste evil forasmuch as ye debarred souls from the way of Allah, and yours should be an awful doom.

And purchase not a small gain at **the price of Allah's Covenant**. Lo! That which Allah hath is better for you, if ye did but know. That which ye have wasteth away, and that which Allah hath remaineth. And verily We shall pay those who are steadfast a recompense in proportion to the best of what they used to do. Whosoever doeth right, whether male or female, and is a believer, him verily we shall quicken with good life, and We shall pay them a recompense in proportion to the best of what they used to do.

And when Thou recitest THIS QUR'AN, seek refuge in Allah from Satan the outcast. Lo! He hath no power over those who believe and put trust in their Lord. His power is only over those who make a friend of him, and those who ascribe partners unto Him. And when We put a Revelation in place of another Revelation--and Allah knoweth best what He revealeth--they say: "Lo! Thou art but inventing." Most of them know not.

Say: "The Holy Spirit hath delivered it from thy Lord with truth, that it may confirm the faith of those who believe, and as guidance and good tidings for those who have surrendered to Allah." And We know well that they say: "Only a man teacheth him. The speech of him at whom they falsely hint is outlandish, and this is clear Arabic speech." Lo! those who disbelieve the Revelations of Allah, Allah guideth them not and theirs will be a painful doom. Only they invent falsehood who believe not Allah's Revelations, and they are the liars.

Whoso disbelieveth in Allah after his belief--save him who is forced thereto and whose heart is still content with the Faith--but whoso findeth ease in disbelief: On them is wrath from Allah. Theirs will be an awful doom. That is because they have chosen **the life of the world** rather than the Hereafter, and because Allah guideth not the disbelieving folk. Such are they whose hearts and ears and eyes Allah hath sealed. And such are the heedless. Assuredly in the Hereafter they are the losers.

Then Lo! Thy Lord--for those who became fugitives after they had been persecuted, and then fought and were steadfast--Lo! Thy Lord afterward is indeed Forgiving, Merciful. On the Day when every soul will come pleading for itself, and every soul will be repaid what it did, and they will not be wronged.

Allah coineth a similitude: a township that dwelt secure and well content, its provision coming to it in abundance from every side, but it disbelieved in Allah's favors, so Allah made it experience the garb of dearth and fear because of what they used to do. And verily there had come unto them a messenger from among them, but they had denied him, and so the torment seized them while they were wrong-doers. So eat of the lawful and good food which Allah hath provided for you, and thank the bounty of your Lord if it is Him ye serve. He hath forbidden for you only carrion and blood and swineflesh and that which hath been immolated in the name of any other than Allah; but he who is driven thereto, neither craving nor transgressing, Lo!Tthen Allah is Forgiving, Merciful.

And speak not, concerning that which your own tongues qualify (as clean or unclean), the falsehood: "This is lawful, and this is forbidden," so that ye invent a lie against Allah. Lo! Those who invent a lie against Allah will not succeed. A brief enjoyment will be theirs; and theirs a painful doom.

And unto those who are Jews We have forbidden that which We have already related unto Thee. And **We wronged them not, but they were wont to wrong themselves.** Then Lo! Thy Lord--for those who do evil in ignorance and afterward repent and amend--Lo! For them Thy Lord is afterward indeed Forgiving, Merciful.

Lo! Abraham was a nation obedient to Allah, by nature upright, and he was not of the idolaters; Thankful for His bounties; He chose him and He guided him unto a straight path. And We gave him good in the world, and in the Hereafter he is among the righteous. And afterward We inspired Thee: "Follow **the Religion of Abraham**, as one by nature upright. He was not of the idolaters."

The Sabbath was appointed only for those who differed concerning it, and Lo! Thy Lord will judge between them on the Day of Resurrection concerning that wherein they used to differ.

Call unto the way of thy Lord with wisdom and fair exhortation, and reason with them in the better way. Lo! Thy Lord is Best Aware of him who strayeth from His way, and He is Best Aware of those who go aright. If ye punish, then punish with the like of that wherewith ye were afflicted. But if ye endure patiently, verily it is better for the patient.

Endure Thou patiently (*O AL-AMIN*). Thine endurance is only by the help of Allah. Grieve not for them, and be not in distress because of that which they devise.

Lo! Allah is with those who keep their duty unto Him and those who are doers of good.

92. Bism'illah Ar-Rahman Ar-Rahim! al- 'Ankabut: THE SPIDER.

Alif. Lam. Mim.

Do men think when they say "We believe" they shall be let alone and not be put to proof?

Lo! We tested those who were before you. Thus Allah knoweth those who are sincere, and knoweth those who feign. Or do those who do ill-deeds imagine that they can outstrip Us? Evil is that which they decide. Whoso looketh forward to the meeting with Allah (let him know that) Allah's reckoning is surely nigh, and He is the Hearer, the Knower. **And whosoever striveth, striveth only for himself**, for Lo! Allah is altogether Independent of His creatures.

And as for those who believe and do good works, We shall remit from them their evil deeds and shall repay them the best that they did. We have enjoined on man kindness to parents; but if they strive to make Thee join with Me that of which Thou hast no knowledge, then obey them not. Unto Me is your return and I shall tell you what ye used to do. And as for those who believe and do good works, We verily shall make them enter in among the righteous.

Of humankind is he who saith: "We believe in Allah," but, if he be made to suffer for the sake of Allah, he mistaketh the persecution of humankind for Allah's punishment; and then, if victory cometh from thy Lord, will say: "Lo! We were with you all the while. Is not Allah Best Aware of what is in the bosoms of His creatures? Verily Allah knoweth those who believe, and verily He knoweth the hypocrites.

Those who disbelieve say unto those who believe: "Follow our way of religion and we verily will bear your sins for you." They cannot bear aught of their sins. Lo! They verily are liars. But they verily will bear their own loads and other loads beside their own, and they verily will be questioned on the Day of Resurrection concerning that which they invented.

And verily we sent Noah as Our messenger unto his folk, and he continued with them for a thousand years save fifty years; and the flood engulfed them, for they were wrong-doers. And We rescued him and those with him in the ship, and made of it a portent for the peoples.

And Abraham! When he said unto his folk: "Serve Allah, and keep your duty unto Him;" that is better for you if ye did but know. Ye serve instead of Allah only idols, and ye only invent a lie. Lo! Those whom ye serve instead of Allah own no provision for you. So seek your provision from Allah, and serve Him, and give thanks unto Him, for unto Him ye will be brought back. But if ye deny, then nations have denied before you. The messenger is only to convey the message plainly.

See they not how Allah produceth creation, then reproduceth it? Lo! for Allah that is easy.

Say: "Travel in the land and see how He originated creation, then Allah bringeth forth the later growth. Lo! Allah is Able to do all things." He punisheth whom He will and showeth mercy unto whom He will, and unto Him ye will be turned. Ye cannot escape from Him in the earth or in the sky, and beside Allah there is for you no friend or helper. Those who disbelieve in the Revelations of Allah and in their Meeting with Him, such have no hope of My mercy. For such there is a painful doom.

But the answer of his folk was only that they said: "Kill him" or "Burn him." Then Allah saved him from the Fire. Lo! herein verily are portents for folk who believe.

He said: "Ye have chosen only idols instead of Allah. The love between you is only in the life of the world. Then on the Day of Resurrection ye will deny each other and curse each other, and your abode will be the Fire, and ye will have no helpers."

And Lot believed him, and said: "Lo! I am a fugitive unto my Lord. Lo! He, only He, is the Mighty, the Wise."

And We bestowed on him Isaac and Jacob, and We established the prophethood and the Scripture among his seed, and We gave him his reward in the world, and Lo! In the Hereafter he verily is among the righteous.

And Lot! When he said unto his folk: "Lo! Ye commit that which is forbidden such as no creature did before you. For come ye not in unto males, and cut ye not the road for travellers, and commit ye not abomination in your meetings?" But the answer of his folk was only that they said: "Bring Allah's doom upon us if thou art a truthteller!"

He said: "My Lord! Give me victory over folk who work corruption."

And when Our messengers brought Abraham the good news, they said: "Lo! We are about to destroy the people of that township, for its people are wrong-doers."

He said: "Lo! Lot is there." They said: "We are best aware of who is there. We are to deliver him and his household, all save his wife, who is of those who stay behind."

And when Our messengers came unto Lot, he was troubled upon their account, for he could not protect them; but they said: "Fear not, nor grieve! Lo! we are to deliver Thee and Thy household, all save thy wife, who is of those who stay behind. Lo! We are about to bring down upon the folk of this township a fury from the sky because they are evil-livers." And verily of that We have left a clear sign for people who have sense.

And unto Midian We sent *ZOROASTER (Shu'ayb) SPENTA MANIYUSH*, their brother. He said: "O my people! Serve Allah, and look forward to the Last Day, and do not evil, making mischief, in the earth." But they denied him, and the dreadful earthquake took them, and morning found them prostrate in their dwelling place.

And A'ad and Thamud! Their fate is manifest unto you from their ruined and deserted dwellings. Satan made their deeds seem fair unto them and so debarred them from the Way, though they were keen observers.

And Korah, Pharaoh and Haman! *MOSES* came unto them with THIS RIGHTEOUS BOOK, but they were boastful in the land. And they were not winners. So We took each one in his sin; of them was he on whom We sent a hurricane, and of them was he who was overtaken by the Awful Cry, and of them was he whom We caused the earth to swallow, and of them was he whom We drowned. It was not for Allah to wrong them, but they wronged themselves.

The likeness of those who choose other patrons than Allah is as the likeness of the spider when she taketh unto herself a house, and Lo! The frailest of all houses is the spider's house, if they but knew. Lo! Allah knoweth what thing they invoke instead of Him. He is the Mighty, the Wise.

As for these similitudes, We coin them for mankind, but **none will grasp their meaning save the wise.**

Allah created the heavens and the earth with truth. Lo! therein is indeed a portent for believers. Recite that which hath been inspired in Thee of the Scripture, and establish worship. Lo! Worship preserveth from that which is frobidden and iniquity, but verily remembrance of Allah is more important. And Allah knoweth what ye do.

And argue not with the People of the Scripture unless it be in a way that is better, save with such of them as do wrong; and say: "**We believe in that which hath been revealed unto us and revealed unto you; our God and your God is One, and unto Him we surrender.**"

In like manner We have revealed unto Thee this Scripture, and those unto whom We gave the Scripture aforetime will believe therein; and of these also there are some who believe therein. And none deny Our Revelations save the disbelievers.

And Thou (O *MUHAMMAD*) wast not a reader of any scripture before it, nor didst Thou write it with Thy right hand, for then might those have doubted, who follow falsehood. But it is clear Revelations in the hearts of those who have been given knowledge, and none deny Our Revelations save wrong-doers. And they say: "Why are not portents sent down upon him from his Lord?" Say: "Portents are with Allah only, and I am but a plain warner."

Is it not enough for them that We have sent down unto Thee this Scripture which is read unto them? Lo! Herein verily is mercy, and a reminder for folk who believe. Say: "Allah sufficeth for witness between me and you. He knoweth whatsoever is in the heavens and the earth. And those who believe in vanity and disbelieve in Allah, they it is who are the losers."

They bid Thee hasten on the doom. And if a term had not been appointed, the doom would assuredly have come unto them ere now. And verily it will come upon them suddenly when they perceive not. They bid Thee hasten on the doom, when Lo! Hell verily will encompass the disbelievers on the day when the doom will overwhelm them from above them and from underneath their feet, and He will say: "Taste what ye used to do!"

O my bondmen who believe! Lo! My earth is spacious. Therefore serve Me only. Every soul will taste of death. Then unto Us ye will be returned. Those who believe and do good works, them verily We shall house in lofty dwellings of the Garden underneath which rivers flow. There they will dwell secure. How sweet the guerdon of the toilers, who persevere, and put their trust in their Lord! And how many an animal there is that beareth not its own provision! Allah provideth for it and for you. He is the Hearer, the Knower.

And if Thou wert to ask them: "Who created the heavens and the earth, and constrained the sun and the moon to their appointed work?" they would say: "Allah." How then are they turned away?

Allah maketh the provision wide for whom He will of His bondmen, and straiteneth it for whom He will. Lo! Allah is Aware of all things.

And if Thou wert to ask them: "Who causeth water to come down from the sky, and therewith reviveth the earth after its death?" they verily would say: "Allah." Say: "Praise be to Allah!" But most of them have no sense.

This life of the world is but a pastime and a game. Lo! The home of the Hereafter--that is Life, if they but knew.

And when they mount upon the ships they pray to Allah, making their faith PURE for Him only, but when He bringeth them safe to land, Behold! They ascribe partners unto Him, that they may disbelieve in that which We have given them, and that they may take their ease. But they will come to know. Have they not seen that We have appointed a Sanctuary immune from violence, while humankind are ravaged all around them? Do they then believe in falsehood and disbelieve in the bounty of Allah?

Who doeth greater wrong than he who inventeth a lie concerning Allah, or denieth the truth when it cometh unto him? Is not there a home in hell for disbelievers?

As for those who strive in Us, We surely guide them to Our PATHS, and Lo! Allah is with the good.

XXIV. JUZ'UN SIPARA VENTIQUATTRO:

93. Bism'illah Ar-Rahman Ar-Rahim! al-Jathiyah: THE KNEELING.

Ha. Mim.

The revelation of the Scripture is from Allah, the Mighty, the Wise.

Lo! in the heavens and the earth are portents for believers. And in your creation, and all the beasts that He scattereth in the earth, are portents for a folk whose faith is sure. And the difference of night and day and the provision that Allah sendeth down from the sky and thereby quickeneth the earth after her death, and the ordering of the winds, are portents for a people who have sense.

These are the portents of Allah which We recite unto Thee with truth. Then in what fact, after Allah and His portents, will they believe? Woe unto each sinful liar, who heareth the Revelations of Allah recited unto him, and then continueth in pride as though he heard them not. Give him tidings of a painful doom. And when he knoweth aught of Our Revelations he maketh it a jest. For such there is a shameful doom. Beyond them there is hell, and that which they have earned will naught avail them, nor those whom they have chosen for protecting friends beside Allah. Theirs will be an awful doom. This is guidance. And those who disbelieve the Revelations of their Lord, for them there is a painful doom of wrath.

Allah it is Who hath made the sea of service unto you that the ships may run thereon by His command, and that ye may seek of His bounty, and that haply ye may be thankful; and hath made of service unto you whatsoever is in the heavens and whatsoever is in the earth; it is all from Him. Lo! herein verily are portents for a people who reflect.

Tell those who believe to forgive those who hope not for the days of Allah; in order that He may requite folk what they used to earn. Whoso doeth right, it is for his soul, and whoso doeth wrong, it is against it. And afterward unto your Lord ye will be brought back.

And verily we gave the Children of Israel the Scripture and the Command and the Prophethood, and provided them with good things and favored them above all peoples; and gave them plain commandments (*mitzvah*). And they differed not until after the knowledge came unto them, through rivalry among themselves. Lo! thy Lord will judge between them on the Day of Resurrection concerning that wherein they used to differ.

And now have We set Thee on a clear road of Our commandment; so follow it, and follow not the whims of those who know not. Lo! They can avail Thee naught against Allah. And Lo! As for the wrong-doers, some of them are friends of others; and Allah is the Friend of those who ward off evil. This is clear indication for humankind, and a guidance and a mercy for a folk whose faith is sure. Or do those who commit ill-deeds suppose that We shall make them as those who believe and do good works, the same in life and death Bad is their judgment! And Allah hath created the heavens and the earth with truth, and that every soul may be repaid what it hath earned. And they will not be wronged.

Hast thou seen him who maketh his desire his god, and Allah sendeth him astray purposely, and sealeth up his hearing and his heart, and setteth on his sight a covering? Then who will lead him after Allah? Will ye not then heed? And they say: "There is naught but our life of the world; we die and we live, and naught destroyeth us save time;" when they have no knowledge whatsoever of all that; they do but guess. And when Our clear Revelations are recited unto them their only argument is that they say: "Bring back our fathers. then, if ye are truthful."

Say: "Allah giveth life to you, then causeth you to die, then gathereth you unto the Day of Resurrection whereof there is no doubt." But most of mankind know not. And unto Allah belongeth the Sovereignty of the heavens and the earth; and on the day when the HOUR riseth, on that day those who follow falsehood will be lost. And Thou wilt see each nation crouching, each nation summoned to its record: "This day ye are requited what ye used to do."

This OUR BOOK pronounceth against you with truth. Lo! We have caused all that ye did to be recorded.

Then, as for those who believed and did good works, their Lord will bring them in unto His mercy. That is the evident triumph.

And as for those who disbelieved: "Were not Our Revelations recited unto you? But ye were scornful and became a guilty folk."

And when it was said: "Lo! Allah's promise is the truth, and there is no doubt of the HOUR's coming," ye said: "We know not what the HOUR is. We deem it naught but a conjecture, and we are by no means convinced."

And the evils of what they did will appear unto them, and that which they used to deride will befall them. And it will be said: "This day We forget you, even as ye forgot the meeting of this your day; and your habitation is the Fire, and there is none to help you. This, forasmuch as ye made the Revelations of Allah a jest, and the life of the world beguiled you." Therefore this day they come not forth from thence, nor can they make amends.

Then praise be to Allah, Lord of the heavens and Lord of the earth, the Lord of the Worlds. And unto Him alone belongeth Majesty in the heavens and the earth, and He is the Mighty, the Wise.

94. Bism'illah Ar-Rahman Ar-Rahim! ar-Ra'd: THE THUNDER.

Alif. Lam. Mim. Ra.

These are verses of the Scripture. That which is revealed unto thee from thy Lord is the Truth, but most of mankind believe not.

Allah it is Who raised up the heavens without visible supports, then mounted the Throne, and compelled the sun and the moon to be of service, each runneth unto an appointed term; He ordereth the course; He detaileth the Revelations, that haply ye may be certain of the meeting with your Lord.

And He it is Who spread out the earth and placed therein firm hills and flowing streams, and of all fruits He placed therein two spouses (male and female). He covereth the night with the day. Lo! Herein verily are portents for people who take thought.

And in the Earth are neighboring tracts, vineyards and ploughed lands, and date-palms, like and unlike, which are watered with one water. And we have made some of them to excel others in fruit. Lo! Herein verily are portents for people who have sense.

And if thou wonderest, then wondrous is their saying: "When we are dust, are we then forsooth to be raised in a new creation?" Such are they who disbelieve in their Lord; such have carcans on their necks; such are rightful owners of the Fire, they will abide therein. And they bid Thee hasten on the evil rather than the good, when exemplary punishments have indeed occurred before them. But Lo! Thy Lord is rich in pardon for mankind despite their wrong, and Lo! Thy Lord is strong in punishment.

Those who disbelieve say: "If only some portent were sent down upon him from his Lord!" Thou art a warner only, and for every folk a guide.

Allah knoweth that which every female beareth and that which the wombs absorb and that which they grow. And everything with Him is measured. He is the Knower of the Invisible and the Visible, the Great, the High Exalted.

Alike of you is he who hideth the saying and he who noiseth it abroad, he who lurketh in the night and he who goeth freely in the daytime. For him are angels ranged before him and behind him, who guard him by Allah's command. Lo! Allah changeth not the condition of a folk until they first **change that which is in their hearts**; and if Allah willeth misfortune for a folk there is none that can repel it, nor have they a defender beside Him.

He it is Who showeth you the lightning, a fear and a hope, and raiseth the heavy clouds. The thunder hymneth His praise and so do the angels for awe of Him. He launcheth the thunderbolts and smiteth with them whom He will while they dispute concerning Allah, and He is mighty in wrath.

Unto Him is the real prayer. Those unto whom they pray beside Allah respond to them not at all, save as is the response to one who stretcheth forth his hands toward water asking that it may come unto his mouth, and it will never reach it. The prayer of disbelievers goeth far astray. And unto Allah falleth prostrate whosoever is in the heavens and the earth, willingly or unwillingly, as do their shadows in the morning and the evening *hours*.

Say : "Who is Lord of the heavens and the earth?" Say: "Allah." Say: "Take ye then others beside Him for protectors, which, even for themselves, have neither benefit nor hurt?" Say: "Is the blind man equal to the seer, or is darkness equal to light?" Or assign they unto Allah partners who created the like of His creation so that the creation seemed alike to them? Say: "Allah is the Creator of all things, and He is the One, the Almighty!"

He sendeth down water from the sky, so that valleys flow according to their measure, and the flood beareth on its surface swelling foam--from that which they smelt in the fire in order to make ornaments and tools riseth a foam like unto it--thus Allah coineth the true and the false. Then, as for the foam, it passeth away as scum upon the banks, while, as for that which is of use to humankind, it remaineth in the earth. Thus Allah coineth the similitudes.

For those who answered **Allah's call is Bliss**; and for those who answered not His call, if they had all that is in the earth, and therewith the like thereof, they would proffer it as ransom. Such will have a woeful reckoning, and their habitation will be hell, a dire abode. Is he who knoweth that what is revealed unto Thee from Thy Lord is the truth like him who is blind? But only men of understanding heed; such as keep the pact of Allah, and break not **the Covenant**; such as unite that which Allah hath commandeth should be joined, and fear their Lord, and dread a woeful reckoning; such as persevere in seeking their Lord's Countenance and are regular in prayer and spend of that which We bestow upon them secretly and openly, and overcome evil with good. Theirs will be the SEQUEL of the Home, Gardens of Eden which they enter, along with all who do right of their fathers and their helpmeets and their seed. The angels enter unto them from every GATE: "Salem be unto you because ye persevered. Ah, passing sweet will be the SEQUEL of the Home!"

And those who break the covenant of Allah after ratifying it, and sever that which Allah hath commanded should be joined, and make mischief in the earth: theirs is the curse and theirs the ill abode.

Allah enlargeth livelihood for whom He will, and straiteneth it for whom He will; and they rejoice in the life of the world, whereas the life of the world is but brief comfort as compared with the Hereafter. Those who disbelieve say: "If only a portent were sent down upon him from his Lord!" Say: "Lo! Allah sendeth whom He will astray, and guideth unto Himself all who turn unto Him, who have believed and whose hearts have rest in the remembrance of Allah. Verily in the remembrance of Allah do hearts find rest!"

Those who believe and do right: **Joy is for them, and bliss their journey's end**. Thus We send Thee unto a nation, before whom other nations have passed away, that Thou mayst recite unto them that which We have inspired in Thee, while they are disbelievers in the Beneficent. Say: "He is my Lord; there is no God save Him. In Him do I put my trust and unto Him is my recourse."

Had it been possible for a Lecture to cause the mountains to move, or the earth to be torn asunder, or the dead to speak, (this Qur'an has done so). Nay, but Allah's is the whole command. Do not those who believe know that, had Allah willed, He could have guided all mankind? As for those who disbelieve, disaster ceaseth not to strike them because of what they do, or it dwelleth near their home until the threat of Allah come to pass. Lo! Allah faileth not to keep the tryst.

And verily messengers were mocked before Thee, but long I bore with those who disbelieved. At length I seized them, and how awful was My punishment! Is He Who is aware of the deserts of every soul as he who is aware of nothing? Yet they ascribe unto Allah partners. Say: "Name them. Is it that ye would inform Him of something which He knoweth not in the earth? Or is it but a way of speaking?" Nay but their contrivance is made seeming fair for those who disbelieve and they are kept from the right road. He whom Allah sendeth astray, for him there is no guide. For them is torment in the life of the world, and verily the doom of the Hereafter is more painful, and they have no defender from Allah.

A similitude of the Garden which is promised unto those who keep their duty: Underneath it rivers flow; its food is everlasting, and its shade; this is the reward of those who keep their duty, while the reward of disbelievers is the Fire.

Those unto whom We gave the Scripture rejoice in that which is revealed unto Thee. And of the clans there are who deny some of it. Say: "I am commanded only that I serve Allah and ascribe unto Him no partner. Unto Him I cry, and unto Him is my return."

Thus have We revealed it, a decisive utterance in Arabic; and if thou shouldst follow their desires after that which hath come unto Thee of knowledge, then truly wouldst Thou have from Allah no protecting friend nor defender.

And verily We sent messengers before Thee, and We appointed for them wives and offspring, and it was not given to any messenger that he should bring a portent save by Allah's leave. For everything there is a time prescribed. Allah effaceth what He will, and establisheth what He will, and with Him is the source of ordinance.

Whether We let Thee see something of that which We have promised them, or make Thee die (before its happening), Thine is but conveyance of the message. Ours the reckoning.

See they not how we aim to the land, reducing it of its outlying parts? When Allah doometh there is none that can postpone His doom, and He is swift at reckoning.

Those who were before them plotted; but all plotting is Allah's. He knoweth that which each soul earneth. The disbelievers will come to know for whom will be the SEQUEL of the Home. They who disbelieve say: "Thou art no messenger of Allah." Say: "Allah, and whosoever hath knowledge of the Scripture, is sufficient witness between me and you!"

95. Bism'illah Ar-Rahman Ar-Rahim! al-Hajj: THE PILGRIMAGE.

O Humankind! Fear your Lord. Lo! The earthquake of the HOUR is a tremendous thing. On the day when ye behold it, every nursing mother will forget her nursling and every pregnant one will be delivered of her burden, and Thou wilt see humankind as drunken, yet they will not be drunken, but the Doom of Allah will be strong upon them.

Among the people is he who disputeth concerning Allah without knowledge, and followeth each froward devil; For him it is decreed that whoso taketh him for friend, he verily will mislead him and will guide him to the punishment of the Flame.

O Humanity! If ye are in doubt concerning the Resurrection, then Lo! We have created you from dust, then from a drop of seed, then from a clot, then from a little lump of flesh shapely and shapeless, that We may make it clear for you. And We cause what We will to remain in the wombs for an appointed time, and afterward We bring you forth as infants, then give you growth that ye attain your full strength.

And among you there is he who dieth young, and among you there is he who is brought back to the most abject time of life, so that, after knowledge, he knoweth naught. And Thou seest the earth barren, but when We send down water thereon, it doth thrill and swell and put forth every lovely kind of growth. That is because Allah, He is the Truth and because He quickeneth the dead, and because He is Able to do all things; and because the HOUR will come, there is no doubt thereof; and because Allah will raise those who are in the graves.

And among the people is he who disputeth concerning Allah without knowledge or guidance or a scripture giving light, turning away in pride to beguile souls from the way of Allah. For him in this world is ignominy, and on the Day of Resurrection We make him taste the doom of burning: "This is for that which thy two hands have sent before, and because Allah is no oppressor of His slaves."

And among the people is he who worshippeth Allah upon a narrow marge so that if good befalleth him he is content therewith, but if a trial befalleth him, he falleth away utterly. He loseth both the world and the Hereafter. That is the sheer loss. He calleth, beside Allah, unto that which hurteth him not nor benefiteth him. That is the far error. He calleth unto him whose harm is nearer than his benefit; verily an evil patron and verily an evil friend! Lo! Allah causeth those who believe and do good works to enter Gardens underneath which rivers flow. Lo! Allah doth what He intendeth.

Whoso is wont to think through envy that Allah will not give him (*Al-AMIN*) victory in the world and the Hereafter and is enraged at the thought of his victory, **let him stretch a rope up to the roof of his dwelling, and let him hang himself.** Then let him see whether his strategy dispelleth that whereat he rageth!

Thus We reveal it as plain revelations, and verily Allah guideth whom He will.

Lo! Those who believe (*AL-AMIN**), and those true believers in Jews, and the Sabaeans and the Christians and the Magians and the Mushrikuny--Lo! Allah will decide between them on the Day of Resurrection. Lo! Allah is Witness over all things. Hast thou not seen that unto Allah payeth *Adoration* whosoever is in the heavens and whosoever is in the earth, and the sun, and the moon, and the stars, and the hills, and the trees, and the beasts, and many of humankind, while there are

---

AL-AMIN is a cognate of SOLOMON that is SOL-AMUN or AMUN-RA the hidden sun. Literally it means the truthfull--the trustworthy one, a title bestowed upon Muhammad by his own people prior to his call and mission as open revelator.

many unto whom the doom is justly due. He whom Allah scorneth, there is none to give him honor. Lo! Allah doeth what He will.

These twain are two opponents who contend concerning their Lord. But as for those who disbelieve, garments of fire will be cut out for them; boiling fluid will be poured down on their heads, whereby that which is in their bellies, and their skins too, will be melted; and for them are hooked rods of iron. Whenever, in their anguish, they would go forth from thence they are driven back therein and it is said unto them: "Taste the doom of burning."

Lo! Allah will cause those who believe and do good works to enter Gardens underneath which rivers flow, wherein they will be allowed armlets of gold, and pearls, and their raiment therein will be silk. **They are guided unto gentle speech**; they are guided unto the path of the Glorious One.

Lo! those who disbelieve and bar souls from the way of Allah and from the **Inviolable Place of Worship**, which **We have *appointed* for mankind together** (for the Oneness of Humanity), the dweller therein and the nomad: whosoever seeketh wrongful partiality therein, him We shall cause to taste a painful doom.

And when We prepared for Abraham the place of the House, saying: "Ascribe Thou no thing as partner unto Me, and PURIFY My House for those who make the round thereof and those who stand and those who bow and make prostration. And proclaim unto humankind the pilgrimage." They will come unto Thee on foot and on every lean camel; they will come from every deep ravine, That they may witness things that are of benefit to them, and mention the name of Allah on appointed days over the beast of cattle that He hath bestowed upon them. Then eat thereof and feed therewith the poor unfortunate. Then let them make an end of their unkemptness and pay their vows and go around the Ancient House. That is the command.

And whoso magnifieth the sacred things of Allah, it will be well for him in the sight of his Lord.

The cattle are lawful unto you save that which hath been told you. So shun the filth of idols, and shun lying speech, Turning unto Allah only, not ascribing partners unto Him; for whoso ascribeth partners unto Allah, it is as if he had fallen from the sky and the birds had snatched him or the wind had blown him to a far-off place. That is the command.

And whoso magnifieth the offerings consecrated to Allah, it surely is from devotion of the hearts, Therein are benefits for you for an appointed term; and afterward they are brought for sacrifice unto the Ancient House.

And for **every nation** have We appointed **a ritual**, that they may mention the name of Allah over the beast of cattle that He hath given them for food; and your God is One God, therefore surrender unto Him. And give good tidings (O *AL-AMIN*) to the humble, Whose hearts fear when Allah is mentioned, and the patient of whatever may befall them, and those who establish worship and who spend of that We have bestowed on them.

And the camels! We have appointed them among the ceremonies of Allah. Therein ye have much good. So mention the name of Allah over them when they are drawn up in lines. Then when their flanks fall dead, eat thereof and feed the beggar and the suppliant. Thus have We made them subject unto you, that haply ye may give thanks. Their flesh and their food reach not Allah, but **the devotion from you reacheth Him**. Thus have We made them subject unto you that ye may magnify Allah that He hath guided you. And give good tidings (*O AL-AMIN*) to the good. Lo! Allah defendeth *those* who are __true__. Lo! Allah loveth not each treacherous ingrate.

__Sanction__ is given unto *those* who fight BECAUSE **they have been wronged**; and Allah is indeed Able to give them Victory; those who have been driven from their homes unjustly only because they said: "Our Lord is Allah!" For had it not been for Allah's repelling *some men* **by means of __others__**, cloisters and churches and oratories and mosques--wherein the name of Allah is oft mentioned--would assuredly have been pulled down. Verily Allah helpeth one who helpeth Him. Lo! Allah is Strong, Almighty! Those who--if We give them power in the land--establish worship and pay the poor-due and enjoin kindness and forbid iniquity.

And Allah's is the SEQUEL of events.

If they deny Thee, even so the folk of Noah, and A'ad and Thamud, before Thee, denied Our messengers; And the folk of Abraham and the folk of Lot; and the dwellers in Midian. And *MOSES* was denied; but I indulged the disbelievers a long while, then I seized them, and how terrible was My abhorrence! How many a township have We destroyed while it was sinful, so that it lieth to this day in ruins, and how many a deserted well and lofty tower! Have they not travelled in the land, and have they hearts wherewith to feel and ears wherewith to hear?

For indeed it is not the eyes that grow blind, but it is the hearts, which are within the bosoms, that grow blind. And they will bid thee hasten on the Doom, and Allah faileth not His promise, but Lo! __A Day with Allah is as a Thousand Years of what ye reckon.__

And how many a township did I suffer long though it was sinful! Then I grasped it. Unto Me is the return. Say: "O People--if there be any Humanity in you at all! I am only a plain warner unto you. Those who believe and do good works, for them is pardon and a rich provision; While those who strive to thwart Our Revelations, such are rightful owners of the Fire."

Never sent We a messenger or a prophet before Thee but when He recited Satan proposed in respect of that which he recited thereof. But Allah abolisheth that which Satan proposeth. Then Allah establisheth His Own Revelations. Allah is the Kowing, the All-Wise! Such that He may make that which the devil proposeth a temptation for those **in whose hearts is a disease**, and those whose hearts are hardened!--Lo: the evil-doers are in open schism!--And that those who have been given this *__knowledge__* may know that *it is* the TRUTH from thy Lord, so that **they may __believe__ therein** and their hearts may graciously submit humbly unto Him. Lo! Allah verily is __guiding__ *those* who believe **unto a __right path__**.

And those who disbelieve will not cease to be in doubt thereof until the HOUR[*] come upon them unawares, or there come unto them the doom of a disastrous day. The Sovereignty on that day will be Allah's, He will judge between them. Then those who believed and did good works will be in Gardens of Na'im (Heb. *Nahum*), While those who disbelieved and denied Our Revelations, for them will be a shameful doom. Those who fled their homes for the cause of Allah and then were slain or died, Allah verily will provide for them a good provision. Lo! Allah, He verily is Best of all who make provision. **Assuredly He will cause them to enter by an Entry that they will Love.** Lo! Allah verily is Knower, Indulgent. That is so.

And whoso hath retaliated with the like of that which he was made to suffer and then hath again been wronged, Allah will *succour* him. Lo! Allah verily is Mild, Forgiving. That is because Allah maketh the night to pass into the day and maketh the day to pass into the night, and because Allah is Hearer, Seer. That is because Allah, He is the True, and that whereon they call instead of Him, it is the false, and because Allah, He is the High, the Great.

Seest Thou not how Allah sendeth down water from the sky and then the earth becometh green upon the morrow? Lo! Allah is Subtile, Aware. Unto Him belongeth all that is in the heavens and all that is in the earth. Lo! Allah, He verily is the Absolute, the Owner of Praise.

Hast Thou not seen how Allah hath made all that is in the earth subservient unto you? And the ship runneth upon the sea by His command, and He holdeth back the heaven from falling on the earth unless by His leave. Lo! Allah is, for mankind, Full of Pity, Merciful.

And He it is Who gave you life, then He will cause you to die, and then will give you life again. Lo! man is verily an ingrate. Unto **each nation** have We given sacred rites **which they *are* to perform**; so let them not dispute with Thee of the matter, but summon Thou unto thy Lord. Lo! thou indeed followest right guidance.

And if they wrangle with Thee, say: "Allah is Best Aware of what ye do. Allah will judge between you on the Day of Resurrection concerning that wherein ye used to differ. Hast Thou not known that Allah knoweth all that is in the heaven and the earth? Lo! It is in a Record. Lo! that is easy for Allah."

And they worship instead of Allah that for which He hath sent down no warrant, and that whereof they have no knowledge. For evil-doers there is no helper. And when Our Revelations are recited unto them, Thou knowest the denial in the faces of those who disbelieve; they all but attack those who recite Our Revelations unto them. Say: "Shall I proclaim unto you worse than that? The Fire!" Allah hath promised it for those who disbelieve. A hapless journey's end!

O Humankind! A similitude is coined, so pay ye heed to it: Lo! those on whom ye call beside Allah will never create a fly though they combine together for the purpose. And if the fly took something from them, they could not rescue it from it. So weak are both the seeker and the sought! They measure not Allah His rightful measure. Lo! Allah is Strong, Almighty.

---

[*]The psycho-Therapeutic HOUR *worth* **every** penny. The Thermonuclear HOUR--not *worth* a **dime**! Group: Priceless!

Allah chooseth from the angels messengers, and also from humankind. Lo! Allah is Hearer, Seer. He knoweth all that is before them and all that is behind them, and unto Allah all things are returned.

O ye who believe! Bow down and prostrate yourselves, and worship your Lord, and do good, that haply ye may prosper. And strive for Allah with the endeavour which is His right (*Hususqu'llah*).

He hath chosen you and hath not laid upon you in religion any hardship; the faith of your father Abraham is yours. He hath named you *Muslims*--those who surrender--of old time and in THIS BOOK, that the messenger **may be a witness against you**, and that ye may be witnesses against humankind. So establish worship, pay the poor-due (*zakat*), and hold fast to Allah. He is your Protecting friend. A blessed Patron and a blessed Helper!

Bism'illah Ar-Rahman Ar-Rahim!

When Allah's succour (an-Nasr) and the triumph cometh
And thou seest mankind Entering the religion of Allah in Troops,
Then hymn the praises of thy Lord, and seek forgiveness of Him.
Lo! He is ever ready to show mercy.

-Rabe'a

ANUBIS!

ANUBIS!

---THE MESSENGERS (*AL-ANBIYA*) OF THE WEIGHTY BALANCE---
Manzil-i-Akhir
Istijlál

Bism'illah Ar-Rahman Ar-Rahim!

RECITE *(aq-Qaara): In the name of thy Lord Who createth,*
Createth man from a clot (al-'Alaq).
RECITE: *And thy Lord is the Most Bounteous,*
Who teacheth by the **PEN**,
Teacheth man that which he knew not.

When Allah's succour (an-Nasr) and the triumph cometh
And thou seest mankind entering the religion of Allah in troops,
Then hymn the praises of thy Lord, and seek forgiveness of Him.
Lo! He is ever ready to show mercy.

XXV. JUZ'UN SIPARA VICESIMO-QUINTO:

96. Bism'illah Ar-Rahman Ar-Rahim! al-A'la: THE MOST HIGH.

PRAISE THE NAME OF THY LORD:[*] **THE MOST HIGH!**

Who createth, then disposeth;
Who measureth, then guideth;
Who bringeth forth the pasturage,
Then turneth it to russet stubble.

We shall make Thee read (O *MUHAMMAD*) so that Thou shalt not forget:
Save that which Allah willeth. Lo! He knoweth the disclosed and that which still is hidden!

And We shall ease thy way unto the state of ease.

Therefore remind (men), for of use is the reminder.
He will heed who feareth,
But the most hapless will flout it,
He who will be flung to the great Fire
Wherein he will neither die nor live.

He is successful who groweth,

---

[*]**Al-Musabbihat** refer to the collective name of the seven surahs that begin with Allah's ***glorification*** 'Subhana,'
'Sabbaha,' and 'Yusabbihu:' *al-Hadid*; *al-Hashr* ; *as-Saff* ; *al-Jumua*; *at-Taghabun* ; *al-Isra*; and *al-Ala*.

253

And remembereth the name of his Lord, so prayeth,
But ye prefer the life of the world
Although the Hereafter is better and more lasting.

Lo! This is in the former scrolls.
The Books of Abraham and of *MOSES*.

97. Bism'illah Ar-Rahman Ar-Rahim! al-Bayyinah va al-Bayan: THIS RIGHTEOUS BOOK!

Those who disbelieve among the *Ahl al-Kitab* (**People of the Book**) and the *Mushrikuny* (**The People of the Collective**) could not have left off (erring) till THIS RIGHTEOUS BOOK came unto them, A messenger from Allah, reading purified pages Containing correct scriptures.

Nor were the *Ahl al-Kitab* (**People of the Book**) divided until after THIS RIGHTEOUS BOOK came unto them. And they are ordered naught else than to serve Allah, keeping religion pure for Him, as men by nature upright, and to establish worship and to pay the poor-due (*zakat*). That is true religion.

Lo! those *who* <u>disbelieve</u>, among the *Ahl al-Kitab* (*People of the Book*) and the *Mushrikuny* (*The People of the Collective--of the Cave--that which conceals*), will abide in fire of hell. They (who disbelieve) are the worst of created beings.

(And) Lo! those *who* <u>believe</u> and do good works are the best of created beings. Their reward is with their Lord: Gardens of Eden underneath which rivers flow, wherein they dwell for ever.

Allah hath pleasure in them and they have pleasure in Him.

This is (in store) for that one who feareth his Lord.

98. Bism'illah Ar-Rahman Ar-Rahim! al-Anbiya: THE PROPHETS.

Their reckoning draweth nigh for mankind, while they turn away in heedlessness. Never cometh there unto them a <u>New Reminder</u> from their Lord but they listen to it while they play, With hearts preoccupied. And they confer in secret.

The wrong-doers say: "Is this other than a mortal like you?" Will ye then succumb to magic when ye see (it)?

He saith: "My Lord knoweth what is spoken in the heaven and the earth. He is the Hearer, the Knower."

Nay, say they, "(These are but) muddled dreams; nay, he hath but invented it; nay, he is but a poet. Let him bring us a portent even as those of old (who were God's messengers) were sent (with portents)."

Not a township believed of those which We destroyed before them (though We sent them portents): would they then believe? And We sent not (as Our messengers) before thee other than men, whom We inspired. Ask the followers of the Reminder if ye know not? We gave them not bodies that would not eat food, nor were they immortals. Then we fulfilled the promise unto them. So we delivered them and whom We would, and We destroyed the prodigals. Now We have revealed unto you a Scripture wherein is your Reminder. Have ye then no sense?

How many a community that dealt unjustly have We shattered, and raised up after them another folk! And, when they felt Our might, behold them fleeing from it! (But it was said unto them): Flee not, but return to that (existence) which emasculated you and to your dwellings, that ye may be questioned.

They cried: "Alas for us! We were wrong-doers." And this their crying ceased not till We made them as reaped corn, extinct.

We created not the heaven and the earth and all that is between them in play. If We had wished to find a pastime, We could have found it in Our presence--if We ever did.

Nay, but We hurl the true against the false, and it doth break its head and Lo! it *vanisheth*. And *yours will be* **woe** *for that which* **ye ascribe** *(unto* **Him***)*.

Unto Him belongeth whosoever is in the heavens and the earth. And those who dwell in His presence are not too proud to worship Him, nor do they weary; They glorify (Him) night and day; they flag not. Or have they chosen gods from the earth who raise the dead?

If there were therein *gods beside Allah*, then verily both (the heavens and the earth) had been disordered. Glorified be Allah, the Lord of the Throne, from all that they ascribe (unto Him). He will not be questioned as to that which He doeth, but they will be questioned.

Or have they chosen other gods beside Him? Say: Bring your proof (of their godhead). This is the Reminder of those with me and those before me, but most of them know not the Truth and so they are averse. And We sent no messenger before thee but We inspired him, (saying): There is no God save Me (Allah), so worship Me.

And they say: "The Beneficent hath taken unto Himself a son. Be He Glorified!" Nay, but (those whom they call sons) are honoured slaves; They speak not until He hath spoken, and they act by His command. He knoweth what is before them and what is behind them, and they cannot intercede except for him whom He accepteth, and they quake for awe of Him. And one of them who should say: Lo! I am a god beside Him, that one We should repay with hell. Thus We Repay wrong-doers.

Have not those who disbelieve known that the heavens and the earth were of one piece, then We parted them, and we made every living thing of water? Will they not then believe? And We have placed in the earth firm hills lest it quake with them, and We have placed therein ravines as roads that haply they may find their way. And we have made the sky a roof withheld (from them). Yet they turn away from its portents. And He it is Who created the night and the day, and the sun and the moon. They float, each in an orbit.

We appointed immortality for no mortal before thee.

What! if Thou *diest*, can they be immortal!
Every soul must taste of death, and We try you with evil and with good, for ordeal. And unto Us ye will be returned.

And when those who disbelieve behold thee, they but choose thee out for mockery, (saying): Is this he who maketh mention of your gods? And they would deny all mention of the Beneficent. Man is made of haste. "I shall show you My portents, but ask Me not to hasten." And they say: "When will this promise (be fulfilled), if ye are truthful?"

If those who disbelieved but knew the time when they will not be able to drive off the fire from their faces and from their backs, and they will not be helped! Nay, but it will come upon them unawares so that it will stupefy them, and they will be unable to repel it, neither will they be reprieved. Messengers before thee, indeed, were mocked, but that whereat they mocked surrounded those who scoffed at them.

Say: Who guardeth you in the night or in the day from the Beneficent? Nay, but they turn away from mention of their Lord! Or have they gods who can shield them from Us? They cannot help themselves nor can they be defended from Us. Nay, but We gave these and their fathers ease until life grew long for them. See they not how we aim to the land, reducing it of its outlying parts? Can they then be the Victors?

Say (*O AL-AMIN*)! I warn you only by the Inspiration. But the deaf hear not the call when they are warned. And if a breath of thy Lord's punishment were to touch them, they assuredly would say: "Alas for us! Lo! We were wrong-doers."

And We set a ***Just Balance*** for the ***Day of Resurrection*** so that no soul is wronged in aught. Though it be of the weight of a grain of mustard seed, We bring it. And We suffice for reckoners. And We verily gave *MOSES* and Aaron the Criterion (of right and wrong: ***Urim-i Thummim: Lights and Perfections***) and **a Light** and **a Reminder** for those who keep from evil, Those who fear their Lord in secret and who dread the HOUR (of doom). This is a blessed **Reminder** that we have revealed: Will ye then reject it?

And We verily gave Abraham of old his proper course, and We were Aware of him, When he said unto his father and his folk: What are these images unto which ye pay devotion?

They said: "We found our fathers worshippers of them."

He said: "Verily ye and your fathers were in plain error."

They said: "Bringest thou unto us the truth, or art thou some jester?" (*Comedian?*)

He said: "Nay, but your Lord is the Lord of the heavens and the earth, Who created them; and I am of those who testify unto that. And, by Allah, I shall circumvent your idols after ye have gone away and turned your backs." Then he reduced them to fragments, all save the chief of them, that haply they might have recourse to it.

They said: "Who hath done this to our gods ? Surely it must be some evil- doer."

They said: "We heard a youth make mention of them, who is called Abraham."

They said: "Then bring him (hither) before the people's eyes that they may testify."

They said: "Is it thou who hast done this to our gods, O Abraham?"

He said, but this: "Their chief hath done it. So question them, if they can speak." Then gathered they apart and We said: "Lo! ye yourselves are the wrong-doers." And they were utterly confounded!

They said: "Well thou knowest that these speak not."

He said: "Worship ye then instead of Allah that which cannot profit you at all, nor harm you? Fie on you and all that ye worship instead of Allah! Have ye then no sense?"

They cried: "Burn him! And stand by your gods, if ye will be doing."

We said: "O fire, be coolness and peace for Abraham!" And they wished to set a snare for him, but We made them the greater losers. And We rescued him and Lot (and brought them) to the land which We have blessed for (all) peoples. And We bestowed upon him Isaac, and Jacob as a grandson. Each of them We made righteous. And We made them chiefs who guide by Our command, and We inspired in them the doing of good deeds and the right establishment of worship and the giving of alms, and they were worshippers of Us (alone).

And unto Lot we gave judgment and knowledge, and We delivered him from the community that did abominations. Lo! they were folk of evil, lewd. And We brought him in unto Our mercy. Lo! he was of the righteous. And Noah, when he cried of old, We heard his prayer and saved him and his household from the great affliction. And delivered him from the people who denied Our revelations. Lo! they were folk of evil, therefore did We drown them all.

And David and Solomon, when they gave judgment concerning the field, when people's sheep had strayed and browsed therein by night; and We were witnesses to their judgment. And We made Solomon to understand (the case); and unto each of them We gave judgment and knowledge. And we subdued the hills and the birds to hymn (His) praise along with David. We were the doers (thereof). And We taught him the art of making garments (of mail: faraday suits) to protect you in your daring. Are ye then thankful?

And unto Solomon (We subdued) the wind in its raging. It set by his command toward the land which We had blessed. And of everything We are Aware. And of the evil ones (subdued We unto him) some who dived (for pearls) for him and did other work, and We were warders unto them.

And Shem (*Job*) Melchizedec, when he cried unto his Lord, (saying): "Lo! adversity afflicteth me, and Thou art Most Merciful of all who show mercy." Then We heard his prayer and removed that adversity from which he suffered, and We gave him his household (that he had lost) and the like thereof along with them, a mercy from Our store, and a remembrance for the worshippers;

And Ishmael, and Enoch (*Idris: 'Akhnukh*) and Tonpa Shenrab Miwo (*Dhu'l-Kifl**). ALL prophets of all indigenous peoples are of the steadfast. And We brought them in unto Our MERCY. Lo! They are ALL among the righteous.

And Garab Dorje (*Dhu'n-Nun*), when he went off in anger and deemed that We had no power over him, but **he cried out in the darkness**: "There is no God save Thee. Be Thou Glorified! Lo! I have been a wrong-doer." Then we heard his *Prayer of Dzogchen* and saved him in Our **GREAT-PERFECTION** from the anguish. Thus we save believers.[†]

***Dhu'l-Kifl** (Lit. "Lord of the Doubles" the "Double Prophets" of India: specifically Buddha of Kapilavastu (the Sakya Sage) and his predecessor in arms Lord Kirshna called Madhusudan in The Gita. The double-folding, therefore includes all avatars of the *Dhyani-Tathagatas Dashavatara (Wuzhi Rulai)* and all *Shivatashvatara* in the doubling. **Kifl** is Kapila. Literally meaning "the double folding" referring to the "double folding" of the two revelations of Buddha and Krishna, of the solar and lunar dynasties: the Revelation of the *Tripitaka* (Three Baskets) and the *Bhagavad Gita* (the Song of God). Kapila is known in the Gita as *the Samkhya Sage*, who founded the School of Kapilavastu whose mission is fulfilled in the progressive teachings of Tonpa Shenrab Miwo *(Dhu'l-Kifl)*, Garab Dorje *(Dhu'n-Nun)* and the *Vajrayāna* (DIAMOND VEHICLE) of Padmasambhava that came after him in his line.

[†]This verse also has another meaning: "And (mention) **Dhu'n-Nun** (Llit. "the Lord of the Fish"--*JESUS*--whose Sign is the "Sign of Jonah" (Matt. 12:39-40 NIV) of the FISH), when he went off (entered the temple with a whip "And when he had made a scourge of small cords, he drove them all out of the temple, and the sheep, and the oxen; and poured out the changer's money, and overthrew the tables (John 2:15 KJV) in anger (Mark 3:5 KJV) and deemed that We had no power over him (John 14:30), but **he cried out in the darkness** ("And when the sixth hour was come, there was darkness over the whole land until the ninth hour" Mark 15:33 KJV), saying: "*Allah-yi, Allah-yi, Lama Sabachthani!* (Mark 15:35 KJV): There is no God save Thee. Be Thou Glorified! Lo! I have been a wrong-doer." Then we heard his prayer (Psalm 22) and saved him from the anguish. Thus we save believers." When *JESUS* fell to silence after the recitation of his prayer to Allah the one thief agreed that he was of the guilty. The other thief declared his innocence. Then the two entered into Paradise that very day (see Luke 23:40-43; and Matt. 27:33-46 for example). Jesus prayed: "My God, my God, why hast thou forsaken me? *why art thou so* far from helping me, *and from* the words of my roaring? O my God, I cry in the daytime, but Thou hearest not; and in the night season, and am not silent. But Thou *art* holy, *O Thou* that inhabitest the praises of Israel. Our fathers trusted in Thee: they trusted, and Thou didst deliver them. They cried unto Thee, and were delivered: they trusted in Thee, and were not confounded. But I *am* a worm, and no man; a reproach of men, and despised of the people. All they that see me laugh me to scorn: they shoot out the lip, they shake the head, *saying*, 'He trusted on the LORD *that* he would deliver Him: let Him deliver him, seeing He delighted in him" (Matt. 27:40, 42). But thou *art* He that took me out of the womb: thou didst make me hope *when I was* upon my mother's breasts. I was cast upon Thee from the womb: thou *art* my God from my mother's belly. Be not far from me; for trouble *is* near; for *there is* none to help. Many bulls have compassed me: strong *bulls* of Bashan have beset me round. They gaped upon me *with* their mouths, *as* a ravening and a roaring lion. I am poured out like water, and all my bones are out of joint: my heart is like wax; it is melted in the midst of my bowels. My strength is dried up like a potsherd; and my tongue cleaveth to my jaws; and thou hast brought me into the dust of death. For dogs have compassed me: **the assembly of the wicked have inclosed me: they pierced my hands and my feet** (*stigma*). I may tell all my bones (the believers are members of my body "of my flesh, and of my bones" Ephesians 5:30 KJV): they look *and* stare upon me (Matt. 27:36). **They**

And Zachariah, when he cried unto his Lord: "My Lord! Leave me not childless, though Thou art the Best of inheritors." Then We heard his prayer, and bestowed upon him John, and adjusted his wife (to bear a child) for him. Lo! they used to *vie* one with the other in good deeds, and they cried unto Us in longing and in fear, and were submissive unto Us.

And she who was Chaste, therefore We breathed into her (something) of Our Spirit and made her and ***her son*** a token for ALL PEOPLES! Lo! this, *your* religion, is ONE RELIGION, and I am your Lord, so worship Me.

And they have broken their religion (into fragments: *furqan*) among them, (yet) ***ALL*** are returning **unto Us**. Then whoso doeth some good works and is a believer, there will be no rejection of his effort. Lo! We record (it) for him.

And there is a ***ban upon any community*** which We have destroyed: that they shall not return. Until, when **Gog and Magog** are let loose, and they hasten out of every mound, And the True Promise draweth nigh; then behold them, staring wide (in terror), the eyes of those who disbelieve! (They say): "Alas for us! We (lived) in forgetfulness of this Holy Qur'an. Ah, but **we were wrong-doers!**" Lo! *ye* and that which *ye worship* **beside** **Allah** are fuel of hell. Thereunto ye will come.

If these had been gods they would not have come thither, but all will abide therein. Therein wailing is their portion, and therein they hear not. Lo! those unto whom kindness hath gone forth before from Us, they will be far removed from thence.

They will not hear the slightest sound thereof, while they abide in that which their souls desire. **The Supreme Horror** will not grieve them, and the angels will welcome them, (saying): "This is your Day which ye were promised; The Day when We shall roll up the heavens as a recorder rolleth up a written scroll." As We began the first creation, We shall repeat it. (It is) a promise (binding) upon Us. Lo! We are to perform it.

And verily we have written in the Scripture, after the Reminder: My righteous slaves will inherit the earth: Lo! there is a plain statement for folk who are devout.

We sent thee not save as a mercy for the peoples.

---

part my garments among them, and **cast lots upon my vesture** (Matt. 27:35). But be not thou far from me, O LORD: O my strength, haste thee to help me. Deliver my soul from the sword; my darling from the power of the dog. Save me from the lion's mouth: for thou hast heard me from the horns of the unicorns. I will declare thy name unto my brethren: in the midst of the congregation will I praise thee. Ye that fear the LORD, praise him; all ye the seed of Jacob, glorify him; and fear him, all ye the seed of Israel. For he hath not despised nor abhorred the affliction of the afflicted; neither hath he hid his face from him; but when he cried unto him, he heard. My praise *shall be* of thee in the great congregation: I will pay my vows before them that fear him. The meek shall eat and be satisfied: they shall praise the LORD that seek him: your heart shall live for ever. All the ends of the world shall remember and turn unto the LORD: and all the kindreds of the nations shall worship before thee. For the kingdom *is* the LORD'S: and he *is* the governor among the nations. All *they that be* fat upon earth shall eat and worship: all they that go down to the dust shall bow before him: and none can keep alive his own soul. A seed shall serve him; it shall be accounted to the Lord for a generation. They shall come, and shall declare his righteousness unto a people that shall be born, that he hath done *this*" (Psalm 22 KJV).

Say: "It is only inspired in me that your God is One God. Will ye then surrender (unto Him)? But if they are averse, then say: "I have warned you all alike, although I know not whether nigh or far is that which ye are promised." Lo! He knoweth that which is said openly, and that which ye conceal.

And I know not but that this may be a trial for you, and enjoyment for a while. He saith: "My Lord! Judge Thou with truth!"

Our Lord is the Beneficent, Whose help is to be implored *against* *that* which <u>ye</u> <u>ascribe</u> (**unto** **Him**).

99. Bism'illah Ar-Rahman Ar-Rahim! Nuh: NOAH.

Lo! We sent Noah unto his people (on *this* mission): "Warn thy people ere the painful doom come unto them." He said: "O my people! Lo! I am a plain warner unto you (Bidding you): Serve Allah and keep your duty unto Him and obey me, That He may forgive you somewhat of your sins and respite you to an appointed term. Lo! the term of Allah, when it cometh, cannot be delayed, if ye but knew!"

He said: "My Lord! Lo! I have called unto my people night and day But all my calling doth but add to their repugnance; And Lo! whenever I call unto them that Thou mayst pardon them they thrust their fingers in their ears and cover themselves with their garments and persist (in their refusal) and magnify themselves in pride. And Lo! I have called unto them aloud, And Lo! I have made public proclamation unto them, and I have appealed to them in private. And I have said: 'Seek pardon of your Lord. Lo! He was ever Forgiving. He will let loose the sky for you in plenteous rain, And will help you with wealth and sons, and will assign unto you Gardens and will assign unto you rivers. What aileth you that ye hope not toward Allah for dignity When He created you by (divers) stages? See ye not how Allah hath created seven heavens in harmony, And hath made the moon a light therein, and made the sun a lamp? And Allah hath caused you to grow as a growth from the earth, And afterward He maketh you return thereto, and He will bring you forth again, a (new) forthbringing. And Allah hath made the earth a wide expanse for you That ye may thread the valley-ways thereof!'" Have they no sense?

Noah said: "My Lord! Lo! they have disobeyed me and followed one whose wealth and children increase him in naught save ruin; And they have plotted a mighty plot, And they have said: 'Forsake not your gods. Forsake not Wadd, nor Suwa', nor Yaghuth and Ya'uq and Nasr'.[*]
And they have led many astray, and Thou increasest the wrong-doers in naught save error. Because of their sins they were drowned, then made to enter a Fire. And they found they had no helpers in place of Allah." Have they no sense?

And Noah said: "My Lord! **Leave not one of the disbelievers in** <u>**the land.**</u> If Thou shouldst leave them, they will mislead Thy slaves and will beget none save lewd ingrates. My Lord! Forgive me and my parents and him who entereth my house believing, and believing men and believing women, and increase not the wrong-doers in aught save ruin." Have they no sense?

---

[*]Five *playnay*.

100. Bism'illah Ar-Rahman Ar-Rahim! Ibrahim: ABRAHAM.

Alif. Lam. Ra.

A Scripture (*Sefer Yotzorah*) which We have revealed unto Thee (O ___KHALIL MY DEAREST AND NEAREST FRIEND!___) that thereby Thou mayst bring forth mankind from Darkness unto Light, by the Permission of their Lord, unto the path of the Mighty, the Owner of "Praise: Allah!" unto Whom belongeth whatsoever is in the heavens and whatsoever is in the earth.

And woe unto the disbelievers from an awful doom; Those who love the life of the world more than the Hereafter, and debar (men) from the way of Allah **and would have it <u>crooked</u>**: such are far astray. And We never sent a messenger save with the language of his folk, that he might make (the message) clear for them. Then Allah sendeth whom He will astray, and guideth whom He will. He is the Mighty, the Wise.

We verily sent *MOSES* with Our revelations, (on ___this___ mission) saying: "Bring ___Thy People forth___ from Darkness unto Light. And remind them of the days of Allah. Lo! therein are revelations for each steadfast, thankful (heart)." And how *MOSES* said unto his people: "Remember Allah's favour unto you when He delivered you from Pharaoh's folk who were afflicting you with dreadful torment, and were slaying your sons and sparing your women; that was a tremendous trial from your Lord. And when your Lord proclaimed: If ye give thanks, I will give you more; but if ye are thankless, Lo! My punishment is dire."

And *MOSES* said: "Though ye and all who are in the earth prove thankless, lo! Allah verily is Absolute, Owner of Praise. Hath not the history of those before you reached you: the folk of Noah, and (the tribes of) A'ad and Thamud, and those after them? None save Allah knoweth them. Their messengers came unto them with THIS RIGHTEOUS BOOK but they thrust their hands into their mouths, and said: 'Lo! we disbelieve in that wherewith ye have been sent, and Lo! we are in grave doubt concerning that to which ye call us.'

"Their messengers said: 'Can there be doubt concerning Allah, the Creator of the heavens and the earth? He calleth you that He may forgive you your sins and reprieve you unto an appointed term.' They said: 'Ye are but mortals like us, who would fain turn us away from what our fathers used to worship. Then bring some clear warrant.' Their messengers said unto them: 'We are but mortals like you, but Allah giveth grace unto whom He will of His slaves. It is not ours to bring you a warrant unless by the permission of Allah. In Allah let believers put their trust!'"

"How should we not put our trust in Allah when He hath shown us our ways? We surely will endure the hurt ye do us. **In Allah let the trusting put their trust.**"

"And those who disbelieved said unto their messengers: 'Verily we will drive you out from our land, unless ye return to our religion.' Then their Lord inspired them, (saying): "Verily We shall Destroy the wrong-doers! And, Verily! We shall make you to dwell in the land after them" **This is for him who feareth My Majesty and feareth My threats.**

"And they sought help (from their Lord) and every froward potentate was bought to naught; Hell is before him, and he is made to drink a festering water, Which he sippeth but can hardly swallow, and death cometh unto him from every side while yet he cannot die, and before him is a harsh doom. **A similitude of those who disbelieve in their Lord**: Their works are as ashes which the wind bloweth hard upon a stormy day. They have no control of aught that they have earned. That is the extreme failure. Hast thou not seen that Allah hath created the heavens and the earth with truth? If He will, He can remove you and bring (in) some new creation; And that is no great matter for Allah. They all come forth unto their Lord. Then those who were despised say unto those who were scornful: 'We were unto you a following, can ye then avert from us aught of Allah's doom?' They say: 'Had Allah guided us, we should have guided you. Whether we rage or patiently endure is (now) all one for us; we have no place of refuge.'

"And Satan saith, 'When the matter hath been decided: Lo! Allah promised you a promise of truth; and I promised you, then failed you. And I had no power over you save that I called unto you and ye obeyed me. So blame not, but blame yourselves. I cannot help you, nor can ye help me, Lo! I disbelieved in that which ye before ascribed to me. Lo! for wrong-doers is a painful doom. And those who believed and did good works are made to enter Gardens underneath which rivers flow, therein abiding by permission of their Lord, their greeting therein: Peace! Seest thou not how **Allah coineth a similitude**: A goodly saying, as a goodly tree, its root set firm, its branches reaching into heaven, Giving its fruit at every season by permission of its Lord? Allah coineth the similitudes for mankind in order that they may reflect. And the similitude of a bad saying is as a bad tree, uprooted from upon the earth, possessing no stability. Allah confirmeth those who believe by a firm saying in the life of the world and in the Hereafter, and Allah sendeth wrong-doers astray. And Allah doeth what He will. Hast thou not seen those who gave the grace of Allah in exchange for thanklessness and led their people down to the **Abode of Loss**, (Even to) hell ? They are exposed thereto. A hapless end! And they set up rivals to Allah that they may mislead (men) from His way. Say: "Enjoy life (while ye may) for Lo! your journey's end will be the Fire" As it is written: "Eat Drink and be Merry! For Tomorrow We Die!"--(Is. 22:13; 1 Cor. 15:32, etc.).

'Tell My bondmen who believe to establish worship and spend of that which We have given them, secretly and publicly, before a day cometh wherein there will be neither traffick nor befriending. Allah is He Who created the heavens and the earth, and causeth water to descend from the sky, thereby producing fruits as food for you, and maketh the ships to be of service unto you, that they may run upon the sea at His command, and hath made of service unto you the rivers; And maketh the sun and the moon, constant in their courses, to be of service unto you, and hath made of service unto you the night and the day. And He giveth you of all ye ask of Him, and if ye would count the bounty of Allah ye cannot reckon it. Lo! man is verily a wrong-doer, an ingrate.'

"And when Abraham said: 'My Lord! Make safe this territory, and preserve me and my sons from serving idols. My Lord! Lo! they have led many of mankind astray. But whoso followeth me, he verily is of me. And whoso disobeyeth me--Still Thou art Forgiving, Merciful. Our Lord! Lo! I have settled some of my posterity in an uncultivable valley near unto Thy holy House, our Lord! that they may establish proper worship; so incline some hearts of men that they may yearn toward them, and provide Thou them with fruits in order that they may be thankful. Our Lord!

262

Lo! Thou knowest that which we hide and that which we proclaim. Nothing in the earth or in the heaven is hidden from Allah. Praise be to Allah Who hath given me, in my old age, Ishmael and Isaac! Lo! my Lord is indeed the Hearer of Prayer. My Lord! Make me to establish proper worship, and some of my posterity (also); our Lord! and accept my prayer. Our Lord! Forgive me and my parents and believers on the day when the account is cast. Deem not that Allah is unaware of what the wicked do. He but giveth them a respite till a day when eyes will stare (in terror), As they come hurrying on in fear, their heads upraised, their gaze returning not to them, and their hearts as air. And warn mankind of a day when the doom will come upon them, and those who did wrong will say: "Our Lord! Reprieve us for a little while. We will obey Thy call and will follow the messengers." (It will be answered): "Did ye not swear before that there would be no end for you? And (have ye not) dwelt in the dwellings of those who wronged themselves (of old) and (hath it not) become plain to you how We dealt with them and made examples for you?" Verily they have plotted their plot, and their plot is with Allah, though their plot were one whereby the mountains should be moved.'

"So think not that Allah will fail to keep His promise to His messengers. Lo! Allah is Mighty, Able to Requite (the wrong). On the day when the earth will be changed to other than the earth, and the heavens (also will be changed) and they will come forth unto Allah, the One, the Almighty, Thou wilt see the guilty on that day linked together in chains, Their raiment of pitch, and the Fire covering their faces, That Allah may repay each soul what it hath earned. Lo! Allah is swift at reckoning. This is a clear message for mankind in order that they may be warned thereby, and that they may know that He is only One God, and that men of understanding may take heed."

XXVI. JUZ'UN SIPARA VICESIMO-SEXTO:

101. Bism'illah Ar-Rahman Ar-Rahim! Yusuf: JOSEPH & THE FAMILY OF JACOB!

Alif. Lam. Ra.

These are verse of the Scripture that maketh plain. Lo! We have revealed it, a Lecture in Arabic, that ye may understand. We narrate unto Thee **THE BEST OF STORIES** in that We have inspired in Thee ***THIS*** Qur'an! Though aforetime thou wast of the heedless.

When Joseph said unto his father: "O my father! Lo! I saw in a dream *eleven planets* and the sun and the moon, I saw them prostrating themselves unto me. He said: "O My Dear Son! Tell not *Thy Brethren* of *Thy* Vision! Lest they plot a plot against thee. **Lo! Satan is for man an open foe**. Thus thy Lord will prefer Thee and will teach Thee the interpretation of events, and will perfect His grace upon thee and upon the **Family of Jacob** as He perfected it upon thy forefathers, Abraham and Isaac. Lo! thy Lord is Knower, Wise."

Verily in Joseph and His Brethren are **Signs** for the *Inquiring!*

When they said: "Verily Joseph and his brother are dearer to our Father than we are, many though we be. Lo! our Father is in plain aberration! Let us: Kill Joseph!... (*silence*)... Or cast him to some (other) land, so that Father's favour may be all-in-all, and *ye may afterward* be righteous *folk*!" Then One among them said: "Kill not Joseph but, if ye must be doing, fling him into the depth of the pit; some caravan will find him."

They said: "O Our Father! Why wilt thou not trust us with Joseph, when Lo! we are good friends to him? Send him with us tomorrow that he may enjoy himself and play. And Lo! we shall take good care of him." He said: "Lo! in truth it saddens me that ye should take him with you, and I fear less **The Wolf** devour him while ye are heedless of him."

They said: "If **The Wolf** (*al-Dhib*) should devour him when we are (so strong) a band, then surely we should have already perished."

Then, when they led him off, and were of one mind that they should place him in the depth of the pit, We inspired in him (on *this* mission): "Thou wilt tell them of this deed of theirs when they know not. "

And they came weeping to their father in the evening. Saying: "O our Father! We went racing one with another, and left Joseph by our things, and **The Wolf** devoured him, and Thou believest not our saying even when we speak the truth." And they came with false blood on his shirt.

He said: "Nay, but your minds have beguiled you into something: *Comely Patience!* And Allah it is Whose help is to be sought in that (predicament) which ye describe."

And there came **a Caravan**, and they sent their waterdrawer. He let down his pail (into the pit). He said: "Good luck! Here is a youth. And they hid him as a treasure, and Allah was Aware of what they did. And they sold him for a low price, **a number of silver coins**; and they attached no value to him. And he of Egypt who purchased him said unto his wife: "Receive him honourably. Perchance he may prove useful to us or we **May Adopt Him as a Son**. Thus we established Joseph in **The Land** that We might teach him the interpretation of events. **And Allah was predominant in His career**, but most of mankind **know not**. And And when he reached his prime We gave him wisdom and knowledge. Thus We reward the good.

And she, in whose house he was, asked of him an evil act. She bolted the doors and said: "Come!" He said: "I seek refuge in Allah! Lo! He is my Lord, who hath treated me honourably. Lo! Wrong-doers never prosper!" She verily desired him, and he would have desired her if it had not been that **he saw** the *Argument* of his Lord. Thus it was, that We might ward off from him adversity and that which is forbidden. Lo! He was of Our chosen slaves.

And they raced with one another to **The Door**, and she tore his shirt from behind, and they met her Lord and Master at **The Door**. She said: "What shall be his reward, who wisheth evil to thy folk, save prison or a painful doom?" "She it was who asked of me an evil act." And a witness of her own folk testified: "If his shirt is torn from before, then she speaketh truth and he is of the liars. And if his shirt is torn from behind, then she hath lied and he is of the truthful."

So when he saw his shirt torn from behind, he said: "Lo! This is of the guile of you women. Lo!" "The guile of you is very great. O Joseph! Turn away from this, and Thou ask forgiveness for thy sin. Lo! thou art of the faulty."

And women in the city said: "The ruler's wife is asking of her slave-boy an ill-deed. Indeed he has smitten her to the heart with love. We behold her in plain aberration."

And when she heard of their sly talk, she sent to them and prepared for them a cushioned couch (to lie on at the feast) and gave to every one of them a knife and said: "Come out unto them!" And when they saw him they exalted him and cut their hands, exclaiming: "Allah Blameless! **This is no human being. This is not other than some gracious angel!**"

She said: "This is he on whose account ye blamed me. I asked of him an evil act, but he proved continent, but if he do not my behest he verily shall be imprisoned, and verily shall be of those brought low."

He said: "O my Lord! Prison is more dear than that unto which they urge me, and if Thou fend not off their wiles from me I shall incline unto them and become of the foolish." So his Lord heard his prayer and fended off their wiles from him. Lo! He is Hearer, Knower.

And it seemed good to them after they had seen **The Signs** (of his innocence) to imprison him for a time. And two young men went to prison with him. One of them said: "I dreamed that I was pressing wine." The other said: "I dreamed that I was carrying upon my head bread whereof the birds were eating." Announce unto us the interpretation, for we see Thee of Those good of THE DREAMING."[*]

He said: "The food which ye are given shall not come unto you but I shall tell you the interpretation ere it cometh unto you. This is of that which my Lord hath taught me. Lo! *I have forsaken the religion* of folk who believe not in Allah and are disbelievers in the Hereafter. *And I have followed* the Religion of *My* Fathers, Abraham and Isaac and Jacob. It never was for *Us* to attribute aught as partner to Allah. This is of the bounty of Allah unto *Us* and unto mankind; but most men give not thanks. **O my fellow-prisoners!** Are *Divers Lords* better, or Allah the One, Almighty? Those whom ye worship beside Him are but *names* which *ye* have *named*, *ye* and *your* fathers! Allah hath revealed **no sanction** for them. The decision rests with Allah only, Who hath commanded you that ye worship none save Him. This is the Right Religion, but most men know not."

"**O my two fellow-prisoners!** As for one of you, *He will Pour out Wine for His Lord to drink*; and as for the other, *He will be Crucified* so that the birds will eat from his head. Thus is the case judged concerning which ye did inquire."

And he said unto him of the twain who he knew would be released: "Mention me in the presence of Thy Lord." But Satan caused him to forget to mention it to His Lord, so he stayed in Prison for some years.

---

[*]The DREAMWALKER: For more see The Book of Daniel, Ezekiel Chapter I, Genesis Chapter I, Isaiah, Jeremiah, Haggai and Zechariah; also *NDoto* and *Alchinga*; *Thingunawat, and Dmoki*; *Milam, Jangwa, Gyurwa* and *Pelwa*; **The Four Oneiroions**: *Asclepeion, Serapeion, Morpheion, and The Coptic Dream Temples of Iemhotep-Pta.*

And the King said: "Lo! I saw in **A Dream** seven fat kine which seven lean were eating; and seven green ears of corn and other dry. O Notables! Expound for me my Vision, if ye can interpret dreams."

They answered: "Jumbled dreams! And we are not knowing in the interpretation of dreams." And he of the two who was released, now at length remembering, said: "I am going to announce unto you the interpretation, therefore send me forth!"

" Joseph! O Thou Truthful One! Expound for us the seven fat kine which seven lean were eating and the seven green ears of corn and other dry, that I may return unto the people, so that they may know."

He said: "Ye shall sow seven years as usual, but that which ye reap, leave it in the ear, all save a little which ye eat. Then after that will come seven hard years which will devour all that ye have prepared for them, save a little of that which ye have stored. Then, after that, will come a year when the people will have plenteous crops and when they will press (*such as* wine and oil)." And the king said: "Bring him unto me." And when the messenger came unto him, he said: "Return unto thy lord and ask him what was the case of the women who cut their hands. Lo! my Lord knoweth their guile." He said: "What happened when ye asked an evil act of Joseph?" They answered: "Allah Blameless! We know no evil of him!" Said the wife of the ruler: "Now the truth is out. I asked of him an evil act, and he is surely of the truthful! This: that he may know that I betrayed him not in secret, and that surely Allah guideth not the snare of the betrayers! I do not exculpate myself. Lo! the soul *enjoineth* unto evil, save that whereon my Lord hath mercy. Lo! my Lord is Forgiving, Merciful."

And the King said: "Bring him unto me that I may attach him to my person." And when he had talked with him he said: "Lo! ***Thou art today in our Presence*** established and trusted."

He said: "Set me over the storehouses of the land. Lo! I am a skilled custodian."

Thus *gave* **We** *power* to Joseph in **The Land**. He was the owner of it where he pleased. We reach with Our mercy whom We will. We lose not the reward of the good. And the reward of the Hereafter is better, for those who ***believe*** and ***ward off***.

And Joseph's Brethren came and presented themselves before him, and he knew them but they knew him not. And when he provided them with their provision he said: "Bring unto me a brother of yours from your Father. See ye not that I fill up the measure and **I am the Best of Hosts**? And if ye bring him not unto me, then there shall be no measure for you with me, nor shall ye draw near. They said: "We will try to win him from his Father: that we will surely do." He said unto his young men: "Place their merchandise in their saddlebags, so that they may know it when they go back to their folk, and so will come again."

So when they went back to their Father they said: "O Our Father! The measure is denied us, so send with us our brother that we may obtain the measure, surely we will guard him well."

266

He said: "Can I entrust him to you save as I entrusted his brother to you aforetime? Allah is better at guarding, and He is the Most Merciful of those who show mercy."

And when they opened their belongings they discovered that *their merchandise <u>had been returned</u> to them*. They said: "O Our Father! What can we ask ? Here is our merchandise returned to us. We shall get provision for our folk and guard our brother, and we shall have the extra measure of a camel. *<u>This</u>* is a light measure!"

He said: "I will not send him with you till ye give me an undertaking in the name of Allah that ye will bring him back to me, unless ye are surrounded." And when they gave him their undertaking He said: "Allah is **<u>The Warden</u>** over what We say!"

And He said: "O My Sons! Go not in by one GATE; go in by different GATES. I can naught avail you as against Allah. Lo! the decision rests with Allah only. **In Him do I put my trust, and in Him let all the trusting put their trust.**"

And when they entered in the manner which their father had enjoined, it would have naught availed them as against Allah; it was but a need of Jacob's soul which he thus satisfied; and Lo! **He was a <u>Lord of Knowledge</u>** because We had taught him; but most of mankind know not.

And when they went in before Joseph, he took his brother unto him, saying: "Lo! I, even I, am Thy brother, therefore sorrow not for what they did."

And when he provided them with their provision, he put the drinking-cup in his brother's saddlebag, and then a crier cried: "O Camel-Riders! Lo! Ye are surely thieves!"

They cried, coming toward them: "What is it ye have lost?"

They said: "We have lost **<u>The King's Cup</u>**, and *<u>he who bringeth it</u>* shall *<u>have a camel</u>-load*, and I am answerable for it."

They said: "By Allah, well ye know we came not to do evil in the land, and are no thieves."

They said: "And what shall be the penalty for it, if ye prove liars?"

They said: "The penalty for it! He in whose bag it's found, he is the penalty for it." Thus We *<u>requite</u>* wrong-doers!

Then he began the search with their bags before his brother's bag, then he produced it from his brother's bag. Thus did We contrive for Joseph. He could not have taken his brother **According to <u>The King's Law</u>** *unless* **Allah willed**. We raise by grades (of mercy) whom We will, and **<u>over</u> *every* <u>Lord of Knowledge</u>** there is *ONE MORE KNOWING!*

They said: "If he stealeth, a brother of his stole before." But Joseph kept it secret in his soul and revealed it not unto them. He said: "Ye are in worse case, and Allah knoweth best that which ye allege."

267

They said: "O Ruler of **The Land**! Lo! He hath a **Very Aged Father**, so take one of us instead of him. Lo! we behold thee of those who do kindness."

He said: "Allah forbid that we should seize save him with whom we found our property; then truly we should be wrong-doers."

So, When they despaired of him, they conferred together apart. The eldest of them said: "Know _ye_ not how _your_ Father took an undertaking from _you_ in Allah's name and how _ye_ failed in the case of Joseph aforetime? Therefore I shall not go forth from **The Land** until My Father giveth leave or Allah judgeth for me. He is the Best of Judges. Return unto _your_ Father and say: 'O Our Father! Lo! Thy Son hath stolen. We testify only to that which we know; **we _are not_ Guardians of the Unseen**! Ask the township where we were, and _The Caravan_ with which we travelled hither. Lo! We speak the truth.'"

He said: "Nay, but your minds have beguiled you into something: _Comely Patience!_ It may be that Allah will bring them all unto me. Lo! He, only He, is the Knower, the Wise!" And He turned away from them and said: "Alas, my grief for Joseph!" And his eyes were whitened with the sorrow that he was suppressing.

They said: "By Allah, Thou wilt never cease remembering Joseph till thy health is ruined or Thou art of those who perish!" He said: "I expose my distress and anguish only unto Allah, and I know from Allah that which ye know not! Go, O My Sons, and ascertain concerning Joseph and his brother, and despair not of the **Spirit of Allah**. Lo! None despaireth of the **Spirit of Allah** save disbelieving folk.

And when they came before him they said: "O Ruler! Misfortune hath touched us and our folk, and we bring but poor merchandise, so fill for us the measure and be charitable unto us. Lo! Allah will requite the charitable..."

He said: "Know ye what ye did unto Joseph and his brother in your ignorance?"

They said: "Is it indeed Thou who art Joseph? He said: "I am Joseph and this is my brother. Allah hath shown us favour. **Lo! He Who Wardeth Off: Endureth**! For Lo! Allah loseth not the wages of the kindly."

They said: "By Allah, verily Allah hath preferred Thee above us, and we were indeed sinful."

He said: "Have no fear this day! May Allah forgive you, and He is the Most Merciful of those who show mercy. Go with this SHIRT OF MINE and lay it on My Father's Face, he will become A SEER; and come to me with all your folk."

When **The Caravan** departed their Father had said: "Truly I am conscious of the breath of Joseph, though ye call me dotard, saying: "By Allah, Lo! Thou art in Thine Old Aberration."

Then, when the bearer of glad tidings came, he laid it on his face and he became A SEER once more. He said: "Said I not unto you that I know from Allah that which ye know not?"

They said: "O Our Father! Ask forgiveness of our sins for us, for Lo! We were sinful."

He said: "I shall ask forgiveness for you of my Lord. Lo! He is the Forgiving, the Merciful."

And when they came in before Joseph, he took his parents unto him, and said: "Come into Egypt safe, if Allah will!" And he placed his parents on the dais and they fell down before him prostrate, and he said: "O My Father! This is the explanation of **My Dream of Old**. My Lord hath made it True! and He hath shown me kindness, since He took me out of **The Prison** and hath brought You from **The Desert** after Satan had made strife between me and my brethren. Lo! My Lord is tender unto whom He will. He is the Knower, the Wise!"

"O my Lord! Thou hast given me of Sovereignty (*sultana*) and hast taught me of the **Understanding of Events**--O THOU CREATOR of the heavens and the earth! **Thou** *art* **My Protecting Guardian** in the world and the Hereafter. *Make* **me** to **DIE MUSLIM**, and *join* **me** to **The Righteous**!

This is of the **Tidings of the Unseen** which We inspire in *THEE. THOU* wast not present with them when they fixed their plan and they were scheming.

And though Thou try much, most men will not believe.

Thou askest them no fee for it. It is naught else than a reminder unto the peoples.

How many a **Portent** is there in the heavens and the earth which they pass by with face averted!

And most of them believe not in Allah except that they attribute partners, Deem they themselves secure from the coming on them of a pall of Allah's punishment, or the coming of the HOUR suddenly while they are unaware?

Say: "This is MY WAY! I call on Allah with **Sure Knowledge** (*Ilm-i Irfani-Iqan*). **I and whosoever followeth me**--Glory be to Allah!--and **I AM** *not* of the Mushrikuny."

We sent not before Thee save men whom We inspired from among the folk of the townships: Have they not travelled in **The Land** and seen the nature of the consequence for those who were before them? And verily the abode of the Hereafter, for those who ward off, is best. Have ye then no sense?

When the messengers despaired and thought that they were denied, until then, came unto them Our Help (*nasr*), and whom We would was saved. And **Our Wrath** cannot be warded from the guilty.

In their history verily there is a lesson for men of understanding. It is no invented story but **A Confirmation of the Existing** and a ***Detailed Explanation*** (*bayan*) ***of Everything*** (*Kulli-Shay'*), and A Guidance and A Mercy for **folk who BELIVE!**

102. Bism'illah Ar-Rahman Ar-Rahim! Musa: MOSES.

Ta. Ha.

We have not revealed unto *THEE* THIS QUR'AN that thou shouldst be distressed! But as a reminder unto him who feareth, A revelation from Him Who created the earth and the high heavens, The Beneficent One, Who is established on the Throne.

Unto Him belongeth whatsoever is in the heavens and whatsoever is in the earth, and whatsoever is between them, and whatsoever is beneath the sod. And if thou ***speakest*** **aloud**, then Lo! He knoweth THE SECRET: *THE MORE HIDDEN.*

Allah! There is no God save Him. **His are The Most Beautiful Names**.

Hath there come unto thee The Story of *MOSES*?

When he saw a fire and said unto his folk: "Lo! Wait! I see A FIRE afar off. Peradventure I may bring you ***a brand*** therefrom or may find GUIDANCE at THE FIRE."

And when he reached it, he was called by name: "O *MOSES*! Lo! I, even I, am Thy Lord, So take off Thy shoes, for Lo! THOU *art* in the **HOLY VALLEY OF TUWA**! And I have *CHOSEN THEE*! So ***hearken*** unto **that which** is *INSPIRED!* Lo! I, even I, am Allah, There is no God save Me. So serve Me and establish worship for My Remembrance. Lo! the HOUR is surely coming. But I will to keep it hidden, that every soul may be rewarded for that which it striveth. Therefore, let not him turn Thee aside from ***IT***--who believeth not therein but followeth his own desire--lest Thou perish--And what is that in thy right hand, O *MOSES*?"

He said: "This is my staff whereon I lean, and wherewith I bear down branches for my sheep, and wherein I find other uses."

He said: "Cast it down, O *MOSES*!"

So he cast it down, and Lo! it was **A Serpent**, ***gliding!***

He said: "Grasp *It* and *Fear Not!* We shall return it to its former state. And thrust *Thy* hand within thine armpit, it will come forth WHITE ***without hurt***: Another token that We may show Thee of **Our Greater Portents!** Go Thou unto Pharaoh! Lo! He hath transgressed!

He said: "My Lord! **Dilate the Expansion of My Heart** and give leeway for me in **My Commad!**" He said: "Lloose a knot from my tongue, that they may understand my saying. Appoint for me a henchman from my folk, Aaron, my Brother. Confirm my strength with him and let him share my task, that we may glorify Thee much and much remember Thee. Lo! Thou art ever Seeing us."

He said: "Thou art granted thy request, O *MOSES*. And indeed, another time, already We have shown thee favour, When we inspired in thy mother that which is inspired, Saying: "Throw him into **The Ark**, and throw it into the river, then the river shall throw it on to **The Bank**, and there an enemy to Me and an enemy to him shall take him." And I endued Thee with love from Me that thou mightest be trained according to My will, when thy sister went and said: "Shall I show you one who will nurse him?" And we restored Thee to Thy mother that her eyes might be refreshed and might not sorrow. And THOU *didst* **kill a man** and We delivered Thee from Great Distress, and tried Thee with a Heavy Trial. And Thou didst tarry years among the folk of Midian. Then camest Thou Providence, O *MOSES*, and **I** *have* **attached Thee to Myself**. Go, Thou and Thy Brother, with My Tokens, and be not faint in remembrance of Me. Go, both of you, unto Pharaoh. Lo! He hath transgressed. And speak unto him a gentle word, that peradventure he may heed or fear."

They said: "Our Lord! Lo! we fear that he may be beforehand with us or that he may play the tyrant. "

He said: "Fear not. **Lo! I am with you** TWAIN, Hearing and Seeing! So go ye unto him and say: 'Lo! we are **Two Messengers** of Thy Lord. So let the children of Israel go with us, and torment them not. We bring Thee a Token from Thy Lord. And peace will be for him who followeth right guidance. Lo! it hath been revealed unto us that the doom will be for him who denieth and turneth away.'"

He said: "Who then is the Lord of *you* TWAIN, O *MOSES*?"

He said: "Our Lord is He Who gave unto everything its nature, then guided it aright."

He said: "What then is the state of the Old Ones?

He said: "The knowledge thereof is with my Lord in **A Record**. My Lord neither erreth nor forgetteth, Who hath appointed the earth as a bed and hath threaded roads for you therein and hath sent down water from the sky and thereby We have brought forth divers kinds of vegetation that eat ye and feed your cattle. Lo! Herein verily are portents for men of thought! Thereof We created you, and thereunto We return you, and thence We bring you forth a second time."

And We verily did show him all Our Tokens, but he denied them and refused.

He said: "Hast come to drive us out from our Land by *thy **Magic***, O *MOSES*? But we surely can produce for Thee magic the like thereof; so appoint **a Tryst** between Us and You, which neither we nor Thou shall fail to keep, at a place convenient." He said: "Your **Tryst** shall be the Day of the Feast, and let the people assemble when the sun hath risen high." Then Pharaoh went and gathered His STRENGTH, then CAME!

MOSES said unto them: "Woe unto you! Invent not a lie against Allah, lest He extirpate you by some punishment. He who lieth faileth miserably."

Then they DEBATED ONE WITH ANOTHER what they must do, and they kept their Counsel SECRET.

They said: "Lo! These are TWO WIZARDS who would drive You out from Your Country by their MAGIC, and destroy Your best traditions! So arrange your plan, and come in battle line. Whoso is uppermost this day will be indeed successful."

They said: O *MOSES*! Either throw first, or let us be the first to throw?"

He said: "Nay, do ye throw! Then lo! their cords and their staves, by their magic, appeared to him as though they ran. And *MOSES* conceived a fear in his mind.

We said: "Fear not! Lo! **Thou** *art* **the Higher**! Throw that which is in Thy right hand! It will eat up that which they have made. Lo! That which they have made is *but a wizard's artifice*, and **a wizard** *shall not* be successful **to whatever point he may attain**."

Then the wizards were (all) flung down prostrate, crying: "We believe in the Lord of Aaron and *MOSES*." He said: "Ye put faith in him before I give you leave. Lo! **He** is *your* **Chief** *who taught you* **MAGIC!** Now surely I shall cut off your hands and your feet alternately, and I shall crucify you on the trunks of palm trees, and ye shall know for certain which of us hath sterner and more lasting punishment!"

They said: "We choose Thee not above THIS RIGHTEOUS BOOK that has come unto us, and above Him Who created us. So decree what Thou wilt decree. Thou wilt end for us only this life of the world. Lo! we believe in our Lord, that He may forgive us our sins and **the magic unto which Thou didst** *force* **Us**. Allah is better and more lasting. Lo! whoso cometh guilty unto his Lord, verily for him is hell. There he will neither die nor live. But whoso cometh unto Him a believer, having done good works, for such are the high stations; Gardens of Eden underneath which rivers flow, wherein they will abide for ever. That is the reward of **him who groweth**."

And verily We inspired *MOSES*, saying: "Take away My slaves by night and strike for them a dry path in the sea, fearing not to be overtaken, neither being afraid." Then Pharaoh followed them with his hosts and there covered them that which did cover them of the sea. And Pharaoh led his folk astray, he did not guide them. "O Children of Israel! We delivered you from your enemy, and we **made a Covenant with you** on the HOLY MOUNTAIN'S SIDE, and sent down on you the manna and the quails! Eat of the good things wherewith We have provided you, and transgress not in respect thereof lest My wrath come upon you: and he on whom My wrath cometh, he is lost indeed. And Lo! verily I am Forgiving toward him who repenteth and believeth and doeth good, and afterward walketh aright. And: What hath made thee hasten from thy folk, O *MOSES*?"

He said: "They are close upon my track. I hastened unto Thee, my Lord, that Thou mightest be well pleased."

He said: "Lo! We have tried Thy folk in Thine absence, and As-Samiri hath misled them."

Then *MOSES* went back unto his folk, angry and sad. He said: "O My People! Hath not your Lord promised you a fair promise? Did the time appointed then appear too long for you, or did ye wish that wrath from your Lord should come upon you, **that ye broke TRYST with me**?"

They said: "We broke not **Tryst** with **Thee of _our own_ will**, but we were laden with burdens of ornaments of the folk, then cast them, for thus As-Samiri proposed. Then he produced for them a calf, of saffron hue, which gave forth a lowing sound. And they cried: 'This is your god and the god of *MOSES*, but he hath forgotten!' See they not, then, that it returneth no saying unto them and possesseth for them neither hurt nor use?"

And Aaron indeed had told them beforehand: "O My People! Ye are but being seduced therewith, for Lo! your Lord is the Beneficent, so follow me and obey my order."

They said: "We shall by no means cease to be its votaries till *MOSES* return unto us."

He said: "O Aaron! What held thee back when thou didst see them gone astray,
That thou followedst me not? Hast thou then disobeyed my order?"

He said: "O Son of My Mother! Clutch not my beard nor my head! I feared lest thou shouldst say: 'Thou hast caused division among the Children of Israel, and hast not waited for my word.'"

He said: "And what hast thou to say, O Samiri?"

He said: "I perceived what they perceive not, so I seized a handful from the footsteps of the messenger, and then threw it in. Thus my soul commended to me."

He said: "Then go! and Lo! In this life it is for Thee to say: 'Touch me not!' and Lo! There is for Thee *A TRYST* Thou canst not break. Now look upon thy god of which thou hast remained a votary. Verily we will burn it and will scatter its dust over the sea. Your God is only Allah, than Whom there is no other God. He embraceth all things in His knowledge. Thus relate We unto Thee some tidings of that which happened of old, and We have given Thee from Our PRESENCE a Reminder. Whoso turneth away from it, he verily will bear a burden on the Day of Resurrection, Abiding under it--an evil burden for them on the Day of Resurrection, The Day when the Trumpet is Blown. **On that Day** we assemble the guilty white-eyed, Murmuring among themselves: 'Ye have tarried but ten.' We are Best Aware of what they utter when their best in conduct say: 'Ye have tarried but a day.' They will ask Thee of **The Mountains**. Say: 'My Lord will break them into scattered dust. And leave it as an empty plain, Wherein thou seest neither curve nor ruggedness. **On that Day** they follow **The Summoner Who Deceiveth** not, and voices are hushed for the Beneficent, and Thou hearest but a faint murmur. **On that Day** no intercession availeth save him unto whom the Beneficent hath given leave and whose word He Accepteth! He knoweth what is before them and what is behind them, while they cannot compass it in knowledge. And faces humble themselves before the Living, the Eternal. And he who beareth wrongdoing is indeed a failure. And he who hath done some good works, being a believer, he feareth not *injustice* nor *begrudging*.'"

Thus We have revealed it as a Lecture in Arabic, and have displayed therein certain threats, that peradventure they may keep from evil or that it may cause them to take heed.

Then exalted be Allah, the True King! And *hasten not with the Qur'an* ere its **Revelation hath been Perfected unto Thee**, and Say: **"O Lord! Increase my Astonishment at THEE!"**

And verily **We made a Covenant of old** with *ADAM*, but he forgot, and We found no constancy in him. And when We said unto the angels: "Fall prostrate before *ADAM*," they fell prostrate save Iblis; he refused. Therefore we said: "O *ADAM*! This is an enemy unto thee and unto Thy wife, so let him not drive you both out of the Garden so that thou come to toil. It is unto Thee that Thou hungerest not therein nor art naked, And that Thou thirstest not therein nor art exposed to the sun's heat."

But the devil whispered to him, saying: "O *ADAM*! Shall I show thee **The Tree of Immortality** and POWER that wasteth not away?" Then they TWAIN ate thereof, so that their shame became apparent unto them, and they began to hide by heaping on themselves some of the leaves of the Garden. And *ADAM* disobeyed his Lord, so went astray. Then his Lord chose him, and relented toward him, and guided him. He said: "Go down hence, both of you, **one of you a foe unto the other.** But when there come unto you from Me a guidance, then whoso followeth My guidance, he will not go astray nor come to grief. But he who turneth away from **Remembrance of Me**, his will be a narrow life, and I shall bring him blind to **The Assembly** (*Knesset*) on the Day of Resurrection. He will say: "My Lord! Wherefore hast Thou gathered me blind, when I was wont to see?" He will answer: "SO MOTE IT BE! Our REVELATIONS came unto Thee but Thou didst forget them. In like manner Thou art forgotten this Day."

Thus do We reward him who is prodigal and believeth not the revelations of his Lord; and verily the doom of the Hereafter will be sterner and more lasting.

Is it not a guidance for them how many a generation We destroyed before them, amid whose dwellings they walk? Lo! Therein verily are **SIGNS** for men of thought!

And but for a Decree that had already gone forth from Thy Lord, and a Term already Fixed, the judgment would have been inevitable. Therefore (O *AL-AMIN*)) bear with what they say and **Celebrate the Praise of Thy** Lord *ere** the **Rising of the Sun** and *ere†* the going down thereof. And glorify Him some *hours‡* of the night and at *the two ends§* of the day, that Thou mayst find acceptance.

And strain not Thine eyes toward that which We cause **some wedded pairs among them to enjoy**, THE FLOWER OF THE LIFE OF THE WORLD, that We may *try them* thereby. The **provision** of thy Lord is better and more lasting.

---

*Fajr.
†*Maghrib.*
‡*Ishaa.*
§*Zuhr va Asr.*

274

And enjoin upon thy people worship, and be constant therein. We ask not of Thee **a provision**: **We provided for Thee**. And the SEQEL is for RIGHTEOUSNESS.

And they say: "If only he would bring us a miracle from his Lord! Hath there not come unto them the proof of THIS RIGHTEOUS BOOK of THAT WHAT is in the former scriptures?

And if we had destroyed them with some punishment before it, they would assuredly have said: "Our Lord! If only Thou hadst sent unto us a messenger, so that we might have followed Thy Revelations before we were humbled and disgraced!"

Say: "Each is awaiting; *SO AWAIT YE!* Ye will **come to know** who are the **Owners of the Path of Equity**, and who is *RIGHT!*

XXVII. JUZ'UN SIPARA VICESIMO-SETTE:

103. Bism'illah Ar-Rahman Ar-Rahim! al-Qasas: THE NARRATIVE.

Ta. Sin. Mim.

These are Revelations of the Scripture that maketh plain.

We narrate unto Thee of the story of *MOSES* and Pharaoh with truth, for folk who believe.

Lo! Pharaoh exalted himself in the earth and **made its people CASTES**. A tribe among them he oppressed, killing their sons and sparing their women. Lo! He was of those who work corruption. And We desired to show favour unto those who were oppressed in the earth, and to make them examples and to make them the inheritors, And to establish them in the earth, and to show Pharaoh and Haman and their hosts that which they feared from them. And We inspired the mother of *MOSES*, (on **this** mission) saying: "Suckle him and, when Thou fearest for him, then cast him into the river and fear not nor grieve. Lo! We shall bring him back unto thee and shall make him of Our messengers."

And the family of Pharaoh took him up, that he might become for them an enemy and a sorrow, Lo! Pharaoh and Haman and their hosts were ever sinning. And the wife of Pharaoh said: "A consolation for me! *And* for Thee! Kill him not. Peradventure he may be of use to Us, or we may choose him for a Son." And they perceived not.

And the heart of the mother of *MOSES became void*, and **she would have betrayed him** if We had not **fortified her heart**, that *she* **might be** of The Believers. And she said unto his sister: "Trace him." So she observed him from afar, and they perceived not.

And We had before forbidden foster-mothers for him, so she said: "Shall I show you a household who will rear him for you and take care of him?" So We restored him to his mother that she might be comforted and not grieve, and that she might know that the promise of Allah is true. But most of them know not.

And when he reached his full strength and was ripe, We gave him wisdom and knowledge. Thus do We reward the good.

And he entered the city at a time of carelessness of its folk, and he found therein two men fighting, one of his own caste, and the other of his enemies; and he who was of his caste asked him for help against him who was of his enemies. So *MOSES* struck him with his fist and killed him. He said: "This is of the devil's doing. Lo! He is an enemy, a mere misleader." He said: "My Lord! Lo! I have wronged my soul, so forgive me." Then He forgave him. Lo! He is the Forgiving, the Merciful.

He said: "My Lord! Forasmuch as Thou hast favoured me, I will nevermore be a supporter of the guilty."

And morning found him in the city, fearing, vigilant, when ***Behold!*** He who had appealed to him the day before cried out to him for help. *MOSES* said unto him: "Lo! Thou art indeed a mere hothead."

And when he would have fallen upon the man who was an enemy unto them both, he said: "O *MOSES*! Wouldst thou kill me as thou didst kill a person yesterday. Thou wouldst be nothing but a tyrant in the land, thou wouldst not be of the reformers." And a man came from the uttermost part of the city, running. He said: "O *MOSES*! Lo! The Chiefs take counsel against Thee to slay Thee: Therefore ***escape***. Lo! I am of those who give thee good advice." So he escaped from thence, fearing, vigilant. He said: "My Lord! Deliver me from the wrongdoing folk." And when he turned his face toward Midian, he said: "Peradventure my Lord will guide me in the right road."

And when he came unto the water of Midian he found there a whole tribe of men, watering. And he found apart from them two women keeping back. He said: "What aileth you ?" The two said: "We cannot give to drink till the shepherds return from the water; and Our Father is a very old man." So he watered for them. Then he turned aside into the shade, and said: "My Lord! I am needy of whatever good Thou sendest down for me."

Then there came unto him one of the two women, walking shyly. She said: "Lo! My Father biddeth Thee, that he may reward Thee with a payment for that thou didst water for Us. Then, when he came unto him and told him the story, He said: "Fear not! Thou hast escaped from the wrongdoing folk."

One of the two women said: "O My Father! Hire him! For the best that Thou canst hire is **The Strong**, **The Trustworthy**. He said: "Lo! I fain would marry Thee to one of these two daughters of mine on condition that thou hirest thyself to me for **eight pilgrimages**. Then if Thou **completest ten** it will be of Thine own accord, for I would not make it hard for thee. Allah willing, thou wilt find me of **The Righteous.** He said: "**LET IT BE** that between Thee and me. Whichever of the two terms I fulfill, there will be no injustice to me, and Allah is Surety over what we say."

Then, when *MOSES* had fulfilled the term, and was travelling with his housefolk, he saw in the distance **A FIRE** and said unto his housefolk: Bide ye. Lo! I see in the distance **A FIRE**; peradventure I shall bring you tidings thence, or **a brand from the fire** that ye may warm yourselves." And when he reached it, he was CALLED from **The Right Side of the Valley** in **The Blessed Field**, from THE TREE: "O *MOSES*! Lo! I, even I, am Allah, the Lord of the Worlds; Throw down thy staff!" And when he *saw* it *writhing* **as it had been a demon**, he turned to flee headlong! "O *MOSES*! Draw nigh and fear not. Lo! Thou art of those who are secure. Thrust thy hand into the bosom of Thy robe *it* will come forth **white without hurt**. And guard thy heart from fear. Then these shall be two proofs from your Lord unto Pharaoh and his chiefs. Lo! they are evil-living folk."

He said: "My Lord! Lo! I killed a man among them and I fear that they will kill me. My Brother Aaron is more eloquent than me in speech. Therefore send him with me as a helper to confirm me. Lo! I fear that they will give the lie to me."

He said: "We will strengthen Thine arm with Thy Brother, and We will give unto you both power so that they cannot reach you for **Our Portents**. Ye TWAIN, and those who follow you, will be the winners."

But when *MOSES* came unto them with Our clear tokens and THIS RIGHTEOUS BOOK, they said: "This is naught but invented magic. We never heard of this among our fathers of old."

And *MOSES* said: "My Lord is Best Aware of him who bringeth guidance from His Presence, and whose will be the sequel of the Home (of bliss). Lo! wrong-doers will not be successful."

And Pharaoh said: "O Chiefs! I know not that ye have a god other than me, so kindle for me (a fire), O Haman, to bake the mud; and set up for me a lofty tower in order that I may survey the God of *MOSES*; and Lo! I deem him of the liars."And he and his hosts were haughty in **the land** without right, and deemed that they would never be brought back to Us. Therefore We seized him and his hosts, and abandoned them unto the sea. Behold the nature of the consequence for evil-doers!

And We made them **Patterns that Invite** unto **the Fire**, and on the Day of Resurrection they will not be helped. And We made a curse to follow them in this world, and on the Day of Resurrection they will be among the hateful. And We verily gave the Scripture unto *MOSES* after We had destroyed the generations of old (Lit. the Old Ones): clear testimonies for mankind, and a guidance and a mercy, that haply they might reflect.

And Thou wast not on the western side when We expounded unto *MOSES* the commandment, and Thou wast not among those present; But We brought forth generations, and their lives dragged on for them. And Thou wast not a dweller in Midian, reciting unto them Our Revelations, but We kept sending (messengers to men). And Thou was not beside the Mount when We did call; but (the knowledge of it is) a mercy from thy Lord that Thou mayst warn a folk unto whom no warner came before Thee, that haply they may give heed.

Otherwise, if disaster should afflict them because of that which their own hands have sent before, they might say: "Our Lord! Why sentest Thou no messenger unto us, that we might have followed Thy Revelations and been of **The Believers**?" But when there came unto them the Truth from Our Presence, they said: "Why is he not given the like of what was given unto *MOSES*?" Did they not disbelieve in that which was given unto *MOSES* of old? They say: "Two *magics* that support each other!" and they say: "Lo! In ***both*** we are disbelievers."

Say: "Then bring a scripture from the presence of Allah that giveth clearer guidance than these two (that) I may follow it, if ye are truthful." And if they answer Thee not, then know that what they **follow is** *their* lusts. And who goeth farther astray than **he who followeth his lust** *without* **Guidance from Allah**. Lo! Allah guideth not wrongdoing folk.

And now Verily We have caused the Word to reach them, that haply they may give heed.

Those unto whom We gave the Scripture before it, they believe in it,

And when it is recited unto them, they say: "We believe in it. Lo! It is the Truth from our Lord. Lo! even before it we were of those who surrender (unto Him)." These will be given their reward twice over, because they are steadfast and repel evil with good, and spend of that wherewith We have provided them, And when they hear vanity they withdraw from it and say: "Unto Us Our works and unto you your works. Peace be unto you! We desire not the ignorant."

Lo! Thou guidest not whom thou lovest, but Allah guideth whom He will. And He is Best Aware of those who walk aright.

And they say: "If we were to follow the Guidance with Thee we should be torn out of our land." Have We not established for them **a Sure Sanctuary**, whereunto the produce of all things is brought (in trade), a provision from Our presence? But most of them know not.

And how many a community have We destroyed that was thankless for its means of livelihood! And yonder are their dwellings, which have not been inhabited after them save a little. And We, even We, were the inheritors. And never did thy Lord destroy the townships, till He had raised up in their mother a messenger reciting unto them Our Revelations. And never did We destroy the townships unless the folk thereof were evil-doers. And whatsoever ye have been given is **a comfort of the life** of the world and an **ornament** thereof; and that which Allah hath is better and more lasting. Have ye then no sense?

Is he whom We have promised a fair promise which he will find like him whom We suffer to enjoy awhile the comfort of the life of the world, then on the Day of Resurrection he will be of those arraigned? On the day when He will call unto them and say: "Where are My partners whom ye imagined?"

Those concerning whom the Word will have come true will say: "Our Lord! These are they whom we led astray. We led them astray even as we ourselves were astray. We declare our innocence before Thee:" Us they never loved nor worshipped!

And it will be said: "Cry unto your (so-called) partners." And they will cry unto them, and they will give no answer unto them, and they will see the Doom. Ah, if they had but been guided!

And on the Day when He will call unto them and say: "What answer gave ye to the messengers?" On that Day (all) tidings will be dimmed for them, nor will they ask one of another. But as for him who shall repent and believe and do right, he haply may be one of the successful. Thy Lord bringeth to pass what He willeth and chooseth. **They have never any choice.** Glorified be Allah and Exalted above all that they associate (with Him)!

And thy Lord knoweth what their breasts conceal, and what they publish.

And He is Allah; there is no God save Him. His is all praise in the former and the latter (state), and His is the Command (*amr*), and unto Him ye will be brought back.

Say: "Have ye thought, if Allah made night everlasting for you till the Day of Resurrection, who is a god beside Allah who could bring you light? Will ye not then hear?"

Say: "Have ye thought, if Allah made day everlasting for you till the Day of Resurrection, who is a god beside Allah who could bring you night wherein ye rest? Will ye not then see?"

Of His mercy hath He appointed for you night and day, that therein ye may rest, and that ye may seek His bounty, and that haply ye may be thankful.

And on the Day when He shall call unto them and say: "Where are My partners whom ye pretended?" And We shall take out from every nation a witness and We shall say: "Bring your proof. Then they will know that Allah hath the Truth, and all that they invented will have failed them."

Now Korah was of *MOSES*' folk, but he oppressed them; and We gave him so much treasure that the stores thereof would verily have been a burden for a troop of mighty men. When his own folk said unto him: "Exult not; Lo! Allah loveth not the exultant; But seek the abode of the Hereafter in that which Allah hath given Thee and neglect not Thy portion of the world, and be Thou kind even as Allah hath been kind to Thee, and seek not corruption in the earth; Lo! Allah loveth not corrupters!" He said: "I have been given it only on account of knowledge I possess." Knew he not that Allah had destroyed already of the generations before him men who were mightier than him in strength and greater in respect of following? The guilty are not questioned of their sins. Then went he forth before his people in his pomp. Those who were desirous of the life of the world said: "Ah, would that we had the like of what hath been given unto Korah! Lo! He is lord of rare good fortune."

But those who had been given knowledge said: "Woe unto you! The reward of Allah for him who believeth and doeth right is better, and only the steadfast will obtain it."

So We caused the earth to swallow him and his dwelling-place. Then he had no host to help him against Allah, nor was he of those who can save themselves. And morning found those who had coveted his place but yesterday crying: "Ah, welladay! Allah enlargeth the provision for whom

He will of His slaves and straiteneth it (for whom He will). If Allah had not been gracious unto us He would have caused it to swallow us (also). Ah, welladay! The disbelievers never prosper!"

As for that Abode of the Hereafter We assign it unto those who seek not oppression in the earth, nor yet corruption. The SEQUEL is for those who ward off. Whoso bringeth a good deed, he will have better than the same; while as for him who bringeth an ill-deed, those who do ill-deeds will be requited only what they did.

Lo! He Who hath given Thee THIS WHOLE (Holy) QUR'AN for a law will surely bring Thee home again. Say: "My Lord is Best Aware of him who bringeth guidance and him who is in error manifest." Thou hadst no hope that the Scripture would **be inspired** in Thee; but it is a mercy from thy Lord, so ***NEVER* be a helper to the disbelievers**.

And let them ***not*** divert Thee from the Revelations of Allah after they have been sent down unto Thee; but CALL unto thy Lord, and be not of those who ***ascribe*** partners. And ***CRY NOT*** unto any other god along with Allah. There is no God save Him. Everything will perish save His Countenance of Love. His is the Command, and unto Him ye will be brought back!

104. Bism'illah Ar-Rahman Ar-Rahim! Hud: MADHUSUDAN KRISHNA OF THE THRONE CHARIOT OF THE GITA OF GOD.

Alif. Lam. Ra.

A Scripture (*Vedas*) the Revelations (*Yugas*) whereof are Perfected (*Bhagavad Gita*) and then Expounded (*Samkhya:* Enumerated) from One Wise, Informed! Serve none but Allah!

Lo! I am unto you from Him a warner and a bringer of good tidings. And Ask pardon of your Lord and turn to Him repentant. He will cause you to enjoy a fair estate until a time appointed. He giveth His Bounty unto every Bountiful One. But if ye turn away, Lo! (then) I fear for you the retribution of an awful Day! Unto Allah is your return, and He is Able to do All Things (*Kull-i Shay'*).

Lo! Now they fold up their breasts that they may hide (their thoughts) from Him. At the very moment when they cover themselves with their clothing, Allah knoweth that which they keep hidden and that which they proclaim. Lo! He is Aware of what is in the breasts (of the individual peoples). And there is not a beast in the earth but the sustenance thereof dependeth on Allah. He knoweth its habitation and its repository. All is in a clear Record.

And He it is Who created the heavens and the earth in <u>six Days</u>--and <u>His Throne</u> was upon the <u>water</u>--that He might try you, which of you is best in conduct. Yet if Thou sayest: "Lo! Ye will be raised again after death!" Those who disbelieve will surely say: "This is naught but mere magic." And if We delay for them the DOOM until a reckoned time, they will surely say: "What withholdeth it?" Verily on the day when it cometh unto them, it cannot be averted from them, and that which they derided will surround them.

And if we cause man to taste some mercy from Us and afterward withdraw it from him, Lo! He is despairing, thankless. And if We cause him to taste grace after some misfortune that had befallen him, he saith: "The ills have gone from me." Lo! He is exultant, boastful; Save those who persevere and do good works. Theirs will be forgiveness and a great reward.

A likely thing, that thou wouldst forsake aught of that which hath been revealed unto Thee, and that Thy breast should be straitened for it, because they say: "Why hath not a treasure been sent down for him, or an angel come with him?" Thou art but a warner, and Allah is in charge of all things. Or they say: "He hath invented it." Say: "Then bring **Ten Sutras**, the like thereof, invented, and call on everyone ye can beside Allah, if ye are truthful!" And if they answer not your call, then know that it is revealed only in the knowledge of Allah; and that there is no God save Him. Will ye then be (of) those who surrender?

Whoso desireth the life of the world and its pomp, We shall repay them their deeds herein, and therein they will not be wronged. Those are they for whom is naught in the Hereafter save THE FIRE. All that they contrive here is vain and all that they are wont to do is fruitless.

Is he (to be counted equal with them) who relieth on THIS RIGHTEOUS BOOK: the proof from his Lord--and *a witness* from Him reciteth it, and before it was the Book of *MOSES*, an example and a mercy? Such believe therein, and whoso disbelieveth therein of the clans, **the Fire** is his appointed place. So be not thou in doubt concerning it. Lo! it is the Truth from thy Lord; but most of mankind believe not.

Who doeth greater wrong than he who inventeth a lie concerning Allah?

Such will be brought before their Lord, and the witnesses will say: "These are they who lied concerning their Lord. Now the curse of Allah is upon wrong-doers, Who debar souls from the way of Allah and would have it crooked, and who are disbelievers in the Hereafter. Such will not escape in the earth, nor have they any protecting friends beside Allah. For them the torment will **be double**. They could not bear to hear, and they used not to see. Such are they who have lost their souls, and that which they used to invent hath failed them. Assuredly in the Hereafter they will be the greatest losers."

Lo! Those who believe and do good works and humble themselves before their Lord: such are rightful owners of the Garden; they will abide therein. The similitude of the two parties is as the blind and the deaf and the seer and the hearer. Are they equal in similitude? Will ye not then be admonished?

And We sent Noah unto his folk (and he said): "Lo! I am a plain warner unto you. That ye serve none, save Allah. Lo! I fear for you the retribution of a painful Day." The Chieftains of his folk, who disbelieved, said: "We see Thee but a mortal like us, and we see not that any follow Thee save the most abject among us, without reflection. We behold in you no merit above us--nay, we deem you liars." He said: "O my people! Bethink you, if I rely on THIS RIGHTEOUS BOOK from my Lord and there hath come unto me a mercy from His presence, and it hath been made obscure to you, can we compel you to accept it when ye are averse thereto?"

And "O my people! I ask of you no wealth therefore. My reward is the concern only of Allah, and I am not going to thrust away those who believe--Lo! They have to meet their Lord!--but I see you a folk that are ignorant."

And, "O my people! Who would deliver me from Allah if I thrust them away? Will ye not then reflect?" I say not unto you: 'I have the treasures of Allah' nor 'I have knowledge of the Unseen,' nor say I: 'Lo! I am an angel!' Nor say I unto those whom your eyes scorn that Allah will not give them good--Allah knoweth best what is in their hearts--Lo! Then indeed I should be of the wrong-doers."

They said: "O Noah! Thou hast disputed with us and multiplied disputation with us; now bring upon us that wherewith thou threatenest us, if thou art of the truthful." He said: "Only Allah will bring it upon you if He will, and ye can by no means escape. My counsel will not profit you if I were minded to advise you, **if** Allah's will is **to keep you astray**. He is your Lord and unto Him ye will be brought back."

Or say they: "He hath invented it? Say: "If I have invented it, upon me be my crimes, but I am innocent of all what that ye commit.

And it was inspired in Noah (in ***this*** mission): "No-one of Thy folk will believe save him who hath believed already. Be not distressed because of what they do. Build the ship under Our eyes and by Our inspiration, and speak not unto Me on behalf of those who do wrong. Lo! they will be drowned."

And he was building the ship, and every time that Chieftains of his people passed him, they made mock of him. He said: "**Though ye make mock of Us, yet We mock at you even as ye mock**! And ye shall know to whom a punishment that will confound him cometh, and upon whom a lasting doom will fall."

So it is till the term appointed when Our commandment came to pass and the oven gushed forth water, We said: "Load therein two of every kind, a reproductive-pair, and Thy household, save him against whom the word hath gone forth already, and those who believe." And but a few were they who believed with him. And he said: "Embark therein! In the name of Allah be its course and its mooring. Lo! my Lord is Forgiving, Merciful."

And it sailed with them amid waves like mountains, and Noah cried unto his Son--and he was standing aloof --O My Son! Come ride with us, and be not with the disbelievers. He said: "I shall betake me to some mountain that will save me from the water." He said: This day there is none that saveth from the commandment of Allah save him on whom He hath had mercy." And the wave came in between them, so he was among the drowned.

And it was said: "O Earth! Swallow thy water and, O Sky! Be cleared of clouds!" And the water was made to subside. And the commandment was fulfilled. And ***It*** came to rest upon **AL-JUDI** and it was said: "A far removal for wrongdoing folk!" And Noah cried unto his Lord and said: "My Lord! Lo! My Son is of my Household! Surely Thy promise is the truth and Thou are the Most Just of Judges."

He said: "O Noah! Lo! He is not of Thy Household; Lo! He is of evil conduct, so ask not of Me that whereof thou hast no knowledge. I admonish Thee lest thou be among the ignorant."

He said: "My Lord! Lo! in Thee do I seek refuge that I should ask of Thee that whereof I have no knowledge. Unless Thou forgive me and have mercy on me I shall be among the lost."

It was said: "O Noah! Go thou down with calm loving-kindness from Us and blessings upon Thee and some nations from those with Thee: nations unto whom We shall give enjoyment a long while and then **a painful doom** from Us will overtake them. "

This is of the tidings of the Unseen which We inspire in Thee. Thou Thyself knewest it not, nor did thy folk before this. Then have patience. Lo! THE SEQUEL is for those who ward off. And unto A'ad (whose regions extended from Hyderabad, Hadhramut, Shambhala, Bamiyan, *al-Rub' al Khali* and adjacent lands), came their Brother, *KRISHNA (Hud) MADHUSUDAN*. He said: "O my people! Serve Allah! Ye have no other God save Him. Lo! ye do but invent. O my people! I ask of you no reward for it. Lo! my reward is the concern only of Him Who made me. Have ye then no sense?"

And, "O my people! Ask forgiveness of your Lord, then turn unto Him repentant; He will cause the sky to rain abundance on you and will add unto you strength to your strength. Turn not away, guilty!" They said: "O *MADHUSUDAN (Hud) THOU KRISHNA*! Thou hast brought us no **proofs** of *THY MISSION* and we are not going to forsake our gods (*Rig Veda*) on Thy mere saying, and we *are not* believers in Thee. We say naught save that one of our gods hath possessed Thee in an *evil way*."

He said: "I call Allah to witness, and do ye (too) bear witness, that I am innocent of (all) that ye ascribe as partners: **Beside Him**. So (try to) circumvent ME, all of you, give me no respite. Lo! I have put my trust in Allah, my Lord and your Lord. Not an animal but He doth grasp it by the forelock! Lo! My Lord is on a straight path. And if ye turn away, still I have conveyed unto you that (*Gita*) wherewith I was sent unto you, and my Lord will set in place of you a folk other than you. Ye cannot injure Him at all. Lo! My Lord is Guardian over all things."

And when Our commandment came to pass We saved *KRISHNA (Hud) MADHUSUDAN* and those (Pandavs and more) who believed with him by a Mercy from Us; We saved them from a **Harsh DOOM (Agnia Fire Weapon)**. And such were A'ad. They denied the revelations of their Lord and flouted His messengers and followed the command of every froward potentate. And a curse was made to follow them in the world and on the Day of Resurrection. Lo! A'ad disbelieved in their Lord. A far removal for A'ad, the folk of *KRISHNA*!

And unto Thamud came their brother *SIDDHARTHA (Salih) THE BUDDHA*. He said: "O my People! Serve Allah, Ye have no other God save Him. He brought you forth from the earth and hath made you husband it. So ask forgiveness of Him and turn unto Him repentant. Lo! My Lord is Nigh, Responsive." They said: O *SIDDHARTHA (Salih) THOU BUDDHA*! Thou hast been among us hitherto as that wherein our hope was placed. Dost Thou ask us not to worship (*anatman*) what our fathers worshipped (*atman*)?" Lo! We verily are in grave doubt concerning that to which Thou callest us!"

283

He said: "O my People! Bethink you: If I have a Revelation (*Tripitakas*) from my Lord to Support ME and there hath come unto me a Mercy (*Kalachakra Tantra*) from Him, who will save me from Allah if I disobey Him? Ye would add to me naught save perdition. O my People! This is the **Diamond Vehicle** (Sanskrit: *Vahana*) of Allah, a token unto you, so suffer her to feed in Allah's earth, and touch her not with harm lest a near torment seize you." But they **hamstrung her**, and then he said: "Enjoy life in your dwelling-place three days! This is a threat that will not be belied!"

So, when Our commandment came to pass, We saved *SIDDHARTHA (Salih) THE BUDDHA*, and those who believed with him (in all his many advancing turns of the WHEEL) , by a Mercy (*Dzogchen*) from Us, from the **Ignominy of that DAY**. Lo, thy Lord! He is the Strong, the Mighty. And the (awful) Cry overtook those who did wrong, so that morning found them prostrate in their dwellings, As though they had not dwelt there. Lo! Thamud disbelieved in their Lord. A far removal for Thamud!

And Our messengers came unto Abraham with good news. They said: "SALEM!" He answered: "SALEM!" And delayed not to bring a Roasted Calf. And when he saw their hands reached not to it, he mistrusted them and conceived a fear of them. They said: "Fear not! Lo! We are sent unto the folk of Lot." And his wife, standing by laughed* when We gave her good tidings (of the the birth) of Isaac, and, after Isaac, of Jacob.

She said: "Oh Woe is Me! Shall I bear a child when I am an old woman, and this my husband is an old man? Lo! This *is* a **strange thing**!" They said: "Wonderest Thou at the commandment of Allah? The mercy of Allah and His blessings be upon you, O people of THE HOUSE! Lo! He is Owner of Praise, Owner of Glory!" And when **THE AWE** departed from Abraham, and the Glad News (gospel) reached him, he pleaded with Us on behalf of the folk of Lot. Lo! Abraham was mild, imploring, penitent. "O Abraham! Forsake this! Lo! Thy Lord's Commandment hath gone forth, and Lo! There cometh unto them a DOOM which cannot be repelled."

And when Our messengers came unto Lot, he was distressed and knew not how to protect them. He said: "This is a Distressful DAY." And his people came unto him, running towards him--and before then they used to commit abominations--He said: "O my People! Here are my daughters! They are purer for you. Beware of Allah, and degrade me not in (the persons of) my guests. Is there not among you any upright man?" They said: "Well thou knowest that we have no right to Thy daughters, and well thou knowest what we want." He said: "Would that I had strength to resist you or had some strong support (among you)!"

They said: "O Lot! Lo! **We are Messengers of Thy Lord**; They shall not reach Thee. So travel with Thy people in a part of the night, and let not one of you turn round--save thy wife. Lo! That which smiteth them will smite her too. Lo! Their **tryst** is at the morning. Is not the morning nigh?"

So when Our commandment came to pass We overthrew (that township) and rained upon it stones of clay, one after another, Marked with FIRE in the Providence of Thy Lord. And they are never far from the wrong-doers.

Isaac means laughter.

And unto Midian came their Brother *ZOROASTER (Shu'ayb) SPENTA MANIYUSH*. He said: "O my People! Serve Allah. Ye have no other God save Him! And give not short measure and short weight. Lo! I see you well-to-do, and Lo! I fear for you the DOOM of a besetting Day.* O my People! Give full measure and full weight in justice, and wrong not people in respect of their goods. And do not evil in the earth, causing corruption. That which Allah leaveth with you is better for you if ye are believers; and I am not a keeper over you."

They said: "O *ZOROASTER (Shu'ayb) SPENTA MANIYUSH*! Doth Thy way of prayer command Thee that we should forsake that which our fathers (used to) worship, or that we (should leave off) doing what we will with our own property. Lo! Thou art the mild, the guide to right behaviour."

He said: "O my people! Bethink you: If I am come on a **Clear Revelation** from my Lord and He hath supplied me with goodly supplies (***The AVESTA***) from Him, and if I will not follow you in that which I Myself forbid you, do I seek aught save **REFORM** so far as I am able? My welfare is only in Allah. In Him I trust and unto Him I turn." And, "O my people! Let not the schism with me cause you to sin so that there befall you that which befell the folk of Noah. The folk of *KRISHNA (Hud) MADHUSUDAN*, and the folk of SIDDHARTHA *(Salih) THE BUDDHA*, and the folk of Lot are ***not far off*** from you! Ask pardon of your Lord and then turn unto Him (repentant). Lo! my Lord is Merciful, Loving."

They said: *ZOROASTER (Shu'ayb) SPENTA MANIYUSH*! We understand not much of that Thou tellest, and Lo! We do behold Thee weak among us. But for **Thy Family** [The Family of **SPITAMO**: Jethro the Midianite father-in-law of *MOSES*†] we should have stoned Thee, for Thou art not strong against us."

He said: "O my People! Is my *Family* more to be honoured by you than Allah? And ye put Him behind you, neglected! Lo! my Lord surroundeth what ye do." And, "O my people! Act according to your power, Lo! I (too) am acting. Ye will soon know on whom there cometh a DOOM that will abase him, and who it is that lieth. And watch! Lo! I am a watcher with you."

And when Our commandment came to pass We saved *ZOROASTER (Shu'ayb) SPENTA MANIYUSH* and those who believed with him by a Mercy (*ZEND*) from Us; and the (Awful) Cry seized those who did injustice, and morning found them prostrate in their dwellings, As though they had not dwelt there. A far removal for Midian, even as Thamud had been removed afar!

---

*Zoroaster was awakened to his mission at the going down of the Sun.
†**Thy Family**: Zoroaster is the promised descendant of Jethro the Midianite through is son Hobob (*Haridar*) who married Rohaya (the grand-daughter of Moses and Tzipora through their son Gershom). Zoroaster is thus the Seventh Generation of **BOTH** MOSES and JETHRO. For this reason of HIS FAMILY--they dared not kill him! This FACT--of his being of the HOLY HOUSEHOLD OF THE HOLY FAMILY--did not deter the peoples from slaying the Blessed *BAB* who was Siyyid (of the House of Muhammad (AFNAN: Lit. "Twigs") of Abraham nor of slaying *JESUS* who was of the House of and Lineage of David (AGHSAN: Lit. BRANCHES (see Zech. 3:8 KJV) of Abraham, through his father Joseph (see Rom. 1:3, 4 KJV: *JESUS* is the sperm-child (male "seed" Gk. *sperma*) of his father Joseph. See my book ***EZEKIEL'S TEMPLE IN MONTANA*** for the Biblical and scientific understanding of the Virgin Birth in this regard according to "Dear Abbey."

285

And verily We sent *MOSES* with Our Revelations and a ***Clear Warrant*** Unto Pharaoh and his Chiefs, but they did follow the command of Pharaoh, and the command of Pharaoh was no right guide. He will go before his people on the Day of Resurrection and will lead them to THE FIRE for watering-place. Ah, hapless is the watering-place (whither they are) led. A curse is made to follow them in the world and on the Day of Resurrection. Hapless is the gift (that will be) given (them).

That is (something) of the tidings of the townships (which were destroyed of old). We relate it unto Thee. Some of them are standing and some (already) reaped. **We wronged them not, but they did wrong themselves**; and their gods (*asurahs va devas*) on whom they call beside Allah availed them naught when came thy Lord's Command; They added to them naught save ruin. Even thus is the grasp of thy Lord when He graspeth the townships while they are doing wrong. Lo! His grasp is painful, very strong.

Lo! Herein verily there is **a Portent** for those who fear the DOOM of the Hereafter. That is a Day unto which all the peoples of the world will be assembled, and that is a Day that will be witnessed! And We defer it only to a term already reckoned.

On the Day when it cometh no soul will speak except by His permission; some among them will be wretched, (others) glad. As for those who will be wretched they will be in **the Fire**; sighing and wailing will be their portion therein, Abiding there so long as the heavens and the earth endure save for that which thy Lord willeth. Lo! thy Lord is Doer of what He will.

And as for those who will be glad (that day) they will be in the Garden, abiding there so long as the heavens and the earth endure save for that which thy Lord willeth: a gift unfailing. So be not Thou in doubt concerning that which these (folk) worship. They worship only as their fathers worshipped aforetime. Lo! We shall pay them their whole due unabated.

And we verily gave unto *MOSES* the Scripture (*TORAH*), and there was strife thereupon; and had it not been for a Word that had already gone forth from Thy Lord, the case would have been judged between them, and Lo! They are in grave doubt concerning it.[*]

And Lo! Unto each thy Lord will verily repay his works in full. Lo! He is Informed of what they do. So tread Thou the straight path as Thou art commanded, and those who turn (unto Allah) with Thee, and transgress not. Lo! He is Seer of what ye do.

And incline not toward those who do wrong ***lest*** the FIRE touch you, and ye have no protecting friends against Allah, and afterward ye would not be helped. Establish worship at the two ends of the day and in some watches of the night. Lo! Good deeds annul ill-deeds. This is reminder for the mindful. And have patience, for **Lo! Allah loseth not the wages of the good**.

---

[*]This refers to the ASSUMPTION OF MOSES: a strife over the body of Moses and concerning *JESUS* (JOSHUA) THE HIGH PRIEST of Zech. ch. 3, that Michael and Satan contested over. See Jude, Zechariah, Haggai, and The Book of Revelation for more.

If only there had been among the generations before you men possessing a remnant (of good sense) to warn (their people) from corruption in the earth, as did a few of those whom We saved from them! The wrong-doers followed that by which they were made sapless, and were guilty. In truth thy Lord destroyed not the townships tyrannously while their folk were doing right. And if thy Lord had willed, He verily would have made all humanity one nation, yet they cease not differing: Save him on whom thy Lord hath Mercy; and for that He did create them.

And the Word of thy Lord hath been fulfilled: "Verily I shall fill hell with the jinn and mankind together." And all that We relate unto Thee of **The Story of the Messengers** is in order that thereby We may make firm Thy Heart and certain Thy Mind! And herein hath come unto Thee the Truth and an exhortation and a reminder for believers. And say unto those who believe not: "Act according to your power. Lo! We (too) are acting. And wait! Lo! We (too) are waiting."

And Allah's is the Invisible of the heavens and the earth, and unto Him the whole matter will be returned. So worship Him and put thy trust in Him. Lo! Thy Lord is not unaware of what ye (mortals) do!

XXVIII. JUZ'UN SIPARA VICESIMO-OTTO:

105. Bism'illah Ar-Rahman Ar-Rahim! al-A`raf: THE ELEVATED PLACES OF ZOROASTER.

Alif. Lam. Mim. Sad.

A Scripture that is revealed unto Thee--so let there be no heaviness in Thy heart therefrom--that Thou mayst warn thereby, and be a Reminder unto believers. "Follow that which is sent down unto you from your Lord, and follow no protecting friends beside Him. Little do ye recollect! How many a township have We destroyed! As a raid by night, or while they slept at noon, Our TERROR came unto them. No plea had they, when Our TERROR came unto them, save that they said: 'Lo! We were wrong-doers.' Then verily We shall question those unto whom We hath been sent, and verily We shall question the messengers. Then verily We shall **narrate *unto* them** with Knowledge, for We **were *not* absent**."

The weighing on that DAY is **the divine standard**. As for those whose scale is heavy, they are the successful. And as for those whose scale is light: those are they who lose their souls because they used to wrong Our Revelations. And We have given you **power** in the earth, and appointed for you therein livelihoods. Little give ye thanks! And We created you, then fashioned you, then told the angels: "Fall ye prostrate before *ADAM*!" And they fell prostrate, all save Iblis, who was not of those who make prostration.

He said: "What hindered Thee that Thou didst not fall prostrate when I bade thee?"

"I am better than him. Thou createdst me of fire while him Thou didst create of mud."

He said: "Then go down hence! It is not for Thee to show pride here, so go forth! Lo! Thou art of those degraded."

He said: "Reprieve me till the DAY when they are raised."

He said: "Lo! Thou art of those reprieved."

He said: "Now, because _**Thou**_ hast sent me astray, verily I shall lurk in ambush for them on Thy Right Path. Then I shall come upon them from before them and from behind them and from their right hands and from their left hands, and Thou wilt not find most of them loyal."

He said: "Go forth from hence, degraded, banished. As for such of them as follow Thee, surely I will fill hell with all of you." And: "O _ADAM_! Dwell thou and thy wife in the Garden and eat from whence ye will, but come not nigh this tree lest ye become wrong-doers."

Then Satan whispered to them that he might manifest unto them that which was hidden from them of their shame, and he said: "Your Lord forbade you from this tree only lest ye should become angels or become of the immortals." And he swore unto them: "Lo! I am a sincere adviser unto you." Thus did he lead them on with guile.

And when they tasted of the tree their shame was manifest to them and they began to hide themselves with some of the leaves of the Garden. And their Lord called them: "Did I not forbid you from that tree and tell you: 'Lo! Satan is an open enemy to you?'"

They said: "Our Lord! We have wronged Ourselves. If thou forgive us not and have not mercy on us, surely we are of the lost!"

He said: "Go down: One of you a foe unto the Other. There will be for you on earth a habitation and provision for a while."

He said: "There shall ye live, and there shall ye die, and thence shall ye be brought forth."

O Children of _ADAM_! We have revealed unto you raiment to conceal your shame, and splendid vesture, but the raiment of restraint from evil, that is best. This is of the revelations of Allah, that they may remember.

O Children of _ADAM_! Let not Satan seduce you as he caused your parents to go forth from the Garden and tore off from them their robe that He might **manifest their shame** to them. Lo! He seeth you--He and His Tribe, from whence ye see Him not. Lo! We have made the devils protecting friends for those who believe not. And when they do some forbidden act (_fahisha_) they say: "We found our fathers doing it and Allah hath enjoined it on us." Say: "Allah, verily, enjoineth not that which is forbidden. Tell ye concerning Allah that which ye know not?" Say: My Lord enjoineth justice." And set your faces upright toward Him at every place of worship and call upon Him, making **religion pure** for Him. As He brought you into being, so unto Him ye shall return!

A party hath He leads aright, while error hath just hold over any other party, for Lo! **They _choose_** the devils for protecting supporters instead of Allah and deem that they are rightly guided.

O Children of *ADAM*! Look to your adornment at every place of worship, and eat and drink, but **be *not* prodigal**. Lo! He loveth not the prodigals.

Say: "Who hath forbidden the adornment of Allah which He hath brought forth for His bondmen, and the good things of His providing?" Say: "Such, on the Day of Resurrection, will be only for those who believed during the life of the world. Thus do we detail Our Revelations for people who have knowledge."

Say: "My Lord forbiddeth only indecencies, such of them as are apparent and such as are within, and sin and wrongful oppression, and **that ye associate with Allah that for which no warrant hath been revealed, and that ye tell concerning Allah that which ye know not.**"
And every nation hath its term, and when its term cometh, they cannot put it off an *hour* nor yet advance it.

O Children of *ADAM*! When messengers of your own come unto you who narrate unto you My Revelations, then whosoever refraineth from evil and amendeth--there shall no fear come upon them neither shall they grieve. But they who deny Our Revelations and scorn them--each are rightful owners of the Fire; they will abide therein.

Who doeth greater wrong than he who inventeth a lie concerning Allah or he who denieth Our tokens? Their appointed portion of the Book reacheth them both till, the time when Our messengers come to gather them, and say: "Where is that to which ye cried beside Allah?" They say: "They have *departed* from us." And thus they **testify against themselves** that they were disbelievers.

He saith: "Enter into the Fire among nations of the jinn and humankind who passed away before you." Every time a nation entereth, it curseth its sister till, when they have all been made to follow one another thither, the last of them saith unto the first of them: "Our Lord! These led us astray, so give them double torment of the Fire." He saith: "For each one there *IS* double, but ye know not." And the first of them saith unto the last of them: "Ye were no whit better than us, so taste the doom for what ye used to earn."

Lo! They who deny Our Revelations and scorn them, for them the GATES of heaven will not be opened nor will they enter the Garden until the camel goeth through the needle's eye.[*] Thus do We requite the guilty. Theirs will be a bed of hell, and over them coverings. Thus do We requite wrong-doers. But those who believe and do good works--We tax not any soul beyond its scope--Such are rightful owners of the Garden. They abide therein. And We remove whatever rancour may be in their hearts. Rivers flow beneath them. And they say: "The praise to Allah, Who hath guided us to this. We could not truly have been led aright if Allah had not guided us. Verily the messengers of our Lord did bring the Truth!" And it is cried unto them: "This is the Garden. Ye inherit it for what ye **used to do**."

_____

[*] The "eye of the needle" is the name for the small door to the city (opened after the main gate was closed at night) that the camels had to crawl through on their knees, after all the baggage had been removed from them in order to enter. (see Matt. 19:16-30; Mark 10:17-31; Luke 18:18-30). A camel could only pass through this smaller door if it was stooped crawling on its knees and had its baggage and all material possessions removed.

And the dwellers of the Garden cry unto the dwellers of **the Fire**: "We have found that which our Lord promised us is the Truth. Have ye also found that which your Lord promised the Truth?" They say: "Yea, Verily!" And a crier in between them crieth: "The curse of Allah is on evil-doers, who debar souls from the path of Allah and would have it crooked, and who are disbelievers in the Last Day! Between them is a veil."

And **on the Heights** are men who know them all by **their marks**. And they call unto the dwellers of the Garden: "Peace be unto you!" They enter it not although they hope. And when their eyes are turned toward the dwellers of the Fire, they say: "Our Lord! Place us not with the wrong-doing folk!" And **the dwellers on the Heights** call unto the peoples whom they know by their marks: "What did your multitude and that in which ye took your pride avail you? Are these they of whom ye swore that Allah would not show them mercy?" "(O Dwellers on the Heights!) Enter the Garden. No fear shall come upon you nor is it ye who will grieve!"

And the dwellers of **the Fire** cry out unto the dwellers of the Garden: "Pour on us some water or some wherewith Allah hath provided you." They say: "Lo! Allah hath forbidden both to those who refuse His guidance, who took their religion for a sport and pastime, and whom the life of the world beguiled!" So this DAY We have forgotten them even as they forgot the meeting of this their Day and as they used to deny Our tokens.

Verily We have brought them a Scripture which We expounded with knowledge, a guidance and a mercy for a people who believe. Await they aught save the fulfilment thereof? On the day when the fulfilment thereof cometh, those who were before forgetful thereof will say: "The messengers of our Lord did bring the Truth! Have we any intercessors, that they may intercede for us? Or can _we_ be returned (to earth), that we may act otherwise than we used to act?" They have lost their souls, and that which they devised hath failed them.

Lo! Your Lord is Allah Who created the heavens and the earth in six Days, then mounted He the Throne.[*] He covereth the night with the day, which is in haste to follow it, and hath made the sun and the moon and the stars subservient by His command. His verily is all creation (*kalq*) and commandment (*amr*). Blessed be Allah, the Lord of the Worlds!

People! Call upon your Lord humbly and in secret. Lo! He loveth not aggressors. Work not confusion in the earth after the fair ordering thereof and call on Him in fear and hope. Lo! The mercy of Allah is nigh unto the good. And He it is Who sendeth the winds as tidings heralding His mercy, till, when they bear a cloud heavy laden with rain, We lead it to a dead land, and then cause water to descend thereon and thereby bring forth fruits of every kind. **Thus bring We forth the dead.** Haply ye may remember.

---

[*]This represents 6 "days" of a thousand years each for a total of 6000 years cycle of Adam from Septmeber 21st, 4000 BC until September 21st, 2001 AD ten days after the 9-11 when the identity of the living Davidic King in exile (**exilarch**--*exiled monarch of King David*: Heb. Resh Galutha; Ar. Ras Al-Jalut) was made known (see also 2 Peter 3:8; Dr. Jensen's *CHILD OF THE EAST*; and David Davidson, *The Great Pyramid: Its Divine Message*, for more.)

As for the good land, its vegetation cometh forth by permission of its Lord; while as for that which is bad, only the useless cometh forth. Thus do We recount the tokens for **people who** *give* **thanks!**

We sent Noah unto his people, and he said: "O my people! Serve Allah. Ye have no other God save Him. Lo! I fear for you the retribution of an Awful Day." The chieftains of his people said: "Lo! **We** *see* Thee surely in plain error."

He said: "O my people! There is no error in me, but I am a messenger from the Lord of the Worlds. I convey unto you the messages of my Lord and give good counsel unto you, and know from Allah that which ye know not. Marvel ye that there should come unto you a Reminder from your Lord by means of a man among you, that he may warn you, and that ye may keep from evil, and that haply ye may find mercy." But they denied him, so We saved him and those with him in the ship, and We drowned those who denied Our tokens. Lo! they were blind folk.

And unto A'ad came their brother, *MADHUSUDAN* (*Hud*) *KRISHNA*. He said: "O my people! Serve Allah. Ye have no other God save Him. Will ye not ward off the adversary?" The chieftains of his people, who were disbelieving, said: "Lo! We surely see thee in foolishness, and Lo! We deem Thee of the liars."

He said: "O my people! There is no foolishness in me, but I am a messenger from the Lord of the Worlds. I convey unto you the messages of my Lord and am for you a true adviser. Marvel ye that there should come unto you a Reminder from your Lord by means of a man among you, that he may warn you? Remember how He made you viceroys after Noah's folk, and gave you growth of stature. Remember all the bounties of your Lord, that haply ye may be successful." They said: "Hast come unto us that we should serve Allah alone, and forsake what our fathers worshipped? Then bring upon us that wherewith Thou threatenest us if Thou art of the truthful!" He said: "Terror and wrath from your Lord have already fallen on you. Would ye wrangle with me over names which ye have named, ye and your fathers, for which no warrant from Allah hath been revealed? Then await the consequence, Lo! I also am of those awaiting." And We saved him and those with him by a mercy from Us, and We **cut the root** of those who denied Our Revelations and were not believers.

And to Thamud came their brother *SIDDHARTHA* (*Salih*) *THE BUDDHA*. He said: "O my people! Serve Allah. Ye have no other God save Him. A wonder from your Lord hath come unto you. Lo! this is the camel (Sanskrit: *Vahana*) of Allah, a token unto you; so let her feed in Allah's earth, and touch her not with hurt lest painful torment seize you. And remember how He made you viceroys after A'ad and gave you station in the earth. Ye choose castles in the plains and hew the mountains into dwellings. So remember all the bounties of Allah and do not evil, making mischief in the earth."

The chieftains of his people, who were scornful, said unto those whom they despised, unto such of them as believed: "Know ye that *SIDDHARTHA* (*Salih*) *THE BUDDHA* is one sent from his Lord?" They said: "Lo! In that wherewith He hath been sent we are believers." Those who were scornful said: "Lo! in that which ye believe we are disbelievers."

So they **hamstrung the white she-camel**, and they flouted the commandment of their Lord, and they said: "O *SIDDHARTHA (Salih) THOU BUDDHA*! Bring upon us that Thou threatenest if Thou art indeed of those God-sent." So the earthquake seized them, and morning found them prostrate in their dwelling-place. And *THE BUDDHA* turned from them and said: "O my people! I delivered my Lord's message unto you and gave you good advice, but ye love not good advisers!"

And Lot! Call to mind when he said unto his folk: "Will ye commit abomination such as no creature ever did before you? Lo! Ye come with lust unto men instead of women. Nay, but ye are wanton folk." And the answer of his people was only that they said one to another: "Turn them out of your township. They are folk, forsooth, who keep pure." And We rescued him and his household, save his wife, who was of those who stayed behind. And We rained a rain upon them. See now the nature of the consequence of evil-doers!

And unto Midian came their brother, *ZOROASTER (Shu'ayb) SPENTA MANIYUSH*. He said: "O my people! Serve Allah. Ye have no other God save Him. Lo! THIS RIGHTEOUS BOOK hath come unto you from your Lord; so give full measure and full weight and wrong not mankind in their goods, and work not confusion in the earth after the fair ordering thereof. That will be better for you, if ye are believers. Lurk not on every road to threaten wayfarers, and to turn away from Allah's path him who believeth in Him, and to seek to make it crooked. And remember, when ye were but few, how He did multiply you. And see the nature of the consequence for the corrupters! And if there is a party of you which believeth in that wherewith I have been sent, and there is a party which believeth not, then have patience until Allah judge between us. He is the Best of all who deal in judgment!"

The chieftains of his people, who were scornful, said: "Surely we will drive Thee out, O Thou *ZOROASTER (Shu'ayb) SPENTA MANIYUSH*, and those who believe with Thee, from our township, unless ye return to our religion." He said: "Even though you force what is not for us? We should have invented a lie against Allah if we returned to your religion after Allah hath **rescued us from it**. It is not for us to return to it unless Allah our Lord should will. Our Lord comprehendeth all things in knowledge. In Allah do we put our trust. Our Lord! Decide with truth between us and our folk, for Thou art the best of those who make decision!"

But the chieftains of his people, who were disbelieving, said: "If ye follow *ZOROASTER (Shu'ayb) SPENTA MANIYUSH*, then truly ye shall be the losers." So the earthquake seized them and morning found them prostrate in their dwelling-place. Those who denied *ZOROASTER (Shu'ayb) SPENTA MANIYUSH* became as though they had not dwelt there. Those who denied *ZOROASTER (Shu'ayb) SPENTA MANIYUSH*, they were the losers. So he turned from them and said: "O my people! I delivered my Lord's messages unto you and gave you good advice; then how can I sorrow for a people that willfully rejected?"

And We sent no prophet unto any township but We did afflict its folk with tribulation and adversity **that haply *they* might *grow* humble**. Then changed We the evil plight for good till they grew affluent and said: "Tribulation and distress did touch our fathers." Then We seized them unawares, when they perceived not. And if the people of the townships had believed and kept from evil, surely We should have opened for them blessings from the sky and from the earth. But unto every messenger they give the lie, and so We seized them on account of what they used to earn. Are the people of the townships then secure from the coming of Our wrath upon them as a night-raid while they sleep? Or are the people of the townships then secure from the coming of Our wrath upon them in the daytime while they play? Are they then secure **from Allah's scheme**? None deemeth himself secure from **Allah's scheme** save folk that perish. Is it not an indication to those who inherit the land after its people are annihilated that, if We will, We can smite them for their sins and print upon their hearts so that they hear not?

Such were the townships. We relate some tidings of them unto Thee. Their messengers verily came unto them with THIS RIGHTEOUS BOOK, but they could not believe because they had before denied. Thus doth Allah print upon the hearts of disbelievers. **We found no loyalty to any <u>covenant</u> in most of them. Nay, most of them We found wrong-doers.**

Then, after them, We sent *MOSES* with our tokens unto Pharaoh and his Chiefs, but they repelled them. Now, see the nature of the consequence for the corrupters! *MOSES* said: "O Pharaoh! Lo! I am a messenger from the Lord of the Worlds, Approved upon condition that I speak concerning Allah nothing but the truth. I come unto you) with THIS RIGHTEOUS BOOK from your Lord. **<u>So let the Children of Israel go with me</u>**." Pharaoh said: "If Thou comest with a token, then produce it, if Thou art of those who speak the truth!"

Then He flung down His staff and Lo! It was a serpent manifest: And He drew forth His hand, and Lo! It was white for the beholders." The Chiefs of Pharaoh's people said: "Lo! This is some knowing wizard, Who would expel you from your land." "Now what do ye advise?" They said: "Put him off--him and his brother--and send into the cities summoners, to bring each knowing wizard unto Thee." And the wizards came to Pharaoh, saying: "Surely there will be a reward for us if we are victors." He answered: "Yes, and surely ye shall be of those brought near to me." They said: "O *MOSES*! Either throw or let us be the first throwers?"

He said: "Throw!" And when they threw they cast a spell upon the people's eyes, and overawed them, and produced **a mighty spell**. And We inspired *MOSES* (in **this** operation): "Throw Thy staff!" And Lo! **It swallowed up their lying show**.

Thus was the Truth vindicated and that which they were doing was made vain.

Thus were they there defeated and brought low.

And the wizards fell down *prostrate!*

Crying: "We believe in the Lord of the Worlds, The Lord of *MOSES* and Aaron!"

Pharaoh said: "Ye believe in Him before I give you leave! Lo! This is the plot that ye have plotted in the city that ye may drive its people hence. But ye shall come to know! Surely I shall have your hands and feet cut off upon alternate sides. Then I shall crucify you every one!" They said:" Lo! We are about to return unto our Lord! Thou takest vengeance on us only forasmuch as we believed the tokens of our Lord when they came unto us. Our Lord! Vouchsafe unto us steadfastness and make us die as men who have surrendered and grow unto Thee!"

The chiefs of Pharaoh's people said: "Wilt Thou suffer *MOSES* and his people to make mischief **in the land**, and flout Thee and Thy gods?" He said: "We will slay their sons and spare their women, for Lo! We are in power over them."

And *MOSES* said unto his people: "Seek help in Allah and endure. Lo! The earth is Allah's. He giveth it for an inheritance to whom He will. And Lo! the SEQUEL is for those who keep their FEALTY." They said: "We suffered hurt before Thou camest unto us, and since Thou hast come unto us." He said: "It may be that your Lord is going to destroy your adversary and make you viceroys in the earth, that He may see how ye behave." And we straitened Pharaoh's folk with famine and dearth of fruits, that peradventure they might heed. But whenever good befell them, they said: "This is ours" and whenever evil smote them they ascribed it to the evil auspices of *MOSES* and those with him. **Surely their evil auspice was only with Allah**. But most of them knew not. And they said: "Whatever portent Thou bringest wherewith to *bewitch* us, we shall not put faith in Thee."

So We sent against them the flood and the locusts and the vermin and the frogs and the blood--**a succession of clear signs**. But they were arrogant and became a guilty folk. And when the terror fell on them they cried: "O *MOSES*! Pray for us unto thy Lord, because He hath **a covenant with Thee**. If thou removest the terror from us we verily will trust Thee and will let the Children of Israel go with Thee." But when We **did remove from them the terror** for a TERM which they must reach, **Behold! They broke their covenant**. Therefore We took retribution from them; therefore We drowned them in the sea: because they denied Our Revelations and were heedless of them.

And **We caused the folk who were despised to inherit** the eastern parts of the land and the western parts thereof which We had blessed. And the fair word of thy Lord was fulfilled for the Children of Israel because of their endurance; and We annihilated all that Pharaoh and his folk had done and that they had contrived. And We brought the Children of Israel across the sea, and they came unto a people who were given up to idols which they had. They said: "O *MOSES*! Make for us a god even as they have gods." He said: "Lo! Ye are a folk who know not. Lo! As for these, their way will be destroyed and all that they are doing is in vain." He said: "Shall I seek for you a god other than Allah when He hath favoured you above all creatures? Remember when We did deliver you from Pharaoh's folk who were afflicting you with dreadful torment, slaughtering your sons and sparing your women. That was a tremendous trial from your Lord."

And then We did appoint for *MOSES* thirty nights of solitude, and added to them ten, and he completed the whole time appointed by his Lord of forty nights; and *MOSES* said unto his brother, Aaron: "Take my place among the people. Do right, and follow not the way of mischief-makers." And when *MOSES* came to Our appointed TRYST and his Lord had spoken unto him, he said: "My Lord! Show me (Thy Self), that I may gaze upon Thee." He said: "Thou wilt not see Me, but gaze upon the mountain! If it stand still in its place, then Thou wilt see Me." And when his Lord revealed the GLORY of His Divine Presence upon the mountain He sent it crashing down. And *MOSES* fell down senseless. And when he woke he said: "GLORY unto Thee! I turn unto Thee repentant, and **I am the first** of believers."

He said: "O *MOSES*! I have preferred Thee above mankind by My messages and by My speaking unto Thee. So hold that which I have given Thee, and be among the thankful." And We wrote for him, **upon The Tablets**, the LESSON to be drawn from all things and the explanation of all things! Then We bade him: "Hold it fast; and command Thy people saying: 'Take the better WAY now made clear therein!' I shall show Thee the abode of evil-livers. I shall turn away from My Revelations those who magnify themselves wrongfully in the earth. And if they **see each token** (ten *mitzvot*/ten *sephirot*) and believe it not; and if they see THE WAY (Hebrew: **torah** (*direction of flow*) literally means the way) of righteousness and choose it not for their way; and if they see the way of error they choose it for their way. That is because they deny Our Revelations and are used to disregaring them. Those who deny Our Revelations and the meeting of the Hereafter, their works are fruitless. Are they requited aught save what they used to do?"

And the folk of *MOSES*, after he left them, chose a calf they fashioned out of their ornaments, of saffron hue, which gave a lowing sound. Saw they not that it spake not unto them nor guided them to any way? They chose it, and became wrong-doers. And when they feared the consequences thereof and saw that they had gone astray, they said: "Unless our Lord have mercy on us and forgive us, we verily are of the lost."

And when *MOSES* returned unto his people, angry and grieved, he said: "Evil is that which ye took after I had left you. Would ye **hasten on the judgment** of your Lord?" And he cast down **The Tablets**, and he seized his brother by the head, dragging him toward him.

He said: "Son of My Mother! Lo! The folk did judge me weak and almost killed me. Oh, make not mine enemies to triumph over me and place me not among the evil-doers."

He said: My Lord! Have mercy on me and on my brother; bring us into Thy mercy, Thou the Most Merciful of all who show mercy!" Lo! Those who choose the calf, terror from their Lord and humiliation will come upon them in the life of the world. Thus do We requite those who invent a lie. But those who do ill-deeds and afterward repent and believe--Lo! For them, afterward, Allah is Forgiving, Merciful.

Then, when the anger of *MOSES* abated, he took up **The Tablets**, and in their inscription there was guidance and mercy for all those who fear their Lord.

And *MOSES* chose of his people seventy men for Our appointed TRYST and, when the trembling came on them, he said: "My Lord! If Thou hadst willed Thou hadst destroyed them long before, and me with them. Wilt thou destroy us for that which the ignorant among us did?" It is but Thy trial of us. Thou sendest whom Thou wilt astray and guidest whom Thou wilt: Thou art our Protecting Friend, therefore forgive us and have mercy on us, Thou, the Best of all who show forgiveness. And ordain for us in this world that which is good, and in the Hereafter that which is good, Lo! We have turned unto Thee!"

He said: "I smite with My punishment whom I will, and My mercy embraceth all things, therefore I shall ordain it for those who ward off evil and pay the poor-due (*zakat*), and those who believe Our Revelations; Those who follow the messenger, the Prophet who can neither read nor write, whom they will find described in the Torah and the Gospel which are with them.

He will enjoin on them that which is right and forbid them that which is wrong. He will make lawful for them all good things and prohibit for them only the foul; and he will relieve them of their burden and the fetters that they used to wear. Then those who believe in him, and honour him, and help him, and follow the light and love which is sent down with him: they are the successful."

Say: O Humanity! Lo! I am the messenger of Allah to you all--the messenger of Him unto Whom belongeth the Sovereignty of the heavens and the earth. There is no God save Him. He quickeneth life and He giveth death. So believe in Allah and His messenger, the Prophet who can neither read nor write, who believeth in Allah and in His Words, and follow him that haply ye may be led aright!"

And of *MOSES*' folk **there is a community [Exilarchate] who lead with truth and establish justice therewith.** We divided them into twelve tribes, nations; and We inspired *MOSES*, when his people asked him for water, saying: "Smite with thy staff the rock!" And there gushed forth therefrom twelve springs, so that each tribe knew their drinking-place. And we caused the white cloud to overshadow them and sent down for them the manna and the quails: "Eat of the good things wherewith we have provided you." They wronged Us not, but they were wont to wrong themselves.

And when it was said unto them: "Dwell in this township and eat therefrom whence ye will, and say 'Repentance,' and enter the GATE *prostrate!* We shall forgive you your sins; We shall increase for the right-doers." But those of them who did wrong changed the word which had been told them for another saying, and We sent down upon them wrath from heaven for their wrongdoing. Ask them of the township that was by the sea, how they did break the Sabbath, how their big fish came unto them visibly upon their Sabbath day and on a day when they did not keep Sabbath came they not unto them. Thus did We try them for that they were evil-livers.

And when a community among them said: "Why preach ye to a folk whom Allah is about to destroy or punish with an awful doom, they said: In order to be free from guilt before your Lord, and that haply they may ward off. And when they forgot that whereof they had been reminded, We rescued those who forbade wrong, and visited those who did wrong with dreadful punishment because they were evil-livers. So when they took pride in that which they had been forbidden, We said unto them: "Be ye apes (*Neanderthals*) despised and loathed!" And remember when Thy Lord proclaimed that He would raise against them till the Day of Resurrection those who would lay on them a cruel torment. Lo! Verily thy Lord is swift in prosecution and Lo! verily He is Forgiving, Merciful.

And We have sundered them in the earth as nations. Some of them are righteous, and some far from that. And We have tried them with good things and evil things that haply they might return. And a generation hath succeeded them who inherited **the Scriptures**. They grasp the goods of this low life and say: "It will be forgiven us." And if there came to them the offer of the like, they would accept it. Hath not **The Covenant of the Scripture** been taken on their behalf that they should not speak aught concerning Allah save the truth? And they have studied that which is therein. And the abode of the Hereafter is better, for those who ward off. Have ye then no sense?

And as for those who guide people to **keep the Scripture**, and establish worship--Lo! We squander not the wages of reformers.

And when We shook the Mount above them as it were a covering, and they supposed that it was going to fall upon them We said: "Hold fast that which We have given you, and remember that which is therein, that ye may ward off. Remember when Thy Lord brought forth from the Children of *ADAM*, from their reins, their seed, and made them testify of themselves, saying: "Am I not your Lord?" They said: "Yea, verily. We testify." That was just so ye couldn't say at the Day of Resurrection: "Lo! Of this we were unaware;" Or lest ye should say: "It was only that our fathers ascribed partners to Allah of old and we were their seed after them. Wilt Thou destroy us on account of that which those who follow falsehood did?"

Thus we detail the Revelations, that haply they may return.

Recite unto them the tale of him to whom We gave Our Revelations, but he sloughed them off, so Satan overtook him and he became of those who lead astray. And had We willed We could have raised him by their means, but he clung to the earth and followed his own lust. Therefore his likeness is as the likeness of a dog: if Thou attackest him he panteth with his tongue out, and if Thou leavest him he panteth with his tongue out. Such is the likeness of the people who deny Our Revelations. Narrate unto them the history of the Old Ones, that haply they may take thought.

Evil as an example are the folk who denied Our Revelations, and were wont to wrong themselves. He whom Allah leadeth, he indeed is led aright, while he whom Allah sendeth astray--they indeed are losers. Already **have We urged unto hell** many of the jinn and humankind, having hearts wherewith they understand not, and having eyes wherewith they see not, and having ears wherewith they hear not. These are as the cattle--Nay, but they are worse! These are the neglectful.

Allah's are the fairest names. **Invoke Him by them**. And leave the company of those who blaspheme His names. They will be requited what they do. And of those whom We created there is a nation [**The Exilarchate**] who guide with the Truth and establish justice therewith.

And those who deny Our revelations--step by step We lead them on from whence they know not. I give them rein for Lo! **My scheme is strong**.

Have they not bethought them that **there is no madness** in their comrade? He is but a plain warner. Have they not considered the dominion of the heavens and the earth, and what things Allah hath created, and that it may be that their own term draweth nigh? In what fact after this will they believe? **Those whom Allah sendeth astray, there is no guide for them.** He leaveth them to wander blindly on in their contumacy.

They ask thee of the HOUR, when will it come to port. Say: "Knowledge thereof is with my Lord only. He alone will manifest it at its proper time. It is heavy in the heavens and the earth. It cometh not to you save unawares." They question Thee as if Thou couldst be well informed thereof. Say: "Knowledge thereof is with Allah only, but most of humanity know not."

Say: "For myself I have no power to benefit, nor power to hurt, save that which Allah willeth. Had I knowledge of the Unseen, I should have abundance of wealth, and adversity would not touch me. I am but a warner, and a bearer of good tidings unto folk who believe."

He it is Who **did create you from a single soul** [Adam/Eve; Atman/Jiva], and therefrom did make his mate that he might take rest in her. And when he covered her she bore a light burden, and she passed unnoticed with it, but when it became heavy they cried unto Allah, their Lord, saying: "If thou givest unto us aright we shall be of the thankful."

But when He gave unto them aright, they ascribed unto Him partners in respect of that which He had given them. High is He Exalted above all that they associate with Him. Attribute they as partners to Allah those who created naught, but are themselves created, And cannot give them help, nor can they help themselves?

And if ye call them to the Guidance, they follow you not. Whether ye call them or are silent is all one for you.

Lo! Those on whom ye call beside Allah are slaves like unto you. Call on them now, and let them answer you, if ye are truthful! Have they feet wherewith they walk, or have they hands wherewith they hold, or have they eyes wherewith they see, or have they ears wherewith they hear? Say: "Call upon your *partners,* and then contrive against me, spare me not!"

Lo! my Protecting Friend is Allah Who revealeth the Scripture. He befriendeth the righteous. They on whom ye call beside Him have no power to help you, nor can they help you, nor can they help themselves. And if ye call them to the guidance they hear not; and Thou seest them looking toward Thee, but they see not.

Keep to forgiveness, and enjoin kindness, and turn away from the ignorant. And if a slander from the devil wound thee, then seek refuge in Allah. Lo! He is Hearer, Knower. Lo! Those who ward off, when **a glamour from the devil** troubleth them, they do but *Remember* and behold them seers! Their brethren plunge them further into error and cease not. And when Thou bringest not a verse for them they say: "Why hast Thou not chosen it?" Say: "I follow only that which is inspired in me from my Lord. THIS RIGHTEOUS BOOK is insight from your Lord, and a guidance and a mercy for a people that believe.

And when THIS QUR'AN is recited, give ear to it and pay heed, that ye may obtain mercy. And do Thou *Remember* thy Lord within thyself humbly and with awe, below thy breath, at morn and evening. And be not Thou of the neglectful. Lo! Those who are with thy Lord are not too proud to do Him service, but they praise Him and adore Him.

XXIX. JUZ'UN SIPARA VICESIMO-NOVA:

106. Bism'illah Ar-Rahman Ar-Rahim! Sad of Samad: THE ROD OF WOOD: THE AGHSAN BRANCHES OF DAVID AND SOLOMON.

Sad.

By THIS RENOWNED QUR'AN: Nay--but those who disbelieve are in false pride and schism.

How many a generation We destroyed before them, and they cried out when it was no longer the time for escape! And they marvel that a warner from among themselves hath come unto them, and the disbelievers say: "This is a wizard, a charlatan. **Maketh he the gods One God**? Lo! That is an astounding thing!"

The Chiefs among them go about, exhorting: "Go and be staunch to your gods! Lo! This is a thing designed. We have not heard of this in later religion. This is naught but an invention! Hath **The Reminder** been unto ***him alone*** among us?" Nay, but they are in doubt concerning **My Reminder**; nay but they have not yet tasted My DOOM!

Or are theirs the treasures of the mercy of thy Lord, the Mighty, the Bestower?

Or is the kingdom of the heavens and the earth and all that is between them theirs? Then let them ascend by ropes! A defeated host are all factions that are there. The folk of Noah before them denied; and A'ad, and Pharaoh firmly planted, and Thamud, and the folk of Lot, and **the Dwellers in the Wood**: these were the factions.

Not one of them but did deny the messengers, therefore My DOOM was justified, these wait for but one Shout, there will be no second thereto. They say: "Our Lord! Hasten on for us our fate before the Day of Reckoning." Bear with what they say, and remember Our bondman David, Lord of Might, Lo! He was ever turning in repentance. Lo! We subdued the hills to hymn the praises of their Lord (Psalms 89)) with him at nightfall and sunrise, and the birds assembled; all were turning unto Him. We made his kingdom strong and gave him wisdom and decisive speech.

And hath the story of the litigants come unto thee? How they climbed the wall into the royal chamber; How they burst in upon David, and he was afraid of them. They said: "Be not afraid! We are two litigants, one of whom hath wronged the other, therefore judge aright between us; be not unjust; and show us the fair way. Lo! this my brother hath ninety and nine ewes while I had one ewe; and he said: 'Entrust it to me,' and he conquered me in speech."

David said: "He hath wronged Thee in demanding Thine ewe in addition to his ewes, and Lo! Many partners oppress one another, save such as believe and do good works, and they are few!"

And David guessed that We had tried him, and he sought forgiveness of his Lord, and he bowed himself and fell down prostrate and repented.

So We *forgave* him that; and Lo! He had access to Our Presence and a happy journey's end. "O David! Lo! We have set Thee as the Government (*Khalifah*) of God in the earth; Therefore judge aright between humankind, and follow not desire that it beguile Thee from the way of Allah. Lo! Those who wander from the way of Allah have an awful doom, forasmuch as they forgot the Day of Reckoning!"

And We created not the heaven and the earth and all that is between them in vain. **That is the opinion of those who disbelieve**. And woe unto those who disbelieve, from the Fire! Shall We treat those who believe and do good works as those who spread corruption in the earth; or shall We treat the pious as the wicked? Thus We give this Scripture that We have revealed unto Thee, full of blessing, that they may ponder its revelations, and that men of understanding may reflect!

And We bestowed on David, Solomon. How excellent a slave! Lo! He was ever turning in repentance. When there were shown to him at eventide lightfooted coursers and he said: "Lo! I have preferred the good things of the world to the Remembrance of my Lord" till they were taken out of sight behind the curtain. "Bring them back to me!" he said, and fell to rubbing his sword on legs and necks. And Verily We tried Solomon, and set upon his throne **a mere body** (*Jasadan*), but he did return (to his throne and kingdom by the Grace of Allah and he did return) and He said: "My Lord! Forgive me and bestow on me sovereignty such as shall not belong to any after me. Lo! Thou art the Bestower.!"

So We made the wind subservient unto him, setting fair by his command whithersoever he intended. And the unruly, every builder and diver made We subservient, and others linked together in chains, Saying: "This is Our gift, so bestow Thou, or withhold, without reckoning." And Lo! He hath favour with Us, and a happy journey's end.

And make mention of Our bondman Job, when he cried unto his Lord: "Lo! the devil doth afflict me with distress and torment." And it was said unto him: "Strike the ground with Thy foot. This spring is a cool bath and a refreshing drink." And We bestowed on him his household and therewith the like thereof, a mercy from Us, and a memorial for men of understanding. And it was said unto him: "Take in Thine hand a branch and smite therewith, and break not Thine oath!" Lo! We found him steadfast, how excellent a slave! Lo! He was ever turning in repentance!

And make mention of Our bondmen, Abraham, Isaac and Jacob, men of parts and vision. Lo! We purified them with a pure thought, remembrance of the HOME! Lo! in Our sight they are verily of the elect, the excellent.

And make mention of Ishmael and Elisha and Tonpa Shenrab Miwo (*Dhu'l-Kifl*[*]). All are of the chosen.

---

[*]***Dhu'l-Kifl*** (Lit. "Lord of the Doubles" the "Double Prophets" of India: specifically Buddha of Kapilavastu (the Sakya Sage) and his predecessor in arms Lord Kirshna called Madhusudan in The Gita. The double-folding, therefore includes all avatars of the *Dhyani-Tathagatas Dashavatara (Wuzhi Rulai)* and all *Shivatashvatara* in the doubling. *Kifl* is Kapila. Literally meaning "the double folding" referring to the "double folding" of the two revelations of Buddha and Krishna, of the solar and lunar dynasties: the Revelation of the *Tripitaka* (Three Baskets) and the *Bhagavad Gita* (the Song of God). Kapila is known in the Gita as *the Samkhya Sage*, who founded the

This is a reminder. And Lo! for those who ward off is a happy journey's end, Gardens of Eden, whereof the GATES are opened for them, Wherein, reclining, they call for plenteous fruit and cool drink that is therein. And with them are those of modest gaze, companions. This it is that ye are promised for the Day of Reckoning. Lo! This in truth is Our provision, which will never waste away. This is for the righteous. And Lo! For the transgressors there with be an evil journey's end, Hell, where they will burn, an evil resting-place. Here is a boiling and an ice-cold draught, so let them taste it, And others of the kind in pairs!

Here is an army rushing blindly with you. No word of welcome for them. Lo! They will roast at the Fire. They say: "Nay, but you! For you there is no word of welcome. Ye prepared this for us. Now hapless is the plight." They say: "Our Lord! Whoever did prepare this for us, oh, give him double portion of the Fire!" And they say: "What aileth us that we behold not men whom we were wont to count among the wicked? Did we take them wrongly for a laughing-stock, or have our eyes missed them?" Lo! that is very truth: the wrangling of the dwellers in the Fire.

Say: "I am only a warner, and there is no God save Allah, the One, the Absolute,
Lord of the heavens and the earth and all that is between them, the Mighty, the Pardoning!"

Say: "It is tremendous tidings Whence ye turn away! I had no knowledge of the Highest Chiefs when they disputed; It is revealed unto me only that I may be a plain warner!"

When thy Lord said unto **The Angels**: "Lo! I am about to create a mortal out of mire, and when I have fashioned him and breathed into him of My Spirit, then fall down before him prostrate," **The Angels** fell down prostrate, every one, saving Iblis; he was scornful and became one of the disbelievers. He said: "O Iblis! What hindereth Thee from falling prostrate before that which I have created with both My hands? Art Thou too proud or art Thou of the high exalted?"

He said: "I am better than him. Thou createdst me of fire, whilst him Thou didst create of clay."

He said: "Go forth from hence, for Lo! Thou art outcast, And Lo! My curse is on Thee till the Day of Judgment."

He said: "My Lord! Reprieve me till the day when they are raised."

He said: "Lo! Thou art of those reprieved Until the day of the time appointed."

He said: "Then, by Thy might, I surely will beguile them every one, save **Thy single-minded** slaves among them."

He said: "The Truth is, and the Truth I speak, that I shall fill hell with Thee and with such of them as follow Thee, together."

School of Kapilavastu whose mission is fulfilled in the progressive teachings of Tonpa Shenrab Miwo *(Dhu'l-Kifl)* and *Garab Dorje (Dhu'n-Nun)* that came after him in his line.

Say: "I ask of you no fee for this, and I am not simulating, nor am I one of the Mutakallifun! Lo! THIS RIGHTEOUS BOOK is naught else than **a Reminder** for all peoples; and *ye* will come **in time** to know **the truth** thereof.

107. Bism'illah Ar-Rahman Ar-Rahim! Saba': SHEBA QUEEN OF THEBES.

Praise be to Allah, unto Whom belongeth whatsoever is in the heavens and whatsoever is in the earth. His is the praise in the Hereafter, and He is the Wise, the Aware.

He knoweth that which goeth into the earth and that which cometh forth from it, and that descendeth from the heaven and that which ascendeth into it. He is the Merciful, the Forgiving.

Those who disbelieve say: "The HOUR will never come unto us." Say: "Nay, by my Lord, but it is coming unto you surely--**He is the Knower of the Unseen**. Not an atom's weight, or less than that or greater, escapeth Him in the heavens or in the earth, but it is in a CLEAR RECORD, that He may reward those who believe and do good works. For them is pardon and a rich provision. But those who strive against Our Revelations, challenging Us, theirs will be a painful DOOM of wrath."

Those who have been given knowledge see that what is revealed unto Thee from thy Lord is the truth and leadeth unto the path of the Mighty, the Owner of Praise.

Those who disbelieve say: "Shall we show you a man who will tell you that when ye have become dispersed in dust with most complete dispersal still, even then, ye will be created anew? Hath he invented a lie concerning Allah, or is there in him a madness?" Nay, but those who disbelieve in the Hereafter are in torment and far error!

Have they not observed what is before them and what is behind them of the sky and the earth? If We will, We can make the earth swallow them, or cause obliteration from the sky to fall on them. Lo! herein surely is a portent for every slave who turneth contrite and repentant.

And assuredly We gave David grace from Us, saying: "O ye hills and birds, echo **his psalms of praise!**" And We made THE IRON supple unto him, saying: "Make Thou long coats of mail and measure the links thereof. And do ye right. Lo! I am Seer of what ye do."

And unto Solomon We gave the wind, whereof the morning course was a month's journey and the evening course a month's journey, and We caused the fount of copper to gush forth for him, and We gave him certain of the jinn who worked before him by permission of his Lord. And such of them as deviated from Our command, them We caused to taste the punishment of flaming Fire.

They made for him what he willed: synagogues and statues, basins like wells and boilers built into the ground. **Give thanks, O House of David!** Few of My bondmen are thankful.

And when We decreed death for him, nothing showed his death to them save a creeping creature of the earth which gnawed away his staff. And when he fell the jinn saw clearly how, if they had known the Unseen, they would not have continued in despised toil.

There was indeed a sign for Sheba in their dwelling-place: Two gardens on the right hand and the left: "Eat of the provision of your Lord and render thanks to Him." A fair land and an indulgent Lord!

But they were froward, so We sent upon them **the Flood of Iram**[*] (*Iram dhat al-'Imad:* whose regions extended from Hyderabad, Hadhramut, Shambhala, Bamiyan, *al-Rub' al Khali* and adjacent lands), and in exchange for their two gardens gave them two gardens bearing bitter fruit, the tamarisk and here and there a lote-tree. This We awarded them because of their ingratitude. Punish We ever any save the ingrates?

And We set, between them and the towns which We had blessed, towns easy to be seen, and We made the stage between them easy, saying: "Travel in them safely both by night and day." But they said: "Our Lord! Make the stage between our journeys longer." And they wronged themselves, therefore We made them bywords in the land and scattered them abroad, a total scattering. Lo! Herein verily are portents for each steadfast, grateful heart.

And Satan indeed found his calculation true concerning them, for they follow him, all save a group of true believers [**The Exilarchate**]. And he had no warrant whatsoever against them, save that We would know him who believeth in the Hereafter from him who is in doubt thereof; and thy Lord taketh note of all things.

Say: "Call upon those whom ye set up beside Allah! They possess not an atom's weight either in the heavens or in the earth, nor have they any share in either, nor hath He an auxiliary among them. No intercession availeth with Him save for him whom He permitteth. Yet, when fear is banished from their hearts, they say: 'What was it that your Lord said?' They say: 'The Truth! And He is the Sublime, the Great.'"

Say: "Who giveth you provision from the sky and the earth? Say: Allah, Lo! We or you assuredly are rightly guided or in error manifest."

Say: "Ye will not be asked of what we committed, nor shall we be asked of what ye do."

Say: "Our Lord will bring **us all together**, then He will judge between us with truth. He is the All-knowing Judge."

Say: "Show me those whom ye have joined unto Him as partners. Nay! For He is Allah, the Mighty, the Wise."

---

[*]Destroyed their extended Kingdom: from beyond the Nile to beyond the Euphrates: North, South, East and West (see Gen. 15:18-21 for more: "On that day the Lord made a covenant with Abram and said, 'To your descendants I give this land, from the Wadi of Egypt to the Great River, the Euphrates--the land of the Kenites, Kenizzites, Kadmonites, Hittites, Perizzites, Rephaites, Amorites, Canaanites, Girgashites and Jebusites.'"

And We have not sent Thee save as a bringer of good tidings and a warner *unto* **all** humankind; but most of humanity know not!

And they say: "When is this promise true if ye are truthful?"

Say: "Yours is the promise of a Day which ye cannot postpone nor hasten by an *hour*."

And those who disbelieve say: "We believe not in **this Qur'an** nor in that which was before it!" But Oh, if Thou couldst see, when the wrong-doers are brought up before their Lord, how they cast the blame one to another; how those who were of despised lower caste say unto those who were proud upper crust: "But for you, we should have been believers." Those who were proud say unto those who were despised: "Did we drive you away from the guidance after it had come unto you? Nay, but ye were guilty." Those who were despised say unto those who were proud: "Nay but it was your scheming night and day, when ye commanded us to disbelieve in Allah and set up rivals unto Him." And they are filled with remorse when they behold the DOOM; and We place carcans on the necks of those who disbelieved. Are they requited aught save what they used to do?

And We sent not unto any suburb a warner, but its **Pampered Ones** declared: "Lo! We are disbelievers in that wherewith ye have been sent." And they say: "We are more than you in wealth and children. We are not the punished!"

Say: "Lo! My Lord enlargeth the provision for whom He will and narroweth it for whom He will. But most of humankind know not. And it is not your wealth nor your children that will bring you near unto Us, but he who believeth and doeth good--he draweth near. As for such, theirs will be twofold reward for what they did and they will dwell secure in lofty halls of the Pavilions of Paradise. And as for those who strive against Our Revelations, challenging, they will be brought to the DOOM."

Say: "Lo! My Lord enlargeth the provision for whom He will of His bondmen, and narroweth it for him. And whatsoever ye spend for good He replaceth it. And He is the Best of Providers."

And on THE DAY when He will gather them all together, He will say unto the angels: "Did these worship you?" They will say: "Be Thou Glorified. **Thou alone art Our Guardian (*vali*), not them!** Nay, but *they* worshipped the jinn; most of them were believers in them."

That day ye will possess no use nor hurt one for another. And We shall say unto those who did wrong: "Taste the doom of the Fire which ye used to deny!"

And if Our Revelations are recited unto them in plain terms, they say: "This is naught else than a man who would turn you away from what your fathers used to worship;" and they say: "This is naught else **than an invented lie**." Those who disbelieve say of the truth when it reacheth them: "**This is naught else than mere magic.**"

And We have given them no scriptures which they study, nor sent We unto them, before Thee, any warner. Those before them denied, and these have not attained a tithe of that which We bestowed on them of old; yet they denied My messengers. How **intense then was My abhorrence**!

Say: "I exhort you unto one thing only: That *YE AWAKE!* for Allah's sake, by twos and singly, and then reflect: "**There *is no* madness in your comrade**. He is naught else than a warner unto you in face of a TERRIFIC DOOM!"

Say: "Whatever reward I might have asked of you is yours. My reward is the affair of Allah only. He is Witness over all things."

Say: "Lo! My Lord hurleth the truth--the Knower of Things Hidden."

Say: "The Truth hath come, and falsehood showeth not its face and will not return."

Say: "If I err, I err only to my own loss, and if I am rightly guided it is because of that which my Lord hath revealed unto me. Lo! He is Hearer, Nigh!"

Couldst Thou but see when they are terrified with no escape, and are seized from near at hand, and then they say: "We *now* believe therein." But how can they reach from afar off, when they disbelieved in it of yore. They aim at **The Unseen** from afar off. And **A GULF is set between them and that which they desire**, as was done for people of their kind of old: The Old Ones. Lo! They were in hopeless doubt.

108. Bism'illah Ar-Rahman Ar-Rahim! al-Ahqaf: THE SHIFTING WIND-CURVED SANDHILLS (HEAPS) OF THE BUDDHA.

Ha. Mim.

The Revelation of the Scripture is from Allah the Mighty, the All-Wise!

We created not the heavens and the earth and all that is between them save with truth, and for a term appointed. But those who disbelieve turn away from that whereof they are warned. Say: "Have ye thought on all that ye invoke beside Allah? Show me what they have created of the earth. Or have they any portion in the heavens? Bring me a scripture before THIS RIGHTEOUS BOOK, or some vestige of knowledge (in support of what ye say), if ye are truthful."

And who is further astray than those who, instead of Allah, pray unto such as hear not their prayer until the Day of Resurrection, and are unconscious of their prayer, and when all humankind are gathered will become enemies for them, and will become deniers of having been worshipped. And when Our clear Revelations are recited unto them, those who disbelieve say of the Truth when it reacheth them: "This is mere magic." Or say they: "He hath invented it?"

Say: "If I have invented it, still ye have no power to support me against Allah. He is Best Aware of what ye say among yourselves concerning it. He sufficeth for a witness between me and you. And He is the Forgiving, the Merciful!"

Say: "I am no new thing among the messengers, nor know I what will be done with me or with you. **I do but <u>follow</u> that which is <u>inspired in me</u>**, and I am but a plain warner."

Bethink you: "If it is from Allah and ye disbelieve therein, and a witness of the Children of Israel hath already testified to the like thereof and hath believed, and ye are too proud (what plight is yours)?" Lo! Allah guideth not wrong-doing folk.

And those who disbelieve say of those who believe: "If it had been good, they would not have been before us in attaining it." And since they will not be guided by it, they say: "This is an Ancient Lie!" When before it there was the Scripture of *MOSES*, an example and a mercy; and THIS RIGHTEOUS BOOK is a confirming Scripture in the Arabic language, that it may warn those who do wrong and bring good tidings for the righteous.

Lo! Those who say: "Our Lord is Allah," and thereafter walk aright, there shall no fear come upon them neither shall they grieve. Such are rightful owners of the Garden, immortal therein, as a reward for what they used to do.

And We have commended unto man kindness toward parents. His mother beareth him with reluctance, and bringeth him forth with reluctance, and the bearing of him and the weaning of him is thirty months, till, when he attaineth full strength and reacheth forty years, he saith: "My Lord! Arouse me that I may give thanks for the favour wherewith Thou hast favoured me and my parents, and that I may do right acceptable unto Thee. And be gracious unto me in the matter of My seed. Lo! I have turned unto Thee repentant, and Lo! I am of those who surrender unto Thee." Those are they from whom We accept the best of what they do, and overlook their evil deeds. They are among the owners of the Garden. This is the true promise which they were promised.

And whoso saith unto his parents: "Fie upon you both! Do ye threaten me that I shall be brought forth again when generations before me have passed away?" And they twain cry unto Allah for help and say: "Woe unto Thee! Believe! Lo! the promise of Allah is true." But he saith: "This is naught save fables of the men of old!" Such are those on whom the Word concerning nations of the jinn and mankind which have passed away before them hath effect. Lo! They are the losers.

And for all there will be ranks from what they do, that He may pay them for their deeds; and they will not be wronged. And on the day when those who disbelieve are exposed to **the Fire** (it will be said): "Ye squandered your good things in the life of the world and sought comfort therein. Now this day ye are rewarded with **the doom of ignominy** because ye were disdainful in **the land** without a right, and because ye used to transgress."

And make mention of the brother of A'ad (whose regions extended from Hyderabad, Hadhramut, Shambhala, Bamiyan, *al-Rub' al Khali* and adjacent lands) when **he warned his folk among the wind-curved sandhills**--and verily warners came and went before and after him (he said, "I am the fifth of five who came and the first of five to come")--saying: "Serve none but Allah. Lo! I fear for you the doom of a tremendous Day."

They said: "Hast come to turn us away from our gods? Then bring upon us that wherewith Thou threatenest us, if Thou art of the truthful."

He said: "The knowledge is with Allah only. I convey unto you that wherewith I have been sent, but I see you are a folk that know not."

Then, when they beheld it as a dense cloud coming toward their valleys, they said: "Here is a cloud bringing us rain."

"Nay, but it is that which ye did seek to hasten, a wind wherein is painful torment, destroying all things by commandment of its Lord!" And morning found them so that naught could be seen save their dwellings. Thus do We reward the guilty folk.

And verily We had empowered them with that wherewith We have not empowered you, and had assigned them ears and eyes and hearts; but their ears and eyes and hearts availed them naught since they denied the revelations of Allah; and what they used to mock befell them.

And verily We have destroyed townships round about you, and displayed for them Our Revelation, that haply they might return.

Then why did those whom they had chosen for gods (*asuras* and *devas*) as a way of approach unto Us not help them? Nay, but they did fail them utterly. And all that was their lie, and what they used to invent. And when We inclined toward Thee **certain of the jinn**, who wished to hear THIS QUR'AN and, when they were in its presence, said: "Give ear!" And, when it was finished, turned back to their people, warning.

They said: "O Our People! Lo! we have heard a Scripture which hath been revealed after *MOSES*, confirming that which was before it, guiding unto the truth and a right road! O Our People! Respond to Allah's summoner and believe in Him. He will forgive you some of your sins and guard you from a painful doom!"

And whoso respondeth not to Allah's summoner he can nowise escape in the earth, and he hath no protecting friends instead of Him. Such are in error manifest.

Have they not seen that Allah, Who created the heavens and the earth and was not wearied by their creation, is **Able to give Life to the Dead**? Aye, He verily is Able to do all things.

And on the day when those who disbelieve are exposed to the Fire We say: "Is not this real?" They say: "Yea, by our Lord!" He will say: "Then TASTE THE DOOM for that ye disbelieved."

Then have patience (*Suriy-i-Sabr*) even as the stout of heart among the messengers had **The Patience of Job**, and seek not to hasten on THE DOOM for them. On the day when they see that which they are promised it will seem to them as though they had tarried but an *Hour* of **Daylight**.

A CLEAR MESSAGE [9-11, 2001]. Shall any be destroyed save evil-living folk?

109. Bism'illah Ar-Rahman Ar-Rahim! Yunus: JONAH AND THE FISH.

Alif. Lam. Ra.

These are verses of the Wise Scripture.

Is it a wonder for mankind that We have inspired a man among them, saying: "Warn mankind and bring unto those who believe the good tidings that they have a sure footing with their Lord?"

The disbelievers say: "Lo! this is a mere wizard."

Lo! your Lord is Allah Who created the heavens and the earth in six Days, then He established Himself upon the Throne, directing all things. There is no intercessor save after His permission. That is Allah, your Lord, so worship Him. Oh, will ye not remind?

Unto Him is the return of all of you; it is a promise of Allah in truth. Lo! He produceth creation, then reproduceth it, that He may reward those who believe and do good works with equity; while, as for those who disbelieve, theirs will be a boiling drink and painful doom because they disbelieved.

He it is Who appointed the sun a splendour and the moon a light, and measured for her stages, that ye might know the number of the years, and the reckoning. Allah created not all that save in truth. He detaileth the revelations for people who have knowledge.

Lo! In the difference of day and night and all that Allah hath created in the heavens and the earth are portents, verily, for folk who ward off.

Lo! Those who expect not the meeting with Us but desire the life of the world and feel secure therein, and those who are neglectful of Our revelations, their home will be the Fire because of what they used to earn.

Lo! Those who believe and do good works, their Lord guideth them by their faith. Rivers will flow beneath them in the Gardens of Delight, their prayer therein will be: "Glory be to Thee, O Allah!" And their greeting therein will be: "Salem!" And the conclusion of their prayer will be: "Praise be to Allah, Lord of the Worlds!"

If Allah were to hasten on for men the ill that they have earned by what they have done to their own selves as they would hasten on the good, their respite would already have expired. But We suffer those who look not for the meeting with Us to wander blindly on in their contumacy.

---

*This refers to the throne of David that is **the throne of God** upon the earth: "Then Solomon sat on **the throne of the LORD** (*YHVH*) as king instead of David his father, and prospered; and all Israel obeyed him" (1 Chron. 29:23 KJV). God "brought forth" His "servant the BRANCH (Zech. 3:8 KJV: Aghsan descendant of King David) on September 21st, 2001 AD--upon the throne of David--in fulfillment of the prophesied 6000 years Cycle of Adam (six days each of 1000 years each (see 2 Peter 3:8).

And if misfortune touch a man he crieth unto Us, while reclining on his side, or sitting or standing, but when We have relieved him of the misfortune he goeth his way as though he had not cried unto Us because of a misfortune that afflicted him. Thus is what they do made seeming fair unto the prodigal.

We destroyed the generations before you when they did wrong; and their messengers came unto them with THIS RIGHTEOUS BOOK but they would not believe. Thus do We reward the guilty folk.

Then We appointed you viceroys in the earth after them, that We might see how ye behave.

And when Our Clear Revelations are recited unto them, they who look not for the meeting with Us say: "Bring a Lecture other than this, or change it." Say: "It is not for me to change it of my accord. I only follow that which is inspired in me. Lo! If I disobey my Lord I fear the retribution of an awful Day."

Say: "If Allah had so willed I should not have recited it to you nor would He have made it known to you. I dwelt among you a whole lifetime before it came to me. Have ye then no sense? Who doeth greater wrong than he who inventeth a lie concerning Allah and denieth His revelations? Lo! the guilty never are successful!"

They worship beside Allah that which neither hurteth them nor profiteth them, and they say: "These are our intercessors with Allah." Say: "Would ye inform Allah of that which He knoweth not in the heavens or in the earth? Praised be He and High Exalted above all that ye associate with Him!"

Humankind were but one community; then they differed; and had it not been for a word that had already gone forth from thy Lord it had been judged between them in respect of that wherein they differ. And they will say: "If only a portent were sent down upon him from his Lord!" Then say: "The Unseen belongeth to Allah." So wait! Lo! I am waiting with you.

And when We cause humanity to taste of mercy after some adversity which had afflicted them, Behold! They have some plot against Our Revelations. Say: "Allah is more swift in plotting. Lo! Our messengers write down that which ye plot."

He it is Who maketh you to go on the land and the sea till, when ye are in the ships and they sail with them with a fair breeze and they are glad therein, a storm-wind reacheth them and the wave cometh unto them from every side and they deem that they are overwhelmed therein; then they cry unto Allah, making their faith pure for Him only: "If Thou deliver us from this, we truly will be of the thankful."

Yet when He hath delivered them, Behold! They rebel in the earth wrongfully. O mankind! Your rebellion is only against yourselves. Ye have enjoyment of the life of the world; then unto Us is your return and We shall proclaim unto you what ye used to do.

The **similitude of the life of the world** is only as water which We send down from the sky, then the earth's growth of that which men and cattle eat mingleth with it till, when the earth hath taken on her ornaments and is embellished, and her people deem that they are masters of her, Our commandment cometh by night or by day and We make it as reaped corn as if it had not flourished yesterday. Thus do we expound the Revelations for people who reflect.

And Allah summoneth **to the Abode of Peace** (Baghdad, Iraq) and leadeth whom He will to a straight path. For those who do good is the best reward and more thereto. Neither dust nor ignominy cometh near their faces. Such are rightful owners of the Garden; they will abide therein. And those who earn ill-deeds, for them requital of each ill-deed by the like thereof; and ignominy overtaketh them--They have no protector from Allah--as if their faces had been covered with a cloak of darkest night. Such are rightful owners of the Fire; they will abide therein.

On the day when We gather them all together, then We say unto those who ascribed partners unto Us: "Stand back, ye and your pretended partners! And We separate them, the one from the other, and their pretended partners say: "It was not us ye worshipped. Allah sufficeth as a witness between us and you, that we were unaware of your worship."

There doth every soul experience that which it did aforetime, and they are returned unto Allah, their rightful Lord, and that which they used to invent hath failed them.

Say: "Who provideth for you from the sky and the earth, or Who owneth hearing and sight; and Who bringeth forth the living from the dead and bringeth forth the dead from the living; and Who directeth the course?" They will say: "Allah." Then say: "Will ye not then keep your duty unto Him? Such then is Allah, your rightful Lord. After the Truth what is there saving error? How then are ye turned away!" Thus is the Word of Thy Lord justified concerning those who do wrong: that they believe not.

Say: "Is there of your partners one that produceth Creation and then reproduceth it?" Say: "Allah produceth Creation, then reproduceth it. How then, are ye misled!" Say: "Is there of your partners one that leadeth to the Truth?" Say: "Allah leadeth to the Truth. Is He Who leadeth to the Truth more deserving that He should be followed, or he who findeth not the way unless he himself be guided. What aileth you? How judge ye?"

Most of them follow not but conjecture. Assuredly **conjecture can by no means take the place of truth**. Lo! Allah is Aware of what they do.

And THIS QUR'AN is not such as could ever be invented in despite of Allah; but it is **a confirmation** of that which was before it and an exposition of that which is decreed for mankind--Therein is no doubt--from the Lord of the Worlds.

Or say they: "He hath invented it?" Say: "Then bring a SURAH like unto it, and call for help on all ye can besides Allah, if ye are truthful." Nay, but they denied that, the knowledge whereof they could not compass, and whereof the interpretation in events (like the 9-11, etc. and the throne) hath not yet come unto them. Even so did those before them deny. Then see what was the consequence for the wrong-doers!

And of them is he who believeth therein, and of them is he who believeth not therein, and thy Lord is Best Aware of the corrupters.

And if they deny Thee, say: "**Unto me my work, and unto you your work. Ye are innocent of what I do, and I am innocent of what ye do.**" And of them are some who listen unto Thee. But canst Thou make the deaf to hear even though they apprehend not? And of them is he who looketh toward Thee. But canst Thou guide the blind even though they see not?

Lo! Allah wrongeth not mankind in aught; but mankind wrong themselves.

And on the day when He shall gather them together, (when it will seem) as though they had tarried but an *hour* of the day, recognising one another, those will verily have perished who denied the meeting with Allah and were not guided. Whether We let Thee behold something of that which We promise them or whether We cause Thee to die, still unto Us is their return, and Allah, moreover, is Witness over what they do.

And for <u>every nation</u> there is a messenger. And when their messenger cometh on the Day of Resurrection and the Judgment) it will be judged between them fairly, and they will not be wronged. And they say: "When will this promise be fulfilled, if ye are truthful?" Say: "I have no power to hurt or benefit myself, save that which Allah willeth. For every nation there is an appointed time. When their time cometh, then they cannot put it off an *hour*, nor hasten it." Say: "Have ye thought: When His DOOM cometh unto you as a raid by night, or in the busy day; what is there of it that the guilty ones desire to hasten? Is it only then, when it hath befallen you, that ye will believe? What! Believe now, when until now ye have been hastening it on through disbelief?" Then will it be said unto those who dealt unjustly "Taste the torment of eternity. Are ye requited aught save what ye used to earn?"And they ask Thee to inform them saying: "Is it true?" Say: "Yea, by my Lord, *verily* it is true, and ye cannot escape."

And if each soul that doeth wrong had all that is in the earth it would seek to ransom itself therewith; and they will feel remorse within them, when they see the DOOM. But it hath been judged between them fairly and they are not wronged. Lo! Verily all that is in the heavens and the earth is Allah's. Lo! verily Allah's promise is true. But most of them know not! He quickeneth and giveth death, and unto Him ye will be returned.

O Humankind! There hath come unto you an exhortation from your Lord, a balm for that which is in the breasts, a guidance and a mercy for believers. Say: "In the bounty of Allah and in His mercy: therein let them rejoice. It is better than what they hoard." Say: "Have ye considered what provision Allah hath sent down for you, how ye have made of it lawful and unlawful? Hath Allah permitted you, or do ye invent a lie concerning Allah?"

And what think those who invent a lie concerning Allah upon the Day of Resurrection? Lo! Allah truly is Bountiful toward mankind, but most of them give not thanks. And Thou art not occupied with any business and Thou recitest not a Lecture from this, and ye perform no act, but

We are Witness of you when ye are engaged therein. And not an atom's weight in the earth or in the sky escapeth your Lord, nor what is less than that or greater than that, but it is written in a CLEAR BOOK.

Lo! Verily the friends of Allah are those on whom fear cometh not, nor do they grieve. Those who believe and keep their duty to Allah, theirs are good tidings in the life of the world and in the Hereafter --there is no changing the Words of Allah--that is the Supreme Triumph.

And let not their speech grieve Thee. Lo! power belongeth wholly to Allah. He is the Hearer, the Knower. Lo! is it not unto Allah that belongeth whosoever is in the heavens and whosoever is in the earth? Those who follow aught instead of Allah follow not partners: They follow only a conjecture, and they do but guess.

He it is Who hath appointed for you the night that ye should rest therein and the day giving sight. Lo! herein verily are portents for a folk that heed. They say: "Allah hath taken a Son"--Glorified be He! He hath no needs! His is all that is in the heavens and all that is in the earth. Ye have no warrant for this. Tell ye concerning Allah that which ye know not? Say: "Verily those who invent a lie concerning Allah will not succeed." This world's portion will be theirs, then unto Us is their return. Then We make them taste a dreadful doom because they used to disbelieve.

Recite unto them the story of Noah, when he told his people: "O my people! If my sojourn here and my reminding you by Allah's Revelations are an offence unto you, in Allah have I put my trust, so decide upon your course of action you and your partners. Let not your course of action be in doubt for you. Then have at me, give me no respite. But if ye are averse I have asked of you no wage. My wage is the concern of Allah only, and I am commanded to be of those who surrender." But they denied him, so We saved him and those with him in the ship, and made them viceroys, while We drowned those who denied Our Revelations. See then the nature of the consequence for those who had been warned.

Then, after him, We sent messengers unto their folk, and they brought them THIS RIGHTEOUS BOOK. But they were not ready to believe in that which they before denied. Thus **print We** on the hearts of the transgressors.

Then, after them, We sent *MOSES* and Aaron unto Pharaoh and his Chiefs with Our Revelations, but they were arrogant and were a guilty folk. And when the Truth from **Our Presence** came unto them, they said: "Lo! this is mere magic." *MOSES* said: "Speak ye so of the Truth when it hath come unto you? Is this magic? Now magicians thrive not."

They said: "Hast Thou come unto us to pervert us from that in which we found our fathers, and that you two may own the place of greatness in the land? We will not believe you two." And Pharaoh said: "Bring every cunning wizard unto me." And when the wizards came, *MOSES* said unto them: "Cast your cast!" And when they had cast, *MOSES* said: "That which ye have brought is magic. Lo! Allah will make it vain. Lo! Allah upholdeth not the work of mischief-makers." And Allah will vindicate the Truth by His words, however much the guilty be averse.

But none trusted *MOSES*, save some scions of his people, and they were in fear of Pharaoh and their Chiefs, that he would persecute them. Lo! Pharaoh was verily a tyrant in the land, and Lo! He verily was of the wanton. And *MOSES* said: "O My People! If ye have believed in Allah then put trust in Him, if ye have indeed surrendered!" They said: "In Allah we put trust. Our Lord! Oh, make us not a lure for the wrongdoing folk; and, of Thy mercy, save us from the folk that disbelieve."

And We inspired *MOSES* and his brother, saying: "Appoint houses for your people in Egypt and make your houses oratories, and establish worship. And give good news to the believers." And *MOSES* said: "Our Lord! Lo! Thou hast given Pharaoh and his Chiefs splendour and riches in the life of the world, Our Lord! That they may lead men astray from Thy way. Our Lord! Destroy their riches and harden their hearts so that they believe not till they see the painful doom."

He said: "Your prayer is heard. Do ye TWAIN keep to the straight path, and follow not the road of those who have no knowledge."

And We brought the **Children of Israel** across the sea, and Pharaoh with his hosts pursued them in rebellion and transgression, till, when **The Drowning** overtook him, he exclaimed: "I believe that there is no God save Him in Whom the Children of Israel believe, and I am of those who surrender."

What! Now! When hitherto thou hast rebelled and been of the wrong-doers?

But this day We save Thee in Thy body that Thou mayst be a portent for those after Thee. Lo! most of mankind are heedless of Our portents.

And We verily did allot unto the Children of Israel a fixed abode, and did provide them with good things; and they **differed not** *until* **the knowledge came unto them**. Lo! Thy Lord will judge between them on the Day of Resurrection concerning that wherein they used to differ.

And if Thou art in doubt concerning that which We reveal unto Thee, then question those who read the Scriptures that came before Thee. Verily the Truth from thy Lord hath come unto Thee. So be not thou of the waverers. And be not thou of those who deny the Revelations of Allah, for then wert Thou of the losers. Lo! Those wrong-doers for whom the word of thy Lord hath effect will not believe, though every token come unto them, till they see the painful doom.

If only there had been a community (of all those that were destroyed of old) that believed and profited by its belief as did the folk of Jonah! When they believed We drew off from them the torment of disgrace in the life of the world and gave them comfort for a while. And if thy Lord willed, **all who are in the earth would have believed together**. Wouldst Thou compel men until they are believers? It is not for any soul to believe save by the permission of Allah. He hath set uncleanness upon those who have no sense.

Say: "Behold what is in the heavens and the earth!" But Revelations and warnings avail not folk who will not believe. What expect they save the like of the days of those who passed away before them? Say: "Expect then! I am with you among the expectant." Then shall We save Our messengers and the believers, in like manner. It is incumbent upon Us to save believers.

Say: "O Humanity! If ye are in doubt of my religion, then know that I worship not those whom ye worship instead of Allah, but I worship Allah Who causeth you to die, and I have been commanded to be of the believers." **And set Thy purpose resolutely for religion**, as a man by nature upright, and be not of those who ascribe partners. And cry not, beside Allah, unto that which cannot profit Thee nor hurt Thee, for if Thou didst so then wert Thou of the wrong-doers. **If Allah afflicteth Thee with some hurt, there is none who can remove it save Him**; and if He desireth good for Thee, there is none who can repel His bounty. He **striketh** with it whom He will of his bondmen. He is the Forgiving, the Merciful.

Say: "O Humankind! Now hath the Truth from your Lord come unto you. So whosoever is guided, is guided only for the good of his soul, and whosoever erreth erreth only against it. And I am not a warder over you." And (O *AL-AMIN*) follow that which is inspired in Thee, and forbear until Allah give judgment. And He is the Best of Judges.

XXX. JUZ'UN SIPARA ULTIMO:

110. Bism'illah Ar-Rahman Ar-Rahim! Miriam: MIRIAM.

Kaf. Ha. Ya. A'in. Sad.

A mention of the mercy of thy Lord unto His servant Zachariah. When he cried unto his Lord a cry in secret, saying: "My Lord! Lo! the bones of me wax feeble and my head is shining with grey hair, and I have never been unblest in prayer to Thee, my Lord. Lo! I fear my kinsfolk after me, since my wife is barren. Oh, give me from Thy presence a successor who shall inherit of me and inherit also of the House of Jacob. And make him, my Lord, acceptable unto Thee."

"O Zachariah! Lo! We bring Thee tidings of a Son whose name is John; we have given the same name to none before him." He said: "My Lord! How can I have a Son when my wife is barren and I have reached infirm old age?" He said: So it shall be." Thy Lord saith: "It is easy for Me, even as I created Thee before, when Thou wast naught." He said: "My Lord! Appoint for me some token." He said: "Thy token is that Thou, with no bodily defect, shalt not speak unto mankind three nights."

Then he came forth unto his people from the Sanctuary, and signified to them: "Glorify your Lord at break of day and fall of night." And it was said unto his Son: "O John! Hold fast the Scripture." And we gave him wisdom when a child, and compassion from Our Presence, and purity; and he was devout, and dutiful toward his parents. And he was not arrogant, rebellious. Blessings on him the day he was born, and the day he dieth and the day he shall be raised alive!

And make mention of Miriam in the Scripture, when she had withdrawn from her people to a chamber looking East, and had chosen seclusion from them. Then We sent unto her Our Spirit and it assumed for her the likeness of a perfect man. She said: "Lo! I seek refuge in the

314

Beneficent One from Thee, if Thou art God-fearing." He said: "I am only a messenger of Thy Lord, that I may bestow on Thee a faultless Son."

She said: "How can I have a Son when no mortal hath touched me, neither have I been unchaste?" He said: "So it shall be." Thy Lord saith: "It is easy for Me. And it will be that We may make of him a Revelation for mankind and a mercy from Us, and it is a thing ordained."

And she conceived him, and she withdrew with him to a far place.

And the pangs of childbirth drove her unto the trunk of the palm-tree. She said: "Oh, would that I had died ere this and had become a thing of naught, forgotten!"

Then cried one unto her from below her, saying: "Grieve not! Thy Lord hath placed a rivulet beneath Thee, and shake the trunk of the palm-tree toward Thee, Thou wilt cause ripe dates to fall upon Thee. So eat and drink and be consoled. And if thou meetest any mortal, say: 'Lo! I have vowed a fast unto the Beneficent, and may not speak this day to any mortal.'"

Then she brought him to her own folk, carrying him. They said: "O Miriam! Thou hast come with an amazing thing. O sister of Aaron! Thy father was not a wicked man nor was thy mother a harlot." Then she pointed to him. They said: "How can we talk to one who is in the cradle, a young boy?" He spake: "Lo! I am the slave of Allah. He hath given me the Scripture and hath appointed me a Prophet, and hath made me blessed wheresoever I may be, and hath enjoined upon me prayer and almsgiving so long as I remain alive, and hath made me dutiful toward her who bore me, and hath not made me arrogant, unblest. Blessing on me the day I was born, and the day I die, and the day I shall be raised alive!"

Such was *JESUS*, son of Miriam: This is a statement of the truth concerning which they doubt. It befitteth not the Majesty of Allah that He should take unto Himself a Son. Glory be to Him! When He decreeth a thing, He saith unto it only: "Be!" and it is. And Lo! Allah is my Lord and your Lord. So serve Him. That is the right path.

The sects among them differ: but woe unto the disbelievers from the meeting of an awful Day. See and hear them on the Day they come unto Us! Yet the evil-doers are today in error manifest. And warn them of the Day of Anguish when the case hath been decided. Now they are in a state of carelessness, and they believe not. Lo! We, only We, inherit the earth and all who are thereon, and unto Us they are returned.

And make mention in the Scripture of Abraham. Lo! He was a saint, a prophet. When he said unto his father: "O My Father! Why worshippest Thou that which heareth not nor seeth, nor can in aught avail Thee? O my father! Lo! **There hath come unto me of knowledge that which came not unto Thee**. So follow me, and I will lead thee on a right path. O my father! Serve not the devil. Lo! The devil is a rebel* unto the Beneficent. O my father! Lo! I fear lest a punishment from the Beneficent overtake Thee so that Thou become a comrade of the devil."

---

*The father of Abraham served Nimrod in the military empire of Babylon.

He said: "Rejectest Thou my gods, O Abraham? If Thou cease not, I shall surely stone thee. Depart from me a long while!"

He said: "Peace be unto Thee! I shall ask forgiveness of my Lord for Thee. Lo! He was ever gracious unto me. I shall withdraw from you and that unto which ye pray beside Allah, and I shall pray unto my Lord. It may be that, in prayer unto my Lord, I shall not be unblest."
So, when he had withdrawn from them and that which they were worshipping beside Allah, We gave him Isaac and Jacob. Each of them We made a prophet. And we gave them of Our mercy, and assigned to them a high and true renown.

And make mention in the Scripture of *MOSES*. Lo! He was chosen, and he was a messenger, a prophet. We called him from the right slope of the Mount, and brought him nigh in communion. And We bestowed upon him of Our Mercy his brother Aaron, a prophet likewise.

And make mention in the Scripture of Ishmael. Lo! He was a keeper of his promise, and he was a messenger, a prophet. He enjoined upon his people worship and almsgiving, and was acceptable in the sight of his Lord.

And make mention in the Scripture of Enoch (*Idris: 'Akhnukh*). Lo! he was a saint, a prophet; and We raised him to high station. These are they unto whom Allah showed favour from among the prophets, of the seed of *ADAM* and of those whom We carried in the ship with Noah, and of the seed of Abraham and Israel, and from among those whom We guided and chose. When the Revelations of the Beneficent were recited unto them, they fell down, adoring and weeping. Now there hath succeeded them a later generation whom have ruined worship and have followed lusts. But they will meet deception. Save him who shall repent and believe and do right. Such will enter the Garden, and they will not be wronged in aught--Gardens of Eden, which the Beneficent hath promised to His slaves in **The Unseen**.

Lo! His promise is ever sure of fulfilment--They hear therein no idle talk, but only Blessings; and therein they have food for morn and evening. Such is the Garden which We cause the devout among Our bondmen to inherit. They say "We come not down save by commandment of Thy Lord. Unto Him belongeth all that is before us and all that is behind us and all that is between those two, and thy Lord was never forgetful--Lord of the heavens and the earth and all that is between them! Therefore, worship Thou Him and be Thou steadfast in His service. Knowest Thou one that can be named along with Him?"

And man saith: "When I am dead, shall I forsooth be brought forth alive?" Doth not man remember that We created him before, when he was naught? And, by thy Lord, verily We shall assemble them and the devils, then We shall bring them, crouching, around hell. Then We shall pluck out from *every sect* **whichever of them was most stubborn in rebellion** to the Beneficent. And surely We are Best Aware of those most worthy to be burned therein.

There is not one of you but shall approach it. That is a fixed ordinance of thy Lord.

Then We shall rescue those who kept from evil, and leave the evil-doers crouching there.

And when Our clear Revelations are recited unto them, those who disbelieve say unto those who believe: "Which of the two parties is better in position, and more imposing as an army?" How many a generation have We destroyed before them, who were more imposing in respect of gear and outward seeming!

Say: "As for him who is in error, the Beneficent will verily prolong his span of life until, when they behold that which they were promised, whether it be punishment, or the HOUR, they will know who is worse in position and who is weaker as an army!" Allah increaseth in right guidance those who walk aright, and the good deeds which endure are better in thy Lord's sight for reward, and better for resort.

Hast Thou seen him who disbelieveth in Our Revelations and saith: "Assuredly I shall be given wealth and children?" Hath he perused the Unseen, or hath he made a pact with the Beneficent? Nay, but We shall record that which he saith and prolong for him a span of torment. And We shall inherit from him that whereof he spake, and he will come unto Us, alone. And they have chosen gods beside Allah that they may be a power for them. Nay, but they will deny their worship of them, and become opponents unto them.

Seest Thou not that We have set the devils on the disbelievers to confound them with confusion? So make no haste against them. We do but number unto them a sum. On the day when We shall gather the righteous unto the Beneficent, a goodly company. And drive the guilty unto hell, a weary herd, they will have no power of intercession, **save him who hath made <u>a covenant with his Lord</u>**.

And they say: "The Beneficent hath taken unto Himself a Son."

Assuredly ye utter a disastrous thing whereby almost the heavens are torn, and the earth is split asunder and the mountains fall in ruins, that ye ascribe unto the Beneficent a Son, when it is not meet for the Magnificence of the Beneficent that He should choose a Son. There is none in the heavens and the earth but cometh unto the Beneficent as a slave. Verily He knoweth them and numbereth them with right numbering.

And each one of them will come unto Him on the Day of Resurrection, **<u>alone</u>**.

Lo! those who believe and do good works, the Beneficent will appoint for them LOVE.
And We make THIS SCRIPTURE easy in Thy tongue, O *AL-AMIN*, only that Thou mayst bear good tidings therewith unto those who ward off, and warn therewith the froward folk. And how many a generation before them have We destroyed! Canst Thou see a single man of them, or hear from them the slightest sound?

111. *Bism'illah Ar-Rahman Ar-Rahim! Muhammad: MUHAMMAD.*

Those who disbelieve and turn souls from the way of Allah, He rendereth their actions vain. And those who believe and do good works and believe in that which is revealed unto *MUHAMMAD*-- and it is the truth from their Lord--He riddeth them of their ill-deeds and improveth their state.

That is because those who disbelieve follow falsehood and because those who believe follow the truth from their Lord. Thus Allah coineth their similitudes for mankind.

Now when you encounter the disbelievers in a battle (*jihad*: the greater and the lesser), strike-off their heads. Take them as captives when they are defeated. **Then you may <u>set them free as a favor to them, with or without a ransom, when the battle is over.</u>** So shall it be. Had God wanted, He could have granted them (the unbelievers) victory, but He wants to TEST you through each other. The deeds of those who are killed for the cause of God will never be without virtuous results. He will guide them and improve their state, and bring them in unto the Garden which He hath made known to them.

O ye who believe! If ye help Allah, He will help you and will make your foothold firm. And those who disbelieve, perdition is for them, and He will make their actions vain. That is because they are averse to that which Allah hath revealed, therefore maketh He their actions fruitless. Have they not travelled in the land to see the nature of the consequence for those who were before them? **Allah wiped them out**. And for the disbelievers there will be the like thereof. That is because Allah is patron of those who believe, and because the disbelievers have no patron.

Lo! Allah will cause those who believe and do good works to enter Gardens underneath which rivers flow; while those who disbelieve **take their comfort in this life** and eat even as the cattle eat, and the Fire is their habitation. And how many a township stronger than Thy township which hath cast Thee out (O *AL-AMIN*), have We destroyed, and they had no helper!

Is he who relieth on THIS RIGHTEOUS BOOK from his Lord like those for whom the evil that they do is beautified while they follow their own lusts?

A similitude of the Garden which those who keep their duty are promised: Therein are rivers of water unpolluted, and rivers of milk whereof the flavour changeth not, and rivers of wine delicious to the drinkers, and rivers of clear-run honey; therein for them is every kind of fruit, with pardon from their Lord. Are those who enjoy all this like those who are immortal in the Fire and are given boiling water to drink so that it teareth their bowels?

Among them are some who give ear unto Thee till, when they go forth from Thy Presence they say unto those who have been given knowledge: "What was that he said just now?" Those are they whose hearts Allah hath sealed, and they follow their own lusts.

While as for those who walk aright, He addeth to their guidance, and giveth them their protection. Await they aught save the HOUR, that it should come upon them unawares? And the beginnings thereof have already come. But how, when it hath come upon them, can they take their warning?

So know that there is no God save Allah, and ask forgiveness for Thy sin and for believing men and believing women. Allah knoweth both your place of turmoil and your place of rest. And those who believe say: "If only a SURAH were revealed! But when a decisive SURAH is revealed and **war** (*jihad:* the greater and the lesser) **is mentioned therein**, Thou seest those in whose hearts is a disease looking at Thee with the look of men fainting unto death. There for **woe** unto them!

Obedience and a civil word. Then, when the matter is determined, if they are loyal to Allah it will be well for them. Would ye then, if ye were given the command, work corruption in **the land** and *sever* your ties of kinship (to the Oneness of All Humanity)? **Such are they whom Allah curseth** so that He deafeneth them and maketh blind their eyes. Will they then not meditate on THIS QUR'AN, or are there locks on the hearts and minds?

Lo! those who turn back after the guidance hath been manifested unto them, Satan hath seduced them, and He giveth them the rein.

That is because they say unto those who hate what Allah hath revealed: "We will obey you in some matters"--and Allah knoweth their secret talk. Then how will it be with them when the angels gather them, smiting their faces and their backs! That will be because they followed that which angereth Allah, and hated that which pleaseth Him. Therefore He hath made their actions vain.

Or do those in whose hearts is a disease deem that Allah will not bring to light their secret hates?

And if We would, We could show them unto Thee so that Thou shouldst know them surely by their marks. And Thou shalt know them by the burden of their talk. And Allah knoweth your deeds. And verily We shall TRY you till We know those of you who strive hard for the Cause and who are of the steadfast, and till We TEST your record.

Lo! Those who disbelieve and turn from the way of Allah and oppose the messenger after the guidance hath been manifested unto them, they hurt Allah not a jot, and He will make their actions fruitless.

O ye who believe! Obey Allah and obey the messenger, and render not your actions vain.
Lo! Those who disbelieve and turn from the way of Allah and then die disbelievers, Allah surely will not pardon them.

So do not falter and cry out for peace when ye are the uppermost, and Allah is with you, and He will not grudge your actions. **The life of the world is but a sport and a pastime.** And if ye believe and ward off adversity, He will give you your wages, and **will not ask of you** your wordly wealth. If He should ask it of you and importune you, ye would hoard it, and He would bring to light your secret hates.

Lo! Ye are those who are called **to spend in the way of Allah**, yet among you there are some who **hoard**. **And as for him who hoardeth, he hoardeth only from his soul.** And Allah is the Rich, and ye are the poor. And if ye turn away He will exchange you for some other folk, and they will not be the likes of you.

Nay, I swear by the Day of Resurrection;
Nay, I swear by the accusing soul that this Scripture is true.
Thinketh man that We shall not assemble his bones?
Yea, verily. We are Able to restore his very fingers!
But man would fain deny what is before him.
He asketh: "When will be this Day of Resurrection?"
But when sight is confounded
And the moon is eclipsed
And sun and moon are united,
On that day Man will cry: "Whither to flee!"
Alas! No refuge!
Unto thy Lord is the recourse that day.
On that day Man is told the tale of that which he hath sent before and left behind.
Oh, but Man is a telling witness against himself,
Although he tender his excuses.
Stir not thy tongue herewith to hasten it.

Lo! Upon Us is the putting together thereof
and the reading thereof of THIS RIGHTEOUS BOOK.
And when We read it, follow Thou the reading!
Then Lo! upon Us *is* **the explanation thereof**.

Nay, but ye do love the fleeting Now
And neglect the Hereafter.
That day will faces be resplendent,
Looking toward their Lord;
And that day will other faces be despondent,
Thou wilt know that some great disaster is about to fall on them.
Nay, but when the life cometh up to the throat
And men say: "Where is the wizard who can save him now?"
And he knoweth that it is the parting;
And agony is heaped on agony;
Unto thy Lord that day will be the driving.
For he neither trusted, nor prayed.
But he denied and flouted.
Then went he to his folk with glee.
Therefore **woe** unto Thee, **woe**!
And, again, **woe** unto Thee, **woe**!*

Thinketh man that he is to be left aimless?
Was he not a drop of fluid which gushed forth?
Then he became a clot; then Allah shaped and fashioned

---

*Or: "Nearer unto Thee and Nearer, Again Nearer unto Thee and Nearer (is the WOE)."

And made of him TWAIN: a pair, the male and female.

Is not He Able, therefore, to bring the dead to life?

113. Bism'illah Ar-Rahman Ar-Rahim! al-Mu'min: THE FORGIVING ONE!

Ha. Mim.

The Revelation of the Scripture is from Allah, the Mighty, the Knower, the Forgiver of sin, the Accepter of repentance, the Stern in punishment, the Bountiful. There is no God save Him. **Unto Him is the journeying.**

None argue concerning the Revelations of Allah save those who disbelieve, so let not their turn of fortune in the land deceive Thee.

The folk of Noah and the factions after them denied their messengers before these, and every nation purposed to seize their messenger and argued falsely, thinking thereby to refute the Truth. Then I seized them, and how terrific was My punishment. Thus was the word of Thy Lord concerning those who disbelieve fulfilled: "That they are owners of the Fire."

Those who bear the Throne, and all who are round about it, hymn the praises of their Lord and believe in Him and ask forgiveness for those who believe saying: "Our Lord! Thou comprehendest all things in mercy and knowledge, therefore forgive those who repent and follow Thy way. Ward off from them the punishment of hell--O Our Lord! And make them enter the Gardens of Eden which Thou hast promised them, with such of their fathers and their wives and their descendants as do right. Lo! Thou, only Thou, art the Mighty, the Wise."

And ward off from them ill-deeds; and he from whom Thou wardest off ill-deeds that day, him verily hast Thou taken into Mercy. That is the supreme triumph.

Lo! Those who disbelieve are **informed by Proclamation**: "Verily Allah's abhorrence is more terrible than your abhorrence one of another, when ye were called unto the faith but did refuse." They say: "Our Lord! Twice hast Thou made us die, and twice hast Thou made us live. Now we confess our sins. Is there any way to go out?"

"This is because, when Allah only was invoked, ye disbelieved, but when some partner was ascribed to Him ye were believing. But the command belongeth only to Allah, the Sublime, the Majestic. He it is Who showeth you His portents, and sendeth down for you provision from the sky. None payeth heed save him who turneth unto Him repentant." Therefore pray unto Allah, making religion PURE for Him, however much the disbelievers be averse--The Exalter of Ranks, the Lord of the Throne.

He causeth the Spirit of His command upon whom He will of His slaves, that He may warn of the Day of Meeting, the day when they come forth, nothing of them being hidden from Allah. Whose is the Sovereignty this day? It is Allah's, the One, the Almighty.

This day is each **soul requited** that which **it hath earned**[*]; no wrong is done this day. Lo! Allah is swift at reckoning.

Warn them (O *AL-AMIN*) of the Day of the approaching DOOM, when the hearts will be choking the throats, when there will be no friend for the wrong-doers, nor any intercessor who will be heard. **He knoweth the traitor of the eyes, and that which the bosoms hide.** Allah judgeth with truth, while those to whom they cry instead of Him judge not at all. Lo! Allah, He is the Hearer, the Seer.

Have they not travelled in the land to see the nature of the consequence for those who disbelieved before them? They were mightier than these in power and in the traces of the ruins which they left behind them in the earth. Yet Allah seized them for their sins, and they had no protector from Allah. That was because their messengers kept bringing them THIS RIGHTEOUS BOOK but they disbelieved; so Allah seized them. Lo! He is Strong, severe in punishment.

And verily We sent *MOSES* with Our revelations and a clear warrant unto Pharaoh and Haman and Korah, but they said: "A lying sorcerer!"

And when he brought them the Truth from Our Presence, they said: "Slay the sons of those who believe with him, and spare their women." But the plot of disbelievers is in naught but error. And Pharaoh said: "Suffer me to kill *MOSES*, and let him cry unto his Lord. Lo! I fear that he will alter your religion or that he will cause confusion in the land."

MOSES said: "Lo! I seek refuge in my Lord and your Lord from every scorner who believeth not in a Day of Reckoning." And Orpheus--a believing man of Pharaoh's family--who hid his faith, said: "Would ye kill a man because he saith: 'My Lord is Allah, and hath brought you THIS RIGHTEOUS BOOK from your Lord?' If he is lying, then his lie is upon him; and if he is truthful, then some of that wherewith he threateneth you will strike you. Lo! Allah guideth not one who is a prodigal, a liar. O My People! Yours is the kingdom today, ye being uppermost in **the land**. But who would save us from the wrath of Allah should it reach us?"

Pharaoh said: "I do but show you what I think, and I do but guide you to wise policy."

And he who believed said: "O my people! Lo! I fear for you a fate like that of the factions of old; A plight like that of Noah's folk, and A'ad and Thamud, and those after them, and Allah willeth no injustice for His slaves." And, "O My People! Lo! I fear for you a Day of Summoning, a day when ye will turn to flee, having no preserver from Allah: and he whom Allah sendeth astray, for him there is no guide. And verily Joseph brought you of old THIS RIGHTEOUS BOOK, yet ye ceased not to be in doubt concerning what he brought you till, when he died, ye said: '**Allah will not send any messenger after him**.' **Thus Allah deceiveth him** who is a prodigal, a doubter. Those who wrangle concerning the revelations of Allah without any warrant that hath come unto

---

[*]It's not the good things you do that get you in--it is the bad things *ye* do that keep you out. "And the dead were judged by what was written in the books, **by what they had done**" "Behold, I am coming soon, bringing my recompense, to **repay every one for what he has done**" (Revelation 20:12; 22:12 RSV).

them, it is greatly abhorrent in the sight of Allah and in the sight of those who believe. Thus doth Allah print on every arrogant, disdainful heart."

And Pharaoh said: "O Haman! Build for me a tower that haply I may reach the Roads, **the Roads of the Heavens**, and may look upon the God of *MOSES*, though verily I think him a liar."

Thus was the evil that he did made fairseeming unto Pharaoh, and he was debarred from THE WAY.[*] The plot of Pharaoh ended but in ruin. And he who believed said: "O My People! Follow me. I will show you the way of right conduct. O My People! Lo! this life of the world is but a passing comfort, and Lo! the Hereafter, that is the enduring home. Whoso doeth an ill-deed, he will be repaid the like thereof, while whoso doeth right, whether male or female, and is a believer, all such will enter the Garden, where they will be nourished without stint." And, "O My People! What aileth me that I call you unto deliverance when ye call me unto the Fire? Ye call me to disbelieve in Allah and ascribe unto Him as partners that whereof I have no knowledge, while I call you unto the Mighty, the Forgiver. Assuredly that whereunto ye call me hath no claim in the world or in the Hereafter, and our return will be unto Allah, and the prodigals will be owners of the Fire. And ye will remember what I say unto you. I confide my cause unto Allah. Lo! Allah is Seer of His slaves."

So Allah warded off from him the evils which they plotted, while a dreadful doom encompassed Pharaoh's folk, **The Fire**; they are exposed to it morning and evening; and on the day when the HOUR upriseth: "Cause Pharaoh's folk to enter the most awful doom."

And when they wrangle in the Fire, the weak say unto those who were proud: "Lo! We were a following unto you; will ye therefor rid us of a portion of the Fire?" Those who were proud say: "Lo! We are all together herein. Lo! Allah hath judged between His slaves." And those in the Fire say unto the guards of hell: "Entreat your Lord that He relieve us of a day of the torment." They say: "Came not your messengers unto you with THIS RIGHTEOUS BOOK?" They say: "Yea, Verily!" They say: "Then do ye pray, although the prayer of disbelievers is in vain."

Lo! We verily do help Our messengers, and those who believe, in the life of the world and on the DAY when **The Witnesses** arise, The day when their excuse availeth not the evil-doers, and theirs is the curse, and theirs the ill abode.

And We verily gave *MOSES* the guidance, and We caused the Children of Israel to inherit the Scripture, a guide and a reminder for men of understanding. Then have patience. Lo! the promise of Allah is true. And ask forgiveness of thy sin, and hymn the praise of thy Lord at fall of night and in the early *hours*.

Lo! Those who wrangle concerning the Revelations of Allah without a warrant having come unto them, there is naught else in their breasts save pride which they will never attain. So take Thou refuge in Allah. Lo! He, only He, is the Hearer, the Seer.

---

[*]"Torah" literarily means, THE WAY (the direction of flow). The term "law" is an unwarranted bad translation of the true Hebrew meanings into English. Likewise "miztvot" refers to cairns--or ten piles of rock--that are guideposts along the way that give the right directions for the journeying at each stage of THE WAY!

Assuredly the creation of the heavens and the earth is greater than the creation of mankind; but most of mankind know not. And the blind man and the seer are not equal, neither are those who believe and do good works equal with the evil-doer. Little do ye reflect!

Lo! the HOUR is surely coming, there is no doubt thereof; yet most of mankind believe not.

And your Lord hath said: "Pray unto Me and I will hear your prayer. Lo! those who scorn My service, they will enter hell, disgraced." Allah it is Who hath appointed for you night that ye may rest therein, and day for seeing. Lo! Allah is a Lord of bounty for mankind, yet most of mankind give not thanks. Such is Allah, your Lord, the Creator of all things, There is no God save Him. How then are ye perverted?

Thus are they perverted who deny the revelations of Allah.

Allah it is Who appointed for you the earth for a dwelling-place and the sky for a canopy, and fashioned you and perfected your shapes, and hath provided you with good things. Such is Allah, your Lord. Then blessed be Allah, the Lord of the Worlds! He is the Living One. There is no God save Him. So pray unto Him, making religion PURE for Him. Praise be to Allah, the Lord of the Worlds!

Say (O *AL-AMIN*): "I am forbidden to worship those unto whom ye cry beside Allah since there have come unto me THIS RIGHTEOUS BOOK from my Lord, and I am commanded to surrender to the Lord of the Worlds! He it is Who created you from dust, then from **a drop of goo**, then from a clot, then bringeth you forth as a child, then ordaineth that ye attain full strength and afterward that ye become old men--though some among you die before--and that ye reach an appointed term, that haply ye may understand. He it is Who quickeneth and giveth death. When He ordaineth a thing, He saith unto it only: Be! and it is."

Hast Thou not seen those who wrangle concerning the Revelations of Allah, how they are turned away?--Those who deny the Scripture and that wherewith We send Our messengers. But they will come to know, when carcans are about their necks and chains. They are dragged through boiling waters; then they are thrust into the Fire. Then it is said unto them: "Where are those that ye used to make partners beside Allah?" They say: "They have failed us; but we used not to pray to anything before. **Thus doth Allah send astray the disbelievers**. "This is because ye exulted in the earth without right, and because ye were petulant. Enter ye the GATES of hell, to dwell therein. Evil is the habitation of the scornful."

Then have patience (O *AL-AMIN*). Lo! The promise of Allah is true.

And whether we let Thee see a part of that which We promise them, or whether We cause Thee to die, still unto Us they will be brought back.

Verily We sent messengers before Thee, among them those of whom We have told Thee, and **some of whom We have not told Thee**; and it was not given to any messenger that he should bring a portent save by Allah's leave, but when Allah's commandment cometh the Cause is judged aright, and the followers of vanity will then be lost.

Allah it is Who hath appointed for you cattle, that ye may ride on some of them, and eat of some--much benefits ye have from them--and that ye may satisfy by their means a need that is in your breasts, and may be borne upon them as upon the ship.

And He showeth you His tokens. **Which, then, of the tokens of Allah do ye deny?** Have they not travelled in **the land** to see the nature of the consequence for those before them? They were more numerous than these, and mightier in power and in the traces which they left behind them as ruins in the earth. But all that they used to earn availed them not. And when their messengers brought them THIS RIGHTEOUS BOOK they exulted in the knowledge they themselves possessed. And that which they were wont to mock befell them.

Then, when they saw Our DOOM, they said: "We believe in Allah only and reject **_ALL_** that we used to associate." But their faith could not avail them when they saw Our DOOM. This is Allah's law which hath ever taken course for His bondmen. **And then the disbelievers will be ruined.**

114. Bism'illah Ar-Rahman Ar-Rahim! al-Muzammil: THE MANTLED ONE.

O thou wrapped up in thy raiment!
Keep vigil the night long, save a little--
A half thereof, or abate a little thereof
Or add a little thereto--and chant THIS QUR'AN in measure,
For we shall charge Thee with a word of weight.
Lo! The vigil of the night is a time when impression is more keen and speech more certain.
Lo! Thou hast by day a chain of business.
So remember the name of thy Lord and devote thyself with a complete devotion--Lord of the East and the West; there is no God save Him; so choose thou Him alone for Thy Defender--And bear with patience what they utter, and part from them with a fair leave-taking. Leave Me to deal with the deniers, lords of ease and comfort (of this life); and do thou respite them awhile.

Lo! With Us are heavy fetters and a raging fire,
And food which choketh the partaker, and a painful doom
On the day when the earth and the hills rock, and **the hills become a heap of running sand**.

Lo! We have sent unto you a messenger as witness against you, even as We sent unto Pharaoh a messenger. But Pharaoh rebelled against the messenger, whereupon We seized him with no gentle grip. Then how, if ye disbelieve, will ye protect yourselves upon **The Day which will turn Children Grey**, the very heaven being then rent asunder.

His promise is to be fulfilled!

Lo! This is a Reminder. Let him who will, then, choose a way unto his Lord.

Lo! thy Lord knoweth how Thou keepest vigil sometimes nearly two-thirds of the night, or sometimes half or a third thereof, as do a party of those with Thee. Allah measureth the night and the day. He knoweth that ye count it not, and turneth unto you in mercy. **RECITE, then**, of THIS QUR'AN that which is *easy for you*. He knoweth that there are sick folk among you, while others travel in the land in search of Allah's bounty, and others still are fighting for the Cause of Allah.

SO RECITE of it that which is *easy for you*, and establish worship and pay the poor-due (*zakat*), and so **lend unto Allah a goodly loan**. Whatsoever good ye send before you for your souls, ye will find it with Allah, better and greater in the recompense. And seek forgiveness of Allah. Lo! Allah is Forgiving, All-Merciful.

al-Baqarah!!!

The MESSENGER Believeth in that which hath been Revealed unto Him from His Lord and so do Believers. Each one Believeth in Allah and His Angels and His Scriptures and His Messengers--**We make no distinction between any of His Messengers**--and They say: "We Hear, and We Obey! Grant us Thy forgiveness, O Our Lord! Unto Thee is the Journeying!"

Allah tasketh not a soul beyond its scope. For it (is only) that which it hath earned, and against it (only) that which it hath deserved.

"Our Lord! Condemn Us not if We Forget, or Miss the Mark! Our Lord! Lay not on Us such a Burden as Thou didst lay on those before Us! Our Lord! Impose not on Us that which we have not the Strength to Bear! Pardon us, absolve Us and have Mercy on Us, Thou, our Protector, and give us **Victory** over the Disbelieving Folk."

CHINVAT-SIRAT: Bism'illah Ar-Rahman Ar-Rahim!

When Allah's succour (an-Nasr) and the triumph cometh
And thou seest mankind Entering the religion of Allah in Troops,
Then hymn the praises of thy Lord, and seek forgiveness of Him.
Lo! He is ever ready to show mercy.

--Oula-

INSHIRAH!

I. JUZ'UN SIPARA PRIMO:

1. *Basmala al-Hadid:* THE ROD OF IRON.
2. *Basmala aq-Qaara:* THE FIRST REVELATION READ ALOUD! RECITE!
3. *Basmala an-Nasr: THE DIVINE SUPPORT--ENTRY BY TROOPS.*
4. *Basmala al-Mudathir:* THE CLOAKED ONE.
5. *Basmala al-Fatihah: THE STRAIGHT PATH.*
6. *Basmala al-Inshirah:* THE EXPANSION: THE OPENING OF THY DILATING HEART.
7. *Basmala al-Kafrun: THE UNBELIEVERS.*
8. *Basmala at-Takwir: BURIED ALIVE.*
9. *Basmala al-Humazah: THE BACKBITING SLANDERER.*
10. *Basmala al-Kauthar: ABUNDANCE.*
11. *Basmala al-Lahab: THE FLAME.*
12. *Basmala al-Ma'un: OUR DAILY BREAD.*
13. Basmala *at-Takthur: WORLDLY GAIN.*
14. *Basmala ad-Duha: THE BRIGHTNESS.*

II. JUZ'UN SIPARA SECUNDO:

15. *Basmala as-Saffat: THE RANGERS.*
16. *Basmala al-Qalam:* THE PEN.

III. JUZ'UN SIPARA TERZO/TERTIO:

17. *Basmala al-Imran: THE FAMILY OF IMRAN!*
18. *Basmala at-Tahrim: THE PROHIBITION.*
19. *Basmala al-Qari'ah:* THE TERRIBLE CALAMITY!

IV. JUZ'UN ISPARA QUARTO:

20. *Basmala al-Layli:* THE NIGHT.
21. *Basmala ash-Shams:* THE SUN.
22. *Basmala al-Qamar:* THE MOON.
23. *Basmala an-Najm:* THE STAR.
24. *Basmala al-Inshiqaq:* THE RENDING.
25. *Basmala al-Waqi'ah:* THAT WHICH IS COMING.
26. *Basmala al-Infitar:* THE CLEAVING ASUNDER.
27. *Basmala al-Haqqah:* THE ULTIMATELY REAL.
28. *Basmala al-Ghashiya:* THE OVERWHELMING CALAMITY.
29. *Basmala al-Zilzal:* THE SHAKING.
30. *Basmala al-Mulk:* THE KINGDOM.

31. *Basmala at-Tariq:* THE NIGHT-COMER.
32. *Basmala ad-Dahr:* THE MAN.
33. *Basmala ad-Dukhan:* THE EVIDENT SMOKE.
34. *Basmala at-Tin:* THE FIG.
35. *Basmala al-'Asr:* TIME.
36. *Basmala at-Tur:* THE MOUNTAIN.

MIRAJ!

V. JUZ'UN SIPARA QUINTO:

37. *Basmala bani Isra'il:* O THOSE WHO STRIVE WITH GOD!
38. *Basmala al-Quraysh:* THE ASSOCIATION.
39. *Basmala al-Aliyah:* THE ASCENT.

VI. JUZ'UN SIPARA SEXTO:

ba . Basmala Hadith al-'Isra' wal-Mi'raj: THE NIGHT JOURNEY!

VII. JUZ'UN SIPARA SETTIMO:

ha. Basmala Sharh-i-Shajarih Namih-i-Mubarakih: THE LOTE TREE OF THE
FARTHEST LIMIT!!

VIII. JUZ'UN SIPARA OTTAVO:

40. *Basmala al-Fatir:* THE CREATOR.
41. *Basmala al-Ma'arij:* THE LADDERS AND ASCENDING STAIRWAYS!
42. *Basmala Ha Mim Sajdah:* REVELATIONS WELL EXPOUNDED.
43. *Basmala al-Qadr:* THE MAJESTY.
44. *Basmala an-Naba':* THE TIDING NEWS.
45. *Basmala Qaf-i-Kuh:* THE GRAND MESA SIMURGH RUKH.
46. *Basmala al-Buruj:* THE CONSTELLATIONS.

JUMU'AH!

IX. JUZ'UN SIPARA NOVA:

47. *Basmala al-'Adiyat:* FIRE-HORSE! THE CHARGERS.
48. *Basmala al-Jumu`ah:* THE DAY OF CONGREGATION.
49. *Basmala al-Ma'idah:* THE OUTSPREAD TABLE OF THE SUPPER OF GOD.

X. JUZ'UN SIPARA DECIMO:

50. *Basmala al-Mu'minun:* THE BELIEVERS.

51. Basmala ar-Rum: THE AMERICANS, RUSSIANS, FRENCH AND ENGLAND.
52. Basmala al-Ahza: THE ALLIES.

XI. JUZ'UN SIPARA UNDICI:

53. Basmala az-Zumar: THE COMPANIES.
54. Basmala ash-Shura: THE COUNSEL.
55. Basmala adh-Dhariyat: THE SCATTERERS.
56. Basmala al-Munafiqun: THE HYPOCRITES.
57. Basmala al-Mursalat: THE EMISSARIES.
58. Basmala at-Tatfif: THE DEFRAUDERS.

XII. JUZ'UN SIPARA DODICI:

59. Basmala at-Taubah: REPENTANCE.
60. Basmala an-Nazi'at: THOSE WHO PULL OUT.
61. Basmala as-Sajdah: THE ADORATION.
　　　　　62. Basmala al-Anfal: THE SPOILS OF WAR.
63. Basmala al-Fath: THE VICTORY!

　　i. The Treaty of Hudaybiyyah 628 AD--
　　ii. The Haramization of Yathrib as The City (Medina)
　　　September 16th, 628 AD--(After the Expedition to Khaybar)
　　　"The center of Yathrib (THE CITY) is sacred
　　　for the people of this document."
　　iii. The Victory Surah Revealed on April 21st, 628 AD

JINN!

XIII. JUZ'UN SIPARA TREDICI:

64. Basmala al-Hashr: THE EXILE.
65. Basmala al-Falaq: THE DAYBREAK.
66. Basmala an-Nas: HUMANITY.
67. Basmala al-Jinn: THE JINN.
　　　　　68. Basmala al-Hijr: THE ROCK.

XIV. JUZ'UN SIPARA QUATTORZICI:

69. Basmala al-Furqan: THE BROKEN PIECES. *

---

*This tern *"Furqan"* comes from the Aramaic *farraqo* that means to "**break up**" "to separate." and refers to those who divide their religion, split their own selves, create sects and divisions; separated the people; scattered the gatherings; and who have cut up the Qur'an into broken up little pieces out of order--thus ruining the message, perverting the song, misleading the people, disrupting the tale and the story from God! Thus have they *broken up* (**al-Firkin**) the Revelation of the Holy Koran into parts, mis-assembled them (from longest fragment and part to shortest) out of their correct order--the Order of Imam Ali, and ABANDONED the true "Statute Book." As it is

70. *Basmala al-Fajr:* THE DAYBREAK.
71. *Basmala ash-Shu'ara':* THE POETS.

XV. JUZ'UN SIPARA QUINTICI:

72. *Basmala al-Baqarah!:* HARUT AND MARUT.
73. *Basmala Ya Sin:* ONE SHOUT!

XVI. JUZ'UN SIPARA DECIMO-SEXTO:

74. *Basmala al-Kahf:* THE CAVE.
75. *Basmala ar-Rahman:* ARRAMAN (THE MERCIFUL).

HOURIS!

XVII. JUZ'UN SIPARA DICIASSETTE:

76. *Basmala at-Taghabun:* THE CHEATING.
77. *Basmala az-Zukhruf:* THE EMBELLISHMENT.
78. *Basmala al-Hujurat:* THE CHAMBERS.

XVIII. JUZ'UN SIPARA DICIOTTO:

79. *Basmala an-Nisa:* WOMEN.

---

written: "On that Day, the wrongdoer will bite his hands, and say, 'If only I had followed the way [the true of Order of the Holy Koran as compiled by Imam Ali and presented by him in person to Exilarch Bostanai]... If only I had followed the way with the Messenger [the true order of the Koran of Muhammad, PBUH]. Oh, woe to me; I wish I never took so-and-so [who dissembled both the book, their faith, and their own souls] for a friend. He led me away from the Message [true order of the Holy Koran] after it had come to me; for Satan has always been a betrayer [abandoner; forsaker; Ar. **Khadhulu**] of human kind.' And the Messenger will say, 'My Lord, my people have abandoned (*Khadhulu*) this Quran [as given by Muhammad to Ali in the correct order].' Likewise, to every prophet We assign enemies from among the wicked. But your Lord suffices as a Guide and Savior. Those who disbelieve say, 'Why was the Quran not revealed to him at once?' Thus in order to strengthen your heart thereby, and **We Revealed it in Stages**. Whatever argument they come to you with, We provide you with the truth, and a better exposition" (*al-Furqan: The BROKEN PIECES*). Thus have the quibbled over the order of the book and dissembled and broken it up into pieces. "The Arabic word FURQAN (Arabic: ناقرف) is the criterion or the standard to distinguish between good and bad. The name "The Criterion" refers to the Qur'an itself as the decisive (Key) factor between the Good and the Evil... The Furqan [also] means the Criterion which separates the truth (Haqq) from falsehood (Baatil) and through it Allah made the truth known to mankind. According to Dr. Sobhy as-Salih, this word is also not Arabic but Aramaic, the original language in which Gospel/ Injil was revealed in. From the language the word Furqan describes something which separates a thing into different parts. In the above ayat Allah used the word Faraqna in describing how He separated the water of the sea into two parts so as to allow *MOSES* (Musa) and his followers to cross the dry path. Verily, those who divide [*Farraqo (break up)*] their religion and break up into sects (all kinds of religious sects), you (O Muhammad) have no concern in them in the least. Their affair is only with Allah" *(al-An'am: THE LIVESTOCK)*. Similarly Allah uses the word Farraqo to describe the evil act of breaking up the religion into separate sects. So again the word is used in reference to **that which separates something into parts.**"

330

80. *Basmala at-Talaq:* THE DIVORCE.

XIX. JUZ'UN SIPARA DICIANNOVA:

81. *Basmala al-Ikhlas va al-Baqarah!!:* THE UNITY.

XX. JUZ'UN SIPARA VICESIMO:

82. *Basmala al-Mumtahanah:* SHE WHO IS TESTED.
83. *Basmala al-Mujadilah:* SHE WHO PLEADETH.
84. *Basmala 'Abasa:* HE FROWNED.
85. *Basmala an-Nur:* THE LIGHT.

LUQMAN AL-HAKIM!

XXI. JUZ'UN SIPARA VENTUNO:

86. *Basmala as-Saff:* THE RANKS.
87. *Basmala Luqman:* LAO TZU.
88. *Basmala al-Fil:* THE ELEPHANT.
89. *Basmala an-Naml:* THE ANT.

XXII. JUZ'UN SIPARA VENTIDUO:

90. *Basmala al-An'am:* THE LIVESTOCK.

XXIII. JUZ'UN SIPARA VENTITERZO:

91. *Basmala an-Nahl:* THE BEE.
92. *Basmala al-'Ankabut:* THE SPIDER.

XXIV. JUZ'UN SIPARA VENTIQUATTRO:

93. *Basmala al-Jathiyah:* THE KNEELING.
94. *Basmala ar-Ra'd:* THE THUNDER.
95. *Basmala al-Hajj:* THE PILGRIMAGE.

ANUBIS!

XXV. JUZ'UN SIPARA VICESIMO-QUINTO:

96. *Basmala al-A'la:* THE MOST HIGH.
97. *Basmala al-Bayyinah va al-Bayan:* THIS RIGHTEOUS BOOK!
98. *Basmala al-Anbiya:* THE PROPHETS.

332

www.ingramcontent.com/pod-product-compliance
Lightning Source LLC
Chambersburg PA
CBHW080526090426
42733CB00015B/2498